alieNATION

Bruce E. Gronbeck and Mitchell S. McKinney
General Editors

Vol. 28

The Frontiers in Political Communication series is part
of the Peter Lang Media and Communication list.
Every volume is peer reviewed and meets
the highest quality standards for content and production.

PETER LANG
New York • Bern • Frankfurt • Berlin
Brussels • Vienna • Oxford • Warsaw

alieNATION

the divide & conquer election of 2012

DIANNE G. BYSTROM
MARY C. BANWART
MITCHELL S. MCKINNEY

EDITORS

PETER LANG

New York • Bern • Frankfurt • Berlin
Brussels • Vienna • Oxford • Warsaw

Library of Congress Cataloging-in-Publication Data

alieNATION: the divide & conquer election of 2012 /
edited by Dianne G. Bystrom, Mary C. Banwart, Mitchell S. McKinney.
pages cm — (Frontiers in Political Communication; vol. 28)
Includes bibliographical references.
1. Elections—United States. 2. Presidents—United States—Election—2012.
3. United States. Congress—Elections, 2012. 4. Political campaigns—United States.
5. United States—Politics and government—2009– I. Bystrom, Dianne G.
JK19682012 .A52   324.973'0932—dc23   2014005958
ISBN 978-1-4331-2554-6 (hardcover)
ISBN 978-1-4331-2553-9 (paperback)
ISBN 978-1-4539-1341-3 (e-book)
ISSN 1525-9730

Bibliographic information published by **Die Deutsche Nationalbibliothek.**
Die Deutsche Nationalbibliothek lists this publication in the "Deutsche
Nationalbibliografie"; detailed bibliographic data are available
on the Internet at http://dnb.d-nb.de/.

The paper in this book meets the guidelines for permanence and durability
of the Committee on Production Guidelines for Book Longevity
of the Council of Library Resources.

© 2014 Peter Lang Publishing, Inc., New York
29 Broadway, 18th floor, New York, NY 10006
www.peterlang.com

Printed in the United States of America

Dedication

We dedicate this book to the memory of Lynda Lee Kaid, a mentor and colleague who taught us all the value of collaborative research. We were always proud and honored to have her as the leader of our research team.

Table of Contents

Acknowledgments

alieNATION: The Divide and Conquer Election of 2012 continues the collaborative efforts of a nationwide team of political communication scholars and researchers. We believe such collaborative efforts are essential to the study of political campaign communication. And, we are pleased with our thematic approach to the study of the 2012 presidential election.

The editors wish to thank our contributing authors who wrote chapters for this volume as well as the members of our national research team who coordinated the collection of data on their university campuses. We thank the following members of our 2012 election team, listed alphabetically by university:

Auburn University, Mike Milford; Emerson College, J. Gregory Payne; Georgia College and State University, Kristin N. English; Iowa State University, Dianne G. Bystrom; Kutztown University, Glenn Richardson; Marquette University, Sumana Chattopadhyay; Ohio University, Jerry Miller and J. W. Smith; Radford University, Scott Dunn; Rhodes College, Amy E. Jasperson and Bob Johnson; Texas State University-San Marcos, John Payne and Hyun Jung Yun; University of Georgia, Itai Himelboim, Anandam Kavoori, and Kaye D. Sweetser; University of Kansas, Mary C. Banwart and Kelly L. Winfrey; University of Memphis, Seth Abrutyn, Eric Groenendyk, and Anna Mueller; University of Missouri, J. Brian Houston, Mitchell S. McKinney, and Benjamin R. Warner; University of Nevada-Reno, Leslie A. Rill; University of Texas-San Antonio,

Andrea Aleman and Mary McNaughton-Cassill; and Worcester State University, Amy Ebbeson. We also acknowledge the contributions of John C. Tedesco, Virginia Tech University, in helping organizing this project.

We hope you learn from the results of our collaborative research efforts.

Dianne G. Bystrom, Mary C. Banwart, and Mitchell S. McKinney

An alieNATION of the U.S. Electorate

The Divide and Conquer Election of 2012

MITCHELL S. MCKINNEY AND DIANNE G. BYSTROM

On the evening of November 6, 2012, just as Fox News awarded the state of Ohio, and the presidential election, to President Barack Obama, Republican strategist Karl Rove voiced his adamant disagreement with the call, asserting in a rather belligerent manner, "I think this is premature … we need to be careful about calling things when we have a … a quarter of the vote yet to count. I'd be very cautious about intruding in this process" (Weinger, 2012, para. 4). Rove's rejection of Fox News' prediction that Obama would be re-elected prompted Fox election co-anchor Megyn Kelly to walk through the studio with live camera in tow where she found two members of the Fox "decision team" and had them defend their projection: "We are actually quite comfortable with the call in Ohio. The largest thing that's outstanding right now is the Cleveland area, is Cuyahoga … This is Democratic territory and we're quite comfortable with the idea that Obama will carry Ohio" (Weinger, 2012, para. 11). Still, back at the Fox anchor desk, a doubting Rove continued to dispute the call—even as Fox's on-screen graphic read "Barack Obama Re-elected President"—prompting election co-anchor Chris Wallace to instruct viewers, "Well, folks, so … maybe not so fast?" (Weinger, 2012, para. 6).

Meanwhile, in the presidential suite at Boston's Westin hotel, Mitt Romney was huddled with top advisers, his wife Ann, their five sons and assorted family members, all fully expecting a Romney-Ryan victory. In fact, so sure of his impending election, Romney confided in reporters earlier that morning that he had just put the finishing touches on his victory address and devoted no thought whatsoever to a concession speech (Weiner, 2012). So, at 11:15 p.m. Eastern Standard Time, with NBC and MSNBC the first networks to report the re-election of Obama (and with each of the other news networks, including Fox, following just minutes later), initial reaction by those in the Romney suite was that of the first predicted emotion following a sudden loss, denial: "they just couldn't believe they had been so wrong. And maybe they weren't: There was Karl Rove on Fox saying Ohio wasn't settled, so campaign aides decided to wait. They didn't want to have to withdraw their concession, like Al Gore did in 2000" (Crawford, 2012, para. 6). As team Romney waited, additional reporting from Ohio only increased Obama's margins in the all important Buckeye State; and, as election eve neared midnight, other intensely fought battleground states such as Colorado and, eventually, Virginia were called for the president. Soon after midnight, as the reality of an Obama victory became clear, a "shellshocked" Romney phoned and congratulated the incumbent president on his re-election and quickly huddled with advisers to prepare an impromptu and rather brief concession speech that he delivered to a stunned group of supporters at 1 a.m. Wednesday morning, nearly one hour and forty-five minutes after the networks announced Obama would continue as the nation's 44th president. Although most candidates on Election Day, even those who might suspect they have little to no chance of victory, will project a brave face and message of confidence for their supporters, by all accounts Romney and Republicans—which obviously included Fox analyst Rove—were fully expecting to hear a president-elect Romney deliver his victory speech that evening. Yet, as a top Romney adviser lamented, "There's nothing worse than when you think you're going to win, and you don't … It was like a sucker punch" (Crawford, 2012, para. 12).

So—from the Republicans' viewpoint—what went wrong? With polling throughout the 2012 campaign consistently showing that more citizens thought the nation was on the "wrong track" rather than "right track," an Obama first-term economic recession of historic proportions with a continued struggling economy and near-record unemployment throughout the land, and with Republican voters registering greater fervor (fueled largely by anti-Obama sentiment) and greater motivation to vote than Democrats—surely these conditions would produce a Romney victory. Indeed, team Romney and their voting models were confident that Obama would be unable to assemble the same winning electoral coalition that in 2008 made him our nation's first African-American president. With African-American and young voters as well as many Hispanic/Latino voters bearing the brunt of our nation's economic woes, certainly these key constituencies would not maintain their loyalty to Obama.

Yet, to the surprise of many, team Obama's own voting models—and messaging machine—produced an impressive electoral re-election victory by strategically targeting desired voters in key states with carefully crafted campaign appeals. For example, Obama's share of the Hispanic/Latino vote actually increased from 67% in 2008 to 71% in 2012, and his margin among African-American voters held relatively steady (at 94% in 2008 vs. 93% in 2012). Although Obama's national support among young voters, those 18-to-29 years old, did decline slightly from 66% in 2008 to 62% in 2012, his support among young voters in key battleground states—including such electoral prizes as Ohio, Florida, and Virginia—actually increased in 2012 (President Exit Polls, 2012).

How was Obama able to beat expectations in 2012—certainly the expectations of many Republicans? And, particularly in such challenging times for the incumbent president, how was he able to even "out perform" his impressive 2008 electoral showing in several key areas? It was only following his re-election that the magnitude of team Obama's technological and digital media dominance became fully evident with reports of how his campaign's "technology nerds" developed sophisticated algorithms that sifted through massive amounts of voter, online, and social media data resulting in strategically targeted messages for likely and desired voters. As *The Atlantic's* Alexis Madrigal (2012, para. 1) described, the Obama victory came at the hands of "a dream team of engineers from Facebook, Twitter and Google who built the software that drove Barack Obama's re-election." Obama's campaign appeals were strategically targeted at the individual voter with carefully crafted personalized messages based on the assessment of numerous data points and repeated messages delivered via digital and social media. Such campaign messaging allowed Obama to connect more efficiently with likely voters all the way down to the specific neighborhood, voter precinct, and county level in the handful of battleground states that would decide the 2012 contest (Madrigal, 2012).

Although the Obama campaign's technological sophistication was lauded as a major reason for his electoral success, our changing American societal landscape was identified as a principal cause for Romney's inability to connect with voters. On election night, Fox News commentator Bill O'Reilly offered this explanation for Romney's defeat: "It's a changing country, the demographics are changing. It's not a traditional America anymore … the white establishment is now the minority" (Hoft, 2012). The next day, yet another leading conservative voice and champion of many Republicans, none other than radio talk show host Rush Limbaugh, interpreted Romney's loss as the outright defeat of our nation: "I went to bed last night thinking we're out numbered. I went to bed last night thinking all this discussion we had about this election being THE election that will tell us whether or not we've lost the country … I went to bed last night thinking we've lost the country! I don't know how else you look at this" (The Young Turks, 2012).

Here, in somewhat glaring terms, we begin to see the contours of our national alienation and hear of the divisions and hostilities that often mark our political and social separations. For O'Reilly, a "traditional" and "white establishment" America is pitted against those demographic segments of our society who would prefer Obama as their national leader. Limbaugh is perhaps even more blunt in his "us" versus "them" construction of our political order, warning his large throng of listeners that "we're out numbered" and "we've lost the country."

Yet, beyond these rather stark examples of the rhetoric of political alienation, our campaign communication in general is replete with the discourse of division, difference, and separation. Candidates' political messaging activity is fueled by all manners of slicing and dicing the American electorate, identifying one's likely voters, and targeting these individuals with appeals that often construct a political enemy (e.g., Edelman, 1988) or suggest some other segment of society must be opposed and defeated to protect one's own interest or values in order to gain or maintain power. Consider just this partial inventory of our many political divides: from red versus blue states; conservatives versus liberals; and young versus older voters to the Occupy movement's 99% versus the 1% (much like Romney's 47% of those "who pay no taxes" vs. those who will "take personal responsibility and care for their lives"); or, perhaps, the well-established gender gap in American politics pitting female versus male voters; or our regular versus irregular and even non-church-attending neighbors; or our nation's growing number of ethnic and racial minorities versus O'Reilly's declining "traditional white establishment." Clearly, we have no shortage of differences, divisions, and separations in contemporary American politics.

In considering our many points of difference, however, we are in no way naive or calling for some sort of "kum ba yah" political order. And, certainly, we understand well that political factions and divisions are nothing new in our democracy. From the earliest time of our republic, we've had factions, coalitions, and organized political parties representing groups whose interests and values conflict and who compete for political power. We understand, too, that the electoral process, at its very base, is about difference—including those who win and those who lose. Yet, we are also mindful of a social order and political process consumed with pitting faction against faction, particularly when our differences breed disaffection and even hostilities toward one another, and when our differences and divisions lead to our "alieNATION." We are by no means the first to sound such alarm, a warning that was actually voiced by our very first national leader who himself refused to align with any organized political party. Upon leaving office, President George Washington admonished those whose task it was to maintain our fledgling nation and government of the dangers of "excessive party spirit" and warned that the "channels of party passions" would likely flame our growing North-South divide, a misguided loyalty he wrote that "serves always to distract the Public Councils, and enfeeble the Public Administration. It agitates the Community with ill-founded jealousies and false alarms; kindles the animosity of one part against another, foments occasionally riot and insurrection" (Prothero, 2012, p. 424).

While as far back as 1796 George Washington feared the consequence of excessive political faction, we fear today that we have become an even more polarized society, with our extreme political polarization contributing to divided and increasingly enfeebled political institutions and processes. As evidence of our politically alienated times, we take note of research by Iyengar, Sood, and Lelkes (2012) who examined citizens' affect political polarization, an attitude whereby individuals identify completely with one political group, yet are unable to identify at all with another. Iyengar et al.'s (2012) analysis found that political polarization has indeed increased within the U.S. electorate over the past few decades. Much has also been made of the "gridlock" that afflicts our hyper-partisan national Congress, unable to transcend party bickering to actually govern the nation. On this front, Brennan and Abdullah (2012) confirm that the 112th U.S. Congress (serving from 2010 through 2012) set a new record as the least productive Congress in terms of enacting legislation since such records have been maintained. And, as of this writing, the current 113th Congress is making great strides at breaking this record for doing the least. Even outside the proverbial Washington beltway, we find that our states are increasingly divided by partisanship and party control. Confessore (2013) reports that "state political monopolies" are at a 60-year high, with either Republicans or Democrats in full control of the state legislative bodies and the governor's offices in 36 states (with 23 states solely controlled by Republicans, and 13 solely by Democrats). Finally, evidence suggests that our color-coded electoral map is taking on an ever so darker hue with states becoming even more deeply red or blue, leaving fewer truly competitive states. As Greenblatt (2013) documents, although Obama's national margin of victory was much closer in 2012 (3.9%) than in 2008 (7.2%), and with a closer election we might expect more tightly contested states, the 2012 presidential election actually featured fewer truly competitive states (defined as those decided by 5 points or less) with six such states in 2008 (Florida, Indiana, Missouri, Montana, North Carolina, and Ohio) and only four truly competitive states in 2012 (Florida, North Carolina, Ohio, and Virginia).

Our claim of increased societal difference and division, often encouraging greater political alienation, is also buttressed by rapid and unmistakable cultural changes that are occurring throughout the land. To paraphrase that great social philosopher Bob Dylan, "the times, they are a changing!" Here, we highlight just a few of these dramatic societal shifts—all with very clear political implications.

First, the U.S. Census Bureau reports that in 2012, for the first time in our nation's history, minority births outnumbered those of whites; and, it is projected that our nation's white majority will gain minority status by 2043 (Blow, 2012). Angier's (2013) excellent portrait of the changing American family describes a sharp decline in marriage rates with 41% of all babies in the United States now born to unmarried parents. Finally, Pew's Religion & Public Life Project ("'Nones' on the Rise," 2012) documents a continued increase in the number of Americans who do not identify with any religion, with 20% of the U.S. population (one in five adults) now saying they are religiously unaffiliated (which includes those who identify as atheist, agnostic, or no particular religious affiliation).

This volume's analysis of campaign communication, from the interpretative lens of our political "alieNATION," examines the ever-widening political fault lines that define our dramatically shifting society and the many differences and divisions that produce campaign argumentation, often pitting group against group and frequently constructing the "other" as political enemy. As illustrated with O'Reilly and Limbaugh's interpretation of the 2012 presidential outcome, for some a political defeat comes at the hands of those fundamentally unlike "us" and who seek to control—perhaps even destroy—"our" country. Electoral campaigns are battles, with some victorious and others defeated; and in our current approach to electioneering—that of slicing and dicing the American electorate—our campaign battles are often waged through a war of words, appeals, and attacks designed to persuade those who think like "us" that some "other" must be vanquished.

The book's first section—**Media and Messages**—features five studies that examine how traditional and new media covered the 2012 presidential election as well as targeted voters, including women and young citizens. As television remains the primary information source among American citizens for campaign news, this section begins with a content analysis of election coverage on the three leading U.S. television networks, with particular focus on the types of frames— strategic game, issue, episodic, thematic, and conflict—employed. In Chapter 1, *Framing the 2012 Presidential Election on U.S. Television: Candidates, Issues, and Sources*, Daniela Dimitrova also examines how the media can influence political coverage through their selection of news sources for their stories.

In Chapter 2, *To Form a More Polarized Electorate? The Effect of Presidential Debates on Polarization, Partisanship and Political Aggression*, Joshua Hawthorne and Mitchell McKinney situate their analysis of this form of candidate communication within Terror Management Theory. They use an experimental design to determine if viewing a presidential and vice presidential debate, as a potential threat to one's cultural worldview, results in increased political polarization, aggression, and partisanship.

Given that the 2012 election broke records both in the amount of television ads aired and dollars spent, Chapter 3 seeks to provide a better understanding of the effectiveness of the messages at the heart of this effort. In *Communicating with Voters 30 Seconds at a Time: Presidential Campaign Advertising 2012*, Kelly Winfrey, Mary Banwart, and Benjamin Warner use an experimental design to compare the effects of television ads intended for a general audience with ones targeted toward female voters, especially with regard to presidential candidate favorability, perceptions of their sincerity, and reported levels of political information efficacy.

The final two chapters of section one examine the use of social media by young citizens. In Chapter 4, *Reaching Young Voters in the Middle: Party Loyalty and Perception of Political Participation*, Kaye Sweetser surveyed 610 first-time voters during the "hot phase" of the presidential campaign to determine how independents, vote changers, and party-line crossers perceived digital tools—including watching political videos on YouTube, joining a political group on Facebook, or following a candidate on Twitter—for political participation. In Chapter 5, "*No One Puts Baby in a Binder*": *The Resonance of Social Media Messages with College Students During the 2012 Presidential Campaign*, Amy Jasperson examines how the presidential candidates framed their appeals on women's issues via actual social media messages that appeared online in the form of a "meme." She uses an experimental design to determine which attempts by the candidates to prime gender identities in young female voters were successful.

The major concerns that framed political discourse before, during, and after the 2012 election are explored in Section 2—**Issues**. As the economy emerged as the top concern of voters in 2012, Jay Childers and R. McKay Stangler explore how this issue was framed by the presidential candidates in Chapter 6, *Defining Fairness in the Economic Rhetoric of the 2012 Presidential Election*. Through a rhetorical analysis, they show how Obama and Romney crafted competing narratives to explain who was to blame for the country's financial struggles and who might save the nation.

Second to the economy on the minds of most voters in 2012 was the issue of health care. In Chapter 7, *Health Care Reform: Core Value Differences Between Liberal and Conservative Candidates and Voters*, Ann Gordon, Brett Robertson, and Lisa Sparks use content analysis to explore how both campaigns framed the issue of health care through their television advertising appeals and incorporate public opinion data to examine the extent to which these messages may have resonated with the electorate.

Another major framework—the so-called Republican "war on women"—that persisted during the 2012 campaign is analyzed in Chapter 8, *Gendered Framing of the 2012 Election: The "War on Women" as Rhetorical Strategy*, by Valerie Hennings and Dianne Bystrom. They use computer-assisted content analysis to examine how this term was used in relation to political actors and issues in 757 items—272 newspaper articles, 74 television transcripts, and 414 postings from 142 political blogs—during the 10 months leading up to the election.

Immigration also emerged as a potentially important—and divisive—issue before the 2012 election. In Chapter 9, *Are Latinos Citizens? Labels, Race, and Politics in News Coverage of Immigration Reform*, Sharon Jarvis and Clariza Ruiz De Castilla use content analysis to monitor how readers of English and Spanish newspapers were invited to imagine the opportunities for and potential barriers to citizenship resulting from Arizona's "Support Our Law Enforcement and Safe Neighborhoods Act." They also consider how the conversation surrounding this legislation may have set the stage for discussions of immigration in the 2012 presidential campaign.

The 2012 election also provided opportunities to test the public's shifting attitudes toward a more favorable view of same-sex marriage. In Chapter 10, *Debating Marriage Equality in the 2012 Elections*, Hayley Cole and Mitchell McKinney employ a rhetorical-critical case analysis to examine state campaigns waged both for and against marriage equality ballot initiatives decided by voters in four states in November 2012.

Finally, in Chapter 11, Dianne Bystrom and Valerie Hennings examine the advocacy of women's interests and issues after the 2012 election through a computer-assisted content analysis of the floor speeches of the record 101 women serving in the U.S. Congress in the first six months of 2013. In their chapter—*Articulating Interests and Advocating Issues: An Analysis of Congresswomen's Political Speech after the 2012 Election*—they compare the content and rhetorical frameworks used in a random sample of 546 speeches by political party, chamber, and the congresswomen's years in office.

The third section of the book—**Electorate**—features chapters focusing on key voting constituencies targeted by the candidates during the 2012 election. As has been the case in presidential elections since at least 1992, women voters once again were the focus of both presidential campaigns in 2012. In Chapter 12, *The Gender Gap in Presidential Vote Preference*, Kate Kenski explains the role that gender played in the 2012 campaign and provides a portrait of how gender was associated with the presidential vote through an analysis of primary and general election exit poll data.

In addition to gender, the race and ethnicity of voters were key considerations in presidential campaign communication in 2012. In Chapter 13, *Black, White, and Latino: Message Strategies for a Divided Electorate*, Charlton McIlwain and Stephen Maynard Caliendo describe how race factored into the 2012 presidential election—the candidates selected to run, the messages they employed, the audiences they targeted, and the means by which they did so—through the narrative of racial division that took root in the empirical results of the 2008 election and, ultimately, pervaded the electoral climate and GOP vote strategy in 2012.

Despite predictions to the contrary, young voters also played a key role in the 2012 election through their political participation and vote choice, especially in key battleground states. In Chapter 14, *Defying Expectations: Young Citizens' Political Attitudes and Participation in the 2012 Election*, Leslie Rill and Mitchell McKinney report the results drawn from the third wave of a national longitudinal study that surveyed a panel of young citizens before and after viewing a presidential or vice presidential debate as well as the week following the election. Specifically, they explore the influence of political cynicism and political information efficacy on young citizens' candidate choice and decision to participate in the electoral process from the responses of 277 participants who completed the post-election survey.

Religion continued to shape campaign rhetoric in the 2012 presidential election, as both Republicans and Democrats utilized faith-based appeals to win support at the ballot box. In Chapter 15, *Altar Calls: Religious Segmentation in Campaign Appeals*, Brian Kaylor explores the religious rhetoric offered by the presidential campaigns and political parties based on a rhetorical analysis of their speeches as well as ethnographic insights from attendance at Republican and Democratic religious-political events during the campaign.

In addition to crafting faith-based appeals, both presidential candidates attempted to tap into voter frustration about the partisan gridlock in the nation's Capitol by employing bipartisan rhetorical strategies. In Chapter 16, *Working Together at Arm's Length: Bipartisan Rhetoric in the 2012 Presidential Campaign*, Mike Milford uses Kenneth Burke's concept of identification to demonstrate how both candidates used bipartisan terminology in their campaign speeches to not only illustrate their ability to act in a bipartisan manner, but also to frame their opponent as incapable of bipartisan action.

Finally, the effect of exposure to political campaign messages is explored by Benjamin Warner and Molly Greenwood in Chapter 17, *Affective Polarization from Campaign Communication: Alienating Messages in the 2012 Presidential Election*. They analyze data collected from five independent samples—surveys conducted before viewing three presidential debates and one vice presidential debate as well as an electronic survey emailed in the week before the election—using scales to measure participants' polarization across time and in relation to their attention to the campaign and engagement in campaign communication.

Collectively, these studies provide a comprehensive and in-depth examination of campaign communication during the 2012 election, including investigations of message content and effects. This book's conceptual principle of "alieNATION" informs the analyses found in many of the following chapters that explore our polity's various divisions and differences. With ever more sophisticated campaign communication techniques that now segment the voting electorate, and with profound demographic and social shifts that increasingly cast group against group and citizen against citizen, our concern is of a divided nation seemingly marked by more *pluribus* than *unum*. Yet, we hasten to acknowledge—and celebrate—that "We the People" have never been fully united, but always arguing, debating, and even battling one another for that "more perfect union." Indeed, we would have it no other way—a contested, often contentious, and hopefully continuing experiment in democracy grounded in communication. As Prothero (2012 p. 1) reminds us—and a particularly useful reminder for students and scholars of political communication—it is "our words [that] unite, divide, and define a nation." And, our "words matter. They move individuals to tears and to action. They make or break communities … words tie people together and tear them apart."

We also concur with Prothero's assessment that "American politics is broken because we have forgotten how to talk with one another. Instead of arguing on behalf of our nation, we argue on behalf of our party" (p. 9). Elections serve as those national conversations during which we argue what sort of nation we should have, when we debate "who is—and who is not—authentically American" (Prothero, 2012, p. 2). Our hope is for a national dialogue and elections that advance our shared interests. In rejecting our all too common "divide and conquer" politicking that pits "us" against "them" with battles over what's mine versus what's yours, we might well remember the words of another great American philosopher, Woody Guthrie, who instructed, "This land is your land, this land is my land … This land was made for you and me."

References

Angier, N. (2013, November 25). The changing American family. *The New York Times.* Retrieved from http://www.nytimes.com/2013/11/26/health/families.html

Blow, C. M. (2012, June 22). Bullies on the bus. *The New York Times.* Retrieved from http://www.nytimes.com/2012/06/23/opinion/blow-bullies-on-the-bus.html?_r=1&emc=eta1

Brennan, A., & Abdullah, H. (2012, June 19). Congress: Same hours, half the work. *CNN.com.* Retrieved from http://www.cnn.com/2012/06/19/politics/congress-productivity/index.html

Confessore, N. (2014, January 11). A national strategy funds state political monopolies. *The New York Times.* Retrieved from http://www.nytimes.com/2014/01/12/us/politics/a-national-strategy-funds-state-political-monopolies.html?hpw&rref=politics

Crawford, J. (2012, November 8). Adviser: Romney "shellshocked" by loss. *CBS News*. Retrieved from http://www.cbsnews.com/8301-250_162-57547239/

Edelman, M. (1988). *Constructing the political spectacle*. Chicago, IL: University of Chicago Press.

Greenblatt, A. (2013, November 27). How Republicans and Democrats ended up living apart. *National Public Radio*. Retrieved from http://www.npr.org/blogs/itsallpolitics/2013/11/26/247362143/how-republicans-and-democrats-ended-up-living-apart?sc=17&f=1001

Hoft, J. (2012, November 6). *Bill O'Reilly: It's not a traditional America anymore*. Retrieved from http://www.youtube.com/watch?v=5uqy5CBWjKw

Iyengar, S., Sood, G., & Lelkes, Y. (2012). Affect, not ideology: A social identity perspective on polarization. *Public Opinion Quarterly, 76*, 405–431.

Madrigal, A. C. (2012, November 16). When the nerds go marching in. *The Atlantic*. Retrieved from http://www.theatlantic.com/technology/archive/2012/11/when-the-nerds-go-marching-in/265325/

"'Nones' on the Rise." (2012, October 9). *Pew Research Religion & Public Life Project*. Retrieved from http://www.pewforum.org/2012/10/09/nones-on-the-rise/

President Exit Polls. (2012). *The New York Times*. Retrieved from http://elections.nytimes.com/2012/results/president/exit-polls

Prothero, S. (2012). *The American bible: How our words unite, divide, and define a nation*. New York, NY: HarperOne Publishers.

The Young Turks. (2012, November 8). *Conservatives: We've lost the country!* Retrieved from http://www.youtube.com/watch?v=kxjXcDT8pzk

Weiner, R. (2012, November 6). Mitt Romney hasn't written concession speech. *The Washington Post.com*. Retrieved from http://www.washingtonpost.com/blogs/post-politics/wp/2012/11/06/mitt-romney-hasnt-written-concession-speech/

Weinger, M. (2012, November 6). Karl Rove: Fox news Ohio call premature. *Politico*. Retrieved from http://www.politico.com/blogs/media/2012/11/kral-rove-fox-news-ohio-call-premature-148745.html

Media & Messages

CHAPTER ONE

Framing the 2012 Presidential Election on U.S. Television

Candidates, Issues, and Sources

DANIELA V. DIMITROVA

Television's role in American elections has been the subject of much scholarly attention since its initial introduction in the late 1940s. The expectations at that time for this great "new medium" were high: It was said to have the potential to reinvigorate American politics and raise the level of political knowledge and interest among the general public. Although these expectations may have yet to be fulfilled, there is no doubt that television has allowed people to become first-hand observers of political history and has brought politicians' images and messages into the homes of ordinary Americans. Television today remains the main source of news for the public and, simply put, has emerged as a "definer and constructor of political reality" (Gurevitch, Coleman, & Blumler, 2009, p. 166). The way television news frames political issues has a substantial impact on the way people make sense of the political world (Cappella & Jamieson, 1997; Iyengar, 1987; de Vreese, 2004).

How the news portrays political issues—going beyond their salience and suggesting certain moral evaluations, causal links and interpretations—is one way through which they exert influence (Entman, 1993). It has been well-documented that media framing, including the selection of the perspectives of different political actors in the news report, has tangible consequences for the public (D'Angelo & Kuypers, 2010). Indeed, how the news media frame politics has significant cognitive, attitudinal, and behavioral effects that are especially important during election campaigns when voters are called upon to elect their political leaders.

Prior research has shown that differential framing can increase or decrease voter knowledge of political issues, change public perceptions of candidates, impact the level of support of certain policies, and ultimately affect public opinion and voting decisions (Iyengar, 1991; de Vreese, 2004).

Given the importance of media framing for public knowledge, candidate perceptions, and policy evaluation as well as the significance of television news for American voters, it is critical to investigate the news framing of the 2012 presidential election campaign. This chapter analyzes the news coverage of the election on the three leading U.S. television networks, ABC, CBS, and NBC. Consistent with previous election news framing research, the analysis shows that the election coverage used strategic game framing at the expense of substantive issue discussion and also tended to be episodic in nature and emphasized conflict. The analysis also demonstrates that domestic politicians dominated the coverage while other sources such as ordinary citizens and experts remained much less visible. The theoretical and practical implications of this type of election news coverage are discussed in the context of journalism practice and democratic governance.

Election News on U.S. Television

Television remains the main vehicle through which the majority of Americans learn about politics (Dimock, Doherty, & Tyson, 2013). Yet both pundits and scholars have frequently criticized television news for failing to provide a comprehensive picture of the election landscape. A rich body of literature on political news framing has demonstrated that the media tend to cover elections as a strategic game, focusing on the horse-race aspects of campaigns rather than on the issues (e.g., Cappella & Jamieson, 1997). Other documented characteristics of news coverage, particularly that on television, are the episodic framing of events when the media fail to provide sufficient context or background to the issues at stake and overemphasize conflict in their coverage (e.g., Iyengar, 1991; Patterson, 1993).

Election news research has identified three main types of frames used by the U.S. media to cover political issues: strategy versus issue frame, episodic versus thematic frame, and conflict frame. The following sections offer a brief review of extant literature for each of these frames.

Politics as a Strategic Game

One of the most common and widely documented trends in election news is the framing of politics as a strategic game, which refers to the media's focus on the horse-race aspects of the campaign rather than issues or policies (Cappella & Jamieson, 1997; Kerbel, Apee, and Ross, 2000; Lawrence, 2000a; Strömbäck & Dimitrova, 2006). Previous research on U.S. elections has clearly shown that the news media tend to report on political campaigns by emphasizing who is winning or losing, what tactics politicians use to move ahead in the polls, or what new strategies they employ to appeal to different voter blocks (Benoit, Stein, & Hansen, 2005; Lawrence, 2000a; Patterson, 1993; Strömbäck & Dimitrova, 2006). These trends, including focusing more on image rather than issues, seem to be true not only for print media (Benoit et al., 2005) but also for television (Kerbel et al., 2000) and not only for news content but also for television advertising (Kaid & Johnston, 2001).

The predominantly strategic or game framing of politics has a number of consequences: It has been shown to increase distrust of the political system and increase disillusionment with the political process as a whole among the American public (Cappella & Jamieson, 1997). Arguably, this type of election coverage does not allow full discussion of political issues or policies, an implicit normative standard of news reporting and democratic governance (Lawrence, 2010). It is also likely to prevent viewers from deeper understanding of the issues at stake and to lead to increased voter cynicism (Cappella & Jamieson, 1997), especially after repeated exposure to such coverage (de Vreese, 2004).

It seems likely that U.S. television news coverage of the 2012 campaign would continue overemphasizing the strategies of political candidates using the game frame at the expense of substantive issue discussion, which provides the basis for the following hypothesis:

H1: Strategic game framing will be more common than issue framing in the television coverage of the 2012 presidential election.

Episodic and Conflict Framing

Another common criticism of U.S. news coverage has been the lack of contextualization of issues or events. From a normative standpoint, this has been particularly troubling in the case of political news reporting. Partly due to limited television time and the structure of television news, most reports tend to be what Iyengar calls "episodic" in nature: They focus on a single event without providing enough context or background to the event beyond the specific instance (Iyengar, 1991). The disadvantage of this kind of reporting is the resulting inability of the viewers to understand the broader issues or the social causes of political phenomena (Iyengar, 1991; Iyengar & Kinder, 1987). This trend is exacerbated on television since the typical newscast has a limited amount of airtime to devote to context

(Entman, 2004). Thus, American viewers are often exposed to brief snippets of information on the campaign with seconds-long sound bites from the main political contenders (Kerbel et al., 2000). In contrast, thematic framing provides more background, contextualization, and in-depth coverage of political issues (Iyengar, 1991).

Previous studies looking at the use of thematic versus episodic framing have determined that when episodic framing is dominant, the audience was left with partial knowledge and sometimes skewed understanding of the issue or event (Iyengar, 1987, 1991; Iyengar & Kinder, 1987). Differential framing also had a significant impact on individual levels of support for government policies such as poverty and unemployment (Iyengar & Kinder, 1987). Finally, when presented with predominantly episodic framing, viewers were also more likely to assign blame to individuals rather than social actors (Iyengar, 1991).

Not only is U.S. television coverage predominantly episodic, it also is heavily focused on conflict in the news. Under increasing commercial pressures (Hamilton, 2004) and following the traditional newsworthiness notion that "conflict sells" (Shoemaker & Reese, 1996), U.S. television networks often display a tendency to overemphasize scandal and conflict (Patterson, 1993). In the follow-up of presidential debates, for example, politicians' viewpoints are often presented as conflicting with those of their opponents by stressing that they disagreed but without explaining what they disagreed about. Conflict framing may be somewhat distracting from core political issues or introduction of new policies (Semetko & Valkenburg, 2000). For example, in covering immigration reform, the media have tended to focus on the conflict between and among the two major political parties regarding immigration legislation. The emphasis on conflict results in less substantial coverage of the policy itself, and this often leaves the American public with little understanding of the specifics of the proposed immigration bill. Conflict framing is not unique to the coverage of political issues; nevertheless it remains a concern for election news coverage in the U.S. media (Patterson, 1993; Strömbäck & Dimitrova, 2006).

Considering the historic trends of increasing episodic and conflict framing on U.S. television, there is no reason to believe that the news media would deviate from their previous patterns of election news reporting in 2012. Therefore, I advance the following hypotheses:

H2: Episodic framing will be more common than thematic framing in the television coverage of the 2012 presidential election.

H3: Conflict framing will be present in the majority of the television coverage of the 2012 presidential election.

News Sources as Framing Devices

The news media can influence the framing of politics either directly or by choosing whose perspectives to highlight in their coverage (Callaghan & Schnell, 2001). Although there is general agreement that news sources constitute one of the most common framing devices (e.g., Entman, 1993; Tankard, 2001), the relationship between news sources and media frames remains understudied. It is often assumed, although rarely tested, that different political actors are likely to promote different message frames (Lawrence, 2010).

News sources are an important and indispensable part of the news making process. On the one hand, sources impact news content by allowing certain political actors to present their viewpoints in the media report and thus influence its meaning and interpretations. On the other hand, the impact of news sources on media discourse may be limited as their placement and selection is ultimately in the hands of the journalists. Although academic debate still continues on whether journalists or politicians take the lead, it is implicitly assumed that the use of sources impacts news framing (Callahan & Schnell, 2001; Gans, 1979; Lawrence, 2000b).

Under the norms of objective reporting, the use of sources is inevitable. Sources perform several key functions in newsgathering and newsmaking. For example, they increase verification of the news account and add credibility to the story (Manning, 2001). Sources also help reduce uncertainty under deadline pressure, avoid accusations of bias, and provide diverse viewpoints about the same issue from multiple stakeholders in society (Manning, 2001; Shoemaker & Reese, 1996; Tuchman, 1978). If a news source is credible, then that credibility is likely to be transferred to the news report. This is one of the reasons why journalists often select the so-called "elite" sources (Manning, 2001; Sigal, 1973). Another reason for choosing official sources on certain topics or issues, especially political issues, is that politicians are considered to have more authoritative voices than average citizens (Callahan & Schnell, 2001; Lawrence, 2000b).

It is not surprising then that the political elite as a whole exerts considerable influence over media content. As Hallin and Mancini (2004) have suggested, it may not be an exaggeration to say that ultimately "the production of news is structured around information and interpretation provided by state officials" (p. 233). Heavy reliance on official sources has been documented as a typical feature of U.S. media coverage in general and of elections coverage in particular (Bennett & Entman, 2001; Gans, 1979; Tuchman, 1978). As stated by Callaghan and Schnell (2001, p.188), "the ability of elites to frame and structure issues for the public via the media is influenced by a political actor's status, credibility, and organizational resources."

As a result, journalists are often criticized for giving politicians more influence and opportunity to present their views in the media as opposed to ordinary citizens who are an important part of the democratic process. Although it is difficult to judge media performance in the absence of clear political news standards, most scholars agree that a diversity of sources is a prerequisite for solid news reporting (see Lawrence, 2010). Giving voice to the perspectives of ordinary citizens, non-partisan experts, and non-government officials (NGOs) is thus assumed to be desirable and necessary from a democratic standpoint.

Another key player in the political arena is the media itself. Recent studies of U.S. media coverage have shown a tendency to insert the viewpoints of other media analysts (that is, journalists outside of those reporting the story) in the news (Dimitrova, Kaid, Williams, & Trammel, 2005; Patterson, 1993). Sometimes called "self-referential" or metacoverage, this tendency demonstrates the increasing influence of media practitioners on media content (Esser & D'Angelo, 2003). The "increasing role of reporters as interpreters in campaign news" (Lawrence, 2010, p. 268) and their impact on the framing of politics needs closer examination.

To examine the use of news sources in the election coverage, the following research question is formulated:

RQ1: What are the main sources used in the television coverage of the 2012 presidential election?

Method

The purpose of this study is to examine the framing of politics in the television coverage of the 2012 U.S. presidential campaign, as television remains the main source of news for the American public (Dimock, Doherty, & Tyson, 2013). The evening newscasts of the top three television networks were selected for analysis, as follows: *ABC World News Tonight with Diane Sawyer*, *CBS Evening News with Scott Pelley*, and *NBC Nightly News with Brian Williams*. The evening news audiences for the three networks combined equaled 22.1 million viewers, with *CBS Evening News* trailing behind *NBC Nightly News* and *ABC World News* (Guskin, Jurkowitz, & Mitchell, 2013).

The content analysis focused on the time period between September 7, 2012, and November 1, 2012. Due to the party nominating conventions that took place in late August and early September in 2012, the analysis did not begin immediately after Labor Day, but it still captured the most intense period of the presidential campaign. The content analysis included all early evening news stories that aired on the three television networks during the selected time period (excluding weekends) and that in words or images explicitly referred to domestic political actors, political institutions, or the presidential election, including stories about voters and political candidates. The actual television news content was examined in its entirety rather than focusing only on keywords, headlines, or news transcripts, which are common limitations of prior studies of television news, especially those relying on computerized content analysis (see Lind & Salo, 2002; Lowry & Xie, 2007).

The unit of analysis was the news story. A news story was defined as a single news item focusing on a particular theme or event. The news story could be introduced by a news anchor or aired on its own as video with voice-over package. When the focus of the news story changed from one theme or event to another, it was counted as a new coding unit. Based on these criteria, 310 news stories were downloaded through the SnapStream television monitoring software and copied for analysis.

The main focus of the study was the media framing of the election campaign. Based on a popular conceptualization, a frame functions to define a problem, suggest a causal link, or propose a solution or a moral evaluation (Entman, 1993). In addition to salience, frames display persistent patterns of emphasis and elaboration in mass media content (Reese, Gandy, & Grant, 2001). Using a deductive approach, the following frames were included in the analysis: strategic game versus issue frame (Cappella & Jamieson, 1996), episodic versus thematic frame (Iyengar, 1991), and conflict frame (Semetko & Valkenburg, 2000). A set of specific questions (listed below) was developed and used to measure the prevalence of each frame in a news story. Each question was coded on a presence/absence basis per story. The questions were summed and then averaged to produce a score ranging from 0 (frame not present) to 1 (frame present), a procedure similar to Semetko and Valkenburg's (2000) framing analysis.

A trained research assistant performed the coding of the news stories. To assess intercoder reliability, another researcher coded 10% of the stories, which were randomly selected from the entire sample. Intercoder reliability across all categories was established at 92.5%, based on Holsti's formula (Holsti, 1969), with an average of 87% for the framing variables and 98% for the source variables.

Results

A total of 310 television news stories were retrieved and analyzed. The stories were approximately equally distributed among the three television news programs: 90

(29%) of the stories aired on *ABC World News*, about the same number of stories (91 or 29.4%) appeared on *NBC Nightly News*, and the remaining 129 (41.6%) of the stories aired on *CBS Evening News*.

Main Topics

Looking at the main topic of the news story, coders could choose from 24 topics plus a category "other." The topics included military and defense, immigration policies, taxes and tax policies, health care, social security/social services, education, the environment, foreign affairs and diplomacy, among others. The most common topic of the news stories was the election campaign as a whole, where specific political or policy issues were not in focus. News about the latest polls, political strategy, fundraising, and campaign events were featured in 232 (74.8%) of the 310 stories. This was by far the main thrust of the television reporting. The second most common topic—perhaps not surprisingly in the context of the 2012 election—was the U.S. economy, including the stock market, gross domestic product, and state/federal budgeting; this topic was dominant in 6.1% of the coverage. A close third were political scandals. Surprisingly, issues such as taxes or health care rarely dominated election news.

Issue Versus Strategic Game Framing

The main topic of the news coverage serves as a harbinger of the overall framing of the election. Politics can be covered via an issue frame or strategic game frame (Cappella & Jamieson, 1997). Four specific questions were developed to evaluate the presence of issue framing. These included whether the story focused on substantive policy issues or solutions, whether it provided politicians' stances on policy issues, whether the story discussed any policy implications for the public, and whether it dealt with real-world problems with policy implications. The use of game framing was accessed with four questions. The first question asked whether the story discussed politicians winning or losing; the second one asked if the story dealt with politicians' strategies for winning; next, it was assessed whether the story dealt with implications or consequences of elections, or how politicians or parties might be affected by elections, governing negotiations, or legislative debates; the last question asked whether the story focused extensively on poll results.

The results of the content analysis showed that only 27 (8.8%) of the stories analyzed focused on substantive policy issues/solutions. Consistent with this finding, only 36 (11.8%) of the coverage examined here provided politicians' stances on policy issues. Less than 10% of the stories (28, or 9.2%) discussed policy implications and slightly more stories (32, or 10.5%) dealt with real-world problems with policy implications. Based on these four questions it can be concluded that issue framing was quite rare.

Looking at the four questions assessing the use of strategic framing, the results showed the following: 249 stories or 80.8% of the coverage dealt extensively with winning or losing the election and 74.7% discussed strategic implications. Poll statistics, as expected, were quite common: politicians' standing in the polls appeared in 70.5% of the coverage. Even more common was discussion of politicians' strategies for winning the election, which appeared in 72.7% of the coverage. By taking the four questions together, it can be concluded that the vast majority of the television coverage included some level of game framing.

After looking at the descriptive statistics for each frame, I developed a score ranging from 0 (frame not present) to 1 (frame present) and tested whether strategic framing was significantly more common compared with issue framing, as predicted by Hypothesis 1. A paired-samples t-test across all stations indicated that there was a statistically significant difference in the expected direction, $t(304) = 20.4, p < .001$. As shown in Table 1, the mean for issue framing ($M = .10$, $SD = .28$) was significantly lower than the mean for game framing ($M = .74$, $SD = .37$). Thus, the expectation that strategic game framing would be more common than issue framing in the 2012 election news coverage was supported.

Table 1. Media Frames by Network in the 2012 Election Coverage

Frames	Network News Channels			Total ($N = 310$)
	ABC	CBS	NBC	
Strategic game frame	.76 (.33)	.71 (.40)	.79 (.35)	.75 (.37)
Issue frame*	.04 (.17)	.14 (.33)	.10 (.27)	.10 (.28)
Episodic frame	.43 (.39)	.38 (.40)	.41 (.38)	.40 (.39)
Thematic frame	.14 (.32)	.24 (.40)	.26 (.39)	.22 (.37)
Conflict frame	.53 (.46)	.50 (.43)	.59 (.44)	.54 (.44)

Note. Table shows means for each frame score with standard deviations in parentheses.
* $p < .05$.

Episodic Versus Thematic Framing

Episodic framing was accessed by asking whether the news story focused just on one particular event, without referring to similar events or relevant background information; whether it provided contextualization to the event; and whether it focused only on a single person's experiences. Thematic framing questions included whether the story dealt with the event in a broader context; whether it placed public issues in a broad, theoretical, or abstract context, for instance, by offering general statistics or examples from other elections; and whether it provided any background of the issue or event.

The data showed the following trends in the 2012 election news coverage. Beginning with episodic framing, the news coverage focused on one particular event in 153 (49.8%) of the cases, without referring to similar events or relevant information. The majority of the televisions stories (151, or 49.2%) did not contextualize the event. Even fewer stories (65, or 21.2%) focused only on a single person's experiences. Taken together, the results showed that about half of the coverage was episodic in nature.

Turning to the level of thematic framing in the 2012 election coverage, the findings showed that the news report dealt with the event in a broader context in 77 (25.2%) of the stories. The news placed public issues in a broad, theoretical, or abstract context, providing general statistics or examples from other elections, in 73 (23.9%) of the coverage. Only 49 (16%) of the election news stories provided background of the issue/event.

To test if the use of thematic framing was substantially lower than that of episodic framing, a paired-samples t-test was conducted to compare the means between the two groups. The results showed that the mean for episodic framing (M = .40, SD = .39) was indeed higher than the mean for thematic framing (M = .22, SD = .37). This difference was statistically significant, $t(305) = 5.2, p < .001$. Thus, hypothesis two was supported.

Conflict Framing

Next, I examined the use of conflict framing in the 2012 television news coverage. The following questions were used to gauge the use of conflict framing: whether the story reflected any disagreement between parties, individuals, or groups; whether it contained disapproval, disappointment, or objection to another party or candidate; and whether it referred to more than one side of an issue or problem. The results show that 175 (57.2%) of the stories reflected disagreement between parties, individuals, or groups. Expressing disapproval, disappointment, or objection to another party or candidate was observed in 138 (45.1%) of the coverage. The majority of the news stories—179 (or 58.5%)—referred to more than one side of an issue or problem, which seems consistent with journalistic conventions.

A one-way ANOVA showed no significant differences between the three television news stations for all but one of the frames. CBS was significantly more likely than ABC or NBC to employ the issue frame in their election coverage, $F(2, 303) = 3.22, p = .04$.

News Sources

Of particular interest to this analysis was the use of news sources. A source was defined as an individual or group that had a directly attributed statement, fact, or quote within the news story. Coders could choose from several different types of sources, including domestic politicians (elected officials or candidates running for office); campaign representatives or party officials; government officials (sources identified as holding either a high or low government position); ordinary citizens (people who are depicted as ordinary citizens, i.e., people who get to speak not due to their position within a certain hierarchy but rather as a "person on the street"); experts (non-partisan political experts such as academics or institutional observers); journalists/media analysts (journalists, correspondents, media analysts, or people identified as working for different media beyond the anchor or the reporter covering a particular story); and partisan commentators/pundits. The number of times a particular type of source was used in the news story was recorded and compared across networks (see Table 2).

Table 2. News Sources by Network in the 2012 Election Coverage

Frames	Network News Channels			Total
	ABC	CBS	NBC	($N = 310$)
Domestic politician***	1.21 (1.11)	.79 (.87)	1.56 (1.51)	1.14 (1.20)
Campaign/party official	.69 (.07)	.33 (.66)	.57 (.98)	.42 (.78)
Ordinary citizen	.44 (1.12)	.40 (1.17)	.31 (.90)	.39 (1.08)
Media analyst*	.19 (.54)	.05 (.21)	.13 (.38)	.12 (.39)
Pundit/commentator**	.11 (.51)	.02 (.15)	.24 (.66)	.11 (.47)
Government official	.03 (.18)	.09 (.42)	.12 (.36)	.08 (.35)
Expert (non-partisan)	.06 (.28)	.05 (.25)	.10 (.34)	.07 (.29)

Note. Table shows means for each source with standard deviations in parentheses.
$^* p < .05.$ $^{**} p < .01.$ $^{***} p < .001.$

Perhaps not surprisingly, the most common news sources were domestic politicians, namely those running in the election. Looking at the descriptive statistics, one can observe that, on average, at least one domestic politician was quoted in each television news story. That number ranged between 0 and 7, meaning that some stories did not include politicians as sources while others quoted as many as seven politicians. Campaign representatives (although the second most common source) and government officials were referenced less frequently, providing some evidence for personality-driven coverage.

Of particular interest was the use of ordinary citizens/average voters as news sources. They came as a distant third ($M = .39$, $SD = 1.08$). Another category trying to capture the use of non-elite sources was that of experts. Experts were cited even less frequently than ordinary citizens ($M = .07$, $SD = .29$). In other words, the use of non-partisan experts was quite rare.

Finally, two source categories were used to capture the influence of media professionals on news coverage. One included commentators/pundits that belonged to or were affiliated with a particular party while the other designated journalists/media analysts beyond those reporting the story. The results showed that media analysts ($M = .12$, $SD = .39$) were slightly more common than partisan commentators ($M = .11$, $SD = .47$).

To see whether there were any significant differences in source use across the three networks, a one-way ANOVA was conducted. The results indicate some interesting differences (see Table 2). First, CBS was significantly less likely than ABC or NBC to use domestic politicians as sources, $F(2, 301) = 11.72$, $p < .000$. Conversely, ABC and NBC were significantly more likely than CBS to incorporate media analysts, $F(2, 301) = 3.85$, $p = .02$, and partisan commentators, $t(303) = 5.53$, $p = .004$, in their election coverage.

Discussion

This chapter examines the news framing of the 2012 presidential election campaign on the leading news networks in the United States. The analysis shows that the television coverage followed patterns identified in previous U.S. elections and lacked thematic and issue framing. The overall findings point to a predominantly horse-race, episodic coverage that generally failed to provide substantive discussion of policy issues. Election news focused on episodic framing and emphasized conflict. As a result, the mainstream American viewer was exposed to coverage that by and large emphasized winners versus losers, current stance in the polls, and future strategies in the presidential race.

What are the possible effects of such predominantly strategic, horse-race media coverage? Scholars have suggested that one unintended consequence of the strategic game frame is the increased level of cynicism toward politicians and the political process in general. As Cappella and Jamieson (1996) eloquently put it, "strategic coverage may remind the audience of the self-interest of actors in winning the campaign …. When the motivations of each side in a campaign … are colored by accusations of self-interested action, one response may be to dismiss both sides and eventually to dismiss the process itself" (p. 81). Such negative consequences of political news framing may gradually accumulate over time.

Ironically, the predominantly strategic election coverage and emphasis on conflict are also likely to contribute to low public confidence in the news media. Other possible effects are disempowering the American public to make informed decisions when the only way for them to learn about political candidates and their policy stances is through the media. Fast-moving, short, and isolated television coverage of political issues is hardly the best way to stay informed or get involved in politics. If, as some have suggested, the media tell the public how to think about politics and how to evaluate politicians (Cappella & Jamieson, 1997; Iyengar & Kinder, 1987; de Vreese, 2004), then media appearances and poll standing may soon matter more than issues and policy.

Another important—although hardly surprising—finding was that elite sources continue to dominate election coverage. Consistent with historical trends, the reliance on official sources remains disproportionately higher than other types of sources (Gans, 1979; Sigal, 1973). One possible change, however, is the ascendance of the individual politician rather than the party or campaign representatives; politicians as personalities are now "front and center" on the national media stage and their increasing dominance has certain implications for the public. First, voters are increasingly exposed to personality-driven coverage, which gives politicians the power to set the public agenda. Second, the heavy focus on the individual politicians leads to more human-interest, image-focused coverage and potentially dilutes issue coverage. Third, the overreliance on elite sources obliterates other viewpoints coming from non-partisan groups such as NGOs, academic experts, or average citizens, which then limits the range of debate (Lawrence, 2010).

The rising importance of politicians as drivers of election coverage suggests there may be a more complex, indirect relationship between sources and media frames. If sources are seen as one of several framing devices, then it is not far-fetched to claim that they influence the dominant frame of the news report. This claim seems supported by the characteristics of the CBS coverage: It was significantly more issue-oriented; at the same time, it relied less on politicians, media analysts, and pundits than the other two networks. The relationship between election news sources and media frames calls for a closer examination.

It is difficult to pinpoint exactly what causes this episodic, conflict-ridden, horse-race coverage. Certainly one culprit is the nature of television news reporting: having only 30 or 60 seconds is hardly enough time to discuss and provide enough background to an issue or policy proposal (Iyengar, 2001). Some blame the nature of contemporary U.S. journalism (Kerbel et al., 2000) on the audience itself, who may be more interested in conflict and celebrity rather than issues and substance (Patterson, 1993). Others see the commercial media system, which forces television networks to shift their focus to personalities and conflict in order to keep ratings high, at fault (Hamilton, 2004).

At the end of the day, the television news coverage of the 2012 presidential election was not substantially different from the patterns observed in previous election campaigns. Despite the promises of hope and "change we can believe in" in the rhetoric of the winning presidential candidate, one thing has not changed: the way the U.S. media frame elections. However, it is important to keep in mind that television news content is the result of multi-layered decisions and processes that are influenced by journalism culture, organizational pressures and constraints, and broader ideological and cultural factors (Shoemaker & Reese, 1996). The link between each of these factors, following Shoemaker and Reese's hierarchy of influences, and the framing of politics in the news is a worthwhile avenue for future research. Future studies should also continue to examine how media frames change with the use of different sources and ultimately influence audience frames and understanding of the political world. This can be achieved through experimental studies or longitudinal research designs.

References

Bennett, W. L., & Entman, R. M. (Eds.) (2001). *Mediated politics: Communication in the future of democracy*. New York, NY: Cambridge University Press.

Benoit, W. L., Stein, K. A., & Hansen, G. J. (2005). *New York Times'* coverage of presidential campaigns. *Journalism and Mass Communication Quarterly, 82*(2), 356–376.

Callahan, K., & Schnell, F. (2001). Assessing the democratic debate: How the news media frame elite policy discourse. *Political Communication, 18*(2), 183–212.

Cappella, J. N., & Jamieson, K. H. (1996). News frames, political cynicism, and media cynicism. *Annals of the American Academy of Political and Social Science, 546*(1), 71–84.

Cappella, J. N., & Jamieson, K. H. (1997). *Spiral of cynicism: The press and the public good.* New York, NY: Oxford University Press.

D'Angelo, P., & Kuypers, J. A. (Eds.) (2010). *Doing news framing analysis: Empirical and theoretical perspectives.* New York, NY: Routledge.

de Vreese, C. (2004). The effects of strategic news on political cynicism, issue evaluations, and policy support: A two-wave experiment. *Mass Communication and Society, 7*(2), 191–214.

Dimitrova, D. V., Kaid, L. L., Williams, A., & Trammell, K. D. (2005). War on the web: The immediate news framing of Gulf War II." *The Harvard International Journal of Press/Politics, 10*(1), 22–44.

Dimitrova, D. V., & Strömbäck, J. (2009). Look who's talking: Use of sources in newspaper coverage in Sweden and the United States. *Journalism Practice, 3*(1), 75–91.

Dimock, M., Doherty, C., & Tyson, A. (2013). *Amid criticism, support for media's 'watchdog' role stands out.* Retrieved from the Pew Research Center for the People & the Press website: http://www.people-press.org/files/legacy-pdf/8-8-2013%20Media%20Attitudes%20Release.pdf

Entman, R. M. (1993). Framing: Toward clarification of a fractured paradigm. *Journal of Communication, 43*(4), 51–58.

Esser, F., & D'Angelo, P. (2003). Framing the press and the publicity process: A content analysis of meta-coverage in campaign 2000 network news. *American Behavioral Scientist, 46*(5), 617–641.

Gans, H. J. (1979). *Deciding What's News: A Study of CBS Evening News, NBC Nightly News, Newsweek and Time.* New York, NY: Pantheon.

Gurevitch, M., Coleman, S., & Blumler, J. G. (2009). Political communication—old and new media relationships. *The Annals of the American Academy of Political and Social Science, 625*(1), 164–181.

Guskin, E., Jurkowitz, M., & Mitchell, A. (2013). *The state of the news media 2013: An annual report on American journalism.* Retrieved from the Pew Research Center's Project for Excellence in Journalism website: http://stateofthemedia.org/2013/network-news-a-year-of-change-and-challenge-at-nbc/

Hallin, D. C., & Mancini, P. (2004). *Comparing media systems. Three models of media and politics.* New York, NY: Cambridge University Press.

Hamilton, J. T. (2004). *All the news that's fit to sell: How the market transforms information into news.* Princeton, NJ: Princeton University Press.

Holsti, O. R. (1969). *Content analysis for the social sciences and humanities.* Reading, MA: Addison-Wesley.

Iyengar, S. (1987). Television news and citizens' explanations of national issues. *American Political Science Review, 81*, 815–832.

Iyengar, S. (1991). *Is anyone responsible? How television frames political issues.* Chicago, IL: University of Chicago Press.

Iyengar, S., & Kinder, D. (1987). *News that matters: Television and American opinion.* Chicago, IL: University of Chicago Press.

Kaid, L. L., & Johnston, A. (2001). Negative versus positive television advertising in presidential campaigns, 1960–1988. *Journal of Communication, 41*(3), 53–64.

Kerbel, M. R., Apee, S., & Ross, M. H. (2000). PBS ain't so different: Public broadcasting, election frames and democratic empowerment. *The Harvard International Journal of Press/Politics, 5*(4), 8–32.

Lawrence, R. G. (2000a). Game-framing the issues: Tracking the strategy frame in public policy news. *Political Communication, 17*(2), 93–114.

Lawrence, R. G. (2000b). *The politics of force: Media and the construction of police brutality.* Berkeley, CA: University of California Press.

Lawrence, R. G. (2010). Researching political news framing: Established ground and new horizons. In P. D'Angelo & J. A. Kuypers (Eds.), *Doing news framing analysis: Empirical and theoretical perspectives* (pp. 265–285). New York, NY: Routledge.

Lind, R. A., & Salo, C. (2002). The framing of feminists and feminism in news and public affairs programs in U.S. electronic media. *Journal of Communication, 52*(1), 211–228.

Lowry, D., & Xie, L. (2007). *Agenda-setting and framing by topic proximity: A new technique for the computerized content analysis of network TV news presidential campaign coverage.* Paper presented at the annual meeting of the International Communication Association, San Francisco, CA.

Manning, P. (2001). *News and news sources: A critical introduction.* London, England: SAGE Publications.

Patterson, T. E. (1993). *Out of order.* New York, NY: Knopf.

Reese, S. D., Gandy, O. H., & Grant, A. E. (Eds.). (2001). *Framing public life: Perspectives on media and our understanding of the social world.* Mahwah, NJ: Lawrence Erlbaum.

Semetko, H. A., & Valkenburg, P. M. (2000). Framing European politics: A content analysis of press and television news. *Journal of Communication, 50*(2), 93–109.

Shoemaker, P. J., & Reese, S. D. (1996). *Mediating the message: Theories of influences on mass media content* (2nd Ed.). White Plains, NY: Longman.

Sigal, L. V. (1973). *Reporters and officials: The organization and politics of newsmaking.* Lexington, MA: D. C. Heath & Co.

Strömbäck, J., & Dimitrova, D. V. (2006). Political and media systems matter: A comparison of election news coverage in Sweden and the United States. *The Harvard International Journal of Press/Politics, 11*(4), 131–147.

Tankard, J. W., Jr. (2001). The empirical approach to the study of media framing. In S. D. Reese, O. H. Gandy, & A. E. Grant (Eds.), *Framing public life: Perspectives on media and our understanding of the social world* (pp. 95–106). Mahwah, NJ: Lawrence Erlbaum.

Tuchman, G. (1978). *Making news: A study in the construction of reality.* New York, NY: Free Press.

CHAPTER TWO

To Form a More Polarized Electorate?

The Effect of Presidential Debates on Polarization, Partisanship, and Political Aggression

JOSHUA HAWTHORNE AND MITCHELL S. MCKINNEY

Following Barack Obama's re-election in November of 2012, hundreds of thousands of angry citizens signed online petitions hosted on the White House webpage advocating for the secession from the union of all 50 states (Kwong, 2012). Although electoral defeat has often sparked notions of secession in the past (Reynolds, 2012), the most recent petitions might be viewed as an indicator of the current state of American democracy. Indeed, a sizable segment of the electorate would rather completely separate from those with whom they disagree politically than work together in reaching consensus on the many difficult issues facing our nation. This lack of ability or effort for citizens and their leaders to compromise has been a growing trend in recent history. For example, consider the 112th U.S. Congress (serving from 2010 through 2012), which set a new record as the least productive Congress to enact legislation since such records have been kept (Brennan & Abdullah, 2012).

The inability of leaders and citizens to compromise becomes even more troubling when we consider that our nation's increasing partisanship tends not to be based on actual policy differences, but rather based on identification with and, conversely, dislike towards social groups (Conover & Feldman, 1981; Conover, 1984, 1988; Zschirnt, 2011). Although close identification within and among social groups is not inherently a bad thing, it can become problematic for a democracy when such extreme identification preempts productive policy debates. Returning to the example of the U.S. Congress, there are many potential causes for legislative inactivity. Yet intractable differences between the political parties, caused by intense identification among opposing social groups, could well be a contributing factor to our nation's current sad state of legislative and public policy "gridlock" and thus should be explored further.

Scholars have described the phenomenon that occurs when individuals identify completely with one political group, yet are unable to identify at all with another as affect political polarization (Iyengar, Sood, & Lelkes, 2012). Iyengar et al. (2012) have found that affect political polarization has increased within the U.S. electorate over the past few decades. As seemingly intractable differences have increased among citizens and our leaders in more recent years, it is important that we explore the potential causes and effects of affect political polarization on voters.

The current investigation of citizens' affect political polarization is guided by terror management theory (TMT), a perspective that describes how individuals in different social groups interact with each other when social group identification is an ingrained part of one's cultural worldview (Greenberg, Pyszczynski, & Solomon, 1986). Cultural worldview serves as an individual's ontological and epistemological base for understanding the universe (Koltko-Rivera, 2004), and this base of knowledge includes stereotypes to which people are expected to conform (Schimel et al., 1999). TMT suggests that when exposed to individuals who challenge or contradict one's cultural worldview, the holder of that worldview may react with aggression and increased dislike for the contradiction, among other less drastic reactions (Greenberg, Solomon, & Pyszczynski, 1997; Miller & Landau, 2005). A contradiction to one's cultural worldview can manifest when exposed to arguments or factual information that leads one to question elements of one's own worldview (Greenberg et al., 1986; Hawthorne & Warner, 2013), and also when exposed to an individual that violates the stereotypes ascribed to other social groups (Schimel et al., 1999). With political ideology acting as a crucial element of cultural worldview for some individuals (Hawthorne & Warner, 2013), TMT might fruitfully be applied in the political campaign context to better understand the consequences of increased affect political polarization.

This project applies TMT to a specific campaign message, the televised presidential campaign debate. Presidential debate viewing has been found to increase affect political polarization (Warner & McKinney, 2013), indicating that at least one political outcome predicted by TMT has been observed from campaign debate exposure. Debate viewing, therefore, may well represent a political message context in which other effects predicted by TMT may also be found. This chapter provides a more extensive review of TMT to situate analysis of campaign communication within the theory, and also to further argue that political ideology functions as part of some individuals' cultural worldview. First, however, the importance of the debate message is established to better understand how political campaign debates can both unite and divide the electorate.

Campaign Debate Messages

Certainly, on one level, general election presidential debates function to unite the electorate by assembling the largest audience of any single televised campaign event (McKinney & Carlin, 2004). As the only moment of the entire campaign where opposing candidates meet face-to-face, so, too, is this the only televised event—except for election night—where partisans on both sides assemble to cheer on their party's candidate. Unlike the televised party conventions or even primary debates that appeal largely to a party's base, general-election presidential debates attract a large audience of competing partisans, so-called independents, and the few remaining undecided voters who have yet to commit to a particular candidate. In fact, the three debates between President Obama and former Gov. Mitt Romney, and the single vice presidential debate between Vice President Joe Biden and Rep. Paul Ryan in 2012 were watched by a total of 243.4 million viewers (Commission on Presidential Debates, 2012).

Early presidential debate research found exposure to the candidates—including the candidate one supports as well as the opposition candidate—achieved beneficial results for both candidates. For example, Chaffee's (1978) analysis revealed that debate viewers experienced reinforcement in previously held views regarding the candidate they supported, while also feeling more positive about the opposition candidate. Chaffee (1978, p. 334) also found debate viewers "learned a good deal of information…and they were as likely to learn it from statements made by the candidate they supported as they were when it came from the opposition candidate." Finally, Lanoue and Schrott (1991) found that debates improved viewers' overall support for the political system, and assessments of both candidates' images improved following debate exposure.

However, other campaign debate research has found very different results in terms of viewers' partisan feelings and candidate evaluations. For example, Miller and MacKuen's (1979) analysis found partisans' assessments of their supported candidates' image became more positive while their views regarding opposition candidates became less favorable after watching a debate. More recent research also has found that citizens' political polarization (Warren & McKinney, 2013) and partisanship (Holbert, LaMarre, & Landreville, 2009) increased after viewing presidential debates. Given discrepant findings regarding the effect of debates on viewers' partisan attitudes, yet relying more on the most recent research in this area, we draw on TMT as a theoretical lens to understand why and how the campaign debate message may increase political polarization, strengthen partisanship, and perhaps even activate expressed political aggression when one's worldview is challenged.

A Closer Look at Terror Management Theory

Terror management theory posits that individuals create cultural worldviews to cope with their existential fear of death (Solomon, Greenberg, & Pyszczynski, 2000). The knowledge of our impending demise, and the parallel existential fear that such knowledge generates, requires a distraction from the fear of death. Cultural worldviews provide this needed distraction and allow us to engage in daily activities that are thought to enhance survival (Greenberg, Solomon, & Pyszczynski, 1997). A cultural worldview represents a belief system held by an individual that gives the universe order and provides rules regarding what should and should not exist (Koltko-Rivera, 2004). Cultural worldviews are shared beliefs with other people in a social group and the existence of shared worldviews is maintained by the support and acknowledgment of others within the group (Becker, 1971, 1973, 1975; Pyszczynski, 2004). Though worldviews are shared between and among group members, each individual has their own unique cultural worldview consisting of many different elements based on their personal life experiences and the various social gropus to which they belong (Anson, Pyszczynksi, Solomon, & Greenberg, 2009). An important component of a cultural worldview is the stereotypes developed through life experience of people who belong to different social groups (Schimel et al., 1999). Terror management theory predicts that individuals, functioning as part of a social group, will gain self-esteem and feel that they are a "valuable member of a meaningful universe" as they contribute to the group (Solomon et al., 2000, p. 201).

An individual's political orientation has been described as a psychological attachment (Simon, 2002), and has been shown to correspond closely with one's associations with chosen social groups (Conover & Feldman, 1981; Conover, 1984, 1988; Zschirnt, 2011). In this way, political parties function as an important element of one's cultural worldview as these social collectives allow their members to contribute to the group (by voting, financial contribution, and/or volunteering) and thereby raise members' self-esteem. Such association and contributions allow members to believe they are contributing to a movement that is larger than self, therefore helping individuals achieve some sense of figurative immortality (Miller & Landau, 2005; Solomon et al., 2000). Therefore, it is likely that one's political ideology, and therefore political party affiliation by proxy, serve as important components of individuals' worldviews (Anson et al., 2009).

Another important component of TMT is the mortality salience prime whereby individuals are challenged with reminders that they will die (Solomon et al., 1991). The psychological processes at work here are based on the fact that cultural worldviews function as a defense from our existential fear of death, and reminders of death will influence people to react in ways that conserve their worldview. Reactions may include the defeat of or increased dislike toward those that threaten one's worldview, among other less drastic reactions (Greenberg et al., 1997). Past studies employing a mortality salience prime have found that participants punish violators of cultural norms more than those not experiencing the prime (Rosenblatt, Greenberg, Solomon, Pyszczynski, & Lyon, 1989); and, increased aggression is directed towards those who threaten one's cultural worldview (McGregor et al., 1998). Furthermore, mortality salience primes are found to enhance stereotypic thinking and enhance preferences for those who conform to one's stereotypes (Schimel et al., 1999).

Descriptions of TMT outline instances in which a threat to one's cultural worldview occurs due to the mere presence of an individual from a different social group, even without an overt challenge or existence of an explicit mortality salience prime (Solomon et al., 1991; Anson et al., 2009). As Solomon, Greenberg, and Pyszczynski (1991) describe:

> [T]he mere existence of others who do not share our central attitudes, beliefs, and values is threatening because, if others do not agree with us, it implies that we might be wrong. Consequently, different others motivate action to eradicate the threat and thereby defend the validity of the worldview. (p. 125)

Whether mere exposure to those who threaten our cultural worldview's validity is enough to trigger a reaction, as predicted by TMT, is a key question of the current study. Although assumptions of TMT suggest this might be the case, there are very few empirical results supporting this assertion and even fewer studies in the context of politics and campaign communication. In seeking to fill this void Hawthorne and Warner (2013) found exposure to rhetoric that challenges one's preferred candidate did in fact increase expressed aggression. Therefore, with those results in mind, the current analysis seeks to determine if a presidential campaign debate, as a potential threat to one's cultural worldview, results in increased affect political polarization and also increased political aggression.

Campaign Debates as Site for Worldview Threats

Miller and Landau (2005) have suggested that "the critical condition for terror management defenses … to occur is heightened accessibility of death-related thoughts outside of conscious awareness" (p. 81). The current project tests this ability in relation to political debate messages and explores whether exposure to individuals and ideas that conflict with one's worldview represents an adequate mortality salience prime that could instigate a worldview defense in the form of increased political polarization and aggression. There are several features of presidential campaign debates that make this message a potentially strong threat to one's worldview. First, Carlin (1992) describes general election debates as focal points of presidential campaigns in which the dominant themes and most powerful arguments from each campaign are offered to the public. Also, candidates in a presidential debate construct their language to highlight clash and difference with one's opponent (Carlin, Howard, Stanfield, & Reynolds, 1991). Finally, as Morello (1988) points out, the televised format and context surrounding these debates further enhances the staged drama and perceived clash that occurs between the candidates due to television production and visual editing techniques.

These various argumentative, verbal and visual components of the debate message coalesce to create several possible threats to one's worldview. When a candidate challenges their opponent and makes the case this individual should not be elected, those that support the candidate who is challenged are confronted with an argument as to why their cultural worldview is flawed. This challenge may be perceived as a direct threat to their cultural worldview and therefore may trigger a reaction of increased aggression (Greenberg et al., 1997; Hawthorne & Warner, 2013). Also, when a candidate that one does not support makes the case as to why they are the superior candidate, this argument may be perceived as violating a stereotype that one holds regarding someone from a different or outside group (Schimel et al., 1999). Individuals who are intensely partisan may believe that those of the opposing party are inherently unelectable and undesirable, and thus exposure to an opposition party member discussing why they should be elected the leader of our nation may cause a negative reaction. Finally, analysis guided by TMT has found that mere exposure to those that are different from one can affect a worldview defense (Hawthorne & Warner, 2013). A similar reaction may occur as one is exposed to individuals with differing political views and the intense arguments found in debate dialogue.

The current study explores threats to one's worldview and possible reactions namely dislike for the opposition political party, its presidential candidate and ideology, and potentially resultant expressed political aggression. Our first hypothesis explores presidential debate viewers' political polarization. Previous research has found that exposure to debates typically increases affect political polarization (Warner & McKinney, 2013), and some evidence suggests that extreme partisans may be even more prone to greater polarization (Holbert et al., 2009). We first explore this relationship that has been found in previous research and also examine how debate exposure may affect pre-existing levels of polarization and also political partisanship:

> H1: Viewers' affect political polarization will increase following exposure to a presidential debate.

> RQ1: Does intensity of change in debate viewers' political polarization relate to pre-debate polarization?

> RQ2: Does intensity of change in debate viewers' political polarization relate to pre-debate partisanship?

Next, our project examines the relationship between affect polarization and political aggression in the debate-viewing context. Also, the relationship between political aggression and different levels of partisanship are explored. With little guidance from past research available, we posit the following exploratory research questions:

> RQ3: Does political aggression relate to one's level of affect political polarization?

> RQ4: Does political aggression relate to one's level of partisanship?

Method

To address our hypothesis and research questions, affect political polarization, political aggression and partisanship scales were included as part of a larger presidential debate effect study. The data were collected from participants who watched the first presidential debate between Obama and Romney on October 3, 2012, and the vice presidential debate between Biden and Ryan that occurred on October 11, 2012 (Commission on Presidential Debates, 2012).

In total, the study included 459 participants, all drawn from a convenience sample, with most consisting of college students who were offered extra credit in exchange for their participation. Although a convenience sample is not ideal for experimental research, its use is justified within the context of the current exploratory study and particularly as meta-analysis of debate effects has shown no significant differences in the effects sizes between convenience and nationally representative samples (Benoit, Hansen, & Verser, 2003). The sample was primarily female (n = 268, 58.5%; male: n = 190, 41.4%) with one person not reporting their sex. The age of participants ranged from 17 to 58 (M = 20.36, SD = 4.22). The sample was also primarily Caucasian (n = 342, 74.5%), but Hispanics (n = 33, 7.2%), African-Americans (n = 29, 6.3%), Asian or Pacific Islanders (n = 19, 4.1%), and individuals identifying as other races/ethnicities (n = 35, 7.6%) were also represented, with one individual not responding. Participants watched the debate at one of nine universities/colleges across the country, as the debate was broadcast nationally, including institutions located in Alabama, Georgia, Massachusetts, Missouri, Tennessee, Texas, Virginia, Washington, and Wisconsin. An online survey tool was used to collect all data; consequently all participants were required to bring a laptop computer or smart phone to complete pre- and post-debate surveys.

Measures

Political Polarization. Polarization was determined using an affect-based measure of polarization (Iyengar et al., 2012; Skitka, Bauman, & Sargis, 2005). Feeling thermometers to assess reactions to liberals, conservatives, Democrats, and Republicans were used. Participants were instructed to report how much they liked (scoring from 50 to 100 on the thermometer) or disliked (scoring from 0 to 50 on the thermometer) each group. The sum of the score on the liberal and Democrat thermometers was subtracted from the sum of the score on the conservative and Republican thermometers resulting in an affect based ideology score ranging from -200 to 200. The absolute value of this score was taken, resulting in a polarization score ranging from 0 (implying the individual was a political moderate) to 200 (implying that the individual had extremely high affect political polarization). The same scale was used on the pre- and posttest surveys to measure affect polarization.

    Political Partisanship. Partisanship was measured on a 10-point scale ranging from extremely liberal (1) to extremely conservative (10).

    Political Aggression. Aggression was measured using an edited version of Kalmoe's (2010) acceptance of political violence scale. The scale has been used in previous research exploring how political rhetoric affects aggression (Hawthorne & Warner, 2013). The scale is made up of 11 statements with participants responding from 1 (completely disagree) to 7 (completely agree). The items include the following statements: "The tree of liberty needs to be nourished with the blood of revolution"; "If we can't find a peaceful solution to the problems facing America, true patriots may need to take matters into their own hands"; "When politics fail, violence is sometimes necessary"; "I can see why some people support violent revolution"; "If elections don't fix America's problems, we may need to pursue 2nd Amendment remedies"; "I can foresee a day when violent measures may need to be taken to protect the United States from itself"; "When politicians are damaging the country, citizens should send threats to scare them straight"; "The worst politicians should get a brick through the window to make them stop hurting the country"; "Sometimes the only way to stop bad government is with physical force"; "Some of the problems citizens have with government could be fixed with a few well-aimed bullets"; and "Citizens upset by government should never use violence to express their feelings" (reverse coded item). An acceptance of political violence scale was used rather than a behavioral scale to ameliorate social desirability bias that could be associated with likelihood of engaging in specific behaviors that measure political aggression. As past research regarding aggression suggests, an individual's thoughts about the appropriateness of violent actions predicts future violent activity (Anderson & Bushman, 2002). Therefore the scale was only administered in the posttest survey to avoid testing bias and achieved very good reliability ($\alpha = .91$).

Analysis

Our hypothesis was evaluated using a simple paired sample t-test. However, the remaining research questions require more sophisticated analysis as they ask how variables vary in relationship to another variable. Therefore, generalized additive models were calculated to understand how the mean of the dependent variables changes at different levels of the predictor variables.[1] Generalized additive models work by fitting a smooth function to the relationship between the predictor and dependent variables.

Results

First, we hypothesized that debate viewers' affect political polarization would increase from pretest to posttest. A simple, paired sample t-test was used to test this hypothesis. The test revealed that posttest levels of affect political polarization ($M = 86.97$, $SD = 53.46$) were significantly higher that pretest levels of polarization ($M = 93.24$, $SD = 59.35$), $t(446) = -5.14$, $p < .001$. Therefore, the finding that debate exposure increases political polarization supports the hypothesis.

Research questions one and two examine the relationship between the magnitude of polarization change at different levels of pre-debate polarization and partisanship. To explore these relationships a single general additive model was computed with affect polarization change (calculated by subtracting posttest affect polarization from pretest affect polarization) as the dependent variable with pretest affect polarization and partisanship as the predictor variables. The model explained 6.29% of the deviance associated with affect polarization change. The smooth curves associated with pretest levels of polarization $F(1.00, 1.00) = 14.11$, $p < .001$, and partisanship, $F(7.12,$

8.25) = 2.49, $p < .05$, were both significant predictors of polarization change. The relationships between these variables can be seen in Figure 1. These findings indicate that those individuals who were less polarized prior to the debate experienced greater polarization change after debate viewing than those who were highly polarized prior to the debate. Also, those most extreme in their partisanship—both extreme liberals and conservatives—experienced greater change in affect polarization following debate viewing than those who were more moderate in their partisanship.

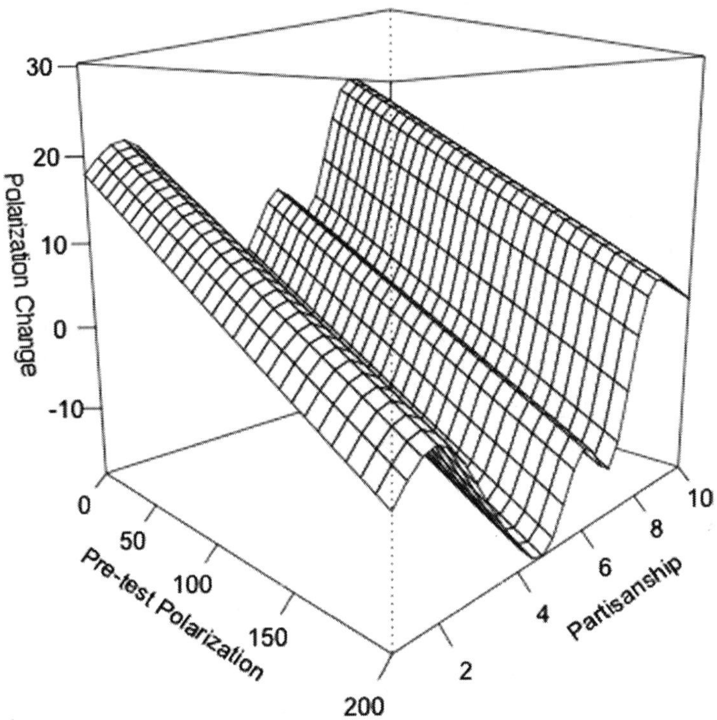

Figure 1. Planar Relationship Between Pretest Polarization, Partisanship, and Polarization Change

Research questions three and four explore the relationship between political aggression as a dependent variable and between pretest levels of polarization and partisanship as predictor variables. Again, a single general additive model was fit to explore this relationship. The model accounted for 6.81% of the deviance associated with the variance on the political aggression variable. The smooth curve associated with pre-test level of polarization variable, $F(2.12, 2.64) = 2.76$, $p < .05$, and partisanship,

$F(2.11, 2.73) = 7.87, p < .001$, were both significant predictors of political aggression. The planar curve of pretest levels of polarization and partisanship against political aggression can be observed in Figure 2. Note that the values of aggression are higher at the low and high ends of the pretest polarization range and that the values of aggression are lower at the middle levels of the pretest polarization scale. Also, it appears that those toward the liberal end of the partisanship variable were less politically aggressive than those toward the conservative end. This indicates that those with lower and higher pretest polarization reported feeling more politically aggressive than those with middle values of pretest polarization and that conservatives were more aggressive than liberals.

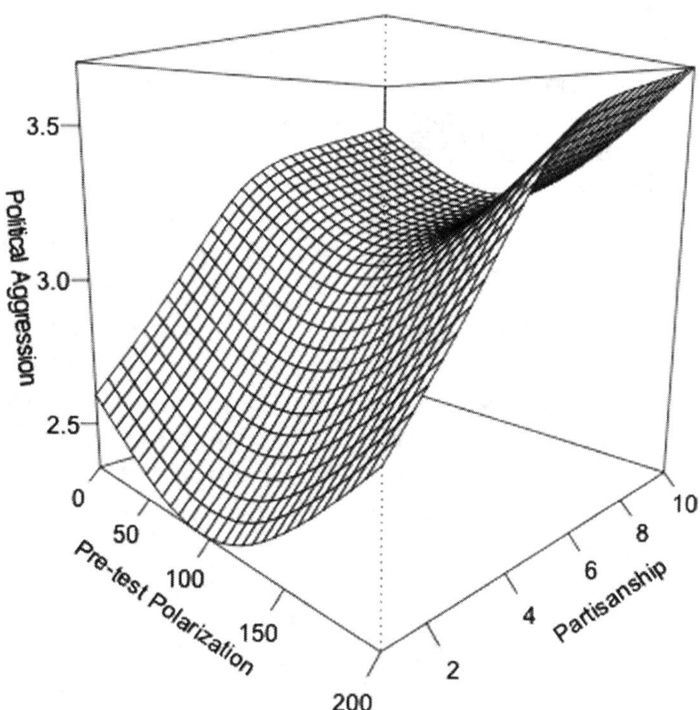

Figure 2. Planar Relationship Between Pretest Polarization, Partisanship, and Political Aggression

Discussion

This project applied terror management theory to the campaign communication context to explore possible negative effects of presidential debate exposure, specifically increased partisanship, political polarization and aggression. Terror management theory posits that when one's cultural worldview is threatened increased dislike and aggression towards the threat will result (Greenberg et al., 1997). A campaign debate provides opportunities for threats to one's political orientation–based cultural worldview and therefore a reaction was predicted and tested following this threat exposure.

The results showed that political polarization increased for all participants following debate viewing no matter one's pre-debate level of polarization. Still, increases in polarization were found to be significantly higher in debate viewers who were less polarized prior to the debate than for participants who were more highly polarized before their debate exposure. Polarization change levels also varied with differences in one's level of partisanship as those who were more extremely liberal or conservative became more polarized following debate exposure compared to those who were more moderate in their political partisanship. The increases in viewers' political polarization found in the current study support previous findings from analysis of campaign debate exposure (Warner & McKinney, 2013). Also, that increases in polarization were greater for those who were more highly partisan supports the notion that debates may strengthen partisanship and especially so for those most extreme in their partisan attitudes (Holbert et al., 2009). This finding also suggests that political orientation may be a more prevalent component of one's cultural worldview among more extreme partisans. Here, it appears that a greater threat to worldview is perceived, and greater reaction in the form of increased polarization occurs, for those who are more extreme in their partisan attitudes.

The fact that those who had the least amount of affect political polarization experienced the greatest increases following debate exposure may likely be due to a "ceiling effect" in which our measurement was unable to capture continued increases in polarization beyond the 100 point upper limit of the feeling thermometer scale. In short, while those less polarized before the debate had ample room to indicate increases in post-debate polarization, those already at the upper limit of our scale had little to no room for additional increases in their polarization. An alternative explanation may be that those who were less polarized before debate viewing represented individuals with less interest and exposure to politics. With less exposure to politics and the ongoing campaign, these individuals may not yet have formed an affective judgment about the two candidates or political parties prior to debate exposure and therefore indicated less pre-debate polarization. Following the debate, however, these individuals may well have felt more confident in their assessments of the candidates and political parties and were more certain as to which political group they most closely associated with based on arguments the candidates made during the debate. This greater knowledge and confidence may have resulted in more clearly discerned differences and increased political polarization.

Our analysis also revealed that political aggression following the debate was higher among individuals whose political polarization was at the extremes—both low and high—prior to debate exposure compared to individuals who had moderate affect polarization before viewing a debate. Also, those who were more conservative reported higher levels of political aggression. Although these results do not point to any causal claims, as participants' political aggression was only measured post-debate, our findings do reveal quite interesting relationships between political aggression, polarization and partisanship.

First, our guiding theoretical perspective suggests that those with higher levels of political aggression may have experienced greater threat to their political worldview from candidates' debate argumentation than those reporting lower levels of aggression. Our findings revealed that individuals who were least and most politically polarized before debate exposure reported the highest levels of political aggression post debate. Here, it may well be that one who is moderate in their political polarization is not prone to aggressive or hostile reaction when confronted with claims that challenge one's political beliefs. Additionally, political moderates may also be more willing to consider alternative views and positions different than their own without reacting in a hostile manner. Still, the fact that participants who were least and most polarized before the debate both reported higher political aggression after the debate seems somewhat at odds.

Yet, as noted previously in our discussion of findings relating to polarization, those participants who were among the least polarized before the debate may represent individuals who do not follow politics very closely and have less interest in the presidential campaign. Once these individuals attune to a 90-minute presidential debate, equipped with less information that might allow them to refute candidate claims that run counter to their worldview beliefs, they may react to such challenge with increased political aggression. Finally, it seems logical that the most highly polarized individuals who often tend to view the political world as an "us" vs. "them" battle might respond to sustained exposure of the competing party's presidential candidate with the highest political aggression. On many fronts, additional investigation is warranted to better understand both causes and effects of political polarization, partisanship and aggression in the campaign communication context.

The findings of our study also raise important questions regarding the role of televised debates in the U.S. political system. Scholars have generally characterized campaign debates as beneficial to democracy, with ample research showing televised debates help inform the electorate about political issues and candidates

(McKinney & Carlin, 2004), and also generate increased interest in the campaign and increased likelihood of voting (McKinney & Chattopadhyay, 2007). The current project, however, has linked debate viewing to what are typically regarded as more negative political outcomes, including increased polarization, partisanship and political aggression. Certainly, it is premature from the results of this single exploratory investigation to proffer any definitive claims or conclusions that the campaign debate message may have deleterious effects on voters and the electoral process. If in fact debate exposure does trigger greater partisanship and polarization, these attitudes may encourage—rather than deter—citizens' political involvement. Although much has been written about the effects of a highly polarized and hyper-partisan polity (e.g., Sunstein, 2007), more research is needed to better understand the influence of campaign messages on such attitudes, including the effects of political campaign debates. This study also has linked polarization and partisanship to expressed political aggression, yet our analysis provides no understanding of the potential behavioral outcomes from increased aggression. Here, one might imagine a range of behavioral consequences, including expressed hostility and even violent behaviors, but also more useful civic engagement such as protest and activist behaviors as well as increased electoral participation. Again, much more work is needed to help us understand the causes and consequences of increased political aggression.

Limitations and Future Study

One limitation of this quasi-experimental study is the lack of a control group that would allow for the testing of differences in key variables of interest between participants viewing the debate message and others with no exposure to the debate. Given the preliminary results of the current study, a true experimental design would likely produce fruitful results in future analysis. Our project also involved a convenience sample of college students; and, although debate experiments using student samples have been shown to have the same effects sizes as those with generalizable samples (Benoit et al., 2003), past research examining political polarization and aggression has found that the age of the participant tends to matter (Anderson & Bushman, 2002). Therefore, the sample used in this project may well have influenced the results and thus future studies should utilize a more generalizable adult sample. Finally, this study's design allowed exploration of only immediate effects of debate exposure. Future research should employ panel and longitudinal analyses to better understand the enduring nature of short-term effects and also potential behavioral outcomes that may follow.

Conclusion

The results of this study found that political polarization increases following debate exposure, and increases in post-debate polarization vary according to the level of polarization and partisanship one brings to the debate viewing experience. The results also show that polarization and partisanship are linked to expressed political aggression following debate exposure. Specifically, we find that the debate message may serve as a threat to the political worldview of some, particularly those who are most liberal and conservative in political ideology, as well as those who are most and least polarized, leading these individuals to respond to the perceived threat with increased political aggression. Although these results potentially implicate the campaign debate message as a cause of some of the more intractable differences in our current state of political affairs, our findings raise intriguing questions for future research.

References

Anderson, C. A., & Bushman, B. J. (2002). Human aggression. *Psychology, 53*(1), 27–51.

Anson, J. M., Pyszczynski, T., Solomon, S., & Greenberg, J. (2009). Political ideology in the 21st century: A terror management perspective on maintenance and change of the status quo. In J. T. Jost, A. C. Kay, & H. Thorisdottir (Eds.), *Social and psychological bases of ideology and system justification* (pp. 210–240). New York, NY: Oxford University Press.

Becker, E. (1971). *The birth and death of meaning* (2nd ed.). New York, NY: Free Press.

Becker, E. (1973). *The denial of death*. New York, NY: Free Press.

Becker, E. (1975). *Escape from evil*. New York, NY: Free Press.

Benoit, W. L., Hansen, G. J., & Verser, R. M. (2003). A meta-analysis of the effects of viewing U.S. presidential debates. *Communication Monographs, 70*, 335–350. doi:10.1080/0363775032000179133

Brennan, A., & Abdullah, H. (2012, June 19). Congress: Same hours, half the work. *CNN*. Retrieved from http://www.cnn.com/2012/06/19/politics/congress-productivity/index.html

Carlin, D. P. (1992). Presidential debates as focal points for campaign arguments. *Political Communication, 9*, 251–265.

Carlin, D. P., Howard, C., Stanfield, S., & Reynolds, L. (1991). The effects of presidential debate formats on clash: A comparative analysis. *Argumentation & Advocacy, 27*, 126–137.

Chaffee, S. H. (1978). Presidential debates—are they helpful to voters? *Communication Monographs*, (45), 330–346.

Commission on Presidential Debates. (2012, October 28). 2012 Debates. Retrieved from http://www.debates.org/index.php?page=2012-debates

Conover, P. J. (1984). The influence of group identifications on political perception and evaluation. *The Journal of Politics, 46*, 760–785. doi:10.2307/2130855

Conover, P. J. (1988). The role of social groups in political thinking. *British Journal of Political Science, 18,* 51–76.

Conover, P. J., & Feldman, S. (1981). The origins and meaning of liberal/conservative self-identifications. *American Journal of Political Science, 25,* 617–645. doi:10.2307/2110756

Greenberg, J., Pyszczynski, T., & Solomon, S. (1986). The causes and consequences of a need for self-esteem: A terror management theory. In R. F. Baumeister (Ed.), *Public self and private self* (pp. 189–212). New York, NY: Springer-Verlag.

Greenberg, J., Solomon, S., & Pyszczynski, T. (1997). Terror management theory of self-esteem and cultural worldviews: Empirical assessments and conceptual refinements. In M.P. Zanna (Ed.), *Advances in experimental social psychology* (Vol. 29, pp. 61–139). Philadelphia, PA: Elsevier, Inc.

Hawthorne, J., & Warner, B. (2013, April). *Hostile rhetoric and aggression.* Paper presented at the annual convention of the Central States Communication Association, Kansas City, MO.

Holbert, R. L., LaMarre, H. L., & Landreville, K. D. (2009). Fanning the flames of a partisan divide: Debate viewing, vote choice, and perceptions of vote count accuracy. *Communication Research, 36,* 155–177. doi:10.1177/0093650208330248

Iyengar, S., Sood, G., & Lelkes, Y. (2012). Affect, not ideology: A social identity perspective on polarization. *Public Opinion Quarterly, 76,* 405–431. doi:10.1093/poq/nfs038

Kalmoe, N. P. (2010, September). *Does violent political rhetoric fuel support for political violence?* Paper presented at the annual meeting of the American Political Science Association, Washington, DC. Retrieved from http://ssrn.com/abstract=1657314

Koltko-Rivera, M. E. (2004). The psychology of worldviews. *Review of General Psychology, 8,* 3–58. doi:10.1037/1089-2680.8.1.3

Kwong, M. (2012, November 20). Divided States of America: Obama win sparks secession mania. *CBC News.* Retrieved from http://www.cbc.ca/news/world/story/2012/11/19/f-us-secession-petitions-kwong.html

Lanoue, D. J., & Schrott, P. R. (1991). *The joint press conference: The history, impact, and prospects of American presidential debates.* New York, NY: Greenwood Press.

McGregor, H. A., Lieberman, J. D., Greenberg, J., Solomon, S., Arndt, J., Simon, L., & Pyszczynski, T. (1998). Terror management and aggression: Evidence that mortality salience motivates aggression against worldview-threatening others. *Journal of Personality and Social Psychology, 74,* 590–605.

McKinney, M. S., & Carlin, D. B. (2004). Political campaign debates. In L. L. Kaid (Ed.), *Handbook of political communication research* (pp. 203–234). Mahwah, N.J.: Lawrence Erlbaum Associates.

McKinney, M. S., & Chattopadhyay, S. (2007). Political engagement through debates: Young citizens' reactions to the 2004 presidential debates. *American Behavioral Scientist, 50,* 1169–1182. doi:10.1177/0002764207300050

Miller, A. H., & MacKuen, M. (1979). Learning about the candidates: The 1976 presidential debates. *Public Opinion Quarterly, 43,* 326–346. doi:10.1086/268525

Miller, C., & Landau, M. (2005). Communication and terrorism: A terror management theory perspective. *Communication Research Reports, 22,* 79–88. doi:10.1080/0882409052000343543

Morello, J. T. (1988). Argument and visual structuring in the 1984 Mondale-Reagan debates: The medium's influence on the perception of clash. *Western Journal of Speech Communication, 52,* 277–290.

Pyszczynski, T. (2004). What are we so afraid of? A terror management theory perspective on the politics of fear. *Social Research, 71,* 827–848.

Reynolds, G. H. (2012, November 19). Column: A solution to secession fever—federalism. *USA Today.* Retrieved from http://www.usatoday.com/story/opinion/2012/11/18/texas-secession-obama-canada/1712241/

Rosenblatt, A., Greenberg, J., Solomon, S., Pyszczynski, T., & Lyon, D. (1989). Evidence for terror management theory: I. The effects of mortality salience on reactions to those who violate or uphold cultural values. *Journal of Personality and Social Psychology, 57,* 681–690.

Schimel, J., Simon, L., Greenberg, J., Pyszczynski, T., Solomon, S., Waxmonsky, J., & Arndt, J. (1999). Stereotypes and terror management: Evidence that mortality salience enhances stereotypic thinking and preferences. *Journal of Personality and Social Psychology, 77,* 905–926.

Simon, A. F. (2002). *The winning message: Candidate behavior, campaign discourse, and democracy.* New York, NY: Cambridge University Press.

Skitka, L. J., Bauman, C. W., & Sargis, E. G. (2005). Moral conviction: Another contributor to attitude strength or something more? *Journal of Personality and Social Psychology, 88,* 895–917. doi:10.1037/0022-3514.88.6.895

Solomon, S., Greenberg, J., & Pyszczynski, T. (1991). A terror management theory of social behavior: The psychological functions of self-esteem and cultural worldviews. *Advances in Experimental Social Psychology, 24,* 93–159.

Solomon, S., Greenberg, J., & Pyszczynski, T. (2000). Pride and prejudice: Fear of death and social behavior. *Current Directions in Psychological Science, 9,* 200–204.

Sunstein, C. R. (2007). *Republic.com 2.0.* Princeton, NJ: Princeton University Press.

Warner, B. R., & McKinney, M. S. (2013). To unite and divide: The polarizing effect of presidential debates. *Communication Studies, 64,* 508–527.

Zschirnt, S. (2011). The origins & meaning of liberal/conservative self-identifications revisited. *Political Behavior, 33,* 685–701. doi:10.1007/s11109-010-9145-6

Note

1. The generalized additive model was fit using R and the package "mgcv," which is a specialized function package for estimating generalized additive models.

CHAPTER THREE

Communicating with Voters 30 Seconds at a Time

Presidential Campaign Advertising 2012

KELLY L. WINFREY, MARY C. BANWART, AND BENJAMIN R. WARNER

Advertising was a critical component of both President Barack Obama's and former Gov. Mitt Romney's campaign strategy in the 2012 presidential election. A record amount of money was spent in the 2012 presidential race, with more than $950 million spent on television advertising to support the candidates. This represents an increase of nearly $350 million from 2008. For that dollar amount, the number of times advertisements aired in support of either Obama or Romney totaled 1,431,939. Although airtime purchased by third-party organizations contributed to this total, the candidates' campaigns represented the greatest effort at reaching voters through television advertising, particularly the Obama campaign. Overall, Obama's campaign bought twice as many placements of their ads as Romney's campaign, airing 511,513 spots on television compared to Romney's 207,984 (Fowler & Ridout, 2012). Given these striking numbers it is clear that the candidates and third parties believed television advertising, as part of an overall campaign strategy, was an essential component for victory.

Television advertising remains one of the greatest expenses and most valuable tools in presidential campaigns. Candidates spend millions of dollars on advertising in an effort to win votes, and research suggests this tactic is effective. Numerous studies have found that campaigns can increase the favorability of their candidate through advertising (Atkin & Heald, 1976; Kahn & Geer, 1994; Kaid, Leland, & Whitney, 1992; Kaid, 1997; Tedesco, 2002; Valentino, Traugott, & Hutchings,

2002). For example, a randomized field experiment during Texas Gov. Rick Perry's 2006 campaign found strong effects from television advertising on vote preference. The results indicated that Perry's position in the polls improved as the advertising buy increased, with the greatest increase of 6% in the polls resulting from an advertising buy totaling 1,000 gross rating points (Gerber, Gimpel, Green, & Shaw, 2011). Furthermore, Gordon and Hartmann (2012) found a significant effect on both voter turnout and vote choice in the 2000, 2004, and 2008 elections. In addition to influencing turnout and vote choice, political advertising increases knowledge of candidates' issue positions (Kaid, Fernandes, & Painter, 2011), interest in the election (Atkin & Herald, 1976), engagement (Freedman, Franz, & Goldstein, 2004), and political efficacy (Kaid, Postelnicu, Landerville, Yun, & LeGrange, 2007).

As the focus on battleground states has increased, media purchasing has allowed candidates to become even more targeted in their advertising messages. In 2012, advertising buys were concentrated within the battleground states and even further concentrated in relatively few media markets, demonstrating the campaigns' focus on specific voters (Scherer, 2012). Did the targeted advertising work in these key battleground states? Of the 15 top media markets targeted by both candidates and their supporters, the Obama campaign held a distinct advantage in 13 markets—located in Nevada, Ohio, Colorado, Florida, and Virginia—when it came to volume of placements (Wesleyan Media Project, 2012). In other words, his ads were, quite simply, viewed more often than Romney's. Although we are, of course, hesitant to suggest causation, it is undeniable that Obama won the states in which these 13 media markets are located.

Although we can suggest from the election's outcome that the targeted placement was in fact likely successful, what remains in question is how the targeted messages might have worked. Women voters were definitively one of the strategically targeted blocks of voters for the Obama and Romney campaigns as we outline below. On Election Day, however, Obama benefitted from a gender gap in eight of the nine battleground states, with women 5% to 15% more likely to vote for Obama than men (Center for American Women and Politics, 2012). Therefore, this study seeks to gain a better understanding of how women might have responded to the candidates' advertising messages, particularly those messages targeted directly toward women compared to those advertisements that contained a broader electoral message.

Targeting the Women's Vote

Although women have often been a focal point for campaign messaging in previous elections, the 2012 election generated a set of messages unheard of in past cycles. Controversial statements about rape from certain Republican congressional candidates, a debate comment from Romney ("binders full of women") that was easily cast in a negative light, and a public debate about such issues as birth control and pay equity all encouraged labeling the general election messaging by Republican candidates as a "war on women." In addition, two weeks before Election Day the majority of undecided voters were women ("The Undecided Voter," 2012). Combined with past electoral data demonstrating that women vote in higher numbers than men (Casserly, 2012), both presidential candidates had very important reasons for specifically targeting women and their concerns. And, both chose television advertising as one vehicle through which to disseminate their targeted messages toward women, although each took very different approaches in designing that message.

For instance, Obama began airing an ad called "First Law" as early as the summer of 2012 to highlight his signing of the Lilly Ledbetter Fair Pay Act. Obama's team also designed and ran ads focusing on the new health care law that he had worked to pass through Congress in 2010 (known as the Affordable Care Act or "Obamacare") and its specific benefits to women, such as insurance-paid birth control. The Obama campaign also sought to clearly contrast his own positions and record on women's issues with that of Romney's, highlighting a comment made by Romney that he would end funding for Planned Parenthood as well as Romney's opposition to both abortion rights and insurance coverage of birth control. In total, Obama's campaign produced nine different ads focused on abortion compared to one ad produced by the Romney campaign (Wilner, 2012).

Romney, on the other hand, employed a very different message strategy in targeting the female vote. In all of his women-targeted ads, Romney focused on making the economy a women's issue. He ran a series of ads featuring various female speakers who, in each ad, emphasized the economy as their greatest concern in the election. Only one ad offered an exception to this rule. That ad, titled "Sarah," began with a direct response to Obama's attack on Romney for his position on abortion. In the Romney response ad, the main character—depicted as a mother—first tells voters that she heard Romney opposed contraception and abortion, but that she decided to do her own research to learn more. She then, amidst video clips of her appearing to research the issues on the computer, assures voters that Romney in fact does not oppose contraception or abortion and that he believes abortion should be an option in certain circumstances. Her next comment reinforces the pattern of Romney's "women care about the economy" focus as she states, "... but I'm more concerned about the debt our children will be faced with." The ad ends with "Sarah" stating she voted for Obama "last time," but that "we can't afford four more years."

Indeed, many presidential campaigns have targeted their advertising to specific voting groups through both content and the amount of time purchased to air the ads, thus increasing the exposure of a specific message created for that target audience. For instance, the 2000, 2004, and 2008 presidential candidates made targeted ad buys with the hope of exposing specific messages to specific demographic groups (Ridout, Franz, Goldstein, & Feltus, 2012). Specifically in 2008, Obama placed twice as many ads than did McCain during "telenovelas," which are programs with a majority Latino audience. In 2008 and 2004, the Obama campaign and John Kerry's campaign, respectively, placed significantly more advertising during programming with predominantly black audiences.

A closer look at 2012 suggests that the advertising purchases of Obama and Romney reflected uniquely different strategies in reaching out to voters. Romney's campaign made what are considered more traditional buys, purchasing airtime mostly during local news programs (Fowler & Ridout, 2012; Wilner, 2012), and were arguably unable to leverage costs to increase their quantity of airtime purchased (Wilner, 2012). However, the Obama campaign designed advertising buys specifically targeted to voter groups, such as purchasing airtime during talk shows, reality shows, and on niche cable networks. As an example, Obama's campaign targeted women through daytime talk shows, who, at the time, represented three-quarters of the viewing audience during those time slots and on cable networks such as the Food Channel, Lifetime, and Hallmark (Fowler & Ridout, 2012).

Past research suggests that these strategies can in fact be very successful among targeted voting groups. For instance, ads focusing on issues important to women have been shown to increase their likelihood to vote (Clinton & Lapinski, 2004), albeit more often so for the Democratic candidate (Schaffner, 2005). Increased placement within programs watched by key voting demographics also has been shown to produce benefits, as the increased placement of advertisements targeted toward Latinos during Latino programming by the Obama campaign in 2008 increased the reported likelihood they would support Obama (Winneg, Hardy, & Jamieson, 2013). Although media sources have validated the Obama campaign's success in targeting key demographic groups in 2012, including women, with the design of their media buys (Fowler & Ridout, 2012; Sherer, 2012; Wilner, 2012) this study seeks to offer additional understanding of how the messages themselves ultimately moved female voters.

Rationale, Expectations, and Questions

Given that the 2012 election broke records both in the number of advertisement spots aired and the dollars spent, this study seeks to better understand the effectiveness of the messages at the heart of this effort. Specifically, we compared the influence of advertising intended for a general audience with advertisements targeted toward female voters. Our first set of hypotheses examined the effects of the messages on candidate favorability, specifically seeking to determine whether favorability differed based on the advertising message shown. Prior research has confirmed that advertisements influence candidate favorability (e.g., Kaid, 1997; Kaid et al., 2011; Tedesco, 2002; Valentino et al., 2002). However, we extended that literature to determine to what extent that favorability might increase among women when the candidate's advertising message is designed to specifically speak to their demographic. By utilizing an experimental design that included exposure to general advertisements, advertisements with a message focused on women, and a control group viewing non-political ads, we tested the following hypotheses and research questions:

> H1: Candidate favorability changes after viewing general message campaign advertisements.

> H2: Candidate favorability changes after viewing targeted message campaign advertisements.

> RQ1: Does candidate favorability change based on the advertising stimulus (general, targeted, or control)?

Prior research also has demonstrated that political advertising influences the image evaluations of candidates (e.g., Kaid et al., 1992; Tedesco & Kaid, 2003). And the sincerity of the candidate has been found to be an extremely important quality to voters (Benoit & McHale, 2004). These perceptions of candidates' image are an important factor in voter decision-making, and have been found to influence election outcomes (Hellweg, 2004; Nimmo & Savage, 1976). Given the focus by both candidates in 2012 on female voters and women's issues, we sought to expand upon image research by examining differences in voters' perceptions of the candidates' sincerity regarding their commitment to women and women's issues and the effect of advertising on those perceptions. Therefore we posed the following research question:

> RQ2: Is there a difference in viewers' perception of candidate sincerity based on advertising stimulus?

Although favorability and image of a candidate are significant predictors of vote choice, key indicators of engagement and turnout are interest in the campaign and political information efficacy. Previous research has demonstrated that women tend to report lower levels of interest in political campaigns than do their male counterparts, and this lack of interest has been related to overall lower levels of political engagement and knowledge (Burns, Scholzman & Verba, 2009; Kenski & Jamison, 2000; Verba, Burns & Scholzman, 1997). In addition to lacking interest, women generally report lower levels of political information efficacy (PIE) (Kaid et al., 2007; Tedesco, 2011), indicating that women are less likely to believe they have the necessary knowledge to participate in politics. These findings are concerning given that low levels of PIE are a significant cause of nonvoting in young people (Kaid, McKinney, & Tedesco, 2007). Although, as previous studies (e.g., Kaid et al., 2011; Kaid et al., 2007) have shown, exposure to political advertising may increase young women's belief that they have the knowledge necessary to participate in the political process. Yet, these studies have typically focused only on general campaign ads with a message designed to target a broader voting audience. Therefore, we designed our study to extend past literature to determine whether women in 2012 continued to report lower levels of interest and information efficacy and whether a targeted message has greater impact on viewers' reported levels of information efficacy. Thus, we posed the following:

H3: Men will report higher levels of interest in the presidential campaign than will women.

H4: Men will report higher levels of political information efficacy than will women.

RQ3: Does political information efficacy change depending on advertising stimulus?

We further sought to determine if there is a relationship between political interest and information efficacy. To that end, we proposed the following hypothesis and research question:

H5: People who are more interested in the campaign will have higher levels of political information efficacy.

RQ4: Does interest in the presidential campaign predict political information efficacy depending on whether the participant is a man or woman?

Method

Participants

Participants completed an online survey containing an advertising stimulus between October 31 and Election Day, November 6, 2012. The participants were recruited from seven colleges and universities across the United States as part of a national research project.[1] The sample included 514 participants ranging in age from 18 to 47 years (M = 20.41, SD = 3.42), of whom 35% (n = 180) were male and 65% (n = 334) were female. Participants were recruited from communication or political science courses and participated for credit or extra-credit. The vast majority of the participants were Caucasian (71.6%).

The majority of the participants (79.6%) indicated they were registered voters, and of these participants, registrations were held in 27 different states. The political party affiliation was relatively evenly split with 35.8% (n = 184) Democrats, 34.4% (n = 177) Republicans, and 29.8% (n = 153) independents/other. The political party affiliation was also relatively split by gender. Among female participants, 35.9% were Democrats, 33.5% were Republican, and 30.5% reported independent/other; among male participants 35.6% were Democrats, 36.1% were Republican, and 28.3% reported independent/other. Participants were also asked how likely they were to vote in the coming presidential election—47.7% indicated they were very likely, somewhat likely, or likely to vote; 21.8% indicated they were either somewhat unlikely, unlikely, or very unlikely to vote; 6.8% reported they were undecided about voting; and 23.7% indicated they had already voted through advanced or absentee voting.

Procedure and Instrumentation

Participants completed an online survey that asked them to evaluate both candidates as well as a series of questions unrelated to the present study. Participants were then randomly assigned to watch one of three advertising conditions. Each condition contained six advertisements viewed in random order. The first stimulus condition—the targeted message condition—contained six advertisements, three from each presidential candidate. The dominant message in each advertisement targeted female voters. The Romney ads included in this condition were titled "Dear Daughter," "Melanie," and "Sarah"; the Obama ads were titled "First Law," "What He'll Do," and "Women's Choices." The second stimulus condition—the general message condition—contained six presidential campaign advertisements with messages not specifically targeted to female voters. The issues discussed in these ads included military issues, leadership, economic issues, and education. The Romney ads included in this condition were titled "Finding a Way," "Bringing People Together," and "Highest Responsibility"; the Obama ads in this condition were titled "Rebuilding," "Challenges," and "Remember." The third condition served as a control group. In other words, participants viewed six commercial advertisements that did not contain political messaging of any kind. After viewing the experimental stimulus, participants in all conditions completed a second questionnaire in which they responded to a number of questions about the candidates, including questions about which candidate would best attend to women's issues, a measure of their political information efficacy, and the measure of candidate favorability.

Candidate favorability. Participants rated each candidate on a scale ranging from 0 (cold/unfavorable) to 100 (warm/favorable) in both the pretest (Obama: $M = 53.51$, $SD = 32.27$; Romney: $M = 43.77$, $SD = 31.61$) and the posttest (Obama: $M = 55.66$, $SD = 32.44$; Romney: $M = 45.74$, $SD = 32.27$). Use of the feeling thermometer as a measure of candidate favorability is consistent with previous research testing evaluations of candidates (e.g., Banwart & Bystrom, 2005; Kaid et al., 2011; Yun, Jasperson, & Kaid, 2010).

Sincerity of candidate. Participants were asked the extent to which they agreed with the following statements for both Barack Obama and Mitt Romney (1 = strongly disagree to 7 = strongly agree): [Candidate] will fight for women; [Candidate] will represent women's issues; and [Candidate] is concerned about women. The items were reliable for both Obama ($M = 5.11$, $SD = 1.30$, a = .921) and Romney ($M = 3.71$, $SD = 1.59$, a = .954).

Political interest. Prior to viewing the advertising stimulus, participants' level of political interest was measured. Participants were asked, "How interested would you say you are in the presidential campaign?" with responses ranging from (1) very uninterested to (5) very interested ($M = 3.67$, SD = 1.16).

Political information efficacy. Political information efficacy (PIE), first developed by Kaid, McKinney, and Tedesco (2007), is a measure of an individual's confidence that s/he has the knowledge and ability to participate in the political process through such behaviors as voting and engaging in political communication. PIE was measured by asking participants to indicate their level of agreement (using a five-point scale from strongly agree to strongly disagree) on four statements reflecting the level of confidence in their political knowledge. The items included: "I consider myself well qualified to participate in politics," "I think that I am better informed about politics and government than most people," "I feel that I have a pretty good understanding of the important political issues facing our country," and "If a friend asked me about the presidential election, I feel I would have enough information to help my friend figure out who to vote for." The items achieved acceptable reliability ($M = 3.21$, $SD = .88$, a = .881).

Results

The first two hypotheses predicted that exposure to general and targeted campaign advertising messages would be associated with a change in the evaluation of the candidate. In testing both questions, an omnibus repeated measures multiple analysis of variance (MANOVA) was run to determine if there was a three-way interaction between the sex of the respondent, whether they were exposed to campaign advertisements, and the main effect of the advertising stimulus. The within-subjects factor was change in favorability from pretest to posttest; the between-subjects factors included sex of respondent and the advertising stimulus.

In response to the first hypothesis, the test revealed a significant three-way interaction between sex, experimental condition, and the main effect of ad stimulus, such that the effect of exposure to the general message condition varied depending on whether the respondent was male or female, $F(1, 510) = 5.43, p < .05$. To account for the three-way interaction, the responses were split by sex for subsequent analyses and paired sample t-tests were conducted to determine whether exposure to campaign advertisements significantly influenced candidate favorability depending on the experimental condition of exposure. As evident in Table 1, exposure to the general message condition did not influence candidate favorability among male participants for either Obama or Romney. However, exposure to the general message condition significantly improved candidate favorability for both Obama and Romney among female participants. Each candidate improved their favorability by approximately five points with women.

Table 1. Effect of Ad Exposure on Candidate Evaluation

Condition	Obama		Romney	
	Pretest M (SD)	Posttest M (SD)	Pretest M (SD)	Posttest M (SD)
Male				
General	52.42 (32.04)	49.62 (32.86)	43.68 (30.72)	45.38 (32.00)
Targeted	54.34 (31.39)	54.90 (32.39)	46.85 (29.21)	47.56 (30.73)
Control	50.81 (35.65)	52.08 (35.17)	44.32 (32.86)	47.55* (31.64)
Female				
General	55.67 (31.98)	60.13*** (31.58)	38.44 (32.13)	43.41*** (33.54)
Targeted	52.66 (32.84)	57.47*** (32.53)	45.17 (31.66)	46.32 (32.53)
Control	54.18 (31.56)	55.29 (31.62)	45.49 (32.29)	45.76 (32.60)

*** = $p < .001$

In response to the second hypothesis, which predicted exposure to targeted ads would significantly influence candidate evaluations, the results were again mixed. For male participants, there was no significant difference in candidate favorability for either Obama or Romney in the targeted message condition. However, for female participants in the targeted message condition, candidate favorability significantly increased for Obama but did not change at a level of significance for Romney. Pretest and posttest scores are displayed in Table 1.

The first research question asked if there was a significant difference in the amount of change in candidate favorability across all conditions, seeking to determine if a change in one condition occurred at a level of significance over and above changes in all other conditions. An analysis of variance (ANOVA) was run for both men and women to determine if change in favorability was significantly different depending on experimental stimulus. With regard to male participants, when evaluating the combination of all conditions, there were no significant differences in changes to candidate favorability for either candidate; changes to candidate favorability across all conditions were statistically equal. Among female participants, changes in candidate favorability were significantly different across conditions for both Obama ($F(2, 331) = 3.13, p < .05$) and Romney ($F(2, 331) = 4.33, p < .05$).

Follow-up analysis using Fisher's least significant difference test revealed that changes in Obama's favorability across the general message condition and the targeted message condition were significantly different than the control condition; however, there were no significant differences between the general message condition and targeted message condition. In other words, changes in female participants' evaluation of Obama's favorability were significantly more likely to increase if they were exposed to Obama's campaign advertising compared to the control condition. Although Obama's favorability increased for female participants in the general message condition and targeted message condition, they did not do so at statistically significant differences across condition.

Follow-up analysis of Romney's favorability revealed that female participants in the general message condition significantly increased their favorability of Romney over and above those in the targeted message condition and the control condition. In other words, Romney's (insignificant) change in favorability in the targeted ad condition was not significantly different from the control condition, but he enjoyed a significant positive change in evaluation from female participants in the general message condition.

The second research question asked if perception of candidate sincerity would differ based on the advertising stimulus viewed depending on the gender of the respondent. To determine whether there were significant differences in evaluations of Obama's sincerity depending on whether the respondent viewed general, targeted, or control ads, and whether this difference varied by gender, a 2x3 ANCOVA was specified with political party as the covariate and gender and ad condition as the between-subjects factors. The analysis revealed that there was no interaction between gender and ad condition and that ad condition did not significantly influence perceptions of Obama's sincerity. However, women were much more likely to rate Obama higher on sincerity ($M = 5.25$, $SD = 1.26$) than men ($M = 4.87$, $SD = 1.35$), $F(1, 500) = 9.68$, $p < .01$. Advertisement exposure did not significantly influence perceptions that Obama would represent women's interests (general: $M = 5.11$, $SD = 1.30$; targeted: $M = 5.14$, $SD = 1.31$; control: $M = 5.09$, $SD = 1.31$).

A 2x3 ANCOVA revealed that there was no interaction between participant gender and ad condition but that women rated Romney significantly lower on sincerity ($M = 3.60$, $SD = 1.63$) than men ($M = 3.90$, $SD = 1.51$), $F(1, 500) = 4.05$, $p < .05$. Although the difference in Romney's score between those in various ad conditions was approaching significance ($p = .073$), follow-up analyses revealed that the only contrast approaching significance was the difference between targeted ads ($M = 3.95$, $SD = 1.62$) and general ads ($M = 3.51$, $SD = 1.60$), $p = .057$, and that there were no differences between those who watched either targeted or general ads and those who were in the control condition ($M = 3.67$, $SD = 1.54$).

As can be seen in Table 2, the third and fourth hypotheses concerning gender differences in interest and information efficacy were also rejected. The third hypothesis in our study predicted that men would report higher levels of interest than women in the presidential campaign; this hypothesis was rejected. An independent samples t-test revealed no significant difference between men and women in their level of interest in the presidential campaign, $t(512) = 1.77$, $p = .08$. The fourth hypothesis predicted that following exposure to political advertisements, men would report higher levels of political information efficacy than would women; this hypothesis was also rejected. An independent samples t-test compared men and women who had been exposed to political advertising, and the analysis revealed no significant difference between men and women in their level of information efficacy after viewing political advertisements, $t(337) = 1.23$, $p = .22$.

Table 2. Interest and Information Efficacy by Participant Gender

	Males M (SD)	Females M (SD)
Interest in Campaign	3.79 (1.16)	3.60 (1.17)
Information Efficacy	3.33 (1.04)	3.21 (.83)

The third research question asked whether political information efficacy (PIE) would be influenced by participant gender and exposure to campaign ads across the three conditions. A 2x3 ANOVA was conducted with the between-subjects factors of gender and advertising stimulus (general, targeted, control). The analysis revealed no significant differences in PIE regardless of the participant's sex or the type of advertising—general message, targeted message, or control messages—to which they were exposed.

The fifth hypothesis predicted that political interest would result in higher levels of PIE. A linear regression analysis revealed that political interest predicted approximately 25% of variance in PIE (R^2 = .251), $F(1, 505)$ = 168.83, $p < .001$) such that people who were more interested in the campaign reported significantly higher levels of PIE, (β = .379, $p < .001$).

The fourth and final research question asked whether the prediction of interest on PIE would depend on the gender of the respondent. To test this, a moderation analysis using the PROCESS macro for SPSS developed by Alexander F. Hayes (2013) was conducted in which interest was specified to predict PIE and whether someone was female was specified as a potential moderator. The results indicated no interaction between gender and political interest. The effect of interest on PIE was consistent for both men and women.

Discussion

The presidential election of 2012 not only set records for the amount of money spent on televised advertising to secure voter favorability, but also broke new ground in terms of targeting voters through television placement (Fowler & Ridout, 2013; Scherer, 2012; Wilner, 2012). To better understand the effectiveness of targeted advertising messages, we designed this experiment to explore effects of advertising exposure on candidate favorability; perceptions of candidate sincerity in representing women; and the relationship between political interest, gender, campaign messages, and political information efficacy. The findings presented in this chapter suggest that although advertising effects were evident among the female participants, male participants were unlikely to be influenced in their candidate favorability evaluation, perceptions of candidate sincerity, or reported political information efficacy. Such results differ, only in part, from prior research and in the following discussion we explore the implications.

Contrary to prior studies of presidential advertising effects on candidate favorability (Kaid et al., 2011; Kaid, Postelnicu et al., 2007), exposure to campaign advertising produced differing results for female and male participants in the current study. Specifically, female participants rated the candidates more favorable in the general message and targeted message conditions over and above the condition in which non-political commercial advertisements were viewed. To be clear, however, the changes were not consistent for both candidates across all conditions. Women in the general message condition and the targeted message condition rated Obama more favorably following exposure to the candidates' advertising, with approximately a 5% increase in both conditions. Although female participants rated Romney more favorably in the general message condition, they did not significantly change their favorability toward Romney after viewing the targeted advertisements. For male participants, changes in favorability for both Obama and Romney remained non-significant across the general message and targeted message conditions.

Certainly, it is not surprising that male participants did not rate either candidate higher following exposure to the targeted advertisements as these ads did not deliver a message designed to persuade men. This lack of change in male participants—and the significant change for female participants—offers encouragement for further exploration of targeted message effects in political campaigns. However, the failure for Romney to benefit from a targeted message bounce in ratings raises an important point in terms of the electoral environment. Data was collected for this study in the final weeks leading in to the election, and a common theme throughout the Republican presidential primary as well as the general election was the Republican candidates'—and Romney's—controversial stands on a variety of women's issues. Quite possibly the framing that resulted from this consistent message in the media and from opponents was strong enough that even targeted advertising messages that reinforced women's support of Romney, reinforced the economy as a woman's issue in the election, and clarified his stand on abortion and birth control was simply too little too late. Given the aforementioned context, our study also suggests that Romney's targeted messaging strategy of framing the economy as a women's issue was less successful than Obama's strategy of focusing on more traditional women's issues such as fair pay, birth control, and reproductive rights.

In an effort to gain additional insight as to the effect of targeted messages on the perceptions of the candidates, we also included a measure to test participants' perception of the candidate's sincerity to represent the demographic targeted in the ads and their issues. For this study, the sincerity measure focused on how sincere the candidate was perceived to be in standing up for women and women's issues. The data revealed that across all conditions participants considered Obama's sincerity to be higher than Romney's. More specifically, women rated Obama higher than men on sincerity and men rated Romney higher than women on sincerity; however, there were no significant differences based on ad condition nor any significant interactions between ad stimulus and gender.

When considering our findings regarding both candidate favorability and sincerity, it is possible to conclude that targeted advertising can be effective in increasing the favorability of a candidate although the advertising messages were not sufficient to generate a unique effect on sincerity. In the 2012 presidential election, Obama was arguably more successful in persuading women voters than Romney as the gender gap would suggest. And, in this current study, Obama was more successful at increasing his favorability rating among female participants through targeted advertising than was Romney. Yet, the data demonstrate that there was no significant difference in the change between Obama's favorability rating in the general message condition and the targeted message condition; in other words, as they changed over time, they did so at similar levels. Therefore, we are unable to claim direct success for Obama from the targeted message condition.

As an added complexity, participants in the targeted message condition did not rate either Obama or Romney any more sincere than did those in the general message condition or the control condition. Certainly, the data in this study were collected at the end of the hyper-covered Republican primary and general election campaigns. Arguably, it had been framed from early in the general election campaign that Obama supported women's issues and that Romney—"aided" by the controversial statements from Republican candidates around the country—was and had been less consistent and less supportive. We posit, then, that exposure to the targeted ads at that late point in the election was unlikely to shift and, for that brief amount of time, was not enough to shift their belief in the candidate's sincerity. Certainly, campaigns are unable to rely on one exposure of an advertisement to sway hearts and minds.

Further, we remain intrigued by the ability—or inability—of a candidate to establish perceptions of sincerity particularly where targeted messages are concerned. Reaching out to specific demographic groups may often be a risky proposition, particularly if that is not a demographic group with which a candidate naturally identifies or is identified. Likely it would not be enough to present a well-tailored message to that group, and—as an outsider—a candidate would need to establish levels of sincerity and credibility in order for the efforts to be fruitful. Ultimately, we propose that these results support a call for further study of political advertising targeted to specific voter demographics in order to more clearly understand the effects and implications on candidate perceptions.

We turn, then, to explore interest in the election and participants' political information efficacy. First, with regard to political interest, young men and young women reported similar levels of interest in the 2012 election. This data is inconsistent with much of the previous literature that shows young males reporting more interest in politics and elections than young females; although in 2004 Banwart (2007) also found no significant differences in young men's and young women's political interest. In addition to no difference in political interest, young men and young women reported similar levels of political information efficacy. Because much of the research examining the influence of communication messages on political information efficacy has indeed found consistent increases following exposure to political messaging, this finding in our study was particularly surprising. And further, young women did not show any increase in political information efficacy following the viewing of the targeted advertisements above the efficacy reported in the general advertisement and control conditions; no differences emerged for young men across conditions either.

One possible explanation may again be the timing of our data collection. Because of the hyper-coverage of the campaign, it is quite possible that even exposure to advertisements—targeted or general messages—were not enough to change their perception of their own ability to participate in the process. We acknowledge that other studies examining political information efficacy have collected data at a similar point in the campaign (e.g., Kaid et al., 2011), seeking to measure changes in response to the viewing of a set of political advertisements. Yet, it is possible that with increased and improved campaign outreach through social media and the tools present in young people's lives, the saturation point even for these citizens may be changing. Further, the message we tested was one that combined long-standing perceptions of issue-ownership (e.g., Democrats are more closely linked with supporting women's issues) with heightened media coverage of the candidates and their stands. And for Romney, it was not just coverage of his positions and comments on the issues, but also the widely reported—and debated—comments of other candidates in his party with which strong associations with Romney were drawn. Thus, once the reports had been heard, there were months in which to debate the issues and come to a firm conclusion on the candidates' positions on and concern for women and women's issues. Further research could certainly more clearly demonstrate the impact of and situational factors under which targeted messages are deemed most effective.

Yet, an important finding in this study is that political interest did predict political information efficacy. With political interest in a campaign being linked to perceptions of one's knowledge level and cynicism (Banwart, 2007), it stands to reason that political interest is also linked to how confident one is to participate in the political process through such behaviors as voting. And, this effect appears consistent across both men and women as the ability of political interest to predict political information efficacy did not differ between them.

On one hand these findings may in fact be interpreted with optimism, in that women's interest in the election was at a level similar to that of men. This, combined with the important outcome variables to which interest is related—information seeking, perceptions of knowledge, and engagement through such activities as talking about politics and running for office—suggests that slowly many of the gaps that have kept women from seeing themselves as active participants in the political arena—beyond the voting booth—may in fact be narrowing. Although an alternative explanation might be that the heightened discussions surrounding women's issues in this election, the coining of the "war on women," and the open fashion with which the candidates were courting the women's vote generated information with which women felt a greater level of connection and, thus, interest for this election cycle. Either way, the findings reported create opportunities to generate as many and more questions for 2016 as they provide answers for 2012.

Conclusion

Undoubtedly, men and women responded to the 2012 presidential candidates differently at the voting booth, as the gender gap suggests. This chapter offers some insight as to how they might have responded to the candidates' messages differently as well. It is important to note the influence that targeted messaging demonstrated for women, as opposed to men, in generating increased candidate favorability. And finally, as further research seeks to discern the complexities of targeted persuasion in political advertising, understanding the framing internalized by voters and used as a lens through which to view targeted advertising will be critical. By doing so, we establish a richer understanding not only of the circumstances in which a targeted advertising message will and will not work, but also the manner in which voters will be likely to accept such a message 30 critical seconds at a time.

References

Atkin, C., & Heald, G. (1976). Effects of political advertising. *The Public Opinion Quarterly, 40*(2), 216–228.

Banwart, M. C. (2007). Gender and young voters in 2004: The influence of perceived knowledge and interest. *American Behavioral Scientist, 50*(9), 1152–1168. doi: 10.1177/0002764207299362

Banwart, M. C., & Bystrom, D. (2005). Gendered reactions: Young voters' responses to the 2004 presidential advertisements. *American Behavioral Scientist, 49*(2), 314–325.

Benoit, W. L. & McHale, J. P. (2004). Presidential candidates' personal qualities: Computer content analysis. In K. L. Hacker (Ed.), *Presidential candidate images* (pp. 49–64). Lanham, MD: Rowman & Littlefield

Burns, N., Scholzman, K., & Verba, S. (2001). *The private roots of public action.* Cambridge, MA: Harvard University Press.

Casserly, M. (2012, November 5). Latest poll shows women's vote will deliver Obama victory. *Forbes*. Retrieved from http://www.forbes.com

Center for American Women and Politics (2012, November 7). Women's votes decisive in 2012 presidential race. Retrieved from http://cawp.rutgers.edu/press_room/news/documents/PressRelease_11-07-12-gendergap.pdf

Clinton, J. D., & Lapinski, J. S. (2004). "Targeted" advertising and voter turnout: An experimental study of the 2000 presidential election. *The Journal of Politics, 66*(1), 69–96.

Freedman, P., Franz, M., & Goldstein, K. (2004). Campaign advertising and democratic citizenship. *American Journal of Political Science, 48*(4), 723–741.

Fowler, E. F., & Ridout, T. N. (2013). Negative, angry, and ubiquitous: Political advertising in 2012. *The Forum, 10*(4), 51–61.

Gerber, A. S., Gimpel, J. G., Green, D. P., & Shaw, D. R. (2011). How large and long-lasting are the persuasive effects of televised campaign ads? Results from a randomized field experiment. *American Political Science Review, 105*(1), 135–150.

Gordon, B. R., & Hartmann, W. R. (2012). Advertising effects in presidential elections. *Marketing Science, 32*(1), 19–35.

Hellweg, S. A. (2004). Campaigns and candidate images in American presidential elections. In K. L. Hacker (Ed.), *Presidential candidate images* (pp. 21–48). Lanham, MD: Rowman & Littlefield.

Kahn, K. F., & Geer, J. G. (1994). Creating impressions: An experimental investigation of political advertising on television. *Political Behavior, 16*(1), 93–116.

Kaid, L. L. (1997). Effects of television spots on images of Dole and Clinton. *American Behavioral Scientist, 40*(8), 1085–1094.

Kaid, L. L., Fernandes, J., & Painter, D. (2011). Effects of political advertising in the 2008 presidential campaign. *American Behavioral Scientist, 55*(4), 437–436. doi: 10.1177/0002764211398071

Kaid, L. L., Leland, C. M., & Whitney, S. (1992). The impact of televised political ads: Evoking viewer responses in the 1988 Presidential campaign. *The Southern Communication Journal, 57*(4), 285–295.

Kaid, L. L., McKinney, M. S., & Tedesco, J. C. (2007). Political information efficacy and young voters. *American Behavioral Scientist, 50*, 1093–1111.

Kaid, L. L., Postelnicu, M., Landerville, L., Yun, H. J., & LeGrange, A. G. (2007). The effects of political advertising on young voters. *American Behavioral Scientist, 50*(9), 1137–1151.

Kenski, K., & Jamieson, K. H. (2000). The gender gap in political knowledge: Are women less knowledgeable than men about politics? In K. H. Jamieson (Ed.), *Everything you think you know about politics and why you're wrong* (pp. 83–92). New York, NY: Basic Books.

McKinney, M. S., & Rill, L. A. (2009). Not your parents' presidential debates: Examining the effects of the CNN/YouTube debates on young citizens' civic engagement. *Communication Studies, 60*(4), 392–406. doi:10.1080/10510970903110001

Nimmo, D., & Savage, R. L. (1976). *Candidates and their images*. Pacific Palisades, CA: Goodyear.

Ridout, T. N., Franz, M., Goldstein, K. M., & Feltus, W. J. (2012). Separation by television program: Understanding the targeting of political advertising in presidential elections. *Political Communication, 29*, 1–23.

Schaffner, B. F. (2005). Priming gender: Campaigning on women's issues in U.S. Senate elections. *American Journal of Political Science, 49*(4), 803–817.

Scherer, M. (2012, November 8). How Obama's data crunchers helped him win. *CNN.com.* Retrieved from http://www.cnn.com/2012/11/07/tech/web/obama-campaign-tech-team/index.html

Tedesco, J. C. (2002). Televised political advertising effects: Evaluating responses during the 2000 Robb-Allen senatorial election. *Journal of Advertising, 31*(1), 37–48.

Tedesco, J. C. (2011). Political information efficacy and internet effects in the 2008 U.S. presidential election. *American Behavioral Scientist, 55*(6), 696–713. doi: 10.1177/0002764211398089

Tedesco, J. C., & Kaid, L. L. (2003). Style and effects of the Bush and Gore spots. In L. L. Kaid, J. C. Tedesco, D. G. Bystrom, & M. S. McKinney (Eds.), *The millennium election: Communication in the 2000 campaign* (pp. 5–26). Lanham, MD: Rowman & Littlefield.

The undecided voter: Just like the unicorn? (2012, October 20). *NPR.* Retrieved from http://www.npr.org/2012/10/20/163309696/the-undecided-voter-just-like-the-unicorn

Valentino, N. A., Traugott, M. W., & Hutchings, V. L. (2002). Group cues and ideological constraint: A replication of political advertising effects studies in the lab and in the field. *Political Communication, 19,* 29–48.

Verba, S., Burns, N., & Schlozman, K. L. (1997). Knowing and caring about politics: Gender and political engagement. *The Journal of Politics 59* (4), 1051-1072.

Wesleyan Media Project (2012, October 24). 2012 shatters 2004 and 2008 records for total ads aired. Retrieved from http://mediaproject.wesleyan.edu/2012/10/24/2012-shatters-2004-and-2008-records-for-total-ads-aired

Wilner, E. (2012, November 9). Romney and Republicans outspent Obama, but couldn't out-advertise him: Targeting and message-control carried the day. Retrieved from http://adage.com/article/campaign-trail/romney-outspent-obama-advertise/238241

Winneg, K. M., Hardy, B. W., & Jamieson, K. H. (2013). The impact of 2008 presidential campaign media on Latinos: A study of Nevada and Arizona Latino voters. *American Politics Research, 4*(2), 244–269.

Yun, H. J., Jasperson, A. E., & Kaid, L. L. (2011). The cumulative effects of televised presidential debates on voters' attitudes across red, blue, and purple political playgrounds. In M. S. McKinney & M. C. Banwart (Eds.), *Communication in the 2008 U.S. election: Digital natives elect a president* (pp. 107–120). New York, NY: Peter Lang Publishing.

Note

1. The national research project through which this data was collected was directed by Dr. Mitchell McKinney (University of Missouri), Dr. Dianne Bystrom (Iowa State University), Dr. John Tedesco (Virginia Tech University), and Dr. Mary Banwart (University of Kansas). The authors thank the 2012 Election Project members for their efforts and participation in obtaining a national data sample.

CHAPTER FOUR

Reaching Young Voters in the Middle

Party Loyalty and Perception of Political Participation

KAYE D. SWEETSER

Winston Churchill once said, "If you're not a liberal at 20 you have no heart, if you're not a conservative at 40 you have no brain." This sentiment encapsulates the idea that, throughout one's life, ideology changes and a voter's allegiances to a party may shift over time. Although such movement in ideology is generally accepted over the course of one's life, society generally paints youth as politically-charged beings who are strongly tied to issues, causes, and even political parties. From the means with which these young voters get political information to the way that they act upon it, the portrait of the first-time voter is constantly evolving.

And as such, changes are afoot in the political sphere as this new generation of voters comes of age and begins participating in a process that they have long been told has shut out their vote. As Lariscy, Tinkham, and Sweetser (2011) point out, young voters are distinctly different from their older counterparts. They see politics, political participation, and the overall election process differently. First-time voters are increasingly forfeiting the opportunity to align themselves with specific political parties and instead are calling themselves "independents" at a greater rate than previous generations (Sweetser, 2013). Even more interesting with regard to party loyalty, those who do identify with a political party are not opposed to crossing party lines once they finally get to the ballot box.

Even anecdotally, it is clear that this latest generation of young voters is diverging from the historical mold of first-time voters as they have grown up in an era witnessing the ever-expanding evolution of political information. Each election cycle finds noticeable advances not only in how information is transmitted (channel or mode), but also in the volume and message diversity of that information. As the availability of information grows by leaps and bounds with each new technological innovation, audiences more than ever have a variety of media from which they can access news. With this growth in media choices, audiences have become increasingly active in their determinations about where to get specific types of news and information. Given that information seeking for news has moved along the continuum where it used to be a rather passive activity to where it now is transformed into a more active engagement-oriented act where, for example, social network users can interact with campaigns and candidates, it becomes clear that political participation deserves more scholarly attention.

Specifically and in keeping with the research of scholars like Erik Bucy (Bucy, 2005; Bucy, D'Angelo, & Newhagen, 1999; Bucy & Gregson, 2001) and Ruthann Lariscy (Lariscy et al., 2011; Sweetser, Lariscy, & Tinkham, 2008), the idea of political participation should be reevaluated to determine whether digital acts, such as engaging with candidates online, might be similar to more traditional acts such as making telephone calls on behalf of a candidate or door-to-door canvassing.

This potential shift in young voter conceptualization of political participation to incorporate broad online and social media uses of political information retrieval and sharing creates an interesting backdrop to the 2012 election. What does this reconceptualization of political participation mean? Are there relationships between online communication retrieval and sharing forms of participation and voting or voting patterns, such as crossing party lines? This chapter addresses these issues, while keeping grounded by the traditional political communication definition of participation.

In doing so, this chapter uses the context of first-time voters in the 2012 election, and it is important to understand the campaign and times as a whole. As if the United States could not appear any more divided in the aftermath of the 2008 presidential election campaign season, the 2012 election showed that the nation remained polarized. The discord in Washington between the Republicans and Democrats that significantly stalled or resulted in inaction on many issues invites attention toward attitudes and behaviors of self-described independents. Who would these voters, who had no loyalty to a particular party and whose votes were up for grabs, end up supporting on Election Day 2012?

Yet, while the media focused their attention on this group of independents, Republicans and Democrats alike began to shift allegiances and change their own votes, suggesting that they too felt alienated by the party to which they belong. Using a survey of young voters ($N = 610$), this study focuses on how independents and party-line-crossing voters in the 2012 election perceive digital tools for political participation. To provide a foundation for this study, I begin with a brief review of previous research.

Social Media Use and Political Participation

For more than a decade, political communication scholars have examined the Internet and its use as a political information tool. From motives as to why one uses the Internet for political information (Johnson & Kaye, 2003; Kaye & Johnson, 2002, 2004) to the idea that involvement online can actually equal political participation (Bucy, 2005; Bucy et al., 1999; Bucy & Gregson, 2001; Lariscy et al., 2011), much has been learned about the Internet as a political forum. During this time, the Internet has evolved from a place where parties and campaigns would provide only "online brochures" as a one-way mass communication broadcast model (Tedesco, 2004) to a more interactive and surprisingly social medium (Zhang, Johnson, Seltzer, & Bichard, 2010). Indeed, the idea that constituents actually build relationships with both political parties (Sweetser, 2013) and candidates (Sweetser & Tedesco, 2014) during the campaign process has begun to emerge as an important context for understanding voter connection beyond the simple act of casting a ballot, and social media has been at the heart of that personalization. Digital political research has, in many cases, focused on the idea that the medium may not transform any given political system, but it can change an individual (Bucy & Gregson, 2001), and that engaging in political discussion as well as information-seeking online can be considered a form of political participation (Bucy, 2005; Bucy et al., 1999; Bucy & Gregson, 2001; Lariscy et al., 2011; Sweetser et al., 2008).

As more interactive forms of communication developed, scholars began considering the proposition that communication activities could actually be considered political participation. Calling the phenomena "media participation," Bucy and Gregson (2001) asserted that this new form of participation was a legitimate and valuable contribution to an individual's political life. Early research in this area noted that call-in political shows and the Internet, both having interactive two-way communication features emblematic of today's social media, were useful and valuable to political life (Bucy et al., 1999). Bucy and Gregson (2001) later investigated what became known as the media participation hypothesis, arguing that online communication activities represent a new form of participation.

Historically, political participation refers to activities performed by citizens that attempt to influence the structure and selection of government policies

(Putnam, 1996). Passive activities—such as supporting political activities and searching and exchanging information—are also considered political participation (Conway, 2000). The more active forms of participation require individuals to share their political ideology and opinions (e.g., listing political ideology on Facebook or sending an email to political organizations). Bucy and Gregson (2001) argued that the sharing of political information in such a mass media forums, like the Internet, invite involvement like donating money to a campaign or joining mobilization efforts. Other forms of online political engagement are less active, such as reading a political blog or searching for information on the Internet. These activities can be characterized as being of a surveillance nature and require little or no information sharing. Given that political experiences online are deemed "real" by the user (Bucy et al., 1999), it has been argued that media participation can indeed influence the actual substance and outcome of politics (Bucy & Gregson, 2001).

Although much research examines political participation, the idea of determining how participatory any specific act is remains a matter of perception with very little scholarly attention. To this point, the so-called media participation hypothesis was developed based on the notion that political participation was an evolving concept to now include a new set of media-use activities. Although Bucy and Gregson (2001) suggested the concept, which was further explicated by Lariscy et al. (2011) and Sweetser et al. (2008), the majority of work has focused on a broad range of generational cohorts rather than a specific group, such as first-time voters. The breakdown of media participation for first-time voters and how it may differ based on political party ideology has not yet been fully investigated and deserves attention in order to understand how this next generation of voters views participation and how this may differ based on their alliance to a particular political party. Indeed, this group is especially interesting because they come to the political process with a fresh perspective and their own way of seeking information and participating. The acts that they adopt during their first election cycle can influence their later behaviors as they become more experienced voters. Thus, this first-time voter analysis allows us a glimpse into the next generation of voters.

Method

This study employed survey methodology as a means to understand how independents, vote changers, and party-line crossers viewed political participation in the 2012 election. A group of nonrandom (convenience sample) first-time voters on a politically active campus during the hot phase of the campaign were surveyed ($N = 610$).

To measure political media participation activities, the Lariscy et al. (2011) scale listing 29 traditional and digital political activities, ranging from attending a rally to listing political ideology on one's Facebook profile, were presented to respondents for their rating of the "participatory" level for each activity. On a Likert-type scale, respondents were asked to rate their perception of whether each individual act was considered a low form of political participation (1, not very participatory) to a high form of political participation (5, very participatory).

Knowing that political parties and their own adoption of social media have been studied and characterized for their differences in approach, political affiliation became an important component to measure here as well. The main political demographic variable here asked respondents to nominally select their political party identification as either Democrat, Republican, or independent. Party strength was measured on a five-point semantic differential scale ranging from weak (1) to strong (5). Vote choice was measured asking respondents for whom they intended to vote during the election. Loyalty was measured two ways: respondents were asked whether they had changed their minds regarding vote choice (yes or no) and whether their vote choice had crossed party lines (yes or no).

Sample

To access the youth vote, this study focused on the first-time voter. The focus on this sample was deliberate for two key reasons. First, Lariscy et al. (2011) found that young voters view political participation differently than their older voting cohorts. Second, research has noted a growing prevalence of noncommittal voters claiming to be independent as opposed to affiliating with one of the two major parties in the United States (Sweetser, 2013). Young voters represent the future of the electoral system, and although there is much criticism suggesting that media and candidates ignore young voters or talk about issues in ways not relevant to young voters, it remains important to assess how young voters view the political process.

As such, a pool of first-time voters was identified using a convenience sampling technique at a large southeastern university. Data were collected via an online survey after the summer nominating conventions, which mark the first significant media events for the general election. The mean age of the sample was just below 20 years old (19.56 years old; SD = 1.47 years), which means the majority of the sample is composed of first-time presidential election voters. The sample was composed of more females (n = 458; 75.1%) than males (n = 145; 23.8%), with seven respondents declining to provide gender data.

The respondents in this study were more commonly self-reported Republicans (n = 345; 56.6%) than Democrats (n = 149; 24.4%) or independents (n = 107; 17.5%), with nine respondents declining to provide political party identification data. These ideological breakdowns are similar to Lariscy et al. (2011).

Research Questions

The following research questions are posed to illuminate how perception of political participation, political affiliation, and various party loyalty variables interplay with one another:

RQ1: How do young voters view political participation?

RQ2: Is there a difference in perception of political participation based on political affiliation?

RQ3a: What role, if any, does loyalty or political participation play in predicting vote changing?

RQ3b: What role, if any, does loyalty or political participation play in predicting whether one's vote will cross party lines?

Results

The majority of respondents in this survey indicated that they were registered voters (n = 474; 77.7%). As might be expected in a group of new affiliates to a political party, strength of party identification was basically neutral among this group (M = 2.73; SD = 1.14), which suggests that those new to the electoral process did not feel completely amalgamated into a political party.

When respondents were asked for whom they would vote if the election were held that day, almost one out of five remained undecided (n = 116; 19.0%). As one might expect based on party identification, more than half of the respondents indicated that they would vote for Republican candidate Mitt Romney (n = 325; 53.3%) and a quarter said Barack Obama (n = 151; 24.8%).

Before analysis could get underway, it was important to review the independents in the sample to ensure that they were not party affiliates hiding under a cloak of noncommittal identification. A chi-square test revealed that independents were equally likely to indicate intent to vote for the Republican candidate (n = 25) as the Democratic candidate (n = 25), $x^2(6, N = 597) = 516.51, p < 001$. A majority of the independents were truly undecided (n = 52), and four were unable to vote in the United States.

Party loyalty was measured by two dichotomous choice questions. The first question asked whether the respondent "changed vote choice during the course of the 2012 election" (yes or no) and the second asked whether "their vote crossed party lines" (yes or no). A chi-square test was used to examine these two questions separately against the categorical variable of political party identification. A total of 13.6% (n = 81) of respondents indicated that they had changed their vote, x^2(2, N = 597) = 31.53, p < 001. Of those who did change their vote, the majority were self-reported Republicans (45.7%), followed by independents (39.5%), and Democrats (14.8%). Next, 13% (n = 77) claimed that their vote would cross party lines, x^2(2, N = 597) = 48.20, p < 001. Those most likely to cross party lines were independents (45.5%), followed by Republicans (35.1%), and Democrats (19.5%). Thus, by being least likely to change their vote and least likely to cross party lines, Democrats in the sample appeared more stable in their vote.

Perception of Political Participation

To answer the first research question, an exploratory factor analysis was conducted on the perception of political participation items used in this survey. As previously done (Lariscy et al., 2011), a principal components factor analysis with varimax rotation was conducted and resulted in a four-factor solution that explained 71.62% of the variance. The first factor was labeled "public participation actions" (α = .97). This factor included publicly observable participation actions, such as volunteering; calling in to a political talk show; attending a political event, such as a political rally; or raising money for a campaign. The second factor was called "private participation actions" (α = .88) and included activities that one might undertake privately without others observing, such as watching a debate on television or talking privately with friends or family about politics. The third factor was named "public political identification actions" (α = .78) as it included items about how one would identify one's political party affiliation or stance publicly, such as listing political ideology on a social network profile or wearing a campaign T-shirt. The final and fourth factor was called "private surveillance actions" (α = .73). This factor was focused around solitary activities that others would not observe, such as reading political blogs as well as candidate blogs. Some items did double-load, which is indicated in the factor loadings provided in Table 1. Standardized factor scores were used in the analysis to represent the weighted extent to which one believed a particular action was political participation.

Traditional activities such as fundraising, door-to-door canvassing, and volunteering were among the strongest activities in first factor defining participation. The more passive, but social circle-limiting and private activities, were represented

Table 1. Rotated Component Factor Loading Scores for Perceived Political Participation

	1	2	3	4
Public Participation Actions (alpha = .97)				
Raising funds for a candidate	.92			
Campaigning for a local candidate	.90			
Contacting a politician	.89			
Door-to-door canvassing	.88			
Volunteering for a political candidate	.86			
Calling a political talk show	.86			
Attending city council/town hall meeting	.84			
Donating money to a campaign/politician	.83			
Emailing political or issue-oriented orgs	.83			
Writing a letter to the newspaper editor	.81			
Attending a political event/rally	.79			
Signing a petition (not e-petition)	.75			
Sending political e-cards	.68			
Posting a political sign in the yard	.60		.55	
Interacting with a candidate on Twitter	.56		.40	
Signing an e-petition	.54		.43	
Private Participation Actions (alpha = .88)				
Watching political TV news shows		.86		
Discussing politics with friends/family		.72		
Voting		.65		
Watching political/issue oriented videos on sites like YouTube		.62		
Searching for political information online		.61		
Public Political Identification Actions (alpha = .78)				
Listing political affiliation on social network profile			.78	
Joining a political Facebook group			.68	
Wearing a political T-shirt	.54		.61	
Private Surveillance Actions (alpha = .73)				
Reading a blog (non-candidate)	.53			.61
Reading a candidate's blog				.56
Following a candidate on Twitter			.52	.53
Variance Explained	48.09%	14.286%	5.34%	3.89%

Note. Items were measured on a five-point Likert scale with 1 = low participation and 5 = high participation.

in the second factor. Here there was a mix of traditional and digital activities, such as watching political news shows or debates, talking about politics with friends or family, and even searching for or watching candidate information online. The third factor represents more public-identity digital activities, like joining a Facebook group or listing ideology on one's Facebook profile. The final factor included more personalized conversation-type digital activities, such as reading political blogs or following a candidate on Twitter.

The loadings in this factor analysis are a distinct departure from those reported elsewhere using the same scale (Lariscy et al., 2011). The current study's factor analysis supported groupings where traditional and digital actions coexisted in factors together, rather than being broken into traditional and Internet-based political participation measures as they were in our 2011 study.

The second research question asked whether there was a difference in the perception of political participation based on the political affiliation of the respondent. In order to investigate a possible difference, a series of one-way analyses of variance was run to separately compare each of the four political participation factor scores based on self-identified political ideology. Significant main effects were found for all but the factor labeled public participation actions. Only one significant finding was associated with the private participation actions factor, which both Democrats and Republicans indicated the highest level, $F(2, 551) = 8.35$, $p < .001$. For this factor, a Tukey's posthoc test showed that Republicans felt more strongly than independents that private actions, such as watching a debate, counted as political participation (mean difference = $.45$, $p < .001$).

Similarly, members of the two main political parties believed public political identification actions were a greater level of participation than independents, $F(2, 551) = 5.04$, $p < .001$. However, a Tukey's posthoc test indicated the only significant difference appeared between Republicans and independents. In fact, for public political identification actions, Republicans showed a standardized factor score of .36 greater than independents, indicating that actions such as posting your political affiliation on your social network profile or wearing a campaign T-shirt were viewed as more participatory by the Republicans ($p < .005$).

For the private surveillance actions factor, independents were significantly more likely than Republicans to indicate that they thought these actions were a form of participation $F(2, 551) = 4.69$, $p < .05$. In this case, a Tukey's posthoc test revealed that independents were significantly more likely than Republicans to indicate that actions such as reading a campaign blog were considered political participation.

Next, a series of independent samples t-tests were run on the perception of political participation variables to compare factor scores based on whether any respondents changed vote or crossed party lines. Two statistically significant results occurred. First, those who crossed party lines were higher in the public participation actions factor score, $t(555) = -2.04$, $p < .05$, but lower in the public political identification factor scores, $t(555) = -2.05$, $p < .05$.

The last two research questions asked what role variables such as political party strength and perception of political party activities might have in predicting vote changing. A stepwise linear regression using vote change as the dependent variable resulted in a weak, though significant, equation ($R^2 = .05$), $F(1, 535) = 27.92$, $p < .001$. Only political party strength was able to predict whether one changed his or her vote ($\beta = .56$, $p < .001$). With regard to party-line crossing with one's vote, a stepwise linear regression resulted in another weak, yet significant, model where political strength ($\beta = .04$, $p < .001$) and the public participation actions factor ($\beta = .03$, $p < .05$) predicted the crossing of party line ($R^2 = .05$), $F(2, 549) = 9.73$, $p < .001$. As such, it appears that vote changers and party-line crossers, for the most part, are not greatly impacted by their perception of political participation activities.

Discussion

As predicted by Lariscy et al. (2011), the definition of political participation is indeed changing in support of Bucy and Gregson's (2001) media participation hypothesis. Just one major election cycle ago, the evolution of political participation compartmentalized traditional activities such as attending a rally or canvassing door-to-door for a candidate separately from digitally-based activities, such as posting one's political ideology on a social network site or searching for political information online. Even with these delineations between the types of participation, young people believed digital activities were indeed real forms of participation. This study demonstrates an evolution in the attempt to define political participation such that the first-time voters surveyed here began to classify political activities by public versus private rather than traditional versus digital categories.

Examining this evolving definition of political participation through the lens of independents and those with low levels of political party loyalty provides an interesting context for understanding the activities in which vote changers and party-line crossers might engage. Though actual participation was not investigated here (instead it was perception of participation activities), one might imagine that if a campaign was able to successfully activate supporters in public participation activities and political identification activities, then the voter may be less likely to change support or cross party lines on Election Day.

Similarly, it becomes important for campaigns to realize that solitary online digital activities like reading candidate blogs, reading political blogs, and searching for political information online are indeed political participation activities by the standards set by our youngest citizens. As such, if campaigns can catch the attention and engage noncommittal voters and independents through online content, then the party may have an opportunity to move these private participation activities into a more publicly observable action like attending a rally or wearing a campaign T-shirt. Although the data here do not speak to that direct path by which activities create support, loyalty, or votes, the argument can be made conceptually that more public displays of support and identification would make it more difficult for one to reconcile changing his or her vote or crossing the party line.

To that end, the results here showed only limited support for the idea that vote changers or party-line crossers are impacted by their perception of political participation activities. This, in itself, is a meaningful finding. Sweetser (2013) argued that political parties in general are losing youth vote support due to a deteriorating relationship between the party and the voter. The findings in this study may suggest such a scenario where these vote changers, party-line crossers, and independents do not view certain acts as political participation because they are not strongly affiliated with a political party or candidate in the first place.

Interestingly, the only political affiliation related significant differences in evaluation of the participatory nature of political activities were between Republicans and independents. Republicans rated two of the four political activity factors—which contained a range of public, private, traditional, and digital political activities—significantly higher than independents. This finding suggests very real differences in the way these voters conceptualize the level of political participation the activity represents.

It is also interesting to note that independents more greatly valued private surveillance types of political actions, such as reading blogs. This may suggest that they want to assimilate into the political landscape under the party radar, yet may also indicate that they want to read political sources outside the traditional media when making political decisions. Furthermore, though the number of independents appears to be growing, it can easily be questioned if they are a rising mass in the shadows of the political system unaware of one another and their size. If they see themselves as politically different and solitary, then independents' reliance on these types of political activities is consistent with their own self-perception.

Paradoxically, people who crossed party lines saw public participation actions as being more participatory than those who did not cross party lines. One might expect the opposite to be true, considering that the loyalty among party-line vote crossers is not high. Loyalty to the party is a characteristic common to base voters, suggesting those with a party allegiance would report this as an important participatory activity. However, those without party allegiance were more likely to indicate public actions were participatory. Along these lines and consistent with the paradox, those who crossed party lines believed private actions were not as participatory. These two findings together suggest that those who cross party lines are quite concerned with appearances—the appearance to campaign for a candidate and donate money are very important. Whether engaging in those acts would have further solidified their relationship with the candidate/party and prevented them from crossing party lines, or whether they are compensating for a dissonant feeling resulting from their desire to cross party lines, deserves further research.

Limitations and Future Research

The greatest limitation lies in the central concept of political participation that was explored here. This study focused on the perception of political participation activities, not the actual frequency with which the respondent undertook the activity. Future research should continue this line and connect both perception of activity as participation and frequency of participation to see if there is a correlation. Furthermore, future research should investigate whether actually engaging in these particular participatory acts (or lack of participating in these acts) might predict vote changing, party-line crossing, or one's status as an independent.

Future research also could investigate whether independents are more predisposed to read blogs and participate in the private surveillance activities or whether participation in such activities turns those with weaker loyalty into independents. To continue this line of research into independents, future studies should investigate the psychological underpinnings at play, any dissonance resulting from party-line crossing, and compensation activities that result from lack of allegiance or loyalty to a major political party.

References

Bucy, E. P. (2005). The media participation hypothesis. In M. S. McKinney, L. L. Kaid, D. G. Bystrom, & D. B. Carlin, *Communicating politics: Engaging the public in democratic life* (pp. 107–122). New York, NY: Peter Lang Publishing.

Bucy, E. P., & Gregson, K. S. (2001). Media participation: A legitimizing mechanism of mass democracy. *New Media & Society, 3*, 359–382.

Bucy, E. P., D'Angelo, P., & Newhagen, J. E. (1999). Engaging the electorate: New media use as political participation. In L. L. Kaid & D. G. Bystrom, *The electronic election: Perspectives on the 1996 campaign communication* (pp. 335–347). Mahwah, NJ: Lawrence Erlbaum Associates.

Conway, M. M. (2002). *Political participation in the US*. Washington D.C.: CQ Press.

Johnson, T. J., & Kaye, B. K. (2003). Around the World Wide Web in 80 ways: How motives for going online are linked to Internet activities among politically interested Internet users. *Social Science Computer Review, 21*(3), 304–325.

Kaye, B. K., & Johnson, T. J. (2002). Online and in the know: Uses and gratifications of the Web for political information. *Journal of Broadcasting & Electronic Media, 46*(1), 54–71.

Kaye, B. K., & Johnson, T. J. (2004). A Web for all reasons: Uses and gratifications of Internet components for political information. *Telematics and Infomatics, 21*, 197–223.

Lariscy, R. W., Tinkham, S. F., & Sweetser, K. D. (2011). Kids these days: Examining differences in political uses and gratifications, Internet political participation, political information efficacy, and cynicism based on age. *American Behavioral Scientist, 55*(6), 749–764.

Putnam, R.D. (1996). The strange disappearance of civic America. *The American Prospect* (24), 34–48.

Sweetser, K. D. (2013, August). *Who's coming to the party? Exploring the political organization-public relationship in terms of relationship, personality, loyalty, and outcomes among first-time voters.* Paper presented at the annual meeting of the Association for Education in Journalism and Mass Communication, Washington D.C.

Sweetser, K.D., Lariscy, R. W., & Tinkham, S. F. (2008, November). *The dabblers, devoted, developing, and disinterested: Examining political uses and gratifications, Internet political sophistication, political information efficacy and cynicism.* Paper presented at the annual meeting of the National Communication Association, San Diego, CA.

Sweetser, K.D., & Tedesco, J.C. (2014). Effects of exposure and messaging on political organization-public relationships exemplified in the candidate-constituent relationship. *American Behavioral Scientist*, forthcoming.

Tedesco, J. (2004). Changing the channel: Use of the Internet for communicating about politics. In L. L. Kaid, *Handbook of political communication research* (pp. 507–532). Mahwah, NJ: Lawrence Erlbaum Associates.

Zhang, W., Johnson, T., Seltzer, T., & Bichard, S. (2010). The revolution will be networked: The influence of social network sites on political attitudes and behaviors. *Social Science Computer Review, 28*(1), 75–92.

CHAPTER FIVE

"No One Puts Baby in a Binder"

The Resonance of Social Media Messages with College Students During the 2012 Presidential Campaign

AMY E. JASPERSON[1]

The Barack Obama and Mitt Romney campaigns both competed for the support of key voting demographics, saturating the social media environment with campaign messages during the 2012 presidential election. In particular, both campaigns targeted women through tailored online appeals. In the 2008 presidential election, 10 million more women than men voted (Casserly, 2012; Riccardi, 2012) and Obama won a majority of the female vote. Yet, in the 2010-midterm elections, more women supported the Republican Party (Doocy, 2012; Pew Research Center, 2010).

This chapter explores how the presidential campaigns' gender-based social media messages resonated with young female voters. Since these female college students have grown up in a time when many rights for women (i.e., access to health care, birth control, and reproductive choice) may be taken for granted, it was unclear as to how campaign messages focused on women's issues and aimed at activating their gender identities would resonate with young female voters.

Both campaigns framed their messages about women's issues in divergent ways. Romney used a "family" frame and an "economic" frame when talking about issues affecting women, whereas Obama used "civil rights" and "female independence" frames. Citizen-generated "memes" commenting on current developments in the campaign added to the gender-focused messages in political discourse, referencing the Dos Equis "Most Interesting Man in the World" ad campaign; Patrick Swayze's character from the movie "Dirty Dancing"; and a cultural icon of female empowerment from World

War II, Rosie the Riveter. Given these competing frames crafted during the campaign speaking to women's issues, were young college women receptive to these social media messages? Which messages framing "women's issues" were most successful at resonating with young voters? This investigation explores how college students used social media during the 2012 presidential campaign and examines the relationship between partisan identification and gender in processing such social media messages. I begin with a review of the literature documenting the effects of traditional and social media.

The Use and Effects of Traditional and Social Media

A wide body of literature has documented the power of traditional media, including print and television sources, to set the public's agenda, perhaps not telling the public what to think, but rather what to think about (Cohen, 1963). As West (2014) notes, campaign advertising messages as well as news media messages set the agenda for voters. Ads have the ability to raise or diminish the importance of particular issues and can be used to provide a strategic advantage for a candidate. "Candidates use election contests to dramatize issues. They also try to de-emphasize matters that may be problematic for them.... Candidates' advertising therefore should be assessed in terms of its ability to change citizens' perceptions of what are the most important priorities" (West, 2014, p. 101). In this way, candidates strategically prime and defuse, or de-emphasize, issues of concern (Shaffner, 2005; West, 2010), altering the standards by which the public evaluates them. Ads like former President George H. W. Bush's "Revolving Door" in 1988 led women more than men to mention crime as the most important issue (West, 2014).

Further, depending upon the issue, if a party is perceived to have ownership of the issue, or greater credibility in handling the issue, the message may be more persuasive (Petrocik, 1996). Republicans have traditionally enjoyed ownership over issues of taxes and foreign policy, whereas Democrats have enjoyed ownership over education and health care. However, when certain issues dominate a campaign, both candidates may attempt to strategically frame the issue to their advantage by emphasizing aspects of the issue that play to each candidate's message strengths.

Framing signifies that political elites, such as candidates, select aspects of an issue to promote a particular "problem definition, causal interpretation, moral evaluation and/or treatment recommendation for the item described" (Entman, 1993, p. 52). Thus, framing has been shown to influence citizens' judgments in a range of situations (Allen, O'Loughlin, Jasperson, & Sullivan, 1994; Gamson, 1992; Iyengar, 1991; Jasperson, Shah, Watts, Faber, & Fan, 1998; Nelson, Clauson, & Oxley, 1997). Democratic candidates have been found to prime women's issues, while Republican candidates have distracted attention away from women's issues (Shaffner, 2005). As noted in *The Responsive Chord*, effective ads attach to something inside of the viewers: "We are not concerned with getting things across to people as much as out of people" (Schwartz, 1972, p. 96). Therefore, viewers' preconceived notions and existing storehouses of experiences make a crucial difference in determining which candidate messages will resonate or fall flat.

Traditional modes of communication are not the only channels that can be utilized to create messages that resonate with voters. As technology evolves, innovations continue to transform campaign communication. For example, Williams and Gulati (2007) investigated the use of Facebook profiles by congressional candidates. They found that Facebook support was an important candidate resource that had a significant impact on the candidate's final vote shares, especially for open-seat candidates. A study of the 2008 presidential campaign found that 40% of the sample studied received news about the presidential campaign from a social networking website at least once a week, similar to the percentage of voters receiving information from cable news outlets (Baumgartner & Morris, 2010).

According to the Pew Research Center, as of May 2013, 72% of online adults use social networking sites; 67% reported using social networking sites in late 2012 around the time of the presidential campaign. Seventy-four percent of women were users of social networking sites compared with 70% of men. Further, 18 to 29 years olds are the most likely age demographic to use a social networking site. The use of social networking sites among young adult Internet users between 18 and 29 years of age rose from 9% in 2005 to 49% in August 2006 and increased subsequently to 89% in May 2013 (Brenner & Smith, 2013). Clearly, political messages on social networking sites were a central path to reaching young voters during the 2012 campaign and, particularly, for reaching young female voters.

This chapter examines how the presidential candidates framed their appeals on women's issues via social media messages and considers the lessons that can be learned about appeals to young voters in the 2012 campaign. How did both candidates attempt to prime gender identities in young female voters and were certain frames more successful than others in activating such identities? Did citizen-generated messages pack the same punch as campaign-related messages?

Method

Participants

Undergraduate and graduate students at participating college and university campuses across eight different states (Georgia, Kansas, Massachusetts, Missouri,

Pennsylvania, Tennessee, Texas, and Virginia) ($N = 732$) participated in this study, which took place online during the four days before Election Day on November 6, 2012. Equal numbers of students were randomly assigned to three experimental groups: subjects who viewed gender-focused political messages, $n = 244$; subjects who viewed general political messages, $n = 245$; and subjects who viewed non-political messages, $n = 243$). Among the participants, 243 students identified themselves as Republicans, 381 students were Democrats, and 97 students were independents. About two thirds of the participants ($n = 511$) were white and one third were ethnic minorities ($n = 221$). The sample had 461 females and 201 males. The mean age was 21.4 years.

For the results that focus specifically on the gender messages condition, this subsample was composed of 32% Republicans, 40% Democrats, and 28% independents; 30% of the subjects in this subset were male and 70% were female. In addition, this subset was 80% white, 12.8% African-American, 6% Asian, 1.8% American Indian, and 13.4% Latino.

Procedure and Measures

Survey participants were recruited by research consortium partners to participate in a study of voters' responses to political campaign messages during 2012. Using the Qualtrics online survey tool, subjects answered questions about their level of political interest, media use, degree of gender group identification, feelings about the country, feelings about the presidential candidates, and they ranked a variety of campaign issues. After answering these initial questions, subjects in the gender messages experimental group were exposed to a series of actual social media messages[2] framed to appeal to women that appeared online in the form of a "meme." The term "meme" signifies a virally transmitted cultural symbol or "an idea, behavior or style that spreads from person to person within a culture" (http://www.merriam-webster.com/dictionary/meme). These ideas gain attention when they go viral and subsequently inspire imitation by others (Ashton, 2013). These images included political messages that were sponsored by the candidates as well as messages generated by citizens, reflective of the social media environment where citizen-generated content co-exists with campaign-sponsored content. The content of these "memes" provides evidence of the candidates' controlled, strategic framing and priming strategies along with citizen-generated understandings of the campaign.

Romney messages. In Romney's "Honors the Family" meme, the text stated, "Any policy that lifts up and honors the family is going to be good for the country, and that must be our goal." In a second Romney meme, "Big Choice," the text explained "women face a big choice this November with very different visions for our nation's future." This graphic contrasted the number of women who are unemployed and living in poverty in the Obama economy versus the potential jobs that Romney will create. In a third meme from the Romney campaign, "Women-Owned Businesses," the message stated that "we need a president who respects and understands what they do."

In each of these three social media messages, Romney directly appealed to female voters, framing issues of concern to women as issues of concern to all voters. Women were just one part of this collective group (whether it be the family, the country, or the business sector), allowing the appeals to women to fit into his larger message framework about jobs and the economy.

Obama messages. Obama's memes also referenced the collective good, but framed it as being achieved through women's control over their own choices and decisions. In Obama's first meme, "Fairly/Equally," the message linked the values of fairness and equality on issues of equal pay and health care decisions to the collective betterment of society. In the second Obama campaign meme in this study, "Back in Time," the message framed "women's reproductive rights" as a Republican attack on women's progress over the last several decades. The text stated, "I had a dream that we went back in time and women had no control of our own health care. Then I realized: That's not my dream—It's the Republican Party's." In the third Obama meme, "Women's Decisions," the text stated, "we shouldn't have a bunch of politicians, a majority of whom are men, making health care decisions on behalf of women."

Overall, these messages framed women's issues through the lens of gender equality and independent choice. The first Obama campaign meme described above framed women as part of the larger collective society. However, the second meme sponsored by Obama placed women in conflict with Republicans, whereas the third meme placed women in conflict with male politicians.

Citizen-generated messages. In addition to candidate-sponsored messages targeted at women, citizens created memes that responded to dynamic events during the campaign. One particular event that generated great attention in the social media environment was the second presidential debate on October 16, 2012, when Romney said that his staff brought him "whole binders full of women" to help him with gender equity in selecting his cabinet (Shear, 2012). After this comment went viral on Twitter, at a rate of 104,704 tweets per minute on the topic (pic.twitter. com/3EjNjfSZ), a Tumblr page sprang up, and memes referencing the binders full of women comment were replicated online at http://bindersfullofwomen.tumblr. com/. These memes were repeated in blog posts and online articles within 24 hours (Johnson, 2012; Ritz, 2012).

In the first citizen-generated meme examined in this study, the image referenced the Dos Equis beer ad campaign's "The Most Interesting Man in the World," saying "I don't always hire women, but when I do, I have binders full of them…" This meme framed the comment as a sexist joke, poking fun at Romney's awkward efforts to address the question about gender equality in the workforce. In the second citizen-generated meme, the image referenced the late actor Patrick Swayze's character, Johnny Castle, and his famous line in the movie, *Dirty Dancing*: "Nobody puts Baby in a corner." In this line, Swayze made the point to Baby's parents that their daughter deserved to be in the spotlight. The campaign-related meme joked, "No One Puts Baby in a Binder," in an imitation of the *Dirty Dancing* line. This message stands in contrast to the Dos Equis meme in that women should not be relegated to the background (or the metaphorical binder).

A third citizen-generated meme focused on women's issues was based on the image of the World War II American icon Rosie the Riveter, seen as a symbol of women's economic power as a factory worker supporting the war effort. In this updated meme, a modern day Rosie was pictured flexing her muscle and saying "hands off our reproductive rights." This meme presented an image of women's empowerment in further contrast to the "most interesting man" meme.

Measures of message resonance. To measure the degree to which the campaigns' message frames resonated with college students' understandings of issues, subjects were asked if they had seen the social media message before, if they would ever "like" this message on Facebook, and if they would ever "share" this message on Facebook. These measures represent the level of subjects' engagement with the message frame. "Liking" a message involves a general affective appraisal with a degree of resonance. "Sharing" a message indicates a more involved degree of resonance, as the choice to share a message serves as a personal and public endorsement of the message for all of one's friends to see in their newsfeed. Open-ended responses provided some sense of why particular messages were rejected, were "liked," or were "shared" with a higher degree of resonance.

Measures of candidate evaluation. Subjects evaluated both candidates on their personal and professional qualities before and after reviewing the social media memes. A personal attribute index was created for each candidate from the mean values of the qualities trustworthy, honest, believable, likable, and pleasant with a high Cronbach's alpha reliability score of .905. The professional attribute index was created from the average value of the qualities intelligent, knowledgeable, smart, strong, poised, good leader, and charismatic for each candidate and achieved a Cronbach's alpha reliability score of .921.

Measures of issue priorities. Subjects also rank ordered their own issue priorities before and after reviewing the social media memes. The degrees of importance of issue priorities were measured on a five-point scale from 1, not at all important, to 5, extremely important. Issue priorities included the economy, health care, protecting women's rights, the budget deficit, taxes, jobs, foreign policy, access to abortion/contraception, and education. Changes in these two measures indicated whether or not the messages primed subjects to alter their issue priorities or to alter their evaluations of the candidates' personal or professional qualities.

Analyses. This study utilized ANOVA, Scheffe post hoc, and difference contrast pair-wise tests simultaneously to find mean differences across different meme exposure groups including interactions with party affiliation, gender, and ethnic status.

Results

General Engagement with Media during Campaign 2012

Young voters in this study rated themselves as informed, with 42.4% considering themselves very to somewhat informed about politics. Sixty-nine percent of subjects were exposed to media coverage of the campaign in the week prior to the survey, while 56.8% of college students had talked with other people about the campaign in the week prior. Eighty-eight percent of subjects reported seeing political advertisements about the presidential campaign via television; 81% reported seeing ads via the Internet; 70% reported seeing ads via Facebook, Twitter, or some other social media outlet; and only 14% had seen ads via emails from friends. These data indicate the growing role of the Internet and social media (and the diminishing role of email) as channels for receiving candidate messages about the campaign.

Focusing exclusively on Facebook, 69.5% of subjects rated it somewhat to very likely that information about the campaign popped up on their Facebook timeline. Fifty-eight percent indicated that they had read a link or watched a video about the campaign that they saw on Facebook, while 77% of subjects indicated that they saw friends discussing the campaign on Facebook. A majority, 53% of subjects, answered that it was somewhat to very likely that they "liked a status update," yet only 36.7% of subjects reported posting a comment themselves in a discussion about the campaign, and only 34.2% posted a status update or shared a link about the campaign. These findings support the notion that "Facebook users across activities tend to receive more from friends than they give to others"; this situation exists due to a small group of "power users" who give more than they get while most others observe and receive (Hampton, Sessions Goulet, Marlow, & Rainie, 2012). Almost 19% said that they would completely ignore Facebook.

Resonance of Social Media Gender Memes

Although college students engaged in "liking" to a greater extent than "sharing" the social media messages seen in this study, not all messages were equally effective in resonating with young voters. Partisan and gender differences emerged in reactions to individual gender-focused memes.

Romney memes. Overall, Romney's appeals to women through these gender-focused memes were not effective in activating gender identities of female students (see Table 1). Results showed no significant differences between male and female students in their prior exposure to the Romney memes, in their decision to like the memes, or in their decision to share the memes. The second Romney meme, "Big Choice," showed the lowest levels of liking (only 13.4% of men "liked" it and only 16.5% of women "liked" it) and sharing (only 8.8% of men "shared" it and only 8.9% of women "shared" it).

However, even with this least popular Romney meme, we found significant differences due to partisan identity. Results showed that 30% of Republican students liked the meme, whereas only 10% of Democrats and 8% of independents liked the meme. Only 18% of Republicans reported that they would share this meme, but even fewer, 5.7% of Democrats and 3.2% of independents, would reportedly share this message with friends. Even more significant partisan differences were seen for the other two more popular memes framing women in "Honors the Family" and "Women-Owned Businesses": 60% of Republicans liked these memes compared to only 11.2% of Democrats, with independents falling closer to the Democrats.

Obama memes. In contrast to the Romney memes, the Obama memes were more effective in activating the gender identities of the female students, although different messages succeeded to varying degrees. A majority of female students "liked" Obama's meme, "Fairly/Equally," and the difference between message resonance in men and women was significant (see Table 1). Almost 56% of women liked the message, whereas only 38.2% of men liked the message; 34% of women reported interest in sharing the message, whereas only 19% of men reported sharing it. Although this meme generated the most dramatic differences between men and women, the differences between partisans were even larger. Almost 78% of Democrats liked the message compared to 21% of Republicans and 46.8% of independents.

Interestingly, the explicitly partisan dig at the Republican Party in "Back in Time" resulted in a significant difference between the resonance of the message with male and female students. Less than a majority of women reported liking or sharing this message. Gender differences were just shy of significance in liking "Women's Decisions"; however, there was a significant difference in reported

Table 1. Message Resonance Percentages by Gender and Political Party

		M	M	M	W	W	W	R	R	R	D	D	D	I	I	I
		SB	L	S	SB	L	S	SB	L	S	SB	L	S	SB	L	S
1	MR – "Honors the Family"	14.7	23.5	15.2	12.7	30.6	14	20***	60***	30***	12.4***	11***	6.8***	8***	19***	8.2***
2	MR – "Big Choice"	2.9	13.4	8.8	8.2	16.5	8.9	7	30*	18*	10	10*	5.7*	1.6	8*	3.2*
3	MR – "Women-Owned Businesses"	8.7	26.1	16.2	10.8	28.5	12.7	19.7**	60***	32.4***	8**	11***	5.7***	8.7**	14.3***	4.8***
4	BO – "Fairly/Equally"	4.3*	38.2*	19*	13.3*	55.7*	34*	4.2*	21.1***	9.9***	16.9*	77.5***	46.6***	7.9*	46.8***	29.5***
5	BO – "Back in Time"	7.2	22.4*	13*	6.3	38.6*	27.2*	4.2	5.6***	7***	10.1	57.3***	39***	48	32.8***	19***
6	BO – "Women's Decisions"	18.8	40.6	20.3*	25.9	54.4	35.7*	14**	19.7***	10***	36**	80***	47***	17.5**	46***	33***
7	"Baby in a Binder"	14.5	18.8	8.8	13.3	29.7	16.6	7	18.3**	13	18	39.3**	21	12.7	19**	8.1
8	"Most Interesting Man"	20.3*	28	10.3	34.8*	23	12.7	21	15.5	4.2*	35	30	15*	33	26	16*
9	"Rosie the Riveter"	23	23.5***	12**	28.5	56.3***	31**	25.4	25.4***	19	32.6	65.2***	33	22.2	45.2***	22

interest in sharing this meme between men and women. Compared to the gender differences, the partisan differences in liking and sharing the latter two memes were significant.

Overall, data reveal that the Obama campaign's social media messages were more successful at framing women's issues in ways that resonated with college students and, in particular, female students, than Romney's frame of women in their roles as members of a family and as business owners. In some cases, Obama's messages activated young women's gender identity when Romney's did not; and in other cases, Obama's messages seemed to resonate with both male and female students. None of Romney's messages or memes earned "likes" from more than 31% of female students.

Citizen-generated memes. The findings described above may not seem surprising given preconceptions about college students' voting allegiances. However, our expectations about the resonance of citizen-generated memes focusing on women's issues are less clear. Although social media messages focusing on "binders full of women" received media coverage after the October 16, 2012, presidential debate, did they strike a responsive chord with women, men, both groups, or neither group? Further, how did partisans process these messages?

Results showed that "Rosie the Riveter," the image with the greatest female empowerment message of the three citizen-generated memes, was most effective in activating gender identity in women. Women were significantly more likely than men (56% compared to 23.5%) to report liking this image. Also significantly, 31% of women reported interest in sharing this meme compared to only 12% of men. This meme also generated the greatest resonance with Democrats, with 65.2% reporting liking the meme's message, compared to the 45.2% of independents and only 25.4% of Republicans. The most disempowering message for women, "The Most Interesting Man in the World" meme, did not activate gender differences. A slightly higher percentage of men reported liking this meme (28% of men to 23% of women), but the difference was not significant. Differences between partisans in response to this meme were not notable either.

Finally, the response to the Patrick Swayze/*Dirty Dancing* meme, "No One Puts Baby in a Binder" was somewhat surprising. Although subjects seemed knowledgeable about the historical Rosie the Riveter reference, several 18- to 24-year-old students indicated through the open-ended responses that they were not aware of the pop cultural reference to *Dirty Dancing* (a 1987 movie). Therefore, they did not understand the humor of the message. There were no significant differences between men and women in liking or sharing this meme. Men rated it second lowest, just ahead of Romney's "Big Choice." Women rated it low, although higher than "Big Choice," "Women-Owned Businesses," and "The Most Interesting Man in the World." Although Democrats were more likely to "like" "Baby in a Binder," Republicans and independents equally disliked this meme, presumably because of its negative representation of Romney's comment about binders full of women. Thus, these citizen-generated attempts at humorous memes reflect resonance with some members of the population, and may earn media attention by resonating with reporters as interesting new angles on campaign coverage, but they are not uniform in the ways that they resonate with different audiences.

Framing and priming gender. Did these social media memes prime college students' evaluation of the candidates' personal and professional qualities? One would expect that subjects would hold more favorable evaluations of their party-affiliated candidate's personal and professional qualities, and this may increase after exposure to their own candidate's messages. Further, when candidates frame their appeals to speak to their strengths, this should increase students' candidate evaluations. The results partially confirmed these expectations. College students more positively evaluated presidential candidates from their own party: Democrats more highly evaluated Obama's personal qualities, $F(2, 611) = 66.8, p \leq .001$, and professional qualities, $F(2, 612) = 46.27, p \leq .001$, whereas Republicans evaluated Romney's personal, $F(2, 599) = 66.56, p \leq .001$, and professional attributes, $F(2, 598) = 36.47, p \leq .001$, more highly.

However, results showed divergent attitude changes between students from different political parties after meme stimulus exposure. Unlike Democrats and independents who did not change their evaluations of candidates' personal and professional attributes, young Republican students' evaluations of Romney's personal and professional qualities declined after viewing the memes. As these numbers indicate, Romney's personal qualities, $F(5, 563) = 3.371, p \leq .035$, and professional attributes, $F(2, 559) = 3.043, p \leq .034$, became more negative after young Republicans viewed the memes. More important, those young citizens who were exposed to gendered memes ($M = -.401, SE = .095$) became more negative in their evaluations of Romney's professional attributes than voters who were exposed to general political ($M = -.063, SE = .101$) or non-political ($M = -.211, SE = .106$) memes, $F(2, 599) = 3.043, p \leq .034$. After meme exposure, the mean changes for young Republican voters' evaluations of Romney's personal and professional attributes decreased by .329 ($SE = .118$) and .454 ($SE = .133$), respectively.

Further, what impact did social media memes have on students' top issue priorities? Results showed that regardless of the type of social media meme exposure (gender memes, general political memes, or non-political memes), students' top issue priorities were the economy and jobs, while their least important issue priorities were women's rights and abortion. One may expect that students in the gender meme condition would be primed to increase their ranking of women's issues after exposure to the memes. At the least, one may expect to see that female students in this condition would increase their ranking of women's issues after exposure to the gender meme stimuli. However, results showed that there was no change in the importance of women's rights for female students after viewing the gendered memes. In fact, women's rights became significantly less important as a campaign issue for male students after viewing the gender memes, $F(2, 576) = 3.074, p \leq .047$.

Discussion

Social media messages are an increasingly important part of strategic communication in political campaigns today. As technological innovations allow candidates to "microtarget" and even "nanotarget" their messages to mobile devices, campaigns work even more carefully to properly tailor their messages to key constituencies. At the same time, candidates have even less control over the groups with which such messages are shared and the ways in which voters interact with these messages. Women are a key demographic group to which both parties must appeal for support. Results from this analysis of social media messages show that gender memes seen in the 2012 presidential campaign varied in their effectiveness in resonating with young female voters. Not all memes are created equal; some (e.g., Obama's "Fairly/Equally") were more effective in speaking the language of the young female voter, whereas other messages (Obama's "Back in Time") fell short with partisan-based attacks or used frames that did not strike a responsive chord (Romney's "Women-Owned Businesses" or "Big Choice") with the target audience. Citizen-generated memes surrounding campaign events and issues showed variation in the degree to which such messages addressed, either explicitly or implicitly, the candidate's positions on women's issues. One such meme, Rosie the Riveter, was just as effective as an Obama-related meme in resonating a gender-based message with young women, suggesting that such social media messages are a part of the campaign communications environment that needs to be considered.

Finally, the online social media environment in 2012 was saturated with citizen-generated content that influenced the public discourse at times. These citizen-generated memes present in the social media environment during this study were negative in tone toward Romney and similar to negative attacks via traditional media channels. Although voters may report disliking negative messages, they may still influence young voters' assessments. Even late in the 2012 campaign, this particular mix of candidate-related and citizen-generated social media messages took a toll on young Republican students' evaluations of both Romney's personal and professional qualities. Although these memes did not significantly impact students' overall assessment at this late stage in the 2012 presidential campaign, the results show that this collection of social media messages did raise doubts about Romney as a candidate among a group that was predisposed to support him.

Further, when it comes to crafting messages on women's issues for young voters, these results suggest that party issue ownership may be at work for the next generation of voters. When young Republicans were exposed to gender memes highlighting women's issues, albeit framed in divergent ways to highlight Romney's and Obama's respective strengths, these students decreased their evaluations of Romney's personal and professional qualities, potentially punishing Romney for treading on the traditionally Democrat Party territory of women's issues. Therefore, in addition to message tone and overall balance of messages in the information environment, issue ownership is another possible explanation to account for the drop in Romney's evaluations as a result of exposure to gendered social media messages.

Given the proximity of this study to Election Day in 2012 and the engagement of the subjects in following the campaign, it could be unrealistic to believe that additional stimuli would prime evaluations of issue priorities and lead to more noticeable shifts in issue importance. It would not be surprising for a ceiling effect to have been reached this late in the campaign. However, instead of seeing a positive impact of gender memes priming an increase in the importance of women's rights as an issue for female students, we do see a defusing of the importance of women's rights as a campaign issue for male students, not in terms of relative ranking (since it was already the lowest ranked issue), but in terms of magnitude. These findings reinforce the point that, even late in the campaign, young voters are still being bombarded regularly with social media messages. Even with the fatigue that comes with such repetition, male students showed evidence of movement away from issues when the messages were communicated in a frame targeted toward a different demographic group that did not resonate with them.

Taken together, these findings suggest that gendered messages can be framed to activate gender identity. It is difficult to discern if the failures to activate gender identity seen here are due to the topical limitations of issue ownership, the specific content of message frames that do not connect with the young female voting demographic, or the late date that this study took place in the campaign. Further, priming does appear to change evaluations of candidates or the importance (or lack of importance) assigned to issue priorities, even at this late date in the campaign in a saturated message environment. This suggests that we do see some limited effects of social media messages through an online survey experiment, and further studies should continue to investigate these factors at a variety of points in time during the campaign.

As women continue to play a key role in elections due to their numbers and as issues of women's rights continue to be the focus of policy-makers' legislative reforms, the questions of how, why, and under what conditions campaign messages influence sentiment and behavior in the changing online environment will continue to be important. Further studies should continue to explore the messages that are able to strike a responsive chord with the newest generation of voters in the interactive, mobile media environment.

References

Ashton, K. (2013, May). How memes are orchestrated by the man. *The Atlantic*. Retrieved from http://www.theatlantic.com/technology/archive/2013/03/how-memes-are-orchestrated-by-the-man/274466/

Allen, B., O'Loughlin, P., Jasperson, A., & Sullivan J. L. (1994). The media and the Gulf War: Framing, priming and the spiral of silence. *Polity, 27(2)*, 255–284.

Baumgartner, J., & Morris, J.S. (2010). Who wants to be my friend? Obama, youth, and social networks in the 2008 campaign. In J. A. Hendricks & R.E. Denton (Eds.), *Communicator in chief: How Barack Obama used new media technology to win the White House* (pp. 51–66). Lanham, MD: Lexington Books.

Brenner, J., & Smith, A. (2013, August 5). 72% of online adults are social networking site users. Pew Internet & American Life Project. Retrieved from http://www.pewinternet.org/Reports/2013/social-networking-sites.aspx

Casserly, M. (2012, June). Where women matter most in election 2012. *Forbes*. Retrieved from http://www.forbes.com/sites/meghancasserly/2012/06/07/election-2012-mitt-romney-obama-women-battleground-states/

Cohen, B. (1963). *The press and foreign policy*. Princeton, NJ: Princeton University Press.

Doocy, P. (2012, March). The fairer half: Presidential campaigns target women voters. *Fox News.com*. Retrieved from http://www.foxnews.com/politics/2012/03/11/fairer-half-presidential-campaigns-target-women-voters/

Entman, R. (1993). Framing: Toward clarification of a fractured paradigm. *Journal of Communication, 43(4)*, 51–58.

Gamson, W. (1992). *Talking politics*. Cambridge, England: Cambridge University Press.

Hampton, K. N., Sessions Goulet, L., Marlow, C., & Rainie, L. (2012). Why most Facebook users get more than they give: The effect of Facebook "power users" on everybody else. Retrieved from Pew Research Center's Internet & American Life Project website: http://pewinternet.org/Reports/2012/Facebook-users.aspx

Jasperson, A., Shah, D., Watts, M., Faber, R., & Fan, D. (1998). Framing and the public agenda: Media effects on the importance of the federal budget deficit. *Political Communication, 15(2)*, 205–224.

Johnson, M. W. (2012, October 16, updated October 17). Romney "binders full of women" debate remark inspires Tumblr, Facebook page and Twitter account. *Huffington Post*.

Retrieved from http://www.huffingtonpost.com/2012/10/16/binders-full-of-women-tumblr-romney-debate_n_1972345.html

McCombs, M., & Shaw, D. (1972). The agenda-setting function of the mass media. *Public Opinion Quarterly, 36,* 176–187.

Nelson, T., Clauson, R., and Oxley, Z. (1997). Media framing of a civil liberties conflict and its effects on tolerance. *American Political Science Review, 91*(3), 567–584.

Petrocik, J. R. (1996). Issue ownership in presidential elections, with a 1980 case study. *American Journal of Political Science, 40*(3), 825–50.

Pew Research Center. (2010, November 17). *A clear rejection of the status quo, No consensus about future policies.* Retrieved from http://www.pewresearch.org/2010/11/03/a-clear-rejection-of-the-status-quo-no-consensus-about-future-policies/

Riccardi, N. (2012, August). Women's vote battle defines 2012 presidential election. *Huffington Post.* Retrieved from http://www.huffingtonpost.com/2012/08/27/womens-vote-2012-election_n_1832825.html

Ritz, E. (2012, October 17). The big story the morning after is … Romney's "binders full of women" remark? See how the left is playing it. *The Blaze.* Retrieved from http://www.theblaze.com/stories/2012/10/17/the-big-story-the-morning-after-is-romneys-binders-full-of-women-remark-see-how-the-left-is-playing-it/

Schwartz, T. (1974). *The responsive chord. How radio and TV manipulate you, who you vote for, what you buy, and how you think.* New York, NY: Anchor Press/Doubleday.

Shaffner, B. (2005). Priming gender: Campaigning on women's issues in U.S. Senate elections. *American Journal of Political Science, 49*(4), 803–817.

Shear, M. D. (2012, October 17). Debate moves women to fore in race for the White House. *The New York Times.* Retrieved from http://www.nytimes.com/2012/10/18/us/politics/obama-and-romney-focus-on-efforts-to-woo-women.html?_r=0

Twitter Government @gov. (2012, October 16). [Chart] Tracking the Presidential #debates: @HofstraU in Hempstead, NY. Retrieved from: https://twitter.com/gov/status/258422696071798784. Also appearing at pic.twitter.com/3EjNjfSZ.

West, D. M. (2010). *Air wars: Television advertising and social media in election campaigns 1952–2008* (5th ed.). Washington, DC: CQ Press.

West, D. M. (2014). *Air wars: Television advertising and social media in election campaigns 1952–2012* (6th ed.). Washington, DC: CQ Press.

Williams, C., & Gulati, G. J. (2007, August-September). *Social networks in political campaigns: Facebook and the 2006 midterm elections.* Paper presented at the annual meeting of the American Political Science Association, Chicago, IL.

Notes

1. The author thanks Dr. Kaye Sweetser and Dr. Hyun Yun for their assistance with this study as well as the participating faculty who were a part of this 2012 research consortium.

2. The memes used in this study were found on these social media links. The titles given to each meme are designators assigned by the author based on message content.

https://www.facebook.com/photo.php?fbid=10151113583361121&set=pb.21392801120.-2207520000.1380744275.&type=3&theater (Romney: Honors the Family)

https://www.facebook.com/photo.php?fbid=10151111566171121&set=pb.21392801120.-2207520000.1380744275.&type=3&theater (Romney: Big Choice)

https://www.facebook.com/photo.php?fbid=513400618670854&set=a.341474035863514.91151.317916771552574&type=1&theater (Romney: Women-Owned Businesses)

https://www.facebook.com/photo.php?fbid=10151257678776252&set=a.10150442734531252.402605.18753646251&type=1&theater (Obama: Fairly/Equally)

https://www.facebook.com/photo.php?fbid=10151220341981252&set=a.10150442734531252.402605.18753646251&type=1&theater (Obama: Back in Time)

https://www.facebook.com/photo.php?fbid=10151133052621252&set=a.10150442734531252.402605.18753646251&type=1&theater (Obama: Women's Decisions)

http://pandawhale.com/post/7699/top-10-binders-full-of-women-images (Citizen-generated: The Most Interesting Man in the World and No One Puts Baby in a Binder)

http://bindersfullofwomen.tumblr.com/post/33750544241/nobody-puts-baby-in-a-binder (Citizen-generated: No One Puts Baby in a Binder)

Issues

Defining Fairness in the Economic Rhetoric of the 2012 Presidential Election

JAY P. CHILDERS AND R. MCKAY STANGLER

In June 2012, the Pew Research Center polled Americans to find out what they believed were the most important issues in that year's presidential election. The top four responses were jobs (35%), the budget deficit (23%), health care (19%), and Social Security (11%)—all economic matters. No other issue, even immigration and gay marriage, garnered more than 5%. In early September, a similar poll conducted by CBS News and *The New York Times* received only two answers shared by more than 10% of the population—the economy and jobs (37%) and health care (11%). And in an exit poll conducted by the *Wall Street Journal* on November 6, 2012, voters identified the economy (59%) and the federal budget deficit (15%) as the most important issues facing the country only moments after casting ballots (King, Lee, & Nelson, 2012). Compared to years like 1988 and 2000 when Gallup found that only 24% and 9%, respectively, of the country thought the economy was the most important problem, the nation's most recent election was clearly and decisively focused on economic concerns.

Anyone paying attention to the United States' economy during the years leading up to the 2012 presidential election would, of course, be quite unsurprised that so many of the American people were focused on pocketbook issues. The nation was still struggling to recover from the biggest economic recession since the Great Depression some 80 years earlier. The unemployment rate in the summer of 2012 stood stuck at 8.2%, which was almost double that of just 4.4% only five years earlier (Whoriskey, 2012). Social mobility—the ability for those born into poor families to climb the economic ladder into financial security and wealth—was lower than it had been in almost a century. People's retirement funds had dried up in a depressed stock market, furloughs and pay cuts had become common, and recent college graduates were moving back home with their parents in droves as they struggled to find jobs and deal with student debt. The American economy was in bad shape, everyone knew it, and there was no way that the two men running for the White House, President Barack Obama and former Gov. Mitt Romney, could avoid talking about it.

And talk about it they did. In fact, both candidates seemed to talk of little else. Although both Obama and Romney had little choice but to focus on what they would do to strengthen the American economy, they did have options for how they talked about both what was behind the current state of the nation's financial problems and what it would take to move forward. Indeed, we focus in this chapter on the rhetorical choices both presidential contenders made in how they talked about the American economy. We do so for three reasons. First, politicians speak the language of politics, which is an ordinary sort of rhetoric that reflects that which most people find comfortable (Hart, Childers, & Lind, 2013, p. 38). Second, how candidates talk does influence election outcomes, mobilizing or demobilizing supporters and helping undecided voters decide (Stuckey, 2005). Third, campaign discourse at the presidential level sets precedents for how future candidates may talk about similar issues due to well-established institutional burdens (Mercieca & Vaughn, forthcoming). For all these reasons, campaign discourse matters.

In fact, we believe that both Obama's and Romney's economic rhetoric in the 2012 general election reveals a great deal about how the American people understood the nation's economic situation and at least part of why Obama was able to defeat Romney in November. Specifically, we claim that the economic discussion in the 2012 election was rooted in a primary concern for fairness that led Obama and Romney to craft competing narratives to explain who was to blame for the country's current financial struggles and who might save the nation. While these narratives are based on a shared assumption about the American dream and track rather predictably along political party assumptions about positive and negative liberty, we argue further that the key element in understanding the economic rhetoric of the presidential election is in how the candidates attacked each other's economic positions. Ultimately, we find that Obama's use of Romney's own words (i.e., "Let Detroit Go Bankrupt," "Big Bird," and "The 47%") against him as synecdochic sound bites proved far more effective than Romney's characterization of Obama as a bad leader who had no new plan for fixing the nation's economy. To make this argument, we begin by outlining the contextual factors that framed the

2012 presidential election and help explain why fairness was so central to both Obama's and Romney's economic rhetoric.

The Great Recession

When it comes to thinking about the economic structure of the United States, the American people have long downplayed the role of institutional forces that might enforce a class system and, instead, emphasized social mobility through an equality of opportunity. This latter focus has, of course, long been referred to as the American Dream, which rhetorical critic Vanessa Beasley (2004) has argued is "the product of the marriage between individualism and capitalism" (p. 38). Given that the United States is predicated upon a commitment to Lockean individualism and a capitalistic economic system, the American Dream asserts that anyone can be successful and find financial security through self-reliance and competitive persistence. If such a dream were true, there would be no place for a rigid caste system in which people are born into clearly defined classes. As Beasley has noted, "in theory, then, individualism and capitalism would indeed seem to be great social levelers within a diverse democracy" (p. 39).

Of course, theory and reality are not the same, and the American myth exists in political ideology and cultural narrative. Economic reality in the United States is quite a different matter. Dana Cloud (1996) has made just this point by noting that the Horatio Algers rags-to-riches narrative has long played a role in the American imagination. As she has further argued, this American Dream rests on the basic assumption that each American citizen be understood as an "autonomous individual who is ostensibly free from structural or economic barriers to fortune" (p. 119). Although this is an inspiring idea, Cloud has also asserted that the dream itself "justifies continuing inattention to structural factors, like race, gender, and class, that pose barriers to the dream for some Americans" (p. 119). This is not to suggest social mobility does not exist in the United States. Instead, it is to draw attention to the reality that different people have different opportunities based on myriad structural obstacles. And American society has always had structural obstacles that create entrenched inequalities.

This disconnect—between the equality of conditions we have traditionally imagined and the systemic inequality we actually face—has made it difficult for modern candidates to successfully discuss class without being accused of "class warfare." Politicians of earlier times, former President Franklin Roosevelt (FDR) chief among them, were comparatively unafraid of attacking the plutocratic class. In his first inaugural address, he attacked "unscrupulous money changers" and began a pattern of criticizing the very wealthy and the very greedy (Roosevelt, 1933). The Great Society programs of the 1960s had a distinct focus on class issues, with former President Lyndon Johnson (1964) saying in his famous University of Michigan speech that the future would be a "battle to give every citizen an escape from the crushing weight of poverty." Even former President Ronald Reagan (1986, para. 4), castigated by the left for a legacy of economic inequality, spoke often of the poor and said the "culture of poverty [is] as inescapable as any chain or bond."

What this discourse reveals is a willingness to discuss both the issue of class and ways to alleviate tensions and deprivations. Roosevelt found an identifiable enemy in the wealthy, and demonized them as responsible for at least part of the Great Depression. He gladly embraced the role of crusader for the forgotten man—which could just as easily be labeled "the poor man"—and many New Deal programs were clearly designed to benefit the lower classes, which had been hardest hit by the crisis. Johnson was just as blatant in his outspoken defense of and support for the poor, and he made poverty and class a centerpiece of his administration. Reagan's discourse about the poor, which admittedly included ways to reduce payments to welfare recipients, nonetheless acknowledged class divisions and framed the stigma of poverty as unacceptable in a wealthy nation. What unites these themes is a willingness to acknowledge, discuss, and address problems relating to the American class divide—no matter the speaker's political party.

But to fully understand the rhetorical choices of Obama and Romney in the 2012 campaign, one needs to understand the economic context within which the election took place. Obama's first term in office began in January 2009, a month that saw 598,000 job losses—the worst since the stagflation and oil shock year of 1974 (Isidore, 2009a). The first three months of Obama's term, in fact, would see more than 2 million jobs lost (Isidore, 2009b). These were losses of an unprecedented scale that no postwar president had ever had to confront. Job losses were just one component of a nation in poor fiscal health, however: the U.S. economy contracted nearly 4% from August 2008 to August 2009, making it the worst economic slump since the Great Depression (Willis, 2009). The housing market, which for most Americans represented their single biggest asset, began a similar free fall. Housing prices fell nationwide by an average of 30% from 2006 to 2009 and, in some areas, price collapses were almost incomprehensible: Las Vegas housing prices fell by 59% in that time (Ellen & Dastrup, 2012). By October 2012, Americans had lost an astonishing $7 trillion in housing wealth in a half-decade.

The Obama administration and the Federal Reserve tried to respond to these crises in a number of ways. Most notably, the Obama administration continued the bank bailouts begun by the Emergency Economic Stabilization Act of 2008, signed by President George W. Bush. This act included more than $700 billion to bail out the nation's biggest banks and financial services companies, but was only a fraction of the government's total efforts (Hulse & Herszenshorn, 2010). The federal government also insured money market accounts, bought troubled securities directly from banks, backstopped federal mortgage issuers, and intervened in the corporate commercial paper market—all of which added up, by early 2011, to more than $12 trillion in federal government commitments to distressed parts of the financial industry ("Adding Up," 2011). For homeowners, the administration began a program to modify mortgages, attempting to reduce principal owed in order to avoid massive foreclosures (Martin, 2011). The Federal Reserve kept interest rates near zero and pledged that it would do so until unemployment rates steadied (da Costa & Bull, 2012). More controversially, the administration elected to use a portion of the bank bailout fund to help take the major automotive companies into managed bankruptcy—a move that stirred outrage when the government announced it would take a $17 billion loss on the intervention (Story, 2010).

As the government worked to help revive the nation's flailing economy, the American people struggled to make sense of the new financial reality. The picture of that new reality was not something many Americans liked very much, especially since they sensed an uneven economic recovery following a recession that had already hit the poor and middle classes much harder than the nation's wealthiest. Nowhere was this unevenness seen more clearly than in the growing income inequality that emerged during the recession. During 2010 as the nation struggled to recover from the Great Recession, those in the top 1% of income earners saw their incomes grow by 11.6%, while the rest of the nation combined only saw a 0.2% increase (Saez, 2013). So few were surprised to find that according to a 2012 Congressional Research Service report, the richest 1% of Americans controlled 34.5% of the nation's wealth, the top 10% controlled 74.5%, and the bottom 50% controlled just 1.1% of the national wealth (Levine, 2012).

Indeed, so salient were these changes that an entirely new social movement emerged and garnered a great deal of national attention. Occupy Wall Street (OWS) brought inequality and economic unfairness to the front lines of all forms of media and to the center of national conversation. For two months in fall 2011, OWS forced national acknowledgment of the consequences of both the recession and the strikingly uneven economic recovery. Its slogan—"We Are the 99%!"—was a direct declaration of class division that implies solidarity on one end and objectionable exclusivity on the other. The nation's uneven economic recovery and growing inequality were simply at levels too significant to ignore, and OWS's slogan captured the attempts to pit one class—made up of nearly every American—

against a much smaller, much richer class. Coming just one year before the 2012 election, the movement could not help but influence national politics.

The political reaction to OWS was mixed. Obama spoke vaguely about sharing the protestors' concerns, saying the movement reflected "broad-based frustration about how our financial system works" (Madison, 2011, para. 1), then mostly used the protests as evidence for the necessity of pending finance-reform legislation. Romney was much more direct, telling one sympathetic protestor that "America's right, and you're wrong" and suggesting that OWS protestors might prefer the economic models of China, Russia, Cuba, or North Korea (Sargent, 2012, para. 4). Both of these reactions reveal a basic unwillingness to engage with the fundamental concerns of the movement. OWS, while never cohering around a single goal, seemed more than anything else to be an expression of widespread, long-term trends in inequality. Since the late 1960s or early 1970s, depending on the calculation, income inequality has increased dramatically in the United States—growing to its widest point in 2011, just a year before the election (Dodge & Dorning, 2012).

The causes of such inequality are diverse and disputed, but they likely include developments in education, globalization, and technological skills. This disparate picture of inequality's causes was reflected in the OWS movement. Indeed, the movement's blog encouraged members of the 99% to take photos of themselves with written descriptions of their tough economic circumstances ("We Are the 99 Percent," 2013). The result is a wide-ranging panorama of fiscal problems, from student loans to deceptive mortgages to cuts in government benefits. The perception one gains from surveying the posts is one of widespread unfairness: that no matter how much effort is accorded to bootstrap-pulling, the economic system of the United States is ineluctably rigged in favor of the richest. Neither candidate's limited responses to OWS displayed an understanding of this concern, though Obama came close when he argued that OWS was "not that different" from the Tea Party protests, saying that Americans "feel that their institutions aren't looking out for them" (Dwyer, 2011, para. 3). Both movements, seen in this light, reflect a sense of unfairness. For the Tea Party, it was unfair that the well-connected political class bailed out certain organizations and certain people. For OWS, it was unfair that the gaps between classes had diverged so sharply. For both, one class had triumphed over another.

This was the scene that greeted Obama and Romney in the 2012 campaign. First, American political tradition demanded a vocal belief in the American dream. Second, the Great Recession and the government's economic response were clearly going to be a campaign issue. Third, various protest movements had brought class inequality and class division to the national spotlight, and ignoring the wealth of statistical evidence proving growing class divisions was not a viable option.

Fairness and the American Dream

Given that the 2012 presidential election took place amidst the backdrop of growing income inequality and a marked decrease on the possibility of social mobility, both Obama and Romney were forced to address the question of fairness. Both men did so directly beginning with their respective acceptance addresses for their parties' nomination. Speaking in Tampa, Florida, Romney noted early in his acceptance address that the many waves of immigrants that come to United States never "doubted that here in America they could build a better life, that in America their children would be more blessed than they" (Romney, 2012a, para. 19). Having established that even immigrants shared equal opportunities and the possibility of achieving the American dream, Romney then suggested things were different in 2012 because "for the first time, the majority of Americans now doubt that our children will have a better future" (para. 20). Having suggested that things were truly different now, Romney then asserted that this new development was not fair because "it is not what we were promised." Indeed, for Romney the ability to build a better economic life was more than a simple promise or some foolish desire: "It's not just what we wanted. It's not just what we expected. It's what Americans deserved" (Romney, 2012a, para. 27). According to Romney, Americans deserved the possibility of social mobility simply because they were Americans. That it was increasingly out of their reach was clearly unfair.

For his part, Obama shared Romney's belief that things in America were not going well and that the weak economy was a direct result of some unfairness. For Obama, the real issue was, as he noted near the beginning of his acceptance address in Charlotte, North Carolina, that something was amiss with "the basic bargain at the heart of America's story, the promise that hard work will pay off, that responsibility will be rewarded, that everyone gets a fair shot and everyone does their fair share and everyone plays by the same rules" (Obama, 2012b, para. 12). That the fairness of this "basic bargain" was central to his re-election campaign became obvious when it was repeated in the assertion at the end of his speech when he said, "if you believe in a country where everyone gets a fair shot, and everyone does their fair share and everyone plays by the same rules, then I need you to vote this November" (para. 75). Framing the opening and closing of his acceptance address, the fairness of the country's basic bargain was clearly a defining theme of Obama's campaign rhetoric.

Having both established fairness as a central factor for their economic rhetoric in the 2012 presidential election, both Obama and Romney had to offer a narrative explanation for how things had gotten so out of order and what might be done to set things right. Like all narratives, this required identifying what rhetorical theorist Barry Brummett (2010) has called a story's "alignment and opposition" (p. 60). Such aligning and opposing allow rhetors to demarcate protagonists and antagonists. It also helps the speaker defend some and blame others.

For both Obama and Romney, their narratives hinged upon an alignment with the middle class, which more often than not was meant synonymously to mean almost all Americans. So clear was Romney's attempt to align himself with collective identity that his entire five-point strategy for improving the nation's economy was called the "Plan for a Stronger Middle Class." This plan was necessary since, as Romney repeatedly noted throughout the campaign, just as he did in the first presidential debate on October 3, 2012, that "the people who are having a hard time right now are middle-income Americans. Under the president's policies, middle-income Americans have been buried. They're just being crushed" (Obama & Romney, 2012a, para. 30). And given that Romney made no mention of the poor or low-income Americans except much later in reference to Medicaid, the middle class clearly represented the vast majority of Americans who were only defined in contrast to "high-income people" (para. 381). In a very similar fashion, Obama suggested the election was really all about the middle class and he also primarily distinguished the middle class from the wealthy in a way that indicated almost all Americans were the middle class. Nowhere was this more apparent than in his final remarks at the first debate, where he said, "four years ago, I … promised that I'd fight every single day on behalf of the American people, the middle class, and all those who were striving to get into the middle class. I've kept that promise and if you'll vote for me, then I promise I'll fight just as hard in a second term" (Obama & Romney, 2012a, para. 384). In these final comments on the night, Obama indicated that his primary concern as president is to fight for the middle class, which he then renamed "the American people," before adding that those who were striving to reach the middle class and, perhaps, become fully American (para. 384). Obama then, like Romney, believed the election was primarily about the defense of the middle class, which represented the American people writ large.

The difference in their narratives came in the form of who the villains were and who might rescue the middle class. For Romney, the villain was the government, or more specifically the Obama administration, and the heroes were the nation's entrepreneurs and small business owners. One of the five aspects of his "Plan for a Stronger Middle Class" was, after all, the need to "champion small business," which were responsible for "two-thirds of American jobs created over the last 15 years" (Romney, 2012b, para. 10). Moreover, one of the key reasons he was confident the nation's economy could fully recover was, as he told the U.S. Hispanic Chamber of Commerce on September 17, 2012, that he believed "in entrepreneurs," and he believed that "the credit for their hard work goes to them, not to the government" (Romney, 2012c, para. 38). In fact, in Romney's explanation of how things ought to be, the only role for government was that it "supports the job creators" (para. 14). This supporting role was evident in some very careful diction that Romney routinely employed with the words *grow* and *create*. As he put this distinction in a campaign address on the economy in Ames, Iowa, on October 26, 2012, his administration would "grow jobs by making America the best possible place for job creators, for entrepreneurs, for small business, for innovators, for manufacturers" (Romney, 2012d, para. 37). In this single line Romney identifies four groups that can actually create jobs and argues that the government can do little more than try to help those job creators, which he believed could be done largely through cutting their taxes.

In contrast to Romney, Obama believed that the villains behind the unfair economic system that had emerged in the United States before he came to office were America's wealthiest citizens and companies. As he recounted what had led the United States into the Great Recession during former President George W. Bush's tenure at a November 1, 2012, campaign speech in Green Bay, Wisconsin, Obama argued, "the wealthiest Americans got tax cuts they didn't need and that we couldn't afford. Companies enjoyed tax breaks for shipping jobs overseas. Insurance companies and oil companies and Wall Street were given free license to do what they pleased" (Obama, 2012d, para. 18). He then suggested that "we shouldn't be ending college tax credits to pay for millionaire tax cuts" (para. 25). So for Obama, the country's wealthiest were to blame because they had been playing unfairly, but more intriguing, the country's wealthiest were also the nation's potential heroes if they could only be persuaded or forced by the government to give back more of their wealth through increased taxes. As he put it later in the speech, the country needed a tax code "to reward companies that create jobs here in America," and "we've also got to ask the wealthiest Americans to go back to the [higher] tax rates they paid when Bill Clinton was in office" (Obama, 2012d, para. 33). According to Obama, the nation's wealthiest, embodied in terms like millionaires and Wall Street, could be transformed from villains to heroes with a little help from the U.S. government.

In many ways, this analysis of Obama's and Romney's economic narratives during the 2012 campaign should not be completely surprising for most readers. Both candidates believed in the myth of the American dream rooted in that nation's long tradition of liberalism. Both candidates championed the middle class. The Democrat Obama offered a solution to the country's economic woes that was somewhat more rooted in positive liberty, the notion that for people to act with economic freedom the government must play an active role in creating the necessary equality of conditions. The Republican Romney engaged a framework of negative freedom, which assumes that people are free to act on their own with the least amount of interference possible. The two candidates argued, that is, about the extent of government regulation. Indeed, little had changed except for the names of those depicted as acting within the narratives. Instead of the "workingmen" of former President William McKinley's era at the end of the 19th century, there was the middle-class American. Instead of the "crooks" that FDR believed were hurting America's consumers, workers, and stockholders, there were millionaires and Wall Street. Instead of the war on poverty lauded by former President Johnson and later derided by former President Richard Nixon, the poor were surprisingly non-existent. So some of the names had changed and everyone was now middle class, except the few wealthiest, but the story was largely the same as it had been for decades—how to create the conditions most likely to create economic security and social mobility. But one thing had changed, and that was the notion of fairness that had emerged as the guiding force behind the narratives. And that, we believe, played a significant role in how Obama and Romney attacked one another on economic issues during the election.

Sound Bites as Synecdoche

For the most part, Romney's portrayal of Obama was what one would expect from a candidate challenging an incumbent president. At its most basic, Romney's strategy was to portray Obama as a bad leader who had hurt the nation's economy. This was the argument Romney put forward in debates, speeches, and campaign advertisements throughout the general election. For instance, in an advertisement Romney released on September 17, 2012 titled "Failing American Families," a voiceover noted that during Obama's four years in office, household income had declined by $4,000 a year and the national debt had risen from $10.6 trillion to more than $16 trillion. These data were then followed by an image of Romney arguing in a speech that "we can't keep buying and spending and passing on debts to our kids." And, in an October 30, 2012, advertisement titled "Can't Afford Another Term," a voiceover begins by noting, "If you want to know President Obama's second term agenda, look at his first." After listing off a series of data that would indicate Obama's failed economic plans, the advertisement ends with another warning about the future under a second term for Obama: "We may have made it through President Obama's first term; it's our children who can't afford a second." This was Romney's basic attack strategy. Again and again, Romney called the nation's attention, as he did during the second debate on October 16, 2012, to Obama's record of failures: "When he took office, 32 million people were on food stamps. Today, 47 million people are on food stamps. …[H]e just hasn't been able to cut the deficit, to put in place reforms for Medicare and Social Security to preserve them, to get us the rising incomes we need. Median incomes are down $4,300 a family and 23 million Americans are out of work" (Obama & Romney, 2012b, para. 347). As evidenced from the sheer repetition of the message, Romney seemed to believe that he could convince the American people to vote for him by listing a series of negative data that suggested Obama's tenure in office had only worsened the already troubled economy.

Although Romney's portrayal of Obama's presidency may have been effective to some who already shared a negative image of the president, his argument failed to gain traction within the dominant economic framework of the election—fairness. By contrast, Obama's negative portrayal of Romney worked specifically to demonstrate that he could not be trusted to create an economic policy that was fair for all Americans. Obama was able to do this by using sound bites of Romney's own words as a synecdoche for Romney's questionable character.

As rhetorical scholar Jeanne Fahnestock (2011) has described it, synecdoche is a trope, or figure of speech, that uses the whole for a part or a part for a whole (p. 101). For instance, one might say that America attacked Iraq, when in fact some portion of the U.S. military attacked the Iraqi military and government. Or one might call for all hands on deck, when what one wants is the whole person. It is in this latter way, the part for the whole, that sound bites can function as synecdoche. Indeed, as Megan Foley (2012) has argued, "the elision of speech into sound bites operates synecdochally" (p. 618). For Foley, this works through a double process of substitution of part for whole and as "a condensation: the sound bite concentrates public speech down to its pithiest core, seeming to capture the quintessence of political oratory at its fullest" (p. 618). It is in this way that Obama focused on three sound bites that were meant to be understood synecdochally as capturing the true Mitt Romney as untrustworthy and unfair. Each of these synecdochic sound bite deserves attention.

Speaking at a campaign rally in Urbandale, Iowa, on September 1, 2012, Obama offered the following comment on Romney's business experience:

> My opponent's experience … has been investing in companies that often were called "pioneers" in the business of outsourcing jobs. And when his advice was to "let Detroit go bankrupt," I said a million jobs were at stake, an iconic American industry is at stake; I'm going to bet on American workers and American manufacturing. And today, the American auto industry has come roaring back. (Obama, 2012a, para. 20)

Obama's reference here to Romney's advice about Detroit was a routine line in his speeches and campaign advertisements. It was also a contentious sound bite that some suggested incorrectly presented Romney's actual argument about Detroit.

The actual four words that Obama used, "let Detroit go bankrupt," come from the title of an opinion piece Romney wrote for *The New York Times* in November 2008. Although Romney did write that "a managed bankruptcy may be the only path to the fundamental restructuring of the [auto] industry needs," the actual title for the opinion piece was an editor's decision at the newspaper (Romney, 2008, para. 14). Even though Romney did not create the title, he did defend his argument and the headline on CBS's "The Early Show" in June 2011 when he argued, "that's exactly what I said. The headline you read, which said 'Let Detroit Go Bankrupt,' points out that those companies needed to go through bankruptcy to shed those costs" (Morgan, 2011, para. 10). In addition, Romney attempted to explain to his interviewer that she was "misunderstanding the word bankrupt" (para. 6). As Obama's campaign understood, she was not the only one to misunderstand that word.

What Romney argued in his editorial was that the auto industry should not be handed a government bailout. Instead, he believed that the industry would survive through a managed bankruptcy that forced them to restructure by allowing "the companies to shed excess labor, pension and real estate costs" (Romney, 2008, para. 14). He did, then, want the auto industry to go through bankruptcy, but he suggested that doing so would allow them to become "newly competitive and viable automakers" (para. 15). Although that was Romney's argument, it was easy to see how many Americans might miss the nuance. Instead, what they largely took away from the often-used quote was that Romney was more than willing to let the auto industry in Detroit collapse, causing thousands of American auto workers to lose their jobs and their pensions. Indeed, that the headline followed Romney's own use of "Detroit" in place of "American auto industry" in his opinion piece was even more rhetorically powerful. Long understood as one of America's blue collar cities, Detroit represented the American worker and American manufacturing. Obama's use of the line, therefore, conveyed an image of Romney as a ruthless businessman who cared nothing for hardworking Americans. He was not someone who could be trusted to play fairly.

The second synecdochic sound bite that Obama employed to great use in the final weeks of the campaign was a reference Romney had made to "Big Bird" of PBS's "Sesame Street" in the first presidential debate. As he was answering a question from moderator Jim Lehrer, the host of the PBS "NewsHour," about his plan to cut government spending, Romney offered the following idea: "I'm going to stop the subsidy to PBS. ... I like PBS, I love Big Bird. Actually like you [Lehrer], too. But I'm not going to keep on spending money on things to borrow money from China to pay for it" (Obama & Romney, 2012a, para. 103). Long seen by some Republicans as a symbol of governmental excess, claiming that he would cut federal funding to the Public Broadcasting System was a clear way for Romney to signal to fiscal conservatives and libertarians that he shared their values. However, naming Big Bird gave the Obama campaign something to use against Romney to further demonstrate his misguided and unfair economic ideas.

And use it they did. Just days after the first debate, Obama released an advertisement simply titled "Big Bird" that was a clear attempt to portray Romney as out of touch with economic reality. Humorously suggesting that Romney was the only person willing to stand up to Big Bird, who the commercial depicted as a secret leader behind a number of recent men imprisoned for financial crimes, the voiceover claimed, "Mitt Romney knows it's not Wall Street you have to worry about; it's Sesame Street." In addition to the commercial, Obama made reference to Big Bird and "Sesame Street" regularly in campaign speeches over the next month, often getting laughter from the crowd, to demonstrate that Romney was not focusing on the real people behind the financial problems facing the country. Indeed, Obama offered the sound bite so often that the Republican National Committee released an advertisement on October 24, 2012, titled, "Big Bird, Binders and Bayonets," to suggest that Obama was using petty attacks on Romney because he did not really have a plan for moving the country forward.

However, Obama's use of the sound bite was effective. Focusing on Big Bird instead of PBS, Obama was able to offer an image of Romney bullying a harmless and beloved children's character. So although Romney had meant to use his love for Big Bird as a way to soften his stance on cutting federal funding for PBS, Obama was able to redeploy the comment as another example of a larger problem—Romney was a ruthless businessman who cared more about securing the wealth of the nation's millionaires than supporting something like "Sesame Street."

The final sound bite that Obama was able to use against Romney was by far the most damaging and not one that Romney had ever meant to be made public. Speaking at a $50,000-per-plate private fundraiser in Boca Raton, Florida, on May 17, 2012, Romney made the following argument:

> There are 47% of the people who will vote for the president no matter what. All right, there are 47% who are with him, who are dependent upon government, who believe that they are victims, who believe the government has a responsibility to care for them, who believe that they are entitled to health care, to food, to housing, to you-name-it—that's an entitlement. And the government should give it to them. And they will vote for this president no matter what. ... These are people who pay no income tax. ... [M]y job is not to worry about those people. I'll never convince them they should take personal responsibility and care for their lives. What I have to do is convince the 5-to-10% in the center that are independents. ("Romney's Speech," 2012, para. 33)

Unbeknownst to him, Romney was being video recorded by the event's bartender. The video eventually made it onto the *Mother Jones* website on September 17,

2012, via James Carter, grandson of former president Jimmy Carter, and then went viral. So damaging was the remark that even Romney admitted in March 2013 on "Fox News Sunday" that "There's no question [the comment] hurt and did real damage to my campaign" ("Romney Relays Disappointment Over Loss," 2013, para. 8). In admitting that, Romney also defended himself by suggesting that his words had come out wrong and did not really express what he meant to say.

Indeed, a generous reading of at least the beginning of Romney's comment would suggest something most political communication scholars already know—the vast majority of voters have already decided who they will vote for long before Election Day arrives. The so-called independent voters are a very small percentage of total voters. However, Romney's description of that 47% of voters as "dependent upon government" and "entitled" is far more difficult to read generously. Indeed, most agreed that Romney was, at best, incorrect. As FactCheck.org noted, "Mitt Romney was wrong when he said the 47% who pay no federal income taxes are 'dependent on the government.' Most of them are working people who simply do not earn very much money" ("Dependency and Romney's 47 Percenters," 2012, para. 1). Moreover, Romney was also wrong in suggesting that all of those in that 47% vote Democrat, as polls showed "Romney is supported by some 40 percent of those earning the lowest income" ("Dependency and Romney's 47 Percenters," 2012, para. 2). So at best, Romney was simply wrong, but it was quite easy for many people to view his comment as more than incorrect. In fact, many people understood it as mean-spirited and yet another sign that Romney did not care about creating economic policy that would be fair for the majority of Americans.

The Obama campaign worked to reinforce the more negative reading of Romney's 47% comment. At times, Obama used the comment to both make Romney look bad and benefit himself. As he put it at a campaign rally in Miami, Florida, on October 11, 2012, "back in 2008, I won, but 47% of the country didn't vote for me. But I didn't just dismiss 47% of the country. What I said was, you may not have voted for me, but I heard your voices, and I'll fight just as hard for you as I will for everybody else" (Obama, 2012c, para. 57). Here Obama asserts that Romney dismissed 47% of the country and then implies that if elected Romney would not be a president for all Americans. At other times, the Obama campaign did far more than imply Romney might not care for all the people. For instance, a campaign advertisement titled "No One Was Looking" released on October 25, 2012, began with a voiceover stating, "it's said that character is what we do when we think no one is looking." Cutting to the footage of Romney at the Boca Raton fundraiser, the voiceover then added, "Romney thought no one was looking when he attacked 47% of Americans." As the advertisement goes on to a list of things that Romney's economic plan would do (e.g., cut millionaire taxes, raise middle-class taxes, turn benefits into vouchers, etc.), the viewers are left in the end with one final message to "Remember what Romney said. And what his plan would do." Voters were told, that is, that no matter what Romney might say in public, his real character shows that he only cares about the nation's wealthiest citizens.

Ultimately, all three sound bites reveal a consistent synecdochic message about Romney. Each is a partial condensation of the whole that is Romney's unwillingness to treat all Americans fairly. Given that the economic discourse in the 2012 election was rooted in a national concern for fairness, it is little wonder that Obama's synecdochic sound bites were an effective rhetorical strategy.

Conclusion

With financial concerns squarely at the forefront of voters' minds during the 2012 election, it was little surprise that both Obama and Romney focused so much of their rhetoric on economic issues. Given the contexts within which the Great Recession had occurred and the nation's attempt to recover from it, it is also rather clear why fairness would have become the dominant theme from which the two candidates constructed their narratives to explain what had happened and then argue for a way forward. What was distinctive about the economic rhetoric in the 2012 presidential campaign were the specific ways that Obama and Romney crafted their narratives and, more importantly, the way in which Obama was able to use Romney's own words against him through what we have termed here synechdochic sound bites. Indeed it is this last observation that we believe may have played an important role in helping to secure Obama's re-election. Put simply, Obama's use of the sound bites to portray Romney as someone who favored millionaires and would not treat all Americans, especially the middle class, fairly may explain why some of Romney's base did not mobilize on Election Day and why some independents opted for Obama.

Given the nature of our analysis, it is, of course, impossible to show a causal connection between Obama's and Romney's economic rhetoric and voters' actual decision about whether and for whom to vote. Voting is a complicated matter influenced by far too numerous factors. However, assuming rhetoric does have the potential to influence the mobilization of a candidate's base and help persuade independent voters, our assessment suggests that Obama's portrayal of Romney was simply more effective.

Moreover, our analysis also helps shed light on how the American people think about economic issues today. As noted in the introduction, presidential candidates must speak a rather pedestrian rhetoric, sounding ordinary so as to give the electorate what they are comfortable hearing. If that is so, then the American people still very much want to believe in the American dream and hope that the system is fair. However, they were also clearly aware in 2012 that the American economic system did not seem to be acting fairly, even if they might have disagreed on why that was so.

Finally, our examination of Obama's and Romney's rhetoric also draws attention to some of the discursive choices that might set a precedent for future presidents. Most obviously, there is both Obama's and Romney's insistence that they were running for office to protect the middle class. In fact, references to the middle class often seemed to imply that almost all Americans were middle class, suggesting that presidential candidates have picked up on what research has shown for decades now—that most Americans, regardless of income, like to think of themselves as middle class (Chandler, 1994; Dugan, 2012). That Obama and Romney chose to reinforce that notion will surely influence future presidential candidates' depictions of the nation. A more interesting discursive development can be found in the distinction between growing and creating both jobs and the economy. Although Romney's rhetoric largely tracked along the distinction between government and small business, Obama's rhetoric seems less consistent, and yet surely the notion that jobs can be grown instead of created implies assumptions about what forces are at work in the national economy.

References

Adding up the government's total bailout tab. (2011, July 24). *The New York Times*. Retrieved from http://www.nytimes.com/interactive/2009/02/04/business/20090205-bailout-totals-graphic.html

Beasley, V. B. (2004). *You, the people: American national identity in presidential rhetoric*. College Station, TX: Texas A&M University Press.

Brummett, B. (2010). *Techniques of close reading*. Thousand Oaks, CA: SAGE Publications.

Cloud, D. L. (1996). Hegemony or concordance? The rhetoric of tokenism in "Oprah" Winfrey's rags-to-riches biography. *Critical Studies in Mass Communication, 13*, 115–137.

da Costa, P., & Bull, A. (2012, December 12). Fed ties rate pledge to a threshold as new stimulus set. *Reuters*. Retrieved from http://www.reuters.com/article/2012/12/12/us-usa-fed-idUS-BRE8BB08A20121212

DeParle, J. (2012, January 4). Harder for Americans to rise from lower rungs. *The New York Times*. Retrieved from http://www.nytimes.com/2012/01/05/us/harder-for-americans-to-rise from-lower-rungs.html?pagewanted=all&_r=0

Dependency and Romney's 47 percenters. (2012, September 18). *FactCheck.org*. Retrieved from http://www.factcheck.org/2012/09/dependency-and-romneys-47-percenters/

Dodge, C., & Dorning, M. (2012, September 12). Rich-poor gap widens to most since 1967 as income falls. *Bloomberg*. Retrieved from http://www.bloomberg.com/news/2012-09-12/u-s-poverty-rate-stays-at-almost-two-decade-high-income-falls.html

Dwyer, D. (2011, October 18). Obama: Occupy Wall Street "not that different" from Tea Party protests. *ABC News*. Retrieved from http://abcnews.go.com/blogs/politics/2011/10/obama-occupy-wall-street-not-that-different-from-tea-party-protests/

Ellen, I. G., & Dastrup, S. (2012). Housing and the great recession. Retrieved from the Russell Sage Foundation and the Stanford Center on Poverty and Inequality website: https://www.stanford.edu/group/recessiontrends/cgi-bin/web/sites/all/themes/barron/pdf/Housing_fact_sheet.pdf

Fahenstock, J. (2011). *Rhetorical style: The uses of language in persuasion*. New York, NY: Oxford University Press.

Foley, M. (2012). Sound bites: Rethinking the circulation of speech from fragment to fetish. *Rhetoric & Public Affairs, 15*, 613–622.

GOP holds early turnout edge, but little enthusiasm for Romney. (2012, June 21). Pew Research Center for the People & the Press. Retrieved from http://www.people-press.org/2012/06/21/gop-holds-early-turnout-edge-but-little-enthusiasm-for-romney/

Greenstone, M., Looney, A., Patashnik, J., & Yu, M. (2013). *Thirteen economic facts about social mobility and the role of education*. Retrieved from The Brookings Institution website: http://www.brookings.edu/research/reports/2013/06/13-facts-higher-education.

Hart, R. P., Childers, J. P., & Lind, J. L. (2013). *Political tone: How leaders talk & why*. Chicago, IL: University of Chicago Press.

Hulse, C., & Herszenshorn, D. (2010, July 10). Bank bailout is potent issue for fall elections. *The New York Times*. Retrieved from http://www.nytimes.com/2010/07/11/us/politics/11tarp.html?_r=0

Isidore, C. (2009a, February 6). Job loss: Worst in 34 years. *CNN*. Retrieved from http://money.cnn.com/2009/02/06/news/economy/jobs_january/

Isidore, C. (2009b, April 3) 2 million jobs lost so far in '09. *CNN*. Retrieved from http://money.cnn.com/2009/04/03/news/economy/jobs_march/

Johnson, L.B. (1964). Commencement address at the University of Michigan in Ann Arbor, Michigan. Retrieved from http://www.pbs.org/wgbh/americanexperience/features/primary-resources/lbj-michigan/

King Jr., N., Lee, C. E., & Nelson, C. M. (2012, November 8). Obama fine-tuned 2008's winning formula. *Wall Street Journal*. Retrieved from http://online.wsj.com/article/SB10001424127887324894104578103432907278390.html#articleTabs%3Darticle

Levine, L. (2012) An analysis of the distribution of wealth across households, 1989-2010. Retrieved from the Congressional Research Service website: http://www.fas.org/sgp/crs/misc/RL33433.pdf

Madison, L. (2011, October 9). Obama: "Occupy Wall Street" reflects "broad-based frustration." *CBS News*. Retrieved from http://www.cbsnews.com/8301-503544_162-20116707-503544/obama-occupy-wall-street-reflects-broad-based-frustration-/

Madison, L. (2012, January 24). Obama: Everyone deserves a "fair shot." *CBS News*. Retrieved from http://www.cbsnews.com/8301-503544_162-57365204-503544/obama-everyone-deserves-a-fair-shot-/

Martin, A. (2011, June 10). A critic's take on the mortgage modification program. *The New York Times*. Retrieved from http://bucks.blogs.nytimes.com/2011/06/10/a-critics-take-on-the-mortgage-modification-program/

Mercieca, J., & Vaughn, J. S. (forthcoming). Barack Obama and the rhetoric of heroic expectations. In J. S. Vaughn & J. Mercieca (Eds.), *The rhetoric of heroic expectations: Establishing the Obama presidency*. College Station, TX: Texas A&M University Press.

Morgan, D. (2011, June 3). Romney: Bankruptcy, not bailouts, saved Detroit. *CBS News*. Retrieved from http://www.cbsnews.com/2100-500202_162-20068606.html

Obama, B. (2012a, September 1). Remarks at a campaign rally in Urbandale, Iowa. Retrieved from http://www.presidency.ucsb.edu/ws/index.php?pid=102002

Obama, B. (2012b, September 6). Remarks accepting the presidential nomination at the Democratic National Convention in Charlotte, North Carolina. Retrieved from http://www.presidency.ucsb.edu/ws/index.php?pid=101968

Obama, B. (2012c, October 11). Remarks at a campaign rally in Miami, Florida. Retrieved from http://www.presidency.ucsb.edu/ws/index.php?pid=102363

Obama, B. (2012d, November 1). Remarks at a campaign rally in Green Bay, Wisconsin. Retrieved from http://www.presidency.ucsb.edu/ws/index.php?pid=102560

Obama, B., & Romney, M. (2012a, October 3). Presidential debate in Denver, Colorado. Retrieved from http://www.presidency.ucsb.edu/ws/index.php?pid=102317

Obama, B., & Romney, M. (2012b, October 16). Presidential debate in Hempstead, New York. Retrieved from http://www.presidency.ucsb.edu/ws/index.php?pid=102343#axzz2h4OBwAuD.

Reagan, R. (1986). Radio address to the nation on welfare reform. Retrieved from http://www.presidency.ucsb.edu/ws/?pid=36875

Romney, M. (2008, November 19). Let Detroit go bankrupt. *The New York Times*, pp. A35.

Romney, M. (2012a, August 30). Address accepting the presidential nomination at the Republican National Convention in Tampa, Florida. Retrieved from http://www.presidency.ucsb.edu/ws/index.php?pid=101966

Romney, M. (2012b, August 30). We believe in America: A plan for a stronger middle class [Press release]. Retrieved from http://www.presidency.ucsb.edu/ws/index.php?pid=102222

Romney, M. (2012c, September 17). Remarks to the U.S. Hispanic chamber of commerce 33rd annual convention in Los Angeles, California. Retrieved from http://www.presidency.ucsb.edu/ws/index.php?pid=102451

Romney, M. (2012d, October 26). Remarks on the economy in Ames, Iowa. Retrieved from http://www.presidency.ucsb.edu/ws/index.php?pid=103076

Romney relays disappointment over loss, admits mistakes, in first sitdown since 2012 election. (2013, March 3). *Fox News*. Retrieved from http://www.foxnews.com/politics/2013/03/03/romney-still-disappointed-over-loss-admits-mistakes-critical-obama-second-term/

Romney's speech from Mother Jones video. (2012, September 19). *The New York Times*. Retrieved from http://www.nytimes.com/2012/09/19/us/politics/mitt-romneys-speech-from-mother-jones-video.html?pagewanted=all

Roosevelt, F. D. (1933, March 4). Inaugural address. Retrieved from http://www.presidency.ucsb.edu/ws/?pid=14473

Saez, E. (2013, September 3). Striking it richer: The evolution of top incomes in the United States (updated with 2012 preliminary estimates). Available at: http://eml.berkeley.edu/~saez/saez-UStopincomes-2012.pdf

Sargent, G. (2012, January 19). Romney to Occupy protestor: Go back to Russia. *The Washington Post*. Retrieved from http://www.washingtonpost.com/blogs/plum-line/post/romney-to-occupy-heckler-go-back-to-russia/2012/01/19/gIQAmrqdBQ_blog.html

Story, L. (2010, October 5). Bailout loss estimated at $29 billion. *The New York Times*. Retrieved from http://www.nytimes.com/2010/10/06/business/economy/06tarp.html?ref=autoindustry.

Stuckey, M. (2005). Swinging the vote in the 2004 presidential election. In R. E. Denton (Ed.), *The 2004 presidential campaign: A communication perspective* (pp. 153–175). Lanham, MD: Rowman & Littlefield.

We are the 99 percent (2013). [Web log]. Retrieved from http://wearethe99percent.tumblr.com/

Willis, B. (2009, August 1). U.S. recession worst since Great Depression, revised data show. *Bloomberg*. Retrieved from http://www.bloomberg.com/apps/news?pid=newsarchive&sid=aNivTjr852TI

Whoriskey, P. (2012, August 3). Job growth "moving sideways." *The Washington Post*, pp. A10.

CHAPTER SEVEN

Health Care Reform

Core Value Differences Between Liberal and Conservative Candidates and Voters

ANN GORDON, BRETT ROBERTSON, AND LISA SPARKS[1]

When President Barack Obama made health care reform his first term priority, he also set the stage for his re-election campaign. Both Obama, and his challenger—former Gov. Mitt Romney—relied heavily on the issue in their appeals to voters. So, when the U.S. Supreme Court handed down its decision on the Patient Protection and Affordable Care Act (PPACA), both campaigns were ready to pounce. It was at the end of June 2012, with the election looming, when the Supreme Court issued its ruling. Chief Justice John Roberts announced that the PPACA, passed by Congress and signed into law two years earlier by Obama, was indeed constitutional.

Reaction from both sides was swift. Obama hailed the decision as a victory for families and sought to frame the policy as providing a measure of economic security. "Here in America, in the wealthiest nation on earth, no illness or accident should lead to any family's financial ruin" (Mears and Cohen, 2012, p. 1). Meanwhile, Romney vowed to undo the law, stating, "What the court did not do on its last day in session, I will do on my first day as president of the United States." For Romney, PPACA was an economic burden and Republicans sought to frame the issue as a tax increase (Zeleny, 2012, p. 1).

Interest groups also jumped into action. For example, within 24 hours of the Supreme Court's ruling, the conservative group Americans for Prosperity announced that it would commit $9 million to an advertising campaign that would emphasize the tax frame and focus on the individual mandate provisions (Gardner, 2012).

More than one million advertisements marked the 2012 presidential race, exceeding the previous record set in 2008. Although Republicans aired fewer advertisements in total, they ended up spending more money, according to the Wesleyan Media Project (2013). This is because the Obama campaign paid for its own advertisements and at a lower rate than outside groups paid. Because the Romney campaign relied more heavily on its allies, the cost was greater. In the final weeks of the election, some 15.5% of the total ad buys by Obama supporters focused on health care, as they had for most of the campaign, and 5.7% of ads supporting Romney were about health care (Wesleyan Media Project, 2013).

In this chapter, we examine the nature of health care advertising appeals through a videostyle analysis. Although the PPACA—commonly referred to as the Affordable Care Act (ACA) or Obamacare—garnered a great deal of attention, perennial issues such as Medicare and abortion also figured into the overall discussion of health policy. We focus on the television advertising strategies employed by both campaigns and their supporters to frame the issue of health care through appeals to core values. After examining the content of these advertisements, we turn to public opinion data in order to examine the extent to which these messages may have resonated with the electorate.

Videostyle as a Framework to Study Political Ads

Videostyle is both a theory and a method used to systematically explore how candidates running for political office use self-presentation in their television advertisements. Conceived by Lynda Lee Kaid and Dorothy Davidson (1986), videostyle attempts to understand the verbal, nonverbal, and production methods of a candidate's presentation. The verbal aspect of videostyle analyzes the linguistic features of the actual message within the presentation. For example, some candidates choose to create advertisements that focus on a policy issue (e.g., health care reform, social security, military spending) whereas others focus on the image of a candidate (e.g., discussing a candidate's background and qualifications). In addition to issue or image emphasis, the verbal content of political ads includes the tone of the message (positive, negative, or comparative).

The nonverbal aspect of videostyle works hand-in-hand with the verbal message, meaning an emphasis is placed on nonlinguistic communication within the advertisement. The nonlinguistic communication examined in a videostyle analysis consists of gestures, facial expressions, appearances, clothing, and/or sounds and sound bites related to the verbal messages. In some instances, nonverbal messages exemplify or speak to how the verbal message is portrayed as positive or negative toward a candidate.

The advertisement's production strategies comprise the final component of videostyle, including the techniques of filmmaking associated with the advertisement. Such techniques include camera angles, sound characteristics, and the presence of certain special effects and editing techniques. The technical production of an advertisement is intended to complement and/or emphasize specific aspects of the verbal and nonverbal content. For instance, a camera moving closer to the subject reveals intimacy, whereas the camera pulling away from the subject reveals a level of distance (Zettl, 1997).

By analyzing advertisements through videostyle, Kaid and Davidson (1986) wanted to understand more than just the rhetoric of political messages; they wanted a complete understanding into how multiple factors (verbal, nonverbal, and production methods) combine to create a message. Videostyle research can help viewers see the message from the perspective of candidates and their communication team. Alternatively, candidates can take a step back and use videostyle to see patterns within their messages, not just how they are portrayed to the public. The framework within videostyle assists candidates in creating a persuasive message that is properly constructed with appropriate images and issue appeals that gets their point across to voters.

Videostyle has been used for more than 25 years to analyze the content of televised political ads of U.S. presidential campaigns beginning with their first use in 1952 as well as candidate advertising at different electoral levels and in numerous countries. Over time, these studies have found that presidential political ads contain a lot of information about issues; feature a variety of speakers, including the candidate, family members, anonymous announcers, and average citizens; and make full use of the range of special effects available in television production (Johnston, 2008).

In the present study, we use videostyle to establish the ways in which candidates framed the issue of health care in their advertisements in the 2012 presidential election. After examining the overall pattern, we turn to a deeper look at some of the more memorable advertisements.

Research Questions and Method

We address three research questions in the present study: First, to what extent was health care the basis of appeals made by candidates and their campaigns? Second, how were issues of health care, abortion, and Medicare framed and presented? Finally, to what extent did a voter's values and ideology influence views on health care policy and did these views play a role in voter decision-making?

We rely on a multi-method approach to answer these questions, including a content analysis of campaign advertisements to understand the messages that were aired during the presidential election, and survey data to assess how voters constructed meaning from those messages. Our content analysis utilizes videostyle methods to explore a sample of the 463 ads.[2] The dataset includes advertisements sponsored by the candidates (51%) or their political party (14%); Super PAC (Political Action Committee) ads that centered on one of the candidates (15%) or formed around issues (2%); and commercials sponsored by independent or third party groups/others (18%).

However, for the purposes of this study we focus solely on television ads with health content, including the ACA and other health care related issues. Overall, some 17% (79) of the sample of 463 ads addressed the issue of health care, abortion/reproductive health, or Medicare/social security/problems of the elderly. Of these, 10% (44) of the advertisements were devoted to health care itself (33) or abortion/reproductive health (11). Our advertising subsample consists of these 44 campaign advertisements focusing on the issue of health care, including reproductive health/abortion. In addition to our content analysis of these television ads, we conducted a post-election web-based survey ($N = 750$) in which we asked voters about their values, ideology, views on health care topics, and how much influence the issue of health care had on their vote choices.

Results

By and large, both candidates, their parties, and supporting interest groups tended to rely on attacks (61.4%) more than comparative (27.3%) or positive (11.4%) messages in the 44 ads analyzed (see Table 1, all figures rounded). Even the comparative ads struck a decidedly negative in tone. Typically, these attacks were delivered by an anonymous announcer (50%), rather than the candidate himself (2.3%) or a surrogate (11.4%). We saw this pattern for both Obama and Romney.

The following is an example of an advertisement from the Obama campaign titled "Remember," which arguably sought to evoke voters' fear of Romney's approach to Medicare and "remember" it on Election Day. The ad began with a shot of a voter in a voting booth and the voiceover stating:

> In here, it's just you—no ads, no debates, just you. So think about this: Mitt Romney's plan rolls back regulations on the banks that crashed our economy. Medicare, voucherized ... That's what Mitt Romney wants to bring here. Remember that when you go here [to the polls]. (Obama for America, 2012a)

Similarly, in the ad below from the Romney campaign titled "Paid In," an anonymous announcer attacked Obama on the issue of health care by telling voters that Medicare is being hurt unfairly by "Obamacare."

> You paid in to Medicare for years. Every paycheck. Now, when you need it, Obama has cut $716 billion from Medicare. Why? To pay for Obamacare. So now the

money you paid for your guaranteed health care is going to a massive new government program that's not for you. The Romney-Ryan plan protects Medicare benefits for today's seniors and strengthens the plan for the next generation. (Romney for President, Inc., 2012a)

Table 1. Health Care Videostyle

	Republican (*n* = 26)	Democrat (*n* = 18)	Total (*n* = 44)
Content of ad			
Issues	73.1 %	72.2 %	72.7%
Image	0	11.1	4.5
Combination	26.9	16.7	22.7[a]
Focus of ad			
Candidate-positive focused	19.2	0	11.4
Opponent-negative focused	57.7	66.7	61.4
Combination-comparative	23.1	33.3	27.3[a]
Appearance in ad			
Candidate or party sponsoring ad appear	38.5	11.1	27.3
Opponent(s) of candidate or party sponsoring ad appear	15.4	61.1	34.1
None	30.8	11.1	27.7
Attack made	80.8	100	88.4
Source of attack			
Candidate attacks opponent	3.8	0	2.3
Surrogate attacks opponent	11.5	11.1	11.4
Anonymous announcer attacks opponent	38.5	66.7	50
Other sources/mixed	26.9	22.5	25
Nature of attack			
Attack on personal characteristics of opponent	4.3	5.6	4.9
Attack on issue stands/consistency of opponent	39.1	88.9	61
Attack on opponent's group affiliations of associations	0	5.6	2.4
Attack on opponent's performance in past office/positions	47.8	0[a]	26.8

Note. [a]Due to rounding, the totals do not add up to 100%.

Approximately 11% of the 44 advertisements analyzed in this study employed the use of a surrogate to attack the opponent. The following is an example of how surrogates were used in a series of attack advertisements sponsored by Priorities USA, a Super PAC that supported Obama's re-election. The advertisement, titled "Understanding," featured a laid-off steel worker, Joe Soptic, whose role in this ad was that of a surrogate for Obama in attacking Romney on health care.

> ....When Mitt Romney and Bain closed the plant, I lost my health care, and my family lost their health care. And a short time after that my wife became ill. I don't know how long she was sick and I think maybe she didn't say anything because she knew that we couldn't afford the insurance, and then one day she became ill and I took her up to the Jackson County Hospital and admitted her for pneumonia and that's when they found the cancer and by then it was stage four. It was, there was nothing they could do for her. And she passed away in 22 days. I do not think Mitt Romney realizes what he's done to anyone. And furthermore I do not think Mitt Romney is concerned.

> Announcer: Priorities USA Action is responsible for the content of this advertisement. (Priorities USA Action, 2012a)

Looking more closely at the negative advertisements in this sample of ads, the vast majority of attacks were on the basis of issues (61%), followed by past performance in office (26.8%). Despite the largely negative tone of the ads in our sample, only (4.9%) of the attacks could be characterized as personal.

Many videostyle analyses of presidential campaign ads indicate that a high percentage of verbal content is focused on candidate issues—including attacks on opponent issue stances—rather than on candidate image (Kaid, 2009). Similarly, in our analysis of the 2012 cycle, we saw very little image content in health care advertisements. Instead, the content of the advertisements relied heavily on issue-based discussion (73.1% for the Republicans and 72.2% for the Democrats) or a combination of issue and image (26.9% for the Republicans, 16.7% for the Democrats).

Keeping the content focused primarily on issues was a sensible strategy for both campaigns as they sought to persuade voters using health care messaging. Both campaigns were seeking to reach voters on a deeper level, where values reside and the framing of issues, particularly with the use of values, has been demonstrated to be effective in persuasion (Gordon and Miller, 2004). As we shall see, both candidates sought to frame health care issues with core values, but the values invoked differed by candidate ideology and were meant to resonate with voters who held these values.

Analysis of Romney's Health Care Advertising

As we look more deeply at the language used in the campaign advertisements focused on health care, we find a pattern of value framing in both Romney's and Obama's appeals. Value-frames, according to Ball-Rokeach and Loges (1996), are the most common justification for individuals to communicate messages regarding why one group's interests are valid. Of note, value-frames must portray values in such a way that viewers of an advertisement would justify or rationalize their current behavior or voting patterns (Schwartz, 1996). In our analysis of the health care advertisements, we argue that Romney and his campaign team sought to use value-framing during the presidential election to entice voters to believe the Affordable Care Act and all its implementations would cause damage to the United States. In touting the negatives of Obama's health care reform plan, Romney framed specific values—such as family, economics, and religious tradition—in order to appeal to a sense of individualism.

For instance, our analysis reveals that Romney used direct appeals to a sense of family or parenthood. In Schwartz's (1996) motivational types of values, family morals can be thought of as a form of tradition. Families, through the socialization process, pass on attitudes, beliefs, customs, and ideas that influence their direct culture. Much of Romney's advertising addressed the influence that the Affordable Care Act could have on families. Specifically, his campaign advertisements discussed the rising costs of health care and the price families would pay. For example, one advertisement claimed the Affordable Care Act would significantly raise taxes for families:

> ....Raising taxes on families making less than $120,000. Free health care comes at a very high price. The Romney-Ryan plan will restore Medicare funding and protect and strengthen the program for the next generation. (Romney for President, Inc., 2012b)

Romney's health care advertising also framed the issue in terms of cost effective measures, with economics serving as a universal, motivational value (Schwartz, 1996). Throughout his advertisements, Romney emphasized that the implementation of the Affordable Care Act would be ultimately costly to the public. By addressing certain provisions in terms of facts and statistics, Romney used primarily an economic frame, but had universal appeal as a value to illustrate that the Affordable Care Act would break and attempt to destroy the welfare and economic well-being of the country and its citizens, particularly middle-class families. By creating a discussion of higher costs, Romney's campaign sought to create a negative image of Obama:

> If Barack Obama is re-elected, what will the next four years be like? One, the debt will grow from 16 trillion to 20 trillion dollars. Two, 20 million Americans could lose their

employer-based health care. Three, taxes on the middle class will go up by $4,000. Four, energy prices will continue to go up. And five, $716 billion in Medicare cuts that hurt current seniors. Five reasons we can't afford four more years of Barack Obama. (Romney for President, Inc., 2012c)

Romney also used a series of advertisements to emphasize the value of tradition and conformity. One specific advertisement, "Be Not Afraid," discussed health care and religion—a topic that certainly Obama had dealt with and for which he received media attention in addressing. We argue that Romney and his team attempted to counteract Obama's messaging strategy with this advertisement, which stated that Obama had created his own "war on religion" with the Affordable Care Act. "Be Not Afraid" included a quotation from and photograph of Pope John Paul II along with an endorsement of Romney by Lech Walesa, the former president of Poland. Regardless of the lack of connection Pope John Paul II actually had with health care reform, the linkage, images, and words established between the two ideas—religion and health care—in this television ad were perhaps enough to encourage people to evaluate their commitment to their traditional values:

> Who shares your values? President Obama used his health care plan to declare war on religion, forcing religious institutions to go against their faith. Mitt Romney believes that's wrong.... When religious freedom is threatened, who do you want to stand with? (Republican National Committee, 2012b)

By focusing on families, affordable health care at a low cost, and religion as a factor of health care reform, Romney's health care advertising can be described as addressing individual freedoms that would be taken away by the Affordable Care Act: the definitions of health care would change within households, people would be "forced" to pay higher costs with certain implementations, and religious choices (e.g., employers and policy on contraceptives) would come into question. Whereas each advertisement often exaggerated this discussion, Romney strategically used values as a means to exemplify just how important individual freedoms are when making health care decisions and how these freedoms can influence individuals and families when taken away.

Analysis of Obama's Health Care Advertising

Because the public's acceptance of the Affordable Care Act was crucial, Obama had much at stake when it came to promoting various implementations of the law. Undoubtedly, Obama and his campaign established many communication objectives regarding his advertising messages. However, based on this analysis, we argue that two objectives were most evident in terms of health care reform: showing the public how their lives would be improved through the Affordable Care Act, and how, if Romney had his way, Americans' lives would be altered for the worse. As a whole, Obama was more visual in explaining his side of the story than was the Romney campaign, and by promoting the Affordable Care Act in terms of an egalitarian approach, Obama was able to illustrate—using values based on equality—that everyone's lives would be enhanced with health care reform implementations.

Based on our analysis, Obama's advertising was more visual than his opponent's because to convey his message he had to show Romney—and America's future under a Romney administration—in a negative light. Obama's health care advertisements often showed pictures of people suffering, which were dramatized through altering the lighting as a production technique. Not surprisingly, then, the lighting was often darker in the images that illustrated the potential for suffering. These images of suffering were juxtaposed with a visual of a lighter, happier world based on the value of universalism (Schwartz, 1996), ultimately illustrating through production techniques, nonverbal content, and verbal content a need to protect the welfare of all people.

For example, one advertisement specifically discussed how Romney's proposed Medicaid cuts would influence middle-class families. Halfway through the ad titled "Care," a series of video clips were all cast in a dark blue tint and featured a young man in a white medical coat holding hands and sitting with an elderly woman, a woman on the telephone with a document in her hand, a man lying in a hospital-style bed, and a young couple discussing and agonizing over a document. The advertisement ended with a clip of Mitt Romney at a podium, then shifted to an image of a woman looking directly at the camera. The voiceover stated:

> More huge tax breaks skewed to the wealthy. While cutting nearly $800 billion from Medicaid even though middle-class families rely on Medicaid to help loved ones cover nursing home care. And it helps parents support children with disabilities. If Mitt Romney really "cares" wouldn't we see it in his priorities? (Obama for America, 2012c)

Obama's attacks on Romney extended far beyond tinted lighting and images of concerned Americans. By using the value of power (Schwartz, 1996), Obama attempted to illustrate how the Romney-Ryan health care proposal (or Romney's future plans of taking apart Obamacare) would be a source of overbearing power and dominance to Americans. In order to portray Romney's actions as harmful, unflattering images of Romney were used. Based on Obama's advertising message, Romney was no longer doing what was in the best interest of egalitarianism, but was instead using his wealth and social status to his personal advantage.

For example, one advertisement titled "Seen" repeated a video clip of Romney stating that if he had the chance he would "be delighted" to sign a bill banning abortions. The voiceover added:

> Banning all abortions? Trying to mislead us. That's wrong. But ban all abortions? Only if you vote for him. (Obama for America, 2012d)

Obama's appeal, specifically toward women with a discussion of Planned Parenthood and access to contraceptives, was not surprising. Nancy Keenan, president of NARAL Pro-Choice America, stated, "Women are making the connection that the person is political" (Thompson, 2012, p. 2). Specifically, the issues of abortion and contraception during the 2012 election were important to women because of how the parties were split over the issue, leading some to believe the value of power could lead to a lack of trust in the candidates.

In attempt to level the field, Obama also crafted advertising appeals toward members of the middle class. By creating a discourse on how Obamacare was actually affordable, especially to members of the middle class, and how the Romney-Ryan plan was not, Obama used the value of universalism to his advantage (Pace and Espo, 2012). Much of Obama's advertising exemplified this notion. Middle-class seniors often received attention, as Obama often touted that the Romney-Ryan plan would raise costs for future retirees. For example, in this ad titled "Facts," an anonymous announcer said:

> The non-partisan AARP says Obamacare "cracks down on Medicare fraud, waste and abuse" and "strengthens guaranteed benefits." And the Ryan plan? AARP says it "would undermine … Medicare and could lead to higher costs for seniors. …" And experts say Ryan's voucher plan could raise future retirees' costs more than $6,000. Get the facts. (Obama for America, 2012b)

By emphasizing the value of universalism, Obama's advertisements created an argument that his policies would benefit the well-being of society. By using vivid imagery and a direct appeal to those who believe in spending less, we suggest that Obama further attempted to balance counterclaims from the opposition and persuade viewers that the Affordable Care Act represents democratic values for our society. Through his health care advertisements, viewers may have interpreted Romney as overbearing, controlling, and whose positions were grounded in a value of power that may not reflect what society wants. In turn, with an emphasis on egalitarianism, Obama's health care advertisements suggested that his policies on health care and the Affordable Care Act represented all interests equally.

Analysis of Political Action Committee Health Care Advertising

Interest groups overall provided significant funding to both candidates during the election, and the health care sector was no exception (Opensecrets.org, 2013). Staying in line with the messaging strategy of each candidate, interest groups and PACs also joined in with their own advertising campaigns. By often featuring one individual in their advertisement, we argue that much of the interest group advertising was designed to directly influence a target audience and seek identification through connection with that individual's story. Further, use of a values-based framework was critical to achieving both the identification and connection among their target audience.

Interests groups—both those who supported Romney and those who supported Obama—used the value of universalism to illustrate how important low-cost health care is to the middle class. The PAC Priorities USA Action was responsible for an advertisement, titled "Sarah," which supported Obama's health care goals. The advertisement featured a young couple at the beginning who claimed, "Mitt Romney is someone who just doesn't understand what it's like to kind of make our way down here," suggesting that Romney was not in touch with all citizens (Priorities USA Action, 2012b). By next highlighting how the Romney-Ryan plan would cut health benefits and Medicare, the voiceover attempted to underscore Romney's inability to understand the wants and needs of middle-class America (Priorities USA Action, 2012b). The universal desire of a healthy well-being and life within the middle class, while also addressing cost-effective measures, was appropriate with the images displayed in the advertisement—the young couple narrating the advertisement served as a voice for these values.

Another value addressed by interest groups was tradition in modern medicine. The PAC Americans for Prosperity aired an advertisement titled, "We Must Replace President Obama," which compared the Affordable Care Act to the Canadian health care system. The advertisement featured a woman from Canada named Shona who needed medical care in the United States, as Canadian health services were not able to treat her. Shona's options were limited as she needed emergency care, or else "she would be dead by September" (Americans for Prosperity, 2012). In the advertisement, Shona stated the United States health care system saved her life, but under Obamacare, it would have threatened traditional, patient-centered values. Therefore, by not re-electing Obama, citizens could protect patient-centered care.

Voting Decisions and Health Care

To what extent did concerns over health care impact voters' decision-making? Relying on the Chapman Public Affairs Survey, conducted after the election, we find that nearly 42% of the 750 people surveyed believed that health care affected their vote choice a lot or a fair amount.[3] However, voters who were most concerned with health care were also more likely to choose Romney (22.4%), who had vowed to repeal the act. Voters who put less weight on health care in their decision (17.1%) reported supporting Obama in the election (see Table 2).

Table 2. Issue of Health Care: Impact on Presidential Choice

	A lot or a fair amount	Only a little	Not at all
Voted for Barack Obama	17.1%	15.3%	11.1%
Voted for Mitt Romney	22.4%	11.1%	4.3%

Surprisingly, the best predictor of whether voters considered health care when choosing a presidential candidate was not ideology. As Table 3 shows, beliefs about specific values influenced voter decision-making. Thus, merely identifying as liberal, conservative, or moderate did not have a statistically significant impact on the importance of health care to the voter. Instead we see specific value orientations playing a role.

Table 3. Importance of Health Care on Vote Choice in the 2012 Presidential Election

	Unstandardized Coefficients		Standardized Coefficients		
	B	Std. Error	Beta	t	Sig.
1 (Constant)	2.412	.286		7.486	.000
The national health care law gives government too big a role in the health care system	.117	.047	.111	2.516	*
If people were treated more equally in this country we would have fewer problems	.097	.048	.081	2.013	*
Newer lifestyles are contributing to the breakdown of our society	.078	.042	.080	1.853	.064
What is your household income?	-.040	.021	-.068	-1.850	.065
Are you male or female?	.184	.092	.073	2.009	*
Political views generally?	-.033	.033	-.044	-.990	.322

*$p < .05$

On the basis of standardized coefficients, voters who were more egalitarian in their value orientation and those who were concerned about big government were the most likely to report that the issue of health care made a difference at the ballot box ($p < .05$). Household income and gender, on the other hand, did not play a role in the importance of health care to vote choice. We also note that at the time of the survey the electorate reported lingering misinformation about the PPACA with half of the respondents (51.1%) reporting they felt certain that the law gives the government the right to decide when to stop care for the elderly—the so-called death panel provision that does not exist. Respondents (64%) also mistakenly believed that PPACA provides coverage to illegal immigrants.

Voters' lack of accurate knowledge and information about the Affordable Care Act may have led them to rely more heavily on framing and peripheral cues in order to understand provisions and implementations of the health care law. As implementation began rolling out in 2010, and different parts of the law came into effect in the following years, it is not surprising that a Washington Post-ABC News poll reported that 60% of Americans did not have the necessary information to fully understand what changes the Affordable Care Act would bring to their lives (Somashekhar and Craighill, 2013). A Pew Research Center poll from September 2013 revealed similar sentiments, stating that only 25% of respondents had a solid understanding of how the law works.

Although the Obama administration worked to educate the public on provisions of the law during and after the election, much misinformation and uncertainty as well as opposition remained a year after the election. For example, we note that some 19% of uninsured Americans, according to a Pew Research Center's September 2013 survey, were generally supportive of the Affordable Care Act and were more likely to view its effects as positive compared to those who have insurance. However, taken as a whole, 53% of respondents disapproved of the health care law. With only a quarter of Americans having an understanding of the content of the law, it is no wonder there is so much confusion about the ACA. That is why value-framing messages played an important role in shaping individuals' peripheral cues during the election. When people who are unaware of the law see candidates and their party's viewpoints portrayed in a television advertisement, their values are shaped into attitudes and beliefs without necessarily having content-specific knowledge.

Conclusion

Although the health care appeals in the 2012 presidential advertising messages were issue focused and comparative in nature rather than purely character attacks, it is very clear that they ultimately were deeply negative. Even the values appeals were meant to evoke fear as evidenced in the Republican National Committee advertisement that warned that health care "threatened" religious freedom. Imagery and videostyle content related to life with—or without—the Affordable Care Act sought to make voters connect fear to their values. Obama's campaign sought to make voters fear that a Romney approach was not only a threat to equality and middle-class citizens, but also could have disastrous results such as preventing the elderly from receiving nursing home care. Other similarly negative appeals invoked fear about the soundness of Medicare and abortion laws. With the negativity and fear appeals so prominent in campaign advertising, it's no wonder that the 2012 election can be characterized as alienating and that during and even after the election, voters reported being unclear about the content and nature of health care reforms.

The division and alienation continued after the election, with health care at the center of the first government shutdown the nation had experienced in 17 years from October 1 through October 16, 2013. In the debate leading up to the government shutdown, we see many of the negative themes and values that were a part of the 2012 campaign advertising echoed in the arguments leading to the shutdown. For example, Speaker of the House John Boehner (R-Ohio) said, on September 30 2013, that the Affordable Care Act "is having a devastating impact.... Something has to be done" (Taylor, 2013, p. 1). Similarly, in the U.S. Senate, a Tea Party–backed Republican took to the floor and spoke for an epic 21 hours in favor of shutting down the federal government in order to gut the Affordable Care Act. During the many hours he held the floor, Sen. Ted Cruz (R-Texas) said, "Everyone in America understands Obamacare is destroying jobs. It is driving up health care costs. It is killing health benefits. It is shattering the economy…" (The Washington Post, 2013, p. 1). Framing the argument in terms of the economy echoed Romney's advertisements that just months earlier had warned Obama's plan would be detrimental to the economy as a whole and health care for individuals and families as well.

Between September 10 and September 30, 2013, the bill to avoid a shutdown had gone through many alterations. House Speaker Boehner refused to bring the amended bill from the Senate to vote on September 30. House Republicans wanted to delay the individual mandate and other provisions of the Affordable Care Act, so another amended bill was created and sent to the Senate. The third version, however, was tabled in the Senate, but not in time. No compromise occurred between Republicans desperately using the Affordable Care Act as leverage, and at the end of the day, the United States government shut down on October 1, 2013.

Some members of the public placed the blame on Tea Party–backed conservatives for the entire 16-day shutdown. However, the Affordable Care Act took some of the brunt of the fault in the eyes of the public. It did not help that toward the end of the shutdown the website Healthcare.gov, the main source for everything related to the Affordable Care Act, faced severe technical log-in problems, fueling conservatives to point out more faults of the health care law.

Sen. Cruz hoped that public pressure would end up forcing Congress to block implementation of the Affordable Care Act. However, a short-term spending bill and the United States debt limit eventually diverted attention away from the Affordable Care Act. In fact, the government shutdown, as a whole, boosted the popularity of the Affordable Care Act by a seven-point increase, according to an NBC-*Wall Street Journal* poll released on October 9, 2013 (Ungar, 2013). At the time of this poll, Sen. Mike Lee (R-Utah), another leader in advocating for the defunding movement, stated the Republican Party was seeking to move past issues related to implementations of the Affordable Care Act for the time being and focus on re-opening the government.

During the duration of the shutdown, Americans strongly felt the domestic effects of federal government operations as well as issues related to foreign policy. On October 16, 2013, Senate Majority Leader Harry Reid (D-Nevada) and Senate Minority Leader Mitch McConnell (R-Kentucky) had reached agreement and advanced a proposal that would keep the government funded until January 15, 2014, as well as keep the debt limited suspended until February 7. The bill passed in the Senate 81 to 18 and was approved by the House 285 to 144. It was signed into law by President Obama shortly after midnight on October 17, 2014.

Even as the shutdown came to an end, television advertisements began to appear, presaging the importance that health care will continue to play in the 2014 election and the ongoing American political process. These ads were similar in videostyle to the 2012 advertisements examined in the present study. For example, one advertisement attacked Speaker Boehner, portraying him as a child having a tantrum:

> "[Baby crying] … Speaker John Boehner didn't get his way on shutting down health care reform, so he shut down the government and hurt the economy. House Majority PAC is responsible for the content of this advertising". (House Majority PAC, 2013)

As with the health care advertisements in the 2012 presidential campaign, the spot was extremely negative and derisive. Versions of this advertisement focused on nine House Republicans from districts around the country. The issue of health care was an alienating issue in the 2012 election, with rhetoric from the presidential campaigns carrying over into the president's second term.

The phenomenon of the permanent campaign is not new, but it is well-illustrated here. Indeed, Sidney Blumenthal's observation that presidents "…must campaign early and often. And the easiest way to do that is to turn governing into a campaign; there is no line of separation" was prescient (1982, p. 26). He also pointed out that this was not merely a strategy. He predicted it was to be the new normal. We believe that health care is likely to be a hot button issue in 2014 and for years to come.

References

Americans for Prosperity. (2012, September 3). *We must replace President Obama* [Video file]. Retrieved from: http://pcl.stanford.edu/campaigns/2012/?adv=We+Must+Replace+Pres.+ Obama+-+Mitt+Romney+%28SPAC%29+-+Sep+3

Ball-Rokeach, S. J., & Loges, W. E. (1996). Making choices: Media roles in the construction of value-choices. In C. Seligman, J. M. Olson, & M. P. Zanna (Eds.), *The psychology of values: The Ontario Symposium, Vol. 8* (pp. 277–298). Hillsdale, NJ: Lawrence Erlbaum Associates.

Blumenthal, S. (1982). *The permanent campaign.* New York: Simon and Schuster.

Gardner, A. (2012, June 28). Supreme Court decision moves health-care debate squarely into political sphere. *The Washington Post.* Retrieved from http://articles.washingtonpost. com/2012-06-28/politics/35462797_1_individual-mandate-president-obama-affordable- care-act

Gordon, A., & Miller, J. L. (2004). Values and persuasion during the first Bush-Gore presiden- tial debate. *Political Communication, 21*(1), 71–92.

House Majority PAC. (2013, October 5). *John Boehner – temper tantrum* [Video file]. Retrieved from http://www.youtube.com/watch?v=SpfmgnjPQ7Y

Johnston, A. (2008). Videostyle. In L. L. Kaid & C. Holtz-Bacha (Eds.), *Encyclopedia of political communication* (pp. 809–811). Thousand Oaks, CA: SAGE Publications, Inc.

Kaid, L. L. (2009). Videostyle in the 2008 presidential advertising. In R. E. Denton, Jr. (Ed.), *The 2008 presidential campaign: A communication perspective* (pp. 200–227). Lanham, MD: Rowman & Littlefield Publishers, Inc.

Kaid, L. L., & Davidson, D. K. (1986). Elements of videostyle: Candidate presentation through television advertising. In L. L. Kaid, D. Nimmo, & K. R. Sanders (Eds.), *New perspectives on political advertising* (pp. 184–209). Carbondale, IL: Southern Illinois University Press.

Mears, B., & Cohen, T. (2012, June 28). Emotions high after Supreme Court upholds health care law. *CNN.* Retrieved from http://www.cnn.com/2012/06/28/politics/supreme-court- health-ruling

Obama for America. (2012a, April 2). *Remember* [Video file]. Retrieved from http://usatoday30. usatoday.com/news/politics/political-ad-tracker/video/848569/barack-obama-remember

Obama for America. (2012b, August 17). *Facts* [Video file]. Retrieved from http://usatoday30. usatoday.com/news/politics/political-ad-tracker/video/826524/barack-obama-facts

Obama for America. (2012c, September 29). *Care* [Video file]. Retrieved from http://pcl. stanford.edu/campaigns/2012/?adv=Care+-+Barack+Obama+-+Sep+29

Obama for America. (2012d, October 18). *Seen* [Video file]. Retrieved from http://pcl.stanford. edu/campaigns/2012/?adv=Seen+-+Barack+Obama+-+Oct+18

Opensecrets.org. (2013, March 25). Health services/HMOs: Selected industry totals. http://www.opensecrets.org/pres12/select.php?ind=H03

Pace, J., & Espo, D. (2012, October 4). Aggressive Romney spars with Obama in first debate. *Associated Press.* Retrieved from http://bigstory.ap.org/article/first-debate-sets-moment-high-risk-theater

Pew Research Center. (2013, September 16). As health care law proceeds, opposition and uncertainty persist. *Pew Research Center.* Retrieved from http://www.people-press.org/2013/09/16/as-health-care-law-proceeds-opposition-and-uncertainty-persist/

Priorities USA Action. (2012a, August 7). *Understands* [Video file]. Retrieved from http://www.youtube.com/watch?v=Nj70XqOxptU

Priorities USA Action. (2012b, October 19). *Sarah* [Video file]. Retrieved from http://pcl.stanford.edu/campaigns/2012/?adv=Sarah+-+Barack+Obama+%28SPAC%29+-+Oct+19

Republican National Committee. (2012a, March 23). *Higher costs* [Video file]. Retrieved from http://usatoday30.usatoday.com/news/politics/political-ad-tracker/video/786832/republican-national-committee-higher-costs

Republican National Committee. (2012b, August 10). *Be not afraid* [Video file]. Retrieved from http://usatoday30.usatoday.com/news/politics/political-ad-tracker/video/822070/mitt-romney-be-not-afraid

Romney for President, Inc. (2012a, August 14). *Paid in* [Video file]. Retrieved from http://www.youtube.com/watch?v=l4gPvToKTWU

Romney for President, Inc. (2012b, August 23). *Nothing's free* [Video file]. Retrieved from http://usatoday30.usatoday.com/news/politics/political-ad-tracker/video/831260/mitt-romney-nothing-s-free

Romney for President, Inc. (2012c, October 20). *The Obama plan* [Video file]. Retrieved from http://www.youtube.com/watch?v=1-dpwYvwmFI

Schwartz, S. H. (1996). *Value priorities and behavior: Applying a theory of integrated value systems.* In C. Seligman, J. M. Olson, & M. P. Zanna (Eds.), *The psychology of values: The Ontario Symposium, Vol. 8* (pp. 1–24). Hillsdale, NJ: Lawrence Erlbaum Associates.

Somashekhar, S., & Craighill, P. M. (2013, September 20). Many Americans confused about health-care law, poll finds. *The Washington Post.* Retrieved from http://articles.washingtonpost.com/2013-09-20/national/42228998_1_health-insurance-health-care-law-insurance-companies

Taylor, A. (2013, October 1). Congress plunges nation into government shutdown. *Yahoo! News.* Retrieved from http://news.yahoo.com/congress-plunges-nation-government-shutdown-071658215--finance.html

Tedesco, J. C., & Dunn, S.W. (2013). Political advertising in the 2012 U. S. presidential election. In R. Denton Jr. (Ed.). *The 2012 Presidential Campaign: A Communication Perspective* (pp. 77–96). Lanham, MD: Rowman & Littlefield Publishers.

The Washington Post. (2013, September 25). Transcript: Sen. Ted Cruz's marathon speech against Obamacare on Sept. 24. *The Washington Post.* Retrieved from http://www.washingtonpost.com/sf/national/2013/09/25/transcript-sen-ted-cruzs-filibuster-against-obamacare/

Thompson, K. (2012, August 24). Obama campaign steps up appeals to female voters. *The Washington Post*. Retrieved from http://www.washingtonpost.com/politics/obama-campaign-steps-up-appeals-to-women-voters/2012/08/24/d9c652ce-ed31-11e1-9ddc-340d5efb1e9c_story.html

Ungar, R. (2013, October 11). Boomerang! Poll reveals GOP's government shutdown bolstered Obamacare's popularity by 20%. *Forbes*. Retrieved from http://www.forbes.com/sites/rickungar/2013/10/11/boomerang-poll-reveals-gops-government-shutdown-bolstered-obamacare-popularity-by-20/

Wesleyan Media Project. (2013, November 2). *Presidential ad war tops 1M airings*. Retrieved from http://mediaproject.wesleyan.edu/2012/11/02/presidential-ad-war-tops-1m-airings/

Zeleny, J. (2012, June 28). G.O.P. vowing to take battle over health care law into November. *The New York Times*. Retrieved from http://www.nytimes.com/2012/06/29/us/politics/republicans-press-on-with-health-law-challenge.html?pagewanted=all&_r=1&

Zettl, H. (1997). *Television production handbook* (6th ed.). Belmont, CA: Wadsworth.

Notes

1. The authors wish to thank Kaela Dalton and Matt Lyons for their research assistance and the Henley Social Science Research Laboratory at Chapman University for supporting this study. Thanks are also due to Dianne Bystrom, Mary Banwart, and Bruce Gronbeck for their helpful suggestions and John Tedesco for contributing his videostyle data for analysis.
2. For a review of the content analytic methods employing the coding scheme used in the current study, see Tedesco and Dunn (2013).
3. The survey was conducted online ($N = 750$), with 27.6% of respondents identifying as Republican, 30.3% as Democrat, and 27.2% as independent. Respondents were 47.3% male and 52% female. The samples were taken from a Survey Monkey panel, which is a group of more than 2 million people who have agreed to take online surveys. The panel is constructed to mirror census statistics in terms of demographics, location, and population density and is routinely benchmarked against other survey data such as Gallup polls. Panel information can be found at: http://www.slideshare.net/SurveyMonkeyAudience/survey-monkey-audience-data-quality-whitepaper-september-2012

CHAPTER EIGHT

Gendered Framing of the 2012 Election

The "War on Women" as Rhetorical Strategy

VALERIE M. HENNINGS AND DIANNE G. BYSTROM

It's just so hard for me to grasp how they [Republicans] can be as anti-woman as they are. I think that the pushback and the guttural reaction from women against the Republicans' agenda out of the gate, the war on women that the Republicans have been waging since they took over the House, I think is not only going to restore but help us exceed the president's margin of victory in the next election. – Democratic Party chairwoman U.S. Rep. Debbie Wasserman Schultz, at a May 26, 2011, breakfast roundtable with reporters. (Bedard, 2011)

If the Democrats said we had a war on caterpillars and every mainstream media outlet talked about the fact that Republicans have a war on caterpillars, then we'd have problems with caterpillars. It's a fiction. – Republican National Committee chairman Reince Priebus, in an April 7, 2012, interview on Bloomberg Television's *Political Capital with Al Hunt.* (Jensen, 2012)

Much of the rhetoric of the 2012 presidential election focused on whether the Democrats or Republicans were waging a so-called "war on women" voters. Prominent Democrats—including U.S. Rep. Debbie Wasserman Schultz of Florida, chairwoman of the Democratic Party, and U.S. Sen. Barbara Boxer of California—charged that Republicans were waging a war on women by introducing bills to restrict their reproductive health care; alleging that their bodies could prevent pregnancy from "legitimate rape"; and opposing bills to increase the minimum wage, support pay equity, and reauthorize the Violence Against Women Act (Boxer, 2012; Ferguson, 2013).

Republicans—including Republican National Committee chairman Reince Priebus and vice presidential candidate U.S. Rep. Paul Ryan of Wisconsin—mocked the Democrats' claims, likening the so-called war on women to a war on caterpillars or left-handed Irishmen (Bassett, 2012; Jensen, 2012). Instead, the Republicans alleged, President Barack Obama was waging the real war on women by not having turned the economy around quickly enough. During the second presidential debate, former Gov. Mitt Romney recited statistics that more women than men had lost their jobs since Obama assumed the presidency and more women were living in poverty (Ferguson, 2013).

The purpose of this chapter is to explore the use of the war on women rhetoric in the 2012 election. We begin with a historical overview of the use of the term "war on women" as a rhetorical strategy followed by a review of the literature on how women voters and issues have been framed in recent political campaigns. Then, we present our research questions, methods, and results before offering our conclusions and directions for future research.

The History of the "War on Women" as a Rhetorical Strategy

Allegations that the Republican Party was waging a war on women date back to at least 16 years prior to the 2012 presidential election. In her 1996 book, *The Republican War Against Women: An Insider's Report from Behind the Lines*, Tanya Melich—a longtime Republican activist and a delegate to the 1992 convention—argued that Republicans adopted an electoral strategy in 1980 that included getting votes by playing on the fear and uncertainty engendered by the civil rights and women's political movements, and continued to use this strategy in the campaigns of 1984, 1988, and 1992. Two books—*The W Effect: Bush's War on Women* (Flanders, 2004) and *George W. Bush and the War on Women: Turning Back the Clock on Progress* (Finlay, 2006)—also have examined the actions and policies of the George W. Bush administration in terms of their impact on women in the United States and abroad.

A collection of essays by journalists and activists, Flander's edited volume (2004) sought to document the Bush administration's incursion into women's rights with reports on such topics as affirmative action, the Patriot Act, welfare reform, sexual freedom, reproductive rights, the impact of the religious right, education funding and Title IX, and public health policy. Finlay's book (2006) argued that Bush's policies and actions reversed or inhibited women's progress over the past three decades not only because of his opposition to abortion, but also by shutting down women's offices in the government, defunding programs that assist women, opposing global women's rights treaties, and supporting anti-feminist organizations.

The more recent use of the term "war on women" dates back to the aftermath of the 2010 midterm election, when the Republican Party won the majority of seats in the U.S. House of Representatives. On January 4, 2011, the day after Congress convened, Kaili Joy Gray of the *Daily Kos* wrote an opinion piece titled "The Coming War on Women." In the article, she outlined many of the measures that Republicans intended to push through the House of Representatives, including personhood and fetal pain laws and an effort to defund Planned Parenthood. In February 2011, U.S. Rep. Jerrold Nadler (D-NY) referred to the proposed No Taxpayer Funding for Abortion Act, which would have changed policy to allow only victims of "forcible rape" or child sex abuse to qualify for Medicaid funding for abortion, as "an entirely new front in the war on women and their families" (Weigel, 2012, "Birth," para.1).

U.S. Rep. Wasserman Schultz (D-FL) began using the term war on women in March 2011 and continued using the term throughout the 2012 election (Weigel, 2012). In his April 12, 2012, article in *Slate*, David Weigel argued that the war on women was over once Democratic strategist Hilary Rosen—who was not affiliated with the Obama campaign or Democratic National Committee—disputed Romney's claim that he stayed in touch with the economy because of his wife, Ann. "His wife has never actually worked a day in her life," Rosen said on CNN on April 11, 2012, unleashing a storm of criticism from Republicans and Democrats alike for seemingly denouncing stay-at-home mothers and women hurt by the economy (Weigel, 2012, para. 2). Weigel also documented Republican efforts to mock the term as well as Democratic attempts to distance themselves from—or even deny starting the use of—the war on women in 2012.

Despite Weigel's pronouncement that the war on women rhetorical strategy was over in April 2012, it lived on throughout the campaign, especially in media reports. Although opinion pieces in *U.S. News and World Report* (Cary, 2012) and *Forbes* (Atlas, 2012) declared that the so-called Republican war on women was fiction, a *New York Times* (2012) editorial and political commentary in *Salon* said the narrative was an accurate description of the "hostile and putative policies" pushed by the Republican Party (Kohn, 2012, para. 2).

After the November 6, 2012, election—in which Obama enjoyed a 10-point gender gap in support from women voters as compared to men (Center for American Women and Politics, 2012)—some media reports declared that the war on women narrative had worked by not only re-electing the president, but also by striking a "historic blow to the religious right" and helping to put a record number of women in the U.S. Senate (M. Goldberg, 2012, para. 2). "But the influence women exercised on this year's results goes beyond electing female representation," Michelle Goldberg wrote for *The Daily Beast*. "Women voters proved that politicians cannot threaten their rights with impunity" (2012, para. 5).

And, as the war on women rhetoric continued to be used in political debates and media commentary well into 2013, *Slate*'s Weigel admitted in an August 2, 2013, article titled "There Will Always be a 'War on Women'" that his declaration that the war on women was dead in April 2012 was his "worst judgment all year" (para. 8).

The war on women narrative used in the 2012 presidential election was not the first time that women voters and issues were framed by political campaigns and the media. Next, we summarize recent research on the framing of women voters and issues during presidential year elections.

Framing Women Voters and Issues in Political Campaigns

In her research on the gender gap—the difference in the proportions of women and men voting for one candidate—political scientist Susan Carroll has documented how groups of women voters are socially constructed by political consultants to win support for their candidates. For example, in the 1996 presidential campaign, so-called "soccer moms"—generally defined as "white, married women with children, presumably of the soccer-playing age, living in the suburbs"—were considered politically important because they were viewed to be swing voters whose demographics had traditionally led them to vote Republican, but could be persuaded to vote Democrat (Carroll, 2010, p. 139). These soccer moms were credited by political pundits and the media for re-electing President Bill Clinton.

In 2004, George W. Bush's presidential campaign targeted "security moms," who shared many similar demographic characteristics with soccer moms in that they were white and married with young children but also preoccupied with keeping their families safe from terrorism (Carroll, 2010). "Both 'soccer moms' and 'security moms' were social constructions, a combination of demographics assigned a catchy name by political consultants with no connection to any existing self-identified group or organizational base," she said (2010, p. 139).

Moreover, campaign and media attention to soccer moms in 1996 and security moms in 2004 deflected attention away from the concerns of other subgroups of women voters, Carroll argued (2010). "As a result, Clinton was re-elected in 1996 and Bush was twice elected to the presidency in 2000 and 2004 without campaigning aggressively on (or, in some cases, even seriously addressing) many of the issues of greatest importance to the majority of women in this country who are not white, middle-class mothers of young children" (p. 140).

In the 2008 election, with the emergence of Alaska Gov. Sarah Palin as the Republican vice presidential candidate, the long-held public connection between motherhood and politics was reframed into the rhetorical narrative of the "hockey mom" (Greenlee, 2010). As a hockey mom who attempted to reach out to other mothers, Palin emphasized her own role as the mother of five children as well as her support for family, family values, and American military troops. According to Greenlee, Palin's strategy was to win middle-class women voters over to the Republican presidential ticket as well as disgruntled supporters of unsuccessful Democratic presidential candidate Hillary Clinton. Thus, the hockey mom rhetorical narrative of 2008 was similar to the soccer mom and security mom appeals of the 1996, 2000, and 2004 campaigns.

In the 2012 presidential campaign, candidates made appeals to female voters not only as mothers but also as single women. Republicans emphasized the impact of the economy on women voters, whereas Democrats charged that the GOP was waging a war on women by attacking Planned Parenthood; limiting access to women's reproductive health care; and opposing legislation to support pay equity, increase the minimum wage, and reauthorize the Violence Against Women Act.

However, similar to Carroll's analysis of the 1996, 2000, and 2004 presidential campaigns, Michaele Ferguson (2013) argued that the emphasis on women in the 2012 election—including the war on women rhetoric—was part of a long-standing trend of presidential candidates paying superficial attention to issues that might turn out female voters rather than addressing structural gender inequality in a more substantive fashion. Conceding that "women were the talk of the 2012 election cycle," Ferguson asserted that both presidential candidates used feminist rhetoric to "appeal to women voters in a way that occludes the possibility of a more radical analysis of the very issues they claimed were important" (2013, para. 4, 5).

Both candidates, Ferguson added, offered a "bland and superficial discussion of 'women's issues' with little or no substantive attention to questions of power, inequity, and oppression" (2013, "Romney: Binders Full of Women," para. 14). For example, Romney talked about women's job losses under the Obama administration without mentioning such root causes for their economic disparity as budget cuts to state and local government, which affected women school teachers and government administrators; the gendered wage gap; or the lack of affordable quality childcare. Obama, on the other hand, acknowledged that women faced structural discrimination in the workplace, but placed the responsibility on women to work hard if they wanted to earn more or advance in the workplace (Ferguson, 2013).

"For all his talk, [Obama's] actions suggest that women's issues matter only when women votes are on the line," Ferguson asserted. "But Romney, despite his criticisms of Obama, behaved in the same way, appealing to women voters by promising to address their interests" (2013, "Women Are an Interest Group," para. 1).

Based on the review of the literature on the framing of women candidates and issues in presidential elections as well as the history of the use of war on women as political rhetoric, we propose the following research questions to study the use of this term in 2012:

RQ1: In what ways did the media use the term, war on women, in relation to the coverage of political actors?

RQ2: In what ways did the media use the term, war on women, in relation to the coverage of policy issues?

Method

We examined these questions through a content analysis of media coverage leading up to and including the day of the 2012 election. In light of previous scholarship that has found significant differences in political coverage across media types (e.g., Bode & Hennings, 2012; Druckman, 2005), we examined coverage that appeared between January 1, 2012, and November 6, 2012, across three separate media: newspapers, television, and blogs.[1]

To construct our collection of coverage, we used the LexisNexis Academic database, which provides users with full-text access to a variety of resources and the ability to search more than 15,000 news, business, and legal publications (LexisNexis, 2013b). Our analysis included articles from three widely-read, national newspapers: *The New York Times*, *The Washington Post*, and *USA Today*.[2] We also analyzed the transcripts of six, top-rated evening television news programs. Three of these national programs aired on broadcast television—*ABC World News with Diane Sawyer*, *NBC Nightly News with Brian Williams*, and *CBS Evening News with Scott Pelley*—and three aired on cable television—*Hardball with Chris Matthews* (MSNBC), *The Situation Room* (CNN), and *Special Report with Bret Baier* (FOX).[3] In addition, we examined the content of 142 government and politics blogs available through the LexisNexis Academic database as archived by Newstex LLC.[4]

Using the term war on women to search the LexisNexis database, we assembled a universe of media coverage. Across the three newspapers selected for this study, we found a total of 272 articles that mentioned the war on women; all of these articles were included in our content analysis. Between January 1, 2012, and November 6, 2012, which encompasses a total of 311 days, 71 stories in *The New York Times*, 188 stories in *The Washington Post*, and 13 stories in *USA Today* mentioned the phrase. Across the six television evening news programs, the war on women was mentioned in 74 transcripts: one each on the *NBC Nightly News with Brian Williams* and *ABC World News with Diane Sawyer*, four on *CBS Evening News with Scott Pelley*, 22 on *The Situation Room* (CNN), 23 on *Special Report with Bret Baier* (FOX), and 23 on *Hardball with Chris Matthews* (MSNBC).[5] We included all 74 transcripts in our content analysis.

In searching blog content, we focused on a subset of postings archived as "Newstex Government and Politics Blogs" within the LexisNexis database.[6] When searching this subset of blogs, a total of 1,336 postings mentioned the war on women. Due to the sheer volume of results, we drew a random sample of 414 postings to include in our sample from the 1,336 found; this sample size meets a 95% confidence level and 4% margin of error. The 414 posts came from 142 different blogs (see Appendix A for a listing of blogs included in the sample). These blogs were then manually coded to ascertain ideological perspective. This evaluation showed that our sample included 172 posts from 51 liberal blogs, 123 posts from 45 conservative blogs, 95 posts from 38 neutral blogs, and 24 posts from 8 blogs whose ideology could not be determined.

Ultimately, our collection of media coverage included 757 items—272 newspaper articles from three national newspapers, 74 television transcripts from six evening news programs, and 414 postings from 142 political blogs—all of which mentioned the war on women. To learn how this phrase was used by these sources in relation to various political actors and policy issues, we conducted a computer-assisted content analysis. This approach provides multiple benefits including the ability to efficiently analyze a large volume of data in a way that can be easily replicated (see Neuendorf, 2002, 2011; and Riffe, Lacy, & Fico 2005 regarding the advantages and disadvantages of computer-assisted content analysis). It is also quite suitable in analyses where the coding unit is a particular word or phrase, such as "abortion" or "Romney." We conducted our analysis using Yoshikoder, which is open-source software that allows users to create custom dictionaries, creates concordances for examining the usage of text in-context, and provides word frequencies (Lowe, 2006).

We coded our sample by creating a custom dictionary of terms to analyze how the media used the war on women phrase in relation to particular policy issues and political actors. We checked this dictionary by manually coding a randomly selected 10% subset of our media coverage sample (76 items out of 757 articles, transcripts, and posts) to confirm that the words used in our dictionary accurately measured the concept of interest. The check certified the validity of the final dictionary used in our study, which includes those terms that were correctly associated with the relevant concepts between 91.5% and 100% of the time.

We generated our dictionary of terms based on a review of the literature, described above, on the framing of women candidates and issues in presidential elections as well as the history of the use of war on women as a rhetorical frame. This review highlighted a variety of political actors and policy issues that we might expect to be discussed in conjunction with the war on women rhetoric used in 2012. Our final dictionary of terms included two categories of words and phrases: political actors and policy issues. The terms relating to political actors included Ann Romney, Democrats, female voters, Hilary Rosen, Obama, Mitt Romney, Paul Ryan, Republican, Rush Limbaugh, Sandra Fluke, Todd Akin, and women voters. The terms used to code policy issues included abortion, birth control, economy, health care, jobs, legitimate rape, minimum wage, Obamacare, pay equity, personhood, Planned Parenthood, rape, reproductive health, Violence Against Women Act, and women's issues.[7]

Results

Our analysis of the media's coverage of the war on women revealed differences in the use of this term in relation to various political actors and policy issues across media types and ideological perspectives. Table 1 presents the results of this analysis. We report risk ratios, which reflect the relative probability of seeing each category of dictionary terms—political actors and policy issues—in the media's discussions of the war on women. This measure essentially allows us to conduct a comparative analysis between subsets of our data collection. For example, we can examine differences in content by comparing coverage by newspaper articles to blog postings or by FOX's *Special Report with Bret Baier* to MSNBC's *Hardball with Chris Matthews*. Risk ratios are calculated from proportions—in this study the risk ratios refer to the number of words coded for each category divided by the total number of words in the sample, which accounts for differences in the length of the items (newspaper articles, television transcripts, and blog postings) being compared.[8]

As an example, to detect differences in mentions of political actors between newspaper and television coverage of the war on women, we divided the proportion of words in newspaper articles coded as political actors by the same proportion

Table 1. Differences in Political Actors and Policy Issues Mentioned in the Media's War on Women Coverage by Media Type and Ideological Perspective

	Newspapers $N = 272$ vs. TV $N = 74$	Newspapers $N = 272$ vs. Blogs $N = 414$	TV $N = 74$ vs. Blogs $N = 414$	FOX $N = 23$ vs. MSNBC $N = 23$	Con Blogs $N = 123$ vs. Lib Blogs $N = 172$
Political Actors	**Newspapers** % Change: 21.69 Risk Ratio: 1.22 [1.17, 1.27]*	**Newspapers** % Change: 11.54 Risk Ratio: 1.12 [1.07, 1.17]*	**Blogs** % Change: -9.10 Risk Ratio: .92 [.88, .96]*	**FOX** % Change: 9.37 Risk Ratio: 1.09 [1.03, 1.17]*	**Conservative Blogs** % Change: 64.57 Risk Ratio: 1.65 [1.52, 1.79]*
Policy Issues	**Newspapers** % Change: 79.82 Risk Ratio: 1.80 [1.66, 1.95]*	**Not Significantly Different** % Change: 2.98 Risk Ratio: 1.03 [.95, 1.12]	**Blogs** % Change: -74.61 Risk Ratio: .57 [.53, .62]*	**Not Significantly Different** % Change: 15.52 Risk Ratio: 1.16 [1.00, 1.34]	**Liberal Blogs** % Change: -28.28 Risk Ratio: .78 [.67, .90]*

Note. Each cell identifies which media—by type or ideological perspective—was more likely to emphasize different policy issues and political actors in their war on women coverage. Percent change, risk ratio estimates, and 95% confidence intervals are also reported for each comparison.

* $p \leq .05$

of actors mentions in television transcripts (see the first data column of Table 1). This produces a risk ratio of 1.22. Ratios greater than 1 mean that the proportion from the first coverage type listed in each set of comparisons—newspapers, television, FOX's *Special Report with Bret Baier*, and conservative blogs (see the columns listed in Table 1)—is greater than the second type. The further away from 1 this ratio is, the greater the difference between the two groups compared. To illustrate whether or not this difference in coverage is statistically significant, we also report a 95% confidence interval for each risk ratio.[9] If that interval does not include 1, the difference between the two groups—in this example, between newspapers and television—is statistically significant (Lowe, 2006). We can then interpret this result as saying that newspaper coverage of the war on women mentioned political actors more often than television coverage and this difference is statistically significant.

To understand how much of a difference is detected between the media coverage compared, we also report percent change. Positive percent change, in those places where a statistically significant ratio is detected, shows a greater likelihood of that category of content appearing in the coverage of the first media type (newspapers, television, FOX, and conservative blogs) in each set of comparisons. In the example discussed above, the percent change in mentions of political actors between newspaper and television coverage of the war on women is about 22% (see Table 1). That is, newspaper coverage of the war on women was 22% more likely than television coverage of the war on women to include mentions of political actors.

When comparing newspaper coverage of the war on women to blogs, we found that newspapers were about 12% more likely to mention political actors. However, in comparisons between television and blog coverage, blogs were approximately 9% more likely to mention political actors. In each set of comparisons, these differences were statistically significant (see Table 1). An article by Kathleen Parker, appearing in *The Washington Post* on October 9, 2012, illustrates how the war on women could be used in framing the discussion of key political actors and policy issues simultaneously:

> Thanks to certain outspoken members/supporters of the GOP, the Democratic Party has been able to capitalize on a fiction created by the Obama campaign—the alleged "war on women." It is not helpful when people such as Rush Limbaugh call Sandra Fluke a "slut" for her position that insurance should cover contraception. Then there was Todd Akin's strange intelligence that victims of "legitimate rape" don't get pregnant, a flourish of rare ignorance. Check the birthrates in countries where rape is employed as a weapon. Finally, some Republican-led states have waved one too many ultrasound wands at women. (Parker, 2012, para. 3)

This excerpt not only shows how the war on women frame was used in discussing relevant actors and issues in the 2012 election, but also how coverage could, not surprisingly, convey a particular ideological stance. To better understand how the war on women frame was used by media sources with conservative and liberal perspectives, we also conducted two analyses that compared coverage between sources with contrasting ideological positions. These analyses build upon previous work that has examined, identified, and discussed the implications of differences in coverage by media sources with varying partisan and ideological leanings (e.g., Baum & Groeling, 2008; Bode & Hennings, 2012; Levendusky, 2013). One comparison included cable television transcripts of *Special Report with Bret Baier* on FOX, which is typically associated with a more conservative ideological perspective, and *Hardball with Chris Matthews* on MSNBC, which tends to be more liberal. Our second comparison looked at conservative blogs in relation to liberal blogs.

We found that the conservative media coverage of the war on women, as found on FOX's *Special Report* and conservative blogs, was more likely to mention political actors than liberal media sources (see Table 1). The FOX program was about 9% more likely to mention political actors and conservative blogs were 65% more likely to do so; both were statistically significant. An excerpt from the October 17, 2012, airing of FOX's *Special Report with Bret Baier* illustrates this finding (Rohrbeck, 2012): "Democrats have invested heavily in the so-called war on women narrative, pinning Romney and Republicans as extreme on everything from contraception to equal pay, a move some think, given Romney's performance in the first two debates, may have backfired."

Our examination of war on women coverage in relation to policy issues also revealed statistically significant differences between media types and ideological perspectives. Among different media types, newspaper and blog coverage of the war on women were respectively 80% and 75% more likely to mention policy issues than television coverage. In considering ideological perspective, liberal blogs mentioned policy issues 28% more often in their war on women discussions than conservative blogs (see Table 1). An April 19, 2012, posting on the liberal-leaning *Ohio Daily Blog* provides an example of how the war on women was used to frame, in this case, the discussion of health care policy (Turner, 2012, para. 4):

> What kind of state are we living in? It is unbelievable that elected officials—stewards of the public interest—would seek to deliberately deny millions of working class and underprivileged women access to high quality healthcare services. This new plan is another vicious, heartless, and unconscionable volley in the Republican war on women. This narrow policy will disproportionately affect low income and rural areas, and will have consequences that will ripple across the state. I urge Ohio's 5.8 million women and the men who love and respect them to speak out against it.

We expanded our examination by conducting a word frequency analysis to determine which particular concepts within the actors and issues categories of our dictionary were the most common throughout our media coverage sample. Our entire sample—newspaper articles, television transcripts, and blog posts combined—included 985,584 words. Overall, 30,613 different words were used. Of the 200 most common, which included words appearing 648 times (the term "something") to 50,534 times ("the"), eight of our dictionary words were found. The terms included four political actors terms—Democrat, Obama, Republican, and Mitt Romney—and four policy issues terms—abortion, economy, jobs, and rape. The saliency of these eight words, and their repeated usage throughout our sample of the media's war on women coverage, makes sense given the context of the 2012 election.

When discussing political actors, mentions of the two 2012 presidential candidates, Obama and Romney, varied across comparisons of media types and ideological perspectives (see Table 2). Newspaper coverage of the war on women was more likely to mention Obama when compared with television and blogs, as exemplified by this quote from Jonah Goldberg's article appearing in the November 5, 2012, edition of *USA Today*:

> Beneath the partisan distortions and hyperbole, Obama's "war on women" rhetoric is the idea that the federal government should be the guarantor of "reproductive freedom"—a malleable term that includes everything from the right to abortion on demand to subsidized birth control pills. Whatever the merits of that argument, the simple fact is that a government that has the power to give you everything you want has the power to take it away, as well. (J. Goldberg, 2012, para. 7).

We also found statistically significant differences between conservative and liberal sources. FOX's *Special Report* was 61% more likely than MSNBC's *Hardball* to mention Obama in its coverage of the war on women. The difference between conservative and liberal blogs was even more pronounced with conservative blogs being 340%, or 3.4 times, more likely to mention Obama than liberal blogs (see Table 2).

We also detected statistically significant differences in the media's mentions of Romney in their framing of the war on women. Television was about 34% more likely to use the term Romney than newspapers; television mentioned Romney more than blogs as well. In comparing newspapers to blogs, we found that newspapers were 27% more likely to refer to Romney than blogs (see Table 2). Also, conservative blogs were 100% more likely to mention the Republican candidate by name than liberal blogs in conjunction with discussions of the war on women as illustrated in this conservative-leaning blog, *Maggie's Notebook*, on October 17, 2012 (Thornton, 2012, para. 7):

> More women now live poverty than they have in 17 years. In my mind, the real war on women has been economic and I know Mitt Romney can turn this economy around. I know he cares, but more important to me, Mitt knows what to do. And, honestly, I'm more concerned about action than talk right now.

When referring to the two major parties, the media also differed significantly. When compared to television coverage of the war on women, newspapers were 129% more likely to refer to Democrats and 56% more likely to refer to Republicans. Blogs also mentioned both parties more often than television coverage (see Table 2). Sources with an ideological leaning connected the parties to the war on women in different ways. Conservative sources like FOX's *Special Report* and conservative blogs mentioned the Democrats more often than liberal sources in relation to the war on women. The opposite held true when examining mentions of the Republican Party: MSNBC's *Hardball* was 34% more likely to mention the Republicans as compared to FOX's *Special Report*. Liberal blogs discussed the Republican Party 54% more often than conservative blogs (see Table 2).

When discussing the policy issues of the economy and jobs, some comparisons between media types and ideological perspectives produced statistically significant differences. Television coverage of the war on women was more likely to mention the economy when compared to coverage by newspapers and blogs (see Table 2). The following excerpt from an April 10, 2012, report by George Stephanopoulos on ABC's *World News with Diane Sawyer* exemplifies how the war on women was linked to the economy (Corn, 2012):

> Mitt Romney is giving a speech tonight where he's gonna try to turn this rhetoric, address the gender gap by turning around this rhetoric on the war on women, saying that women are the real victims of the Obama economy. Here's the statistics they're going to use. They say that women account for 92% of the jobs lost under President Obama. You know the Obama campaign will go back at that. But that's where it's gonna start.

FOX's *Special Report* and conservative blogs were also more likely to discuss the economy than their liberal counterparts. Newspapers and television were more likely, 32% and 17% respectively, than blogs to mention jobs in relation to the war on women. The same was true for conservative blogs, which were 43% more likely, as compared to liberal blogs, to mention jobs in relation to the war on women (see Table 2).

We also found statistically significant differences across media types and ideological perspectives when it comes to mentions of abortion and rape within the war on women coverage. A marked difference between newspaper and television coverage was found with newspapers being 281%, or 2.8 times, more likely to mention the issue of abortion. This excerpt from an opinion piece by Nicholas

Table 2. Differences in the Most Common Political Actors and Policy Issues Mentioned in the Media's War on Women Coverage by Media Type and Ideological Perspective

	Newspapers N = 272 vs. TV N = 74	Newspapers N = 272 vs. Blogs N = 414	TV N = 74 vs. Blogs N = 414	FOX N = 23 vs. MSNBC N = 23	Con Blogs N = 123 vs. Lib Blogs N = 172
Political Actors					
Democrat	**Newspapers** % Change: 129.84 Risk Ratio: 2.30 [2.07, 2.55]*	**Not Significantly Different** % Change: -3.04 Risk Ratio: .97 [.88, 1.07]	**Blogs** % Change: -136.84 Risk Ratio: .42 [.38, .47]*	**FOX** % Change: 42.45 Risk Ratio: 1.43 [1.18, 1.72]*	**Conservative Blogs** % Change: 81.26 Risk Ratio: 1.81 [1.52, 2.16]*
Obama	**Newspapers** % Change: 17.40 Risk Ratio: 1.17 [1.08, 1.27]*	**Newspapers** % Change: 26.02 Risk Ratio: 1.26 [1.15, 1.39]*	**Not Significantly Different** % Change: 7.34 Risk Ratio: 1.07 [.98, 1.17]	**FOX** % Change: 60.95 Risk Ratio: 1.60 [1.43, 1.81]*	**Conservative Blogs** % Change: 340.23 Risk Ratio: 4.40 [3.64, 5.33]*
Republican	**Newspapers** % Change: 56.23 Risk Ratio: 1.56 [1.45, 1.69]*	**Not Significantly Different** % Change: 2.21 Risk Ratio: 1.02 [.94, 1.11]	**Blogs** % Change: -52.85 Risk Ratio: .65 [.61, .71]*	**MSNBC** % Change: -34.29 Risk Ratio: .75 [.64, .86]*	**Liberal Blogs** % Change: -54.40 Risk Ratio: .65 [.55, .76]*
Romney	**TV** % Change: -33.75 Risk Ratio: .75 [.69, .81]*	**Newspapers** % Change: 26.69 Risk Ratio: 1.27 [1.15, 1.40]*	**TV** % Change: 69.45 Risk Ratio: 1.70 [1.56, 1.84]*	**Not Significantly Different** % Change: -6.50 Risk Ratio: .94 [.85, 1.04]	**Conservative Blogs** % Change: 100.12 Risk Ratio: 2.00 [1.68, 2.39]*

Policy Issues					
Abortion	Newspapers	Not Significantly Different	Blogs	Not Significantly Different	Liberal Blogs
	% Change: 281.94 Risk Ratio: 3.82 [3.26, 4.47]*	% Change: 3.30 Risk Ratio: 1.03 [.91, 1.12]	% Change: -269.74 Risk Ratio: .27 [.23, .32]*	% Change: -3.52 Risk Ratio: .97 [.69, 1.36]	% Change: -62.86 Risk Ratio: .61 [.48, .79]*
Economy	TV	Not Significantly Different	TV	FOX	Conservative Blogs
	% Change: -27.05 Risk Ratio: .79 [.65, .96]*	% Change: 4.00 Risk Ratio: 1.04 [.82, 1.32]	% Change: 32.14 Risk Ratio: 1.32 [1.08, 1.62]*	% Change: 74.40 Risk Ratio: 1.74 [1.32, 2.30]*	% Change: 75.26 Risk Ratio: 1.75 [1.18, 2.61]*
Jobs	Not Significantly Different	Newspapers	TV	Not Significantly Different	Conservative Blogs
	% Change: 12.47 Risk Ratio: 1.13 [.98, 1.30]	% Change: 32.49 Risk Ratio: 1.32 [1.11, 1.58]*	% Change: 17.81 Risk Ratio: 1.18 [1.01, 1.38]*	% Change: 10.73 Risk Ratio: 1.11 [.89, 1.38]	% Change: 43.30 Risk Ratio: 1.43 [1.07, 1.92]*
Rape	Newspapers	Not Significantly Different	Blogs	MSNBC	Liberal Blogs
	% Change: 251.63 Risk Ratio: 3.52 [2.84, 4.36]*	% Change: 7.05 Risk Ratio: 1.07 [.89, 1.29]	% Change: -228.46 Risk Ratio: .30 [.25, .38]*	% Change: -129.42 Risk Ratio: .44 [.20, .93]*	% Change: -242.66 Risk Ratio: .29 [.19, .45]*

Note. Each cell identifies which media—by type or ideological perspective—was more likely to emphasize the most common policy issues and political actors in their war on women coverage. Percent change, risk ratio estimates, and 95% confidence intervals are also reported for each comparison.

* $p \leq .05$

Kristof in the November 4, 2012, edition of *The New York Times* demonstrates how the issue of abortion would be highlighted using the war on women frame:

> In this year's campaign furor over a supposed "war on women," involving birth control and abortion, the assumption is that the audience worrying about these issues is just women. Give us a little credit. We men aren't mercenaries caring only for Y chromosomes. We have wives and daughters, mothers and sisters, and we have a pretty intimate stake in contraception as well. This isn't like a tampon commercial on television, leaving men awkwardly examining their fingernails. When it comes to women's health, men as well as women need to pay attention. Just as civil rights wasn't just a "black issue," women's rights and reproductive health shouldn't be reduced to a "women's issue." (Kristof, 2012, para. 1–3)

A similarly pronounced difference arose between television and blogs—blogs were 269% more likely to discuss abortion than television. Liberal blogs also mentioned abortion more, by about 63%, than conservative blogs in discussions of the war on women (see Table 2).

Newspapers and blogs were more likely than television to mention rape in association with the war on women. As with mentions of abortion, the differences between media types were statistically significant and large: newspapers were 252% more likely and blogs were 228% more likely to discuss rape in terms of the war on women as compared to television (see Table 2). Sources with a more liberal perspective, MSNBC's *Hardball* and liberal blogs, also mentioned rape more often than their conservative counterparts. MSNBC's *Hardball* was 129% more likely to mention rape than FOX's *Special Report*. This difference was even larger between blogs—liberal blogs were 243% more likely to mention rape in their discussions of the war on women than conservative blogs (see Table 2).

Conclusion

From the results described above, we gain three key insights regarding the media's use of the war on women rhetoric in the 2012 election—all of which can be used as starting points for future studies. First, our exploration of this particular rhetorical strategy reveals that different types of media—newspapers, television, and blogs—did in fact employ this frame in their 2012 election coverage, thus contributing to the continued life and development of the war on women term as a way for understanding women voters and issues in political campaigns. As noted in the historical overview of the term's usage, the war on women frame did not originate with the 2012 election. Instead, we can interpret our findings as evidence of the perennial nature of the rhetorical term. In other words, we may very well see this frame employed again in other political campaign contexts. Future research on these additional contexts should continue to situate the use of the term as part of a pattern of usage—doing so will provide a better understanding of the political context of interest as well as the progression of the war on women framing strategy.

Second, our study shows differences in the ways different media—by type and ideological perspective—discussed the war on women in relation to key political actors and concepts. Additionally, we can explain differences across media coverage in relation to particularly salient terms included in our content analysis dictionary. Generally speaking, we see that between more traditional media, newspapers and television, the former tended to use the war on women frame in relation to political actors and policy issues more often. The notable exceptions are seen in the analysis of particular actors and issues—Romney and the economy—when television coverage emphasized these items more than newspapers. When comparing traditional media types to blogs, we see interesting differences arise. In places where statistically significant differences emerged, newspapers were more likely to mention political actors and issues than blogs. This may be explained, in part, by the differing roles newspapers and blogs play in the political sphere. Newspapers have been found to play a significant role in informing the public and facilitating voter learning (Druckman, 2005) whereas blogs, while providing information and opinion to readers, can also serve as a space in which to mobilize individuals through direct calls for political action (Wallsten, 2008).

We did not see such a consistent pattern in comparing television to blogs. When we consider the eight most commonly referenced terms from our dictionary, we see that blogs, a type of new media, were more likely to use the war on women frame in relation to key women's issues like abortion and rape as well as in discussing the two major political parties. Television coverage, a more traditional media type, was more likely to reference Romney in relation to the war on women as well as the economy and jobs. It is possible that these findings are ultimately detecting differences in how traditional versus new media use the war on women frame. Future research may wish to delve into this more to see if a pattern can be found in additional instances where the war on women frame is employed as well as in cases where other rhetorical frames are used.

Our analysis also shows that conservative media sources, such as FOX's *Special Report* and conservative blogs, were more likely to use the war on women frame when discussing political actors. This holds true when considering specific terms, except in the case of the term Republican. This is likely the result of liberal sources emphasizing the "Republican war on women" and conservative sources striving to simultaneously disassociate the concept with Republicans in the 2012 election and redefine it in ways that would reap election support for their partisan and ideological positions—both are framing strategies we would expect given the differing ideological perspectives. In terms of policy issues, liberal blogs were more likely to mention issues of particular interest to women such as abortion and rape while conservative blogs linked the war on women to the economy and jobs.

Again, these findings align with the rhetorical strategies we would expect sources with different ideological perspectives to employ in the 2012 election context. Although this analysis provides an important step in understanding how the war on women frame is used in different ways to discuss political actors and policy issues, future research may wish to expand upon our work by incorporating an analysis of content tone that could shed additional light on the usage of this rhetorical frame.

Third, in certain cases, our results indicate prominent differences in how various media types and ideological perspectives discussed certain political actors and issues in their coverage of the war on women. As examples, conservative blogs were 3.4 times more likely to mention Obama than liberal blogs and newspapers were 2.5 times more likely to mention abortion and 2.8 times more likely to mention rape than television (see Table 2). The magnitude of these differences in usage, alongside the understanding that any such differences exist, suggests an additional path for future research—a consideration of the influence of the war on women frame, and the different ways it is used across media types and ideological perspectives, on the public's perceptions of the political actors and policy issues discussed through this rhetorical strategy.

Appendix A
Sample of Blogs Included in Analysis by Ideology
Total Blogs = 142

<u>Liberal (51 blogs)</u>
AMERICAblog
The American Prospect Blogs
Asian American Action Fund
Barefoot and Progressive
The Bilerico Project
BloggingBlue
Blue Virginia
Brutally Honest
Burnt Orange Report
D.C. Now
The Democratic Daily

Democracy for New Mexico
DownWithTyranny
The Dreyfuss Report
Editor's Cut
Electablog
Electronic Urban Report
Hot Dish Politics
Jezebel
The Jane Dough
Jobsanger
Lawyers, Guns and

Money
Left in Alabama
Liberal Values
Malia Litman's Blog
Michael-In-Norfolk
Michiganliberal.com
MN Progressive Project
mnpACT!
The Nation's Blogs
The Notion
Off the Kuff
Ohio Daily Blog
Pensito Review
Plunderbund.com
The Progressive
Professor
ReidBlog
Rep. Gwendolynne
    Moore
Rhode Island's Future
Rhymes With Right
The Richmond Democrat
The Richmonder
Scholars and Rogues
Show Me Progress
The Sin City Siren
Tapped
Taylor Marsh
The Texas Independent
They Gave Us A
    Republic
Uppity Wisconsin
Wonkette

Conservative (45 blogs)

Atlas Shrugs
Bearing Drift
Betsy's Page
BizzyBlog
Blogs for Victory
California Yankee
Capital Eye Blog
CaptainKudzu
Cato@Liberty
A Chequer-Board of
    Nights & Days
Colorado Peak Politics
ColoradoPols.com
Connecticut
    Commentary
Conservative Hideout
Conservatively Speaking
ConWebBlog
Creating Orwellian
    Worldview
Crowley Political
    Report
Dakota Voice
Don Surber
Ed Driscoll.com
GayPatriot
Getting Upset
The Jawa Report
The Lid
The Lonely
    Conservative
Maggie's Notebook
The Marc Chamot
Report News and
    Opinions
Massachusetts
    Conservative
    Feminist
Montana Watchdog
Newsbusters.org
Political Realities
Prairie Pundit
Protein Wisdom
Publius Forum

Rep. Cathy McMorris
Rodgers
Right Wing News
Rush Limbaugh Report
Sense on Cents
Spin Control
Tea Party at Perrysburg
Tony Phyrillas
Weapons of Mass
Discussion
Western Front America
Wigderson Library &
Pub

<u>Neutral (38 blogs)</u>
2 Political Junkies
The Agonist
Attytood
Blisstree
Blogcritics.org
Blue Mass Group
Bookworm Room
Broward Politics
The Business Insider
Capitol Commentary
CBS News
Daily Pundit
Dr. Roy's Thoughts
The Grindstone
Huckleberries Online
Jeremy Scahill
Lexington's Notebook
Liberty's Lifeline

Mediate
The Moderate Voice
Naked Capitalism
NH Insider
Opinion L.A.
Parents
The Periscope Post
Phoenix Network
Planet Moron
The Reality-Based
Community
Ruminations
Say Anything
The Shad Plank
Talking Points Memo
Texas on the Potomac
The Turner Report
Toonari Post
Trail Blazers Blog
US Daily Review
Watch Blog

<u>Could Not Be Determined</u>
<u>(8 blogs)</u>
CT Politics 2011
Fired Up! Missouri
The Florida Independent
Juice
Just Politics
The Politics Blog
Politics Daily
Postcard

References

Atlas, S. W. (2012, November 2). The Republican's "war on women" is a fiction of the liberal media elite. *Forbes*. Retrieved from http://www.forbes.com/sites/scottatlas/2012/11/02/the-republicans-war-on-women-is-a-fiction-of-the-liberal-media-elite/

Bassett, L. (2012, October 19). Paul Ryan mocks "war on women" at private fundraiser. *Huffington Post*. Retrieved from http://www.huffingtonpost.com/2012/10/19/paul-ryan-war-on-women-private-fundraiser_n_1987290.html

Baum, M.A., & Groeling, T. (2008). New media and the polarization of American political discourse. *Political Communication, 25*, 345–365.

Bedard, P. (2011, May 26). New DNC boss calls GOP anti-women. *U.S. News and World Report*. Retrieved from http://www.usnews.com/news/blogs/washington-whispers/2011/05/26/new-dnc-boss-calls-gop-anti-women

Bode, L., & Hennings, V. (2012). Mixed signals? Gender and the media's coverage of the 2008 vice presidential candidates. *Politics & Policy, 40*, 221–257.

Boxer, B. (2012, April 15). Foul play: War on women is real. *Politico*. Retrieved from http://www.politico.com/news/stories/0412/75143.html

Cable news ratings 2012: Top 30 programs of the year (2012, December 14). *Huff Post Media*. Retrieved from http://www.huffingtonpost.com/2012/12/14/cable-news-ratings-2012_n_2300780.html

Carroll, S. J. (2010). Voting choices: The politics of the gender gap. In S. J. Carroll & R. L. Fox (Eds.), *Gender and elections: Shaping the future of American politics* (2nd ed.)(pp. 117–143). New York, NY: Cambridge University Press.

Cary, M. K. (2102, August 29). Five myths about the so-called "Republican war on women." *U.S. News and World Report*. Retrieved from http://www.usnews.com/opinion/articles/2012/08/29/five-myths-about-the-so-called-republican-war-on-women

Corn, M. (Producer). (2012, April 10). *World news with Diane Sawyer* [Television broadcast]. New York, NY: American Broadcasting Company. Retrieved from LexisNexis database.

Druckman, J. N. (2005). Media matter: How newspapers and television news cover campaigns and influence voters. *Political Communication, 22*, 463–481.

Ferguson, M. (2013). "Women are not an interest group": The issue of women's issues in the 2012 presidential campaign. *Theory & Event, 16(1)*. Retrieved from http://muse.jhu.edu/journals/theory_and_event/v016/16.1.ferguson.html

Finlay, B. (2006). *George W. Bush and the war on women: Turning back the clock on progress.* New York, NY: Palgrave Macmillan.

Flanders, L. (Ed.) (2004). *The W effect: Bush's war on women.* New York, NY: Feminist Press.

Goldberg. J. (2012, November 5). Why are elections so scary? *USA Today*. Retrieved from http://www.usatoday.com/story/opinion/2012/11/05/presidential-election-romney-obama-voting/1684277/

Goldberg, M. (2012, November 9). The war on women backfires. *The Daily Beast*. Retrieved from http://www.thedailybeast.com/newsweek/2012/11/11/gop-s-war-on-women-backfires.html

Gray, K. J. (2011, January 2). The coming war on women. *Daily Kos*. Retrieved from http://rhrealitycheck.org/article/2011/01/03/coming-women/

Greenlee, J. S. (2010). Soccer moms, hockey moms and the question of "transformative" motherhood. *Politics & Gender, 6*, 405–431.

Guskin, E., Jurkowitz, M., & Mitchell, M. (2013). Network news: A year of change and challenge at NBC. *The State of the News Media in 2013: An Annual Report on American Journalism*. Retrieved from http://stateofthemedia.org/2013/network-news-a-year-of-change-and-challenge-at-nbc/#evening-news-audiences

Jensen, K. (2012, April 5). Priebus says gender battle fictional as caterpillar war. *Bloomberg*. Retrieved from http://www.bloomberg.com/news/2012-04-05/priebus-says-gender-battle-as-fictonal-as-caterpillar-war.html

Kohn, S. (2012, August 24). GOP: The anti-women warriors. *Salon*. Retrieved from http://www.salon.com/2012/08/24/mitt_romney_the_anti_woman_warrior/

Kristof, N. (2012, November 4). How Romney would treat women. *The New York Times*. Retrieved from http://www.nytimes.com/2012/11/04/opinion/sunday/kristof-how-romney-would-treat-women.html? R=0

Levendusky, M. S. (2013). Why do partisan media polarize viewers? *American Journal of Political Science, 57*, 1–13.

LexisNexis. (2013a). Blogs. Retrieved from http://wiki.lexisnexis.com/academic/index.php?title=Blogs

LexisNexis. (2013b). LexisNexis Academic. Retrieved from http://www.lexisnexis.com/en-us/products/lexisnexis-academic.page

Lowe, W. (2006, September). *Yoshikoder: An open source multilingual content analysis tool for social scientists*. Paper presented at the annual meeting of the American Political Science Association, Philadelphia, PA.

Lulolfs, N. (2013, April 30). The top 25 newspapers for March 2013. Retrieved from the Alliance for Audited Media website: http://www.auditedmedia.com/news/blog/top-25-us-newspapers-for-march-2013.aspx

Melich, T. (1996). *The Republican war against women: An insider's report from behind the lines.* New York, NY: Bantam Books.

Neuendorf, K. A. (2002). *The content analysis handbook.* Thousand Oaks, CA: SAGE Publications.

Neuendorf, K. A. (2011). Content analysis: A methodological primer for gender research. *Sex Roles, 64*, 276–289.

Newstex. (2013). About Newstex. Retrieved from http://newstex.com/about/

Parker, K. (2012, October 9). What women voters want. *The Washington Post*. Retrieved from http://articles.washingtonpost.com/2012-10-09/opinions/35498754_1_women-voters-women-split-women-care

Rohrbeck, D. (Producer). (2012, October 17). *Special report with Bret Baier* [Television broadcast]. Washington, DC: FOX News Channel. Retrieved from LexisNexis database.

Riffe, D., Lacy, S., & Fico, F. G. (2005). *Analyzing media messages: Using quantitative content analysis in research* (2nd ed.). Mahwah, NJ: Lawrence Erlbaum Associates Inc.

The campaign against women. (2012, May 19). *The New York Times*, p. SR10.

Thornton, M. (2012, October 17). Women who worked with Romney campaign for him. *Maggie's Notebook*. Retrieved from http://www.maggiesnotebook.com/

Turner, N. (2012, April 19). Vicious, heartless, and unconscionable. *Ohio Daily Blog*. Retrieved from http://www.ohiodailyblog.com/

Wallsten, K. (2008). Political blogs: Transmission belts, soapboxes, mobilizers, or conversation starters? *Journal of Information Technology & Politics, 4*, 19–40.

Weigel, D. (2012, April 12). The "war on women" is over. *Slate*. Retrieved from http://www.slate.com/articles/news_and_politics/politics/2012/04/hilary_rosen_ann_romney_the_birth_adolescence_and_death_of_the_democrats_war_on_women_talking_point_.html

Weigel, D. (2013, August 2). There will always be a "war on women." *Slate*. Retrieved from http://www.slate.com/blogs/weigel/2013/08/02/there_will_always_be_a_war_on_women.html

Notes

1. We thank Hallie Golay and Morgan Todd of the Carrie Chapman Catt Center for Women and Politics at Iowa State University for their assistance in collecting and organizing our media coverage samples.

2. As of March 21, 2012, the total average circulation, print and digital, of these newspapers was as follows: *USA* Today, 1,817,446 (2nd largest total average circulation), *The New York Times*, 1,586,757 (3rd largest total average circulation), and *The Washington* Post, 507,615 (7th largest total average circulation) (Lulolfs, 2013).

3. We selected these programs based on three criteria: time slot, network, and viewership. Each program airs during an evening news slot, between the hours of 5 and 7 p.m. We included an equal number of shows from broadcast and cable television, representing six different networks. Each show is aired to a national audience and is the top-rated evening news program on each of the six network sources represented in our sample. The average numbers of viewers for the three broadcast news programs are: *NBC Nightly News with Brian Williams*, 8.50 million; *ABC World News with Diane Sawyer*, 7.50 million; and *CBS Evening News with Scott Pelley*, 6.14 million average (Guskin, Jurkowitz, & Mitchell, 2013). The average numbers of viewers for the three cable news show are: *Special Report with Bret Baier* (FOX), 1.95 million; *Hardball with Chris Matthews* (MSNBC), 861,000; and *The Situation Room* (CNN), 547,000 ("Cable News Ratings 2012," 2012). This selection also accounts for differences in partisan and ideological perspectives associated with certain television networks, particularly MSNBC and FOX.

4. The LexisNexis Academic database provides the content of more than 3,000 blogs as gathered through a content archival service known as Newstex LLC (LexisNexis, 2013a). Newstex collects content from a variety of media sources, including blog postings from corporate and independent bloggers (Newstex, 2013).

5. During the time period considered (311 days), the LexisNexis Academic database included the following number of transcripts for the six shows: 220 transcripts of *ABC World News with Diane Sawyer*, 219 transcripts of *NBC Nightly News with Brian Williams*,

219 transcripts of *CBS Evening News with Scott Pelley*, 222 transcripts of *Special Report with Bret Baier* (FOX), 216 transcripts of *Hardball with Chris Matthews* (MSNBC), and 220 transcripts of *The Situation Room* (CNN). Each transcript included the content of a single evening's worth of programming; these numbers account for separate and distinct broadcasts of each show.

6. According to LexisNexis, the "'Newstex Government and Politics Blogs' source includes all of the syndicated Newstex blogs that are political in nature" (2013a).

7. The words included in our final dictionary were coded using a wildcard search so as to include singular and plural versions of the word.

8. As a formula, the risk ratio (RR) can be stated as:

$$RR = p_1 / p_2 \quad \text{where}$$

p_1 = number of category terms in first sample/number of total words in first sample and

p_2 = number of category terms in second sample/number of total words in second sample

9. To generate a 95% confidence interval, we first calculate

$$\text{Ln(RR)} \pm 1.96 \sqrt{\frac{(n_1 - x_1)/x_1}{n_1} + \frac{(n_2 - x_2)/x_2}{n_2}}$$

and then take the antilog (exp) of the lower and upper limits. When the 95% confidence interval does not include the null value (RR = 1), the result is statistically significant.

CHAPTER NINE

Are Latinos Citizens?

Labels, Race, and Politics in News Coverage of Immigration Reform

SHARON E. JARVIS AND CLARIZA RUIZ DE CASTILLA

On April 23, 2010, Arizona Gov. Jan Brewer signed SB 1070 ("Support Our Law Enforcement and Safe Neighborhoods Act") into law. This piece of legislation, which was modified a week later (by Arizona House Bill 2162), represented the "broadest and strictest anti-illegal immigration measure in the United States in decades" (Archibold, 2010, p. A1). The law was written to require: illegal aliens to register with the U.S. government and to carry registration documents at all times; law enforcement officials to enforce strict immigration laws; and citizens of Arizona to curb practices of sheltering, hiring, and transporting illegal aliens.

Early reactions to the legislation were mixed. On one hand, it was applauded for taking the issue of immigration seriously—there had been more illegal crossings of the United States–Mexico border in Arizona than in any other state—(Spagat, 2010), supported in national opinion polls by 50% to 70% of American citizens (Wood, 2010), and praised by some Republican figures who questioned the lack of national attention to immigration (although it was also questioned by some Republican leaders for alienating Latino citizens). On the other hand, it was critiqued for encouraging racial profiling (Cooper, 2010); protested by tens of thousands of individuals in cities such as Phoenix, Los Angeles, Dallas, and Chicago (Thompson, 2010); opposed by up to 70% of Latinos in polls of that ethnic group (Holub, 2010); and lambasted by U.S. President Barack Obama for being "misguided" and by Mexico's President Felipe Calderon as a "violation of human rights" (Montopoli, 2010).

To date, however, the conversation surrounding the legislation has yet to be examined for how the news media helped individuals make sense of it. We believe that such a study is critical for at least three key reasons:

1. Theoretically, individuals are far more likely to encounter the talk surrounding political events than actual political events themselves (Edelman, 1964; Williams, 1976). An analysis of the language surrounding the Arizona immigration law will inform how news outlets encouraged individuals to make sense of the issue of immigration, the concept of citizenship, the stakes in Arizona, and how such matters might influence public life.
2. Politically, there were dramatically different reactions to this reform effort based on race and location. An analysis of the coverage of the legislation—appearing in both English and Spanish language news media—may help shed light on the differences in support for this law across racial groups and across more liberal and more conservative communities.
3. Practically, political labels play a subtle, but powerful, role in shaping the political landscape. The key terms that get repeated regularly become the "language habits of a group" that "unconsciously" build up understandings of public life (Whorf, 1956, p. 134; see also Fromkin & Rodman, 1974; Kress & Hodge, 1981). Labels that appear in media coverage of politics, in particular, can provide cues to audiences regarding what types of ideas and actors are important or insignificant, sensible or untrustworthy, and agreeable or objectionable (Jarvis, 2005).

This chapter tracks the political labels English and Spanish language journalists used in coverage of SB 1070. The goals are to monitor how readers were invited to imagine the opportunities for and potential barriers to citizenship in this 2010 case and to consider how the conversation surrounding this legislation may have set the stage for discussions of immigration in the 2012 presidential campaign. Accordingly, this chapter is guided by two research questions: What labels did English and Spanish language news use to refer to Latinos in coverage of SB 1070? How were the labels in English and Spanish language news connected to issues of immigration, citizenship, and American politics? We begin with a review of the literature on the use of political labels, particularly for Latinos, and news coverage of the issue of immigration.

Political Labels

Researchers from a variety of disciplines have pointed to the power of naming and the impact of labels for general-market audiences. Schudson (1986), for example, has argued that "little is more important than naming, marking, and reminding" (p. xxi). In his mind, individuals learn culture by observing how things are named, and people learn the importance of things given how often they are reminded to think about them. Because attention is a "scarce resources that culture organizes and directs," prominent and visible names "become backed with the authority of a society" and can focus a public's attention on one given direction as opposed to another (p. xxi). For these reasons, Schudson has urged scholars to pay special attention to the names and labels that become so customary that they escape notice, so normalized that they appear benign, and so common that they do not call attention to themselves. Even though "most of the names an adult encounters in a normal day are familiar … this does not make them unimportant," he has insisted, because their very repetition makes them "actionable" (p. xxii).

Jamieson (1993) also has observed the power of names, illustrating how naming processes can lead to political outcomes. In her analysis of the 1988 presidential campaign, she detailed how former President George H. W. Bush's team was able to rename a criminal (from "William Horton" to "Willie Horton"), to label his actions (from rape and murder to "torture" and "terrorize"), to define a policy (a furlough program became "weekend passes" and a "revolving door"), and to entice the media to include such phrasings in their news reports. The Bush campaign's proactivity in these rhetorical matters shifted the ways in which Americans came to know an issue (the furlough program), and the Bush team's discipline in sticking to this language increased the likelihood that citizens heard these terms again and again.

In his work on poverty, Edelman (1977) has shown how labels can aid or prevent the creation of public policy by giving choices to politicians and the public. Specifically, he has discussed how when a phrase such as "the deserving poor" is introduced into a policy debate, new choices emerge. Should the government help the "deserving" poor? What should be done with the "undeserving" poor (a rhetorical byproduct of the deserving poor)? Do both groups deserve help? The very creation of a label for the deserving poor, Edelman has concluded, encourages government to do nothing for millions of poor people (after verbally categorizing them as undeserving), and impoverished citizens to regard other poor people as "undeserving" (siding with governmental elites rather than identifying with those who share their economic condition). For him (1977), political labels are "not simply an instrument for describing events but become a part of events, shaping their meaning and helping to shape the political roles officials and the general public play" (p. 4).

Political Labels and Latinos

Scholars also have observed how labels connected to minority groups appear in political discourses. Their work has come from at least three perspectives. Some have looked at labels in political texts to learn more about cultural forces and representational histories. Flores (2003), for instance, has observed that "contemporary images of immigrants, such as that of the illegal alien, do not emerge in a vacuum" (p. 363). Instead, she has noted, "they are part of our nation's history of immigration, race, and nation; they bring with them varied meanings reflecting their origins and uses" (p. 363). To understand them fully in the present, she has concluded, people must consider how they have been deployed in a variety of contexts and political moments.

Others have focused on how label use influences policy discussions (Hadley, 1965; Hardy, 2003; Ono & Sloop, 2002). Ono and Sloop (2002), for example, have argued that labels in "contemporary mainstream media … provide a specific locale, a space, where social issues collide, where political issues are struggled over, and subject positions … are constituted" (p. 2). Accordingly, how Latinos are discussed can influence how people think about borders, conceive of power relations, and understand immigration policy (p. 5).

Still others have located how the labels and symbols connected to Latinos are often portrayed negatively (Brader, Valentino, & Suhay, 2008; Hopkins, 2010; Santa Ana, 1999; Simon & Lynch, 1999). Pande's (2006) work has shown how news coverage was twice as likely to stress the costs of immigration as the benefits between 1995 and 2005. Streitmatter's (1999) analyses have revealed how immigrants have been treated as a "problem" and a "disease" in coverage, as journalists have constructed them as immoral and troublesome (p. 675). These researchers have asserted that the heavy emphasis on the negative aspects of immigration (Hopkins, 2010) as well as the unflattering metaphors connected to immigrants of Latino origin (Santa Ana, 1999) merits continued attention as it may facilitate and enable anti-immigration (and anti-immigrant) sentiment in the United States.

News Coverage of Immigration

Related scholarly works help to create a set of expectations for how labels would be treated in news coverage of SB 1070 (Hofstetter & Loveman, 1982; Miller, 1994). Perhaps most important, prior studies on news coverage of immigration issues have shown that since the 1980s, immigration has been primarily constructed as a U.S.-Mexican phenomenon. On one hand, this focus makes sense, for as Cornelius (2009) has observed, Mexico was the single-most important source country for immigrants entering the United States, both legally and illegally, during the 1980s and 1990s. On the other hand, however, it offers a myopic focus, for, as Cornelius has argued, "the proportion of Mexicans arise to slightly more than a quarter of all immigrants—far less than the Irish-dominated U.S. immigration in the mid-nineteenth century" (p. 177). Thus, the emphasis on immigration as a U.S.-Mexican issue may address the present, but not with sensitivity to the waves of the past.

Immigration has also been represented as involving primarily one gender: men. Chavez's (2001) study tracking the visual images connected to immigration on magazine covers of more than a 40-year period offers intriguing statistics on this score. This study found that males accounted for almost 80% of the photographs on magazine covers since 1965 (for a total of 225 of 284 images) and accounted for 73% of the illustrations on such covers. For Chavez, two key conclusions emerged from these statistics: immigration is identified as an issue involving men and immigration images emphasized the threats of non-native men coming to the United States.

Scholars have investigated how the often threatening emphasis on Mexico, Mexicans, and Mexican men in coverage of immigration has shaped attitudes. Some works suggest that proximity to the U.S.-Mexico border and greater familiarity with Mexican-Americans have dampened the effects of threatening and negative portrayals in the news. Survey data has shown that individuals who live near high concentrations of Mexican immigrants have better impressions of this group and are less likely than their counterparts in low concentration areas to fear that these individuals are trying to take away their jobs (Pew Research Hispanic Trends Project, 2006). Moreover, people who live near higher concentrations of Latinos were considerably more likely to agree that Latinos strengthened the United States through hard work and talent (47%) than individuals living in low concentration areas (27%, Pew Research Hispanic Trends Project, 2006).

Other studies have emphasized, however, that despite where they live, Americans are poorly informed about immigration, often uncertain about it, and easily influenced by mediated images (Brader, Valentino, & Suhay, 2008). One set of studies has focused on how news reports highlighting outgroup cues of immigrants, often immigrant men, can trigger anxiety in audiences. Such findings have led Brader, Valentino, and Suhay (2008) to worry that these mediated outgroup cues may lead to distortions in public opinion about immigration as well as "provide incentives, or justifications, for officials to enact biased or overreaching public policies" (p. 963). Espenshade (1997), too, has observed how the concentrated emphasis on Mexicans in press coverage has led to some hotbeds of anti-immigrant activism—even in places where individuals have lived experience with Mexican-Americans. This research has uncovered how southern California saw greater conflicts in the early 1990s in response to emphases on Mexican immigration in the news than some other states (a key comparison state being New Jersey—home to a diverse immigrant population, broader waves of immigrant populations from earlier eras, and a place where there is no single numerically dominant minority group).

Less is known about how Spanish language newspapers in the United States address issues of immigration. The lack of research here merits inquiry, for Latinos are more likely than other ethnic minority groups to trust coverage appearing in their native-tongue outlets ("Ethnic Media Overview," 2004). Although a few studies have compared how political messages appear in Spanish and English language media, there are more questions than answers about how Spanish language journalists approach political issues and conceive of the political appetites of their audiences (Jarvis & Connaughton, 2005).

Inspired by the influence of labels in political life, this chapter examines how English and Spanish language newspapers used them in their coverage of the Arizona legislation. Our goal is to study coverage of SB 1070 to see how journalists encourage readers to imagine the issues of immigration and citizenship as they relate to political life.

Method

To learn more about these concerns, texts were collected from six news sources: two from Phoenix, Arizona (*Arizona Republic* and *Prensa Hispana*), two from Los Angeles, California (*Los Angeles Times* and *La Opinion*), and two from Miami, Florida (*Miami Herald* and *Diario Las Americas*). This sample was drawn to study the key papers in Arizona as well as widely researched papers in Los Angeles and Miami that add a bit of political perspective—as the English speaking and Latino populations in Los Angeles have been known to lean to the left, often supporting Democratic candidates, and the English speaking and Latino populations in Miami, which have been known to lean to the right, often supporting Republican candidates (see Espino, Leal, & Meier, 2007).

All issues of these six newspapers were searched for articles addressing immigration and the SB 1070 reform efforts in Arizona from December 1, 2009, to May 15, 2010. This search yielded 759 articles (n = 464,143 words). Specifically, the study included 184 articles from *Arizona Republic* (n = 140,892 words), 125 articles from

Prensa Hispana (*n* = 42,159 words), 125 articles from *Los Angeles Times* (*n* = 94, 278 words), 212 articles from *La Opinion* (*n* = 124,104 words), 63 articles from *Miami Herald* (*n* = 37,157 words), and 50 articles from *Diario Las Americas* (*n* = 25,553 words).

After digitized versions of these articles were collected, they were submitted to the Concordance e-management software where wordlists were created both for English and Spanish language articles. These wordlists were studied to search for the most commonly appearing terms used to refer to Latinos, immigration, citizenship, and political life based on the premise that the frequency of label use can have a considerable impact on "perceiving, organizing, and interpreting" and on "drawing inferences" from news coverage (Pan & Kosicki, 1993).

After the wordlists were created, a close textual analysis was conducted on the data—both to interpret the appearance of the word counts in context and to compare and contrast themes across the English and Spanish language texts. This dual method of searching for quantitative frequency and close textual analysis has been employed in related projects to capture and interpret patterns in English and Spanish texts (see Subervi-Vélez, Brindel, Taylor, & Espinosa, 2008). It also allows researchers to uncover the presence and absence of rhetorical patterns surrounding political labels (Hart, Jarvis, Jennings, & Smith-Howell, 2005). The second author translated all Spanish news texts; and all Spanish spellings, accents, and translations were double-checked by an additional bilingual editor. The paragraphs below present key findings, featuring both word count data as well as qualitative examples that unpack the nuances of the quantitative patterns.

Results

Quantitative Patterns in English and Spanish Language Coverage

Our first research question inquired into the types of labels used to refer to Latinos in coverage of SB 1070. Table 1 presents raw data as well as density ratio data[1] to enable comparisons across the newspapers. If one looks at the overall quantitative patterns, it appears that English language journalists deployed a higher concentration of most labels than did Spanish language journalists.[2]

Focusing in on the specific labels, themselves, the table illustrates both similarities and differences across the languages. Table 1 is organized to display the most commonly occurring terms across the English-speaking papers (see the ratio data in the total column). That column reveals that the most commonly appearing terms in English were "immigration" (.77), "illegal" (.47), "immigrant(s)" (.46), "Mexican(s)" (.20), "citizen(s)" (.13), "Latino(a)(os)(as)" (.11), and "alien(s)" (.02).

Table 1. Most Commonly Appearing Labels in Coverage

	LA Times n (%)	*La Opin.* n (%)	*Miami Her.* n (%)	*D.L. Amer.* n (%)	*Ariz. Rep.* n (%)	*Pren. Hisp.* n (%)	Total n (%)
Immigration/	732 (.78)		332 (.89)		1,040 (.74)		2,104 (.77)
Inmigración		345 (.28)		106 (.41)		90 (.21)	541 (.28)
Illegal(s)(ity)(ly)/	475 (.50)		135 (.36)		685 (.49)		1,295 (.47)
Ilegal(es)(idad)(mente)		112 (.09)		74 (.29)		47 (.11)	233 (.12)
Immigrant(s)/	530 (.56)		240 (.65)		484 (.35)		1,254 (.46)
Inmigrante(s)		410 (.33)		143 (.56)		121 (.29)	674 (.35)
Mexican(s)/	126 (.13)		32 (.09)				558 (.20)
Mexicano(a)(os)(as)		126 (.10)		19 (.07)	400 (.28)	68 (.16)	213 (.11)
Citizen(s)(ship)/	103 (.11)		62 (.17)		198 (.14)		363 (.13)
Ciudadano(s)(ia)		105 (.08)		35 (.14)		25 (.06)	165 (.09)
Latino(a)(os)(as)/	198 (.21)		26 (.07)		66 (.05)		290 (.11)
Latino(a)(os)(as)		106 (.09)		8 (.03)		37 (.08)	151 (.08)
Alien(s)/	13 (.01)		4 (.01)		36 (.03)		53 (.02)
Extranjero(a)(os)		23 (.02)		14 (.05)		4 (.01)	41 (.02)

Note. n = the number of labels appearing in each newspaper. % = the number of labels divided by the total number of words in each newspaper multiplied by 100.

The most commonly appearing terms in Spanish ranked differently for the top three labels—"inmigrant(es)" (.35), "inmigración" (.28), and "illegal(es)" (.12)—but the next four terms follow the English language rankings exactly: "Mexicano(a)(os)(as)" (.11), "(con)ciudadanos" (.09), "Latino(a)(os)(as)" (.08), and "extranjero(as)" (.02).

Although the differences in the top three terms across the languages might initially appear subtle, they contribute to Edelman's (1964, 1977) contention that label use can aid or prevent the creation of public policy by giving choices to politicians and the public. Indeed, English language journalists were more likely to deploy the terms "immigration" (.77) and "illegal" (.47) than were the Spanish language journalists ["inmigración" (.28), "illegal(es)" (.12)]. In contrast, the Spanish language journalists were more likely to use the term "inmigrant(es)" (.35) than "inmigración" (.28). As we read examples of these labels, we saw that the terms "illegal" and "immigration" were regularly paired in English, suggesting that SB 1070 was drafted in response to a troubling situation imposed on the United States by actors who do not respect American laws. In contrast, the relative presence of the term "inmigrant(es)" and less frequent use of "illegal(es)" and "inmigración" in Spanish led to portrayals that put a face on the targets of the legislation and that were less alarmist in tone. As shown by the following section, these patterns contributed powerfully to how audiences were invited to think about the politics surrounding this legislation.

Qualitative Patterns in English and Spanish Language Coverage

Our second research question asked how the labels in English and Spanish coverage connected to issues of citizenship and political life. To learn more about such matters, we consulted our wordlist data to spot other frequently occurring labels. Table 2 displays how the detachment in English coverage and personalization in Spanish coverage led to a set of thematic differences in how SB 1070 was portrayed across the languages. Namely, English coverage treated SB 1070 as an inconvenient problem, imposed by criminals, that incited political conflicts, and that invited sympathy for law enforcement officials. In contrast, the Spanish language coverage depicted SB 1070 as an instance in which individuals were targeted, the instigators were identified, and an imbalance in power was inevitable.

Themes in English language coverage.

An opening theme that emerged from our close reading of the English language texts addresses how SB 1070 was depicted as a response to an inconvenient problem that was imposed by criminals. As Table 2 shows, the terms "law(s)" (.70),

Table 2. Other Key Labels Appearing in Coverage

	LA Times n (%)	La Opin. n (%)	Miami Her. n (%)	D.L. Amer. n (%)	Ariz. Rep. n (%)	Pren. Hisp. n (%)	Total n (%)
Problem/Criminals							
Law(s)/	72 (.08)		230 (.62)		1,617 (1.15)		1,919 (.70)
Ley(es)		636 (.51)		97 (.38)		381 (.90)	1,114 (.58)
Crime(s)(*al*)(s)/	178 (.19)		47 (.13)		312 (.22)		537 (.20)
Crimen(nes)(ales)		69 (.06)		21 (.08)		(.16)	159 (.08)
Arrest(s)(ed)/	65 (.07)		26 (.07)		155 (.11)		246 (.09)
Arrestado(os)(estar)		32 (.03)		8 (.03)		10 (.02)	50 (.03)
Conflict/Instigators							
Republican(s)/	177 (.19)		58 (.16)		144 (.11)		379 (.14)
Republicano(s)		157 (.13)		89 (.35)		15 (.04)	261 (.14)
Democrat(s)/	73 (.08)		22 (.06)		85 (.06)		180 (.07)
Democrata(s)		98 (.07)		6 (.02)		6 (.01)	110 (.06)
Law Enforcement							
Police/Cop(s)/	220 (.23)		63 (.17)		344 (.24)		627 (.23)
Policia(s)(ales)(cial)		136 (.11)		30 (.12)		42 (.10)	208 (.11)
Power Imbalance							
Protest(or)(s)('s)/	34 (.04)		24 (.06)		125 (.09)		183 (.07)
Protesta(as)(antes)		68 (.05)		7 (.03)		45 (.11)	120 (.06)
(aron)(ar\ando)(ante)							
Activist(s)/	49 (.05)		29 (.08)		29 (.02)		107 (.04)
Activista(s)		115 (.09)		15 (.06)		28 (.07)	158 (.08)

Note. *n* = the number of labels appearing in each newspaper. % = the number of labels divided by the total number of words in each newspaper multiplied by 100.

"crime" (.20), and "arrest(s)(ed)" (.09) appeared more commonly in English than Spanish news. These pairings led to coverage informing readers of both the predicament and its propagators. Journalists informed audiences that "by 2005, central Arizona was seething over illegal immigration" (Riccardi, 2009, p. A1) and how many "Americans feel powerless before the many social changes wrought by Latin American immigration" (Tobar, 2010, p. A2). They also placed the blame on a set of actors, as evidenced in the following texts (emphasis added):

> Most *illegal immigrants* either entered the country illegally, or stayed after their visas expired. (González, 2010, p. B1)

> 'Right now, we have killers coming across the border as *illegal immigrants*,' she (an Arizona resident) said. (Rau, 2010, p. A8)

> But a report issued this month … which backs tighter *immigration* controls, said many of the *immigrants* who legalized their status under IRCA did so fraudulently. (Chardy, 2010a, p. 2C)

After setting a context that the legislation was a response to such concerns, many English language articles then addressed how SB 1070 incited political conflicts between political elites. There were several dimensions to this theme. In some cases, the tension was placed between Arizona legislators and the voters who might not return them to office if they did not pass SB 1070. For instance, as Roberts (2010) reported, "a whopping 84 percent of Republicans support SB 1070, according to the latest Rasmussen Poll of likely voters" (p. B1) and, as Douglas (2010) depicted, "failing to overhaul the nation's immigration system … could play a pivotal role in key mid-term elections" (p. A1). In other cases, the tension was located between Latinos/Latino advocates and the Republican Party. For example, Tan and Lee (2010) shared, "advocates for putting the roughly 11 million illegal residents on a path to citizenship will face resistance from many Republicans" (p. A1). Tensions were even witnessed inside the Republican Party. As Riccardi (2010a) informed, "Brewer's situation mirrors struggles of Republicans in other states who face challenges from a resurgent right wing of the party" (p. A10). And, as Nowicki (2010) reported, "some local Republicans believe he (Senator John McCain) has a long history of putting his personal political interests ahead of conservative principles" (p. A1).

While the portrayals of these political groups (e.g., voters, Latinos, Republicans) were largely balanced in English language coverage, one set of professionals did receive special treatment—law enforcement officials (see Table 2). Perhaps because the politicians were portrayed as too busy arguing with each other to solve the immigration problem, news narratives invited readers to identify with the "cops" and "police" (.23). Readers learned that these law enforcement professionals would, eventually, be empowered to step in and stop "crime," make "arrests," and be the ones to protect citizens from "illegal immigrants."

Law enforcement officials were praised collectively and individually. When they were addressed as a group, they were credited as being trusted, as in this column by Serrano and Linthicum (2010) that relayed how "some polls indicate that as many as 70% are in favor of giving local police the authority to check on someone's legal status in the United States" (p. A1). They were also depicted as being in touch with their communities and as having wise judgment, as in this article by Reinhard (2010), which described how "the law gives local police the power to question people suspected of being in the U.S. illegally" (p. A1). They were even described as welcoming the challenge, as in this piece by Esquivel (2010) that reported how "The Phoenix Law Enforcement Assn., a union that represents thousands of officers in the Phoenix Police Department, strongly endorsed the bill, saying it would address the crime of illegal immigration and allow police officers to do their work unimpeded by unnecessary restrictions" (p. A1).

Individualized praise often went to one of the more visible faces connected to immigration in Arizona: Maricopa County Sheriff Joe Arpaio. He was recognized as someone who had "long railed against the influx of illegal immigrants" (Serrano & Linthicum, 2010, p. A1) and was identified as being "wildly popular in Arizona" (Riccardi, 2010c, p. A1) because he got results. One article described how "Arpaio says his tactics have enabled his deputies to identify 6,000 illegal immigrants and refer them to federal immigration authorities. In the jails he runs, 32,000 others have been identified, usually after being arrested by another police department" (Riccardi, 2010b, p. A1). Another article revealed how "at a news conference, Arpaio said his deputies caught 26 illegal immigrants in a car being driven out of Phoenix and 10 other people on outstanding warrants or other violations" (Riccardi, 2010b, p. A5). Although not all statements on Arpaio were this positive (indeed, a few Democrats and Latino activists were quoted as questioning his efforts), the law enforcement community was given more praise and expertise in newspaper coverage than other groups.

Taken together, these English language articles encouraged audiences to believe that immigration was an inconvenient problem, imposed by criminals, that incited political conflicts and invited sympathy and respect for law enforcement professionals. Because the labels under investigation were placed in this type of storyline, the recommending force of the English language articles was that the only resolution would be to hand the unruly matter of illegal immigration over to the cops.

Themes in Spanish language coverage.

The labels in the Spanish language coverage were connected to another set of themes—almost all of which stemmed from a more balanced discussion of "inmigrant(es)"(.35) and "inmigración" (.28). To begin, this emphasis often humanized the individuals being targeted by SB 1070. In one article, these "inmigrant(es)" were people who could be counted:

> Del total de *inmigrantes* indocumentados, un 34% tiene entre 25 a 34 años de edad; un 27% entre 35 a 44 años y un 13% entre 18 y 24 años.

> [Of the total of undocumented *immigrants*, 34% are 25-to-34-years-old; 27% are 35-to-44-years-old and 13% are between 18-and-24-years-old. (Cádiz, 2010a, p. 1A)]

And, in another article, they were depicted as persons who had died while attempting to come to the United States:

> Miles de cruces son cargadas por *inmigrantes* en recordación de las muchas personas que han fallecido en su intento por cruzar la frontera.

> [Thousands of crosses are carried by *immigrants* in remembrance of the many people who have died in their attempt to cross the border. (Cádiz, 2010b, p. 1A)]

Statements like these led to a different type of tone. By offering richer details on the backgrounds and life experiences of immigrants, the Spanish language coverage put a face on the topic. Whereas most of the personalization in English coverage focused on the partisans fighting over SB 1070 (and the cops who would eventually have to take over), the Spanish language coverage reminded readers that legal (and illegal) immigrants were human beings with stories.

In addition, the targets of the legislation were depicted as being pursued by a set of forces. Notice how, in the examples below, they were sought out by the legislation itself, by citizen groups (e.g., the Minutemen), and by coyotes (i.e., individuals attempting to bring "inmigrant(es)" over the border illegally):

> La ley de Arizona, que aguarda la firma de la gobernadora Jan Brewer, criminaliza la presencia ilegal en el estado fronterizo y permite que la policia arreste a quienes sospeche que son *indocumentados*.

> [The law of Arizona, which awaits the signature of Gov. Jan Brewer, criminalizes illegal presence in the border state and allows the police to arrest those suspected of being *undocumented*. (Peña, 2010, p. 1A)]

El grupo [Cuerpo Civil Minuteman de Defensa], creado en abril de 2005, llegó a tener en sus filas a unos 12.000 miembros que se han turnado para detectar a *inmigrantes* indocumentados a lo largo de la frontera de EEUU con México y hacer que los detenga la Patrulla Fronteriza.

[The group (Minuteman Civil Defense Corps), created in April 2005, came to have in their ranks some 12,000 members who have taken turns to detect undocumented *immigrants* along the U.S. border with Mexico and make Border Patrol detain them. ("Disuelven a los Minuteman," 2009, p. 1A)]

La investigación continúa; los presuntos "coyotes" fueron encarcelados y los *inmigrantes* indocumentados están bajo la custodia de las autoridades.

[The investigation continues; the alleged "coyotes" were imprisoned and the undocumented *immigrants* are in the custody of the authorities. (Félix, 2010, p. 2C)]

As Table 2 shows, the second most frequently occurring label in Spanish coverage was "Republicano(s)." Both English and Spanish language newspapers gave more attention to "Republican(s)" (.14) and "Republicano(s)" (.14), than "Democrat(s)" (.07) and "Democrata(s)" (.06). As we read the coverage of these labels closely, we saw that while these political actors were largely in conflict with each other in English coverage, Spanish coverage identified "Republicano(s)" as the instigators of this reform effort and paid modest attention to the conflicts it may have created with "Democrata[s]" or even efforts "Democrata[s]" might have engaged in to oppose the legislation. Articles in Spanish emphasized how Republicano(s) had specific attitudes about "inmigrant(es)" and were even "antiinmigrantes":

El senador estatal republicano Russell Pearce dijo ... que en su opinión los *inmigrantes* indocumentados no tienen por qué gozar de los beneficios de este país. "Estas personas se aprovechan del sistema y dejan sin oportunidad a los que sí lo merecen y lo necesitan," dijo Pearce, quien aseguró que ... presentará una nueva propuesta que podría convertir en un delito estatal la sola presencia de un *inmigrante* indocumentado en Arizona.

[Republican State Senator Russell Pearce said ... that in his opinion undocumented immigrants should not enjoy the benefits of this country. "These people are taking advantage of the system and leave no opportunity for those who deserve it and need it," said Pearce, who assured that ... he will present a new proposal that could convert the mere presence of an undocumented immigrant in Arizona into a state crime. ("Hijos estadounidenses," 2009, p. 3A)]

Es posible que los republicanos pudieran enmendar algunas de las que ya presentaron y proponer más medidas *antiinmigrantes*.

[It is possible that Republicans could amend some of those already presented and propose more *anti-immigrant* measures. (Ortega, 2010, p. 1A)]

Even though the Spanish language coverage placed a tension between "Republicano(s)" and "inmigrantes," it did not forecast that this conflict would have implications for future electoral participation. Instead, the labels in Spanish suggested that this imbalance in power between Republican elites and the Latino public was inevitable. Some articles mentioned how groups might boycott Arizona ("boicotear a Arizona" see "Proponen en San Francisco," 2010). Others mentioned "protest(or)(s)('s)/protesta(as)" (.06) and "activist(s)/activista('s)" (.08), but—curiously—did not depict them as politically influential. Instead, the most vivid stories of protest focused on "los jóvenes activistas" (the young activists) and "hijos" (children). These articles were less likely to focus on if or how protests could hold elites accountable for their actions and more likely to address them as innocent and harmless acts or as activities parents could engage in with their children (Truax, 2010). In these ways, this coverage helped neutralize an appetite for political participation and naturalize the inescapable power of elected officials. Although the Spanish language articles put a richer face on the individuals affected by SB 1070, they did little to invite people to imagine meaningful political opposition to the law.

Conclusion

This chapter has examined the labels used to refer to Latinos, citizenship, and political life in English and Spanish language coverage of SB 1070. Because individuals are more likely to come to know politics through language than actual political events, the goal has been to monitor how readers have been invited to imagine the opportunities for—and potential barriers to—citizenship for this ethnic group. Primary findings reveal how English coverage treated SB 1070 as an inconvenient problem, imposed by criminals, that incited political conflicts, and invited sympathy for law enforcement officials. In contrast, the Spanish language coverage depicted SB 1070 as an instance in which individuals were targeted, the instigators were identified, and an imbalance in power between Republican elites and the Latino public was inevitable. The emphasis on immigration as a political showdown between elites in English language news might not surprise political communication scholars (Fallows, 1997). The relative personalization and lack of advocacy in the Spanish language news coverage, however, raises new questions about the role(s) of Spanish language journalists and opportunities for Latino news audiences to become politically aware in the United States.

To begin, prior works on English language news emphasize how journalists set political agendas, socialize audiences, and whet appetites for politics. Less attention has focused on such concerns in Spanish language news. Alexandre and Rehbinder (2008) contend that Spanish language reporters could play an important role in drawing out "politicians' positions and parties' platforms on issues like Latin America and immigration" (p. 175). Journalists can either push these issues—thereby holding political elites accountable for their positions and educating audiences on them—or fail to help Latinos think critically about their place in the political landscape. Our data invite greater attention to when journalists depoliticize topics and political moments as well as being open to times when they might offer more thorough or critical coverage than studied here.

These findings also raise questions for both general-market and Latino news audiences. If English language coverage of legislative efforts like SB 1070 continues to emphasize law and order language, and if Spanish language coverage continues to naturalize an imbalance in power between elites and non-elites, U.S. news audiences are denied an opportunity to consume news reports that invite them to think about Latino citizenship in rich and complex ways. News that is detached (e.g., in English) or that downplays how legislative efforts like SB 1070 could be challenged via political participation (e.g., in Spanish) does little to involve audiences in a vital political conversation—that of when, if, and how Latinos are considered citizens in the United States.

Moreover, these findings offer a few insights to the key theme of this book: "alieNATION" in campaign 2012. On the topic of voter turnout, the news was mixed for Latinos in that election. On one hand, they comprised a larger segment of the total electorate in 2012 than ever before (10% in 2012, compared to 9% in 2008, and 8% in 2004; see Lopez & Taylor, 2012). On the other hand, however, Latino turnout dropped to 48% in 2012 (from 49.9% in 2008) marking a slight decrease in participation for this group (Lopez & Gonzalez-Barrera, 2013). As for vote choice Latinos supported President Obama (71%) over Republican Mitt Romney (27%; see Lopez & Taylor, 2012). Their support for Romney was considerably lower than for other recent Republican candidates; indeed, George W. Bush received 44% of the Latino vote in 2004 and John McCain received 31% in 2008 (Rodriquez, 2012). Latino support for Romney in Arizona (25%) was also slightly lower than the national average (CNN, 2012).

Polls revealed that border concerns were not the defining issue for Latinos in campaign 2012. Instead, 60% of Latinos identified the economy as the most important issue facing the country—nearly identical to 59% of the general electorate who identified this same issue as their top concern (Lopez & Taylor, 2012). Yet, there is a sense in elite political circles that the tone that the major political parties took toward this ethnic group mattered. Pundits have commented on the perception in Latino communities that the Democratic Party cared more and was more respectful of Latinos as people than was the Republican Party (Foley, 2012). This sentiment was voiced by President Obama in October 2012 when he told Iowa reporters that—if re-elected—his administration would work on immigration reform, stating, "and since this is off the record, I will just be very blunt. Should I win a second term, a big reason ... is because the Republican nominee and the Republican Party have so alienated the fastest-growing demographic group in the country, the Latino community" (Yellin, 2012).

Naturally, there are limitations to all studies and this chapter is no exception. The findings advanced here come from a study of a set of labels appearing in four newspapers. Other projects examining other data might yield different results. It would be helpful, for instance, (1) to conduct studies of English and Spanish language television and radio coverage, (2) to pay attention to visual images appearing in English and Spanish language news, and (3) to interview Spanish language journalists and audiences to learn more about their instincts for and reactions to these types of coverage in order to complement the patterns described in this chapter. All such studies could enrich the data discussed here.

Ultimately, this chapter identifies a few previously stated, but understudied, notions. First, Chavez (2001, 2008) has argued that a "Latino threat" exists between Latinos and English speaking media whereby English language news paints an unnecessarily menacing picture of this ethnic group. The current findings encourage researchers to attend to the portrayals of Latinos in Spanish speaking news media to uncover if a reverse type of "power imbalance" appears there as well. The reluctance of these three Spanish language newspapers to cover SB 1070 in terms of political opportunities for Latinos encourages future investigation. Second, Subervi and colleagues (2008) and Connaughton and Jarvis (2004; Jarvis & Connaughton, 2005) have critiqued politicians and political parties for not reaching out to Latinos in campaign messages.

Although these admonishments may be well-intentioned, our data show a more pervasive and subtle pattern connected to missed opportunities for the political socialization of Latinos—political news coverage in Spanish language news. Latinos have been labeled the "sleeping giant" in American politics, a force that once woken could organize to change representation in several key battleground states.

Our data show that candidates, political parties, and English speaking news outlets may not be the only forces discouraging Latinos from thinking of themselves as political actors; Spanish language coverage, too, may dampen political appetites. These patterns encourage us to return to the question that starts this chapter: are Latinos citizens? Not according to a close reading of the labels in the English or Spanish news coverage we studied. At least not yet.

References

Alexandre, L., & Rehbinder, H. (2008). Watching the 2000 presidential campaign on *Univisión* and *Telemundo*. In F. A. Subervi-Vélez (Ed.), *The mass media and Latino/a politics* (pp. 154–177). New York, NY: Taylor and Francis.

Archibold, R. C. (2010, April 24). U.S.'s toughest immigration law is signed in Arizona. *The New York Times*, p. A1.

Brader, T., Valentino, N.A., Suhay, E. (2008). What triggers public opposition to immigration? Anxiety, group cues, and immigration threat. *American Journal of Political Science, 52(4)*, 959–978.

Cádiz, A. (2010a, February 10). Cae población de indocumentados [Undocumented population falls]. *La Opinión*, pp. A1, A8.

Cádiz, A. (2010b, March 22). Inmigrantes expresan urgencia por la reforma [Immigrants express urgency for reform]. *La Opinión*, pp. A1, A12.

Chardy, A. (2010a, January 12). Economic impact of legalization debated. *Miami Herald*, pp. C1, C2.

Chavez, L. (2001). *Covering immigration: Popular images and the politics of the nation*. Berkeley, CA: University of California Press.

CNN (2012, December 10). President: Arizona. *CNN.com*. Retrieved from http://www.cnn.com/election/2012/results/state/AZ/president

Connaughton, S. L., & Jarvis, S. E. (2004). Apolitical politics: GOP efforts to foster identification from Latinos, 1984–2000. *Communication Studies, 55(3)*, 464–481.

Contreras, H. (1976). *A theory of word order with special reference to Spanish*. New York, NY: North Holland Publishers.

Cooper, J. J. (April 26, 2010). Arizona immigration law target of protest. *MSNBC News*. Retrieved from http://www.msnbc.msn.com/id/36768649/

Cornelius, W. A. (2009/2002). Ambivalent reception: Mass public responses to the "new" Latino immigration to the United States. In M. M. Suárez-Orozco & M. M. Páez (Eds.), *Latinos: Remaking America*, (pp. 165–189). Berkeley, CA: University of California Press.

Disuelven a los Minuteman. [Minuteman are dissolved]. (2010, March 30). *Diario Las Américas*, pp. A1, A5.

Douglas, W. (2010, February 9). Immigration overhaul called a vital issue. *Miami Herald*, p. A1.

Edelman, M. (1964). *The symbolic uses of politics*. Urbana, IL: University of Illinois Press.

Edelman, M. (1977). *Political language*. New York, NY: Academic Press.

Espenshade, T. J. (1997). *Keys to successful immigration: Implications of the New Jersey experience*. Washington, DC: Urban Institute Press.

Espino, R., Leal, D. L., & Meier, K. J. (Eds). (2007). *Latino politics: Identity, mobilization, and representation*. Charlottesville, VA: University of Virginia Press.

Esquivel, P. (2010, May 24). Moving deeper into Arizona's shadows. *Los Angeles Times*, p. A1.

Ethnic media overview. (2004). The state of news media: An annual report on American journalism. Retrieved from http://www.stateofthenewsmedia.com/2004/ narrative_ethnic-alternative_ethnic.asp?media=9

Fallows, J. (1997). *Breaking the news: How the media undermines American democracy.* New York, NY: Vintage Books.

Félix, L. (2010, January 6). Desmantelan casa de seguridad en Phoenix [Dismantling the safehouse in Phoenix]. *Prensa Hispana*, p. 2C.

Flores, L. A. (2003). Constructing rhetorical borders: Peons, illegal aliens, and competing narratives of immigration. *Critical Studies in Media Communication, 40*(4), 362–387.

Fromkin, V., & Rodman, R. (1974). *An introduction to language.* New York, NY: Holt.

Foley, E. (2012, November 7). Latino voters in Election 2012 help sweep Obama to re-election. *Huffington Post*, Retrieved from http://www.huffingtonpost.com/2012/11/07/latino-voters-election-2012_n_2085922.html

González, D. (2010, February 21). Questions over drop in migrant population. *Arizona Republic*, pp. B1, B7.

Hadley, E. M. (1956). A critical analysis of the wetback problem. *Law and Contemporary Problems, 21*(2), 334–357.

Hardy, V. K. (2003). *Metaphoric myth in the representation of Hispanics* (Master's thesis). Retrieved from http//www.georgetown.edu/grad/cct/academics/theses/ValerieHardy.pdf

Hart, R. P., Jarvis, S. E., Jennings, W. P., & Smith-Howell, D. (2005). *Political keywords: Using language that uses us.* New York, NY: Oxford University Press.

"Hijos estadounidenses de indocumentados serán los más afectados por nueva ley" [American children of undocumented [immigrants] will be affected the most by new law]. (2009, December 4). *Diario Las Américas*, pp. A1, A3.

Hofstetter, C. R., & Loveman, B. (1982). Media exposure and attitude consistency about immigration. *Journalism Quarterly, 59*, 298–302.

Holub, H. (2010, May 9). Public support for SB 1070 drops. *Tucson Citizen*. Retrieved from http://tucsoncitizen.com/view-from-baja-arizona/2010/05/09/public-support-for-sb-drops/

Hopkins, D. J. (2010). Politicized places: Explaining where and when immigrants provoke local opposition. *American Political Science Review, 104*, 40–60.

Jamieson, K. H. (1993). The subversive effects of a focus on strategy in news coverage of campaigns. In K. H. Jamieson, K. Auletta & T. E. Patterson (Eds.), *1–800 president: The report of the Twentieth Century Fund Task Force on Television and the Campaign of 1992* (pp. 35–61). New York, NY: Twentieth Century Fund Press.

Jarvis, S. E. (2005). *Talk of the party: Political labels, symbolic capital & American life.* Lanham, MD: Rowman & Littlefield.

Jarvis, S. E., & Connaughton, S. L. (2005). Audiences *implicadas e ignoradas* in English and Spanish language questions in the 2002 Texas gubernatorial debates. *Howard Journal of Communications, 16*(2), 1–18.

Kress, G., & Hodge, R. (1981). *Language as ideology.* London, England: Routledge.

Lanson, J., & Stephens, M. (2007). *Writing and reporting the news*. New York, NY: Oxford University Press.

Lopez, M. H., & Gonzalez-Barrera, A. (2013, June 3). Inside the 2012 Latino electorate. *Pew Research Hispanic Trends Project*, Retrieved from http://www.pewhispanic.org/2013/06/03/inside-the-2012-latino-electorate/

Lopez, M. H., & Taylor, P. (2012, November 7). Latino voters in the 2012 election. *Pew Research Hispanic Trends Project*, Retrieved from http://www.pewhispanic.org/2012/11/07/latino-voters-in-the-2012-election/

Miller, J. J. (1994). The magazine *Charities* and the Italian immigrants, 1903–14. *Journalism Quarterly, 44*, 91–98.

Montopoli, B. (2010, April 27). Obama again hits Arizona immigration bill. *CBSNews.com*, Retrieved from http://www.cbsnews.com/8301-503544_162-20003600-503544.html

Nowicki, D. (2010, January 6). Migrant issue could haunt McCain in race. *Arizona Republic*, p. A1.

Ono, K. A., & Sloop, J. M. (2002). *Shifting borders: Rhetoric, immigration, and California's Proposition 187*. Philadelphia, PA: Temple University Press.

Ortega, A. M. (2010, February 23). Caen planes antiinmigrantes [Anti-immigrant plans fail]. *La Opinión*, p. A1.

Pan, Z., & Kosicki, G. M. (1993). Framing analysis: An approach to news discourse. *Political Communication, 10*, 55–75.

Pande, K. (2006). *The effects of September 11, 2001 on media discourse and public opinion toward immigration*. Unpublished senior honors thesis, University of Michigan, Ann Arbor, MI.

Peña, M. (2010, April 21). McCain arriesga una derrota en las urnas [McCain risked defeat at the polls]. *Diario Las Américas*, pp. A1, A5.

Pew Research Hispanic Trends Project. (2006, March 30). *America's immigration quandary*. Retrieved from http://people-press.org/reports/pdf/274.pdf

"Proponen en San Francisco, California boicot a Arizona" [Proposed in San Francisco, California boycotts Arizona]. (2010, April 28). *Diario Las Américas*, p. B4.

Rau, A. B. (2010, March 20). Arizona may toughen laws on illegal immigration. *Arizona Republic*, pp. A1, A8.

Reinhard, B. (2010, May 14). Florida candidates back Arizona immigration law. *Miami Herald*, p. A1.

Riccardi, N. (2009, December 12). Crusading sheriff takes on his foes. *Los Angeles Times*, p. A1.

Riccardi, N. (2010a, April 21). Governor faces tough choices on Arizona's 2 toughest issues. *Los Angeles Times*, p. A10.

Riccardi, N. (2010b, April 30). First lawsuits are filed challenging Arizona's illegal-immigration law. *Los Angeles Times*, pp. A1, A5.

Riccardi, N. (2010c, May 1). Racial profiling a reality now? An Arizona sheriff's illegal-immigration 'sweeps' already target Latinos, critics say. *Los Angeles Times*, p. A1.

Roberts, L. (2010, April 24). Desperation leads Arizona to police state. *Arizona Republic*, p. B1.

Rodriguez, C. (2012, November 9). Latino vote key to Obama's re-election. *CNN.com*, Retrieved from http://www.cnn.com/2012/11/09/politics/latino-vote-key-election/index.html

Santa Ana, O. (1999). "Like an animal I was treated": Anti-immigrant metaphor in US public discourse. *Discourse & Society, 10,* 191–224.

Schudson, M. (1986). *Advertising: The uneasy persuasion.* New York, NY: Basic Books.

Serrano, R. A., & Linthicum, K. (2010, May 27). Arizona law faces federal challenges. *Los Angeles Times,* p. A1.

Simon, R., & Lynch, J. (1999). A comparative assessment of public opinion toward immigrants and immigration practices. *International Migration Review, 33,* 455–67.

Spagat, E. (2010, May 13). Other border states shun Arizona's immigration law. *MSNBC News.* Retrieved from http://www.msnbc.msn.com/id/37116159

Streitmatter, R. (1999). The nativist press: Demonizing the American immigrant. *Journalism & Mass Communication Quarterly, 76,* 673–683.

Subervi-Vélez, F. A., Brindel, M., Taylor, J., & Espinosa, R. (2008). Spanish-language daily newspapers and presidential elections. In F. A. Subervi-Vélez (Ed.), *The mass media and Latino politics* (pp. 87–130). New York, NY: Routledge.

Tan, C., & Lee, D. (2010, March 22). Huge border reform march. *Los Angeles Times,* p. A1.

Taylor, P. (2013, May 10). Politics and race: Looking ahead to 2060. *Pew Research Hispanic Trends Project.* Retrieved from http://www.pewresearch.org/fact-tank/2013/05/10/politics-and-race-looking-ahead-to-2060/

Thompson, K. (2010, April 30). Protesters of Arizona's new immigration law try to focus boycotts. *The Washington Post.* Retrieved from http://www.washingtonpost.com/wp-dyn/content/article/2010/04/30/ AR2010043001027.html

Tobar, H. (2010). Immigrants also frustrated. *Los Angeles Times,* p. A2.

Truax, E. (2010, March 14). Se refuerzan lazos migratorios [Migration ties are strengthened]. *La Opinión,* p. A3.

Whorf, B. (1956). *Language, thought, and reality.* New York, NY: Wiley.

Williams, R. (1976). *Keywords: A vocabulary of culture and society.* London, England: Fontana.

Wood, D. B. (2010, April 30). Opinion polls show broad support for tough Arizona immigration law. *The Christian Science Monitor.* Retrieved from http://www.csmonitor.com/USA/Society/2010/0430/Opinion-polls-show-broad-support-for-tough-Arizona-immigration-law

Yellin, J. (2012, October 24). Obama 'confident' about immigration reform in a second term. *CNN. com,* Retrieved from http://politicalticker.blogs.cnn.com/2012/10/24/obama-confident-about-immigration-reform-in-a-second-term/.

Notes

1. Density ratio data were calculated by dividing the number of appearances of a particular label by the total number of words in a sample of interest and multiplying this figure by 100. For example, the density ratio in the first column of Table 1 shows the number of appearances of the word immigration divided by the total number of words in our sample from the *Los Angeles Times* multiplied by 100. Because some newspapers offered more

words in their coverage than others (see the methods section), these density ratio data offer a stronger comparison of the proportions of label use in news across newspapers (as they account for the number of appearances of a label of interest divided by the total number of words per newspaper type).

2. This quantitative finding could be influenced by an emphasis in shorter sentences in English than Spanish language reporting as well as observations that Spanish language sentences can run longer than those in English, contributing to lower ratios of labels per sentence (see Contreras, 1976; Lanson & Stephens, 2007).

CHAPTER TEN

Debating Marriage Equality in the 2012 Elections

HAYLEY J. COLE AND MITCHELL S. MCKINNEY

In the last decade of the 20th century, the issue of same-sex marriage caught the attention of the United States Congress in what has become an ongoing battle between state and federal legislative and judicial purview. We might now look back at Hawaii as the state that sparked our national same-sex marriage debate, a social struggle that has only intensified and continues even today. Events in Hawaii instigated national and state legislative battles regarding the legality of same-sex marriage, and efforts in the "Aloha State" to grant marriage equality prompted the U. S. Congress to adopt the Defense of Marriage Act (DOMA) in 1996 (Library of Congress, 1996, p. 10101). In 1993, the Supreme Court of Hawaii ruled that Hawaii's marriage law limiting marriage to heterosexual couples was unconstitutional because it violated the state's equal rights amendment, which ensured that no one would be discriminated against on the basis of sex (Stevens, 2002, p. 7). This ruling held that limiting marriage to heterosexuals denied "same-gender couples equal protection rights in violation of article I, Section 5 of the Hawaii Constitution" (State of Hawaii, 1995, preface). Although Hawaii's Supreme Court was the "first court in the United States to recognize same-sex marriage" (W. S. Rogers, 2010), it was the passage of DOMA at the federal level that became the catalyst for a string of individual states to adopt their own restrictions on marriage equality. As J. Rogers (2010, p. 99) explains:

Proponents of same-sex marriage were forced to pursue marriage equality state by state. Likewise, opponents of same sex marriage focused their efforts, even more than they had prior to the passage of DOMA, on legislation and constitutional amendments at the state level.

The primary arguments offered in favor of DOMA at the time of its passage included the need to protect the federal government and its operations from what were viewed by some federal legislators as ill-advised decisions made by so-called "activist" courts, and particularly judicial bodies at the state level; fiscal arguments suggesting it would be more cost efficient in terms of federal programs (such as federal aid, social support programs and tax policies) to limit marriage only to heterosexual couples; and arguments based largely in religious terms that "traditional" heterosexual marriage is vital to the stability and perpetuation of culture and American society (Library of Congress, 1996). These various arguments proffered by DOMA's supporters contributed to an urgency in adopting the federal legislation. Specifically, DOMA was presented as a pressing measure needed to protect the federal government from Hawaii's imminent recognition of same-sex marriage and also from any other states that might follow in sanctioning same-sex unions (Stevens, 2002, p. 8). The arguments made in opposition to DOMA included claims that the legislation was clearly discriminatory against same-sex couples; and that DOMA was an unconstitutional overreach of federal powers as marriage laws had been traditionally left to the states (Library of Congress, 1996).

With just weeks before President Bill Clinton was re-elected to a second term, and with Gallup polling reporting the vast majority of the American public did not favor same-sex marriage (Newport, 2011), the U. S. Congress approved and President Clinton signed DOMA into law on September 21, 1996 (Library of Congress, 1995–1996a). There are at least two important implications regarding the federal government's rejection of same-sex unions as codified by DOMA. First, states did not have to recognize same-sex marriages from other jurisdictions; and, second, the federal government would only recognize heterosexual marriages (Merin, 2002, p. 274). DOMA defined marriage as "mean[ing] only a legal union between one man and one woman as husband and wife, and the word 'spouse' refers only to a person of the opposite sex who is a husband or a wife" (Library of Congress, 1995–1996b). DOMA's marriage definition, therefore, relies on biological determinism and treats assigned sex at birth as the core feature of one's identity in determining a couple's future eligibility for marriage.

Prompted largely by DOMA's provision that each of the states could decide if they would recognize a same-sex marriage performed in another state, a majority of individual U.S. states eventually sought to adopt constitutional amendments that would limit marriage to heterosexual couples. In fact, one of the very first states to do so was

Hawaii, in response to its Supreme Court's decision to recognize marriage equality. In 1998, just two years after DOMA was adopted and during midterm congressional elections, Hawaii and Alaska became the first two states to ratify ballot initiatives amending their states' constitutions limiting legal marriage to heterosexual couples. From 1998 until 2012, a total of 33 ballot initiatives and one "people's veto" (Maine in 2009) sought to restrict marriage rights to heterosexual couples. All except one of these measures were approved by the voters; and Arizona, the only state whose initial vote to limit marriage to heterosexual couples was narrowly defeated, held a second vote just two years later when the voters of Arizona amended their state constitution to prohibit same-sex marriage (see Table 1).[1] Certainly, with a vast majority of states having now voted to restrict marriage to heterosexual couples, and as Table 1 shows the votes in most of these states were by a rather wide margin against same-sex marriage, one might conclude that our nation's democratic process had produced public policy reflecting the will of the people. Yet, throughout the past two decades the overwhelming trend to prohibit legal marriage and deny same-sex couples the many associated civil rights and privileges highlights a fundamental limitation of our nation's democratic system. Minority populations have often been subjected to control, discrimination, or tyranny by the will of a democratic majority. Indeed, throughout U.S. history direct democracy has often "produced its share of policies that are abusive to minorities" (Bowler & Donovan, 2000, p. 9).

Table 1. Same-Sex Marriage State Ballot Initiatives Prior to 2012

State	Year	Ballot Initiative	Type	Pass / Fail	%Yes	%No
HI	1998	Question 2	Constitutional	Pass	69.2%	28.6%
AK	1998	Measure 2	Constitutional	Pass	68.11%	31.89%
NV	2000	Question 2 (1st Vote)	Constitutional	Pass	65.38%	34.62%
NE	2000	Initiative 416	Constitutional	Pass	70.1%	29.9%
CA	2000	Proposition 22	State Statute	Pass	61.4%	38.6%
NV	2002	Question 2 (2nd Vote)	Constitutional	Pass	67.2%	32.8%
UT	2004	Amendment 3	Constitutional	Pass	65.9%	34.1%
OR	2004	Measure 36	Constitutional	Pass	56.63%	43.37%
OK	2004	Question 711	Constitutional	Pass	75.59%	24.42%
OH	2004	Issue 1	Constitutional	Pass	61.71%	38.29%
ND	2004	Marriage Amendment	Constitutional	Pass	73.23%	26.77%
MT	2004	Measure CI-96	Constitutional	Pass	66.56%	33.44%
MO	2004	Amendment 2	Constitutional	Pass	70.6%	29.4%
MS	2004	Amendment 1	Constitutional	Pass	86.01%	14.99%

State	Year	Ballot Initiative	Type	Pass / Fail	%Yes	%No
MI	2004	Marriage Amendment	Constitutional	Pass	58.62%	41.38%
LA	2004	CA No.1 Act 926-2004	Constitutional	Pass	77.78%	22.22%
KY	2004	Marriage Amendment	Constitutional	Pass	74.56%	25.44%
GA	2004	Amendment 1	Constitutional	Pass	76.2%	23.8%
AR	2004	Amendment 3	Constitutional	Pass	74.95%	25.05%
TX	2005	Proposition 2	Constitutional	Pass	76.25%	23.75%
KS	2005	Marriage Amendment	Constitutional	Pass	69.96%	30.05%
WI	2006	Question 1	Constitutional	Pass	59.43%	40.57%
VA	2006	Amendment 1	Constitutional	Pass	57.06%	42.94%
TN	2006	Amendment C	Constitutional	Pass	81.25%	18.75%
SD	2006	Amendment C	Constitutional	Pass	51.83%	48.17%
SC	2006	Amendment 1	Constitutional	Pass	77.97%	22.03%
AL	2006	Amendment 774	Constitutional	Pass	81.2%	18.8%
AZ	2006	Proposition 107	Constitutional	Fail	48.2%	51.8%
CO	2006	Amendment 43	Constitutional	Pass	55.02%	44.98%
ID	2006	H.J.R. 2	Constitutional	Pass	63.35%	36.65%
AZ	2008	Proposition 102	Constitutional	Pass	56.2%	43.8%
CA	2008	Proposition 8	Constitutional	Pass	52.3%	47.7%
FL	2008	Proposition 2	Constitutional	Pass	61.9%	38.1%
ME	2009	Question 1	Popular Refer.	Pass	52.9%	47.1%

Note. Information obtained from Secretaries of States websites.

Shifting Public Opinion

Since 1998 and until just recently, U.S. citizens have consistently voted to reject the right of same-sex couples to marry. More recent legislative and ballot actions, however, indicate citizens have been willing to grant domestic partnerships the same rights and privileges of marriage, especially when the legal status of marriage is somehow "protected" or reserved for heterosexual couples. For more than a decade, states' votes against same-sex marriage (see Table 1) reflected public opinion against marriage equality (see Figure 1; Newport, 2011). Gallup polling from 1996 through 2010 found that a majority of Americans were not supportive of same-sex marriages. Yet, in 2011 Gallup polling revealed for the first time since it began its polling on this issue that a majority of Americans agreed that marriage between same-sex couples "should be recognized by the law as valid, with the same rights as traditional marriages" (Newport, 2011). Similarly, a Pew Research Center

(2012) poll also found that 47% favored allowing gay and lesbian couples to marry, whereas 43% were opposed. In addition, the Public Religion Research Institute (2012) found 52% supported the full and legal marriage of gay and lesbian couples, although 44% opposed such marriage.

Figure 1. Gallup Poll Results from 1996–2012 Indicating Public Support for Same-Sex Marriage

Do you think marriages between same-sex couples should or should not be recognized by the law as valid, with the same rights as traditional marriages?

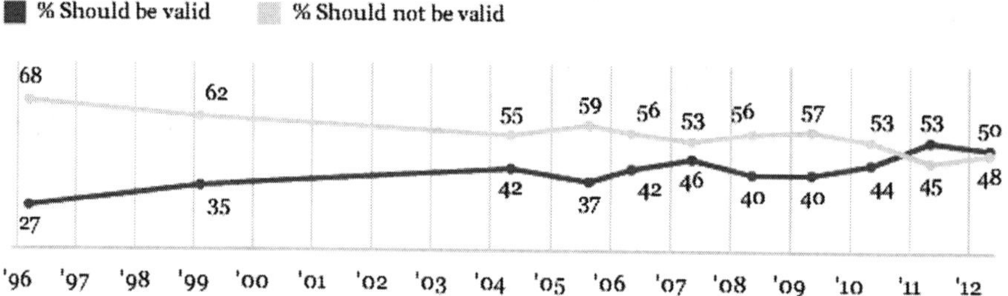

Note: Trend shown for polls in which same-sex marriage question followed questions on gay/lesbian rights and relations
1996-2005 wording: "Do you think marriages between homosexuals ..."

Note. The source for this figure is Newport, 2012.

Therefore, in just over a decade, public sentiment has turned from largely against same-sex marriage (68% to 27% in 1996) to public opinion that, although somewhat evenly divided, has now tilted slightly in favor (with 50% approving and 48% not approving legal marriage for same-sex couples in 2012, according to Gallup polling). This period of evolving public opinion was perhaps most aptly exemplified by the changing attitudes of none other than our nation's leader. When first elected to public office, President Barack Obama supported civil unions for same-sex couples while reserving the status of legal marriage for heterosexuals. In May 2012, however, Obama described his own "wrenching personal transformation" on this issue when he became the first U.S. president to publically declare support of full marriage equality for same-sex couples (Calmes & Baker, 2012). With public opinion trending in favor of legalizing same-sex marriage, and with the occupant of our nation's bully pulpit now arguing for such change, the dynamics of our national marriage equality debate has clearly shifted. Several state ballot initiatives in the fall of 2012 would serve as the latest front on which this contentious social struggle would be fought. Through a rhetorical-critical case analysis of the state campaigns waged both for and against same-sex marriage, this chapter examines the historic marriage equality ballot initiatives that voters decided in November 2012.

2012 Marriage Equality Battlegrounds

To claim that the marriage equality votes of 2012 were historic is an assertion that can be supported on at least two counts. First, ballot initiatives in three states (Washington, Maryland, and Maine) represented the very first popular votes in U. S. history in which citizens were asked to legalize same-sex marriage and thus add to the small number of states that had already achieved marriage equality through state legislative or judicial action. For the past 14 years, previous states' votes had asked citizens to amend their constitutions or approve state statutes that sought to ban same-sex marriage and limit legal marriage to heterosexuals. In all three of these states in 2012, citizens made history by legalizing marriage equality at the ballot box. Furthermore, Minnesota was the fourth state in November of 2012 to include a marriage initiative on its ballot—again, a constitutional amendment to limit legal marriage to heterosexuals—and this measure was rejected by the voters of Minnesota. Therefore, with three states affirming same-sex marriage and one state rejecting the limiting of legal marriage to only heterosexuals, marriage equality was clearly the winning option at the ballot boxes in the fall of 2012. The votes in these four states—bolstered by subsequent U.S. Supreme Court decisions that we note in the conclusion of this chapter—may well represent the turning point for greater acceptance and approval of marriage equality in the United States.

As public attitudes shift in favor of marriage equality and with the forces seeking legal recognition now taking an offensive political stance by pursuing public affirmation of this position, it seems useful at this crucial moment in the marriage equality movement to examine the rhetoric surrounding this important civil rights debate. In this chapter, we are particularly interested in the persuasive appeals of the marriage equality campaigns that challenge our national hetero-normativity and seek to open up spaces for legal marriage and greater inclusion of all citizens no matter who they may love. This study also contributes to the scholarship of political campaign rhetoric as much of the existing work in electoral campaign communication has largely ignored examination of ballot initiatives. Before we turn to analysis of the rhetoric from campaigns both for and against marriage equality, we first provide an overview of our four case studies, describe the specific ballot measures in each state, and note the leading campaign organizations behind each of the ballot initiatives.

Minnesota

Minnesota was the only state in 2012 that directly sought to constitutionally limit marriage to heterosexuals, a measure that was narrowly rejected by that state's voters (51.2% voted no, 47.4% voted yes, and 1.4% of the ballots cast were left blank on this question) (Minnesota Secretary of State, 2012). The two major campaigns for and against marriage equality in Minnesota included Minnesota for Marriage and Minnesotans United for All Families (Helgeson, 2012). Minnesota for Marriage was the campaign working to adopt the constitutional amendment limiting marriage to heterosexuals, and at the national level, the National Organization for Marriage (NOM) was the primary funder of this state group (Eckholm, 2012). The campaign manager for Minnesota for Marriage was Frank Schubert, who led the successful Yes on Prop 8 campaign in California in 2008 restricting marriage to heterosexual couples (Eckholm, 2012). Minnesotans United for All Families, the campaign in support of marriage equality, was "an umbrella organization for more than 600 groups working to defeat the amendment" (Helgeson, 2012, para. 22).

Washington

In February 2012, the Washington state legislature approved a measure legalizing same-sex marriage that was signed by the state's governor (La Corte, 2012). This legislative measure, however, included a "veto referendum" provision by which the citizens of Washington could accept or reject this change in state law (Shannon, 2012). Thus, in November 2012, voters were presented with Referendum 74, asking them to approve or reject marriage equality within the state of Washington (Washington Secretary of State, 2012a). If a majority of voters had voted "no" on the referendum, the same-sex marriage legislation approved by the legislature and signed by the governor would not become law. However, a majority of voters in Washington upheld the legalization of same-sex marriage through their "yes" votes on the referendum (with 53.7% approving and 46.3% voting no) (Washington Secretary of State, 2012b). The two major campaigns that worked for and against Referendum 74 in Washington were Washington United for Marriage, the organization working to approve the referendum, and Preserve Marriage Washington, which was working to defeat Referendum 74. As with the campaign against same-sex marriage in Minnesota, Schubert served as the campaign manager for Preserve Marriage Washington (Eckholm, 2012). The Human Rights Campaign (HRC) was also a large player in Washington's United for Marriage campaign, with HRC proclaiming this was one of the largest voter mobilization efforts in its organization's history (Rafter, 2012).

Maryland

Similarly, in Maryland there was also a referendum petition—Question 6—placed on the state's fall ballot that, if rejected, would have repealed the Civil Marriage Protections Act (CMPA), a measure adopted by the Maryland legislature in March 2012 legalizing same-sex marriage (Leaderman, 2012). Yet, Maryland voters narrowly supported the referendum (with 52.4% voting to uphold the law, and 47.6% voting against the measure) (Maryland State Board of Elections, 2012). Thus, CMPA became law in January 2013 allowing same-sex couples to obtain marriage licenses in Maryland (Equality Maryland, 2012; Leaderman, 2012). The two major campaigns working for and against Question 6 were Marylanders for Marriage Equality and the Maryland Marriage Alliance (Lavers, 2012; Wagner, 2012). Marylanders for Marriage Equality, like the name suggests, sought support for marriage equality and a yes vote on Question 6, whereas the Maryland Marriage Alliance pursued a no vote on 6 and was against marriage equality (Lavers, 2012; Wagner, 2012). Maryland Marriage Alliance was the organization that collected the required signatures and initiated the referendum to overturn the same-sex marriage law that Gov. Martin O'Malley had signed into law earlier in the year (Lavers, 2012). Just like the other states' campaigns against marriage equality in 2012, NOM was leading the fight with Maryland Marriage Alliance and Schubert served as the campaign manager for the Maryland Marriage Alliance (Eckholm, 2012). Marylanders for Marriage Equality was the leading campaign supporting the marriage equality referendum in Maryland, an organization that was founded and funded by the Human Rights Campaign (Human Rights Campaign, 2012).

Maine

Finally, in November 2012 the citizens of Maine actively sought to overturn their state's ban on same-sex marriage with the passage of Question 1, a citizen-initiated ballot measure that asked voters a very simple question: "Do you want to allow the State of Maine to issue marriage licenses to same-sex couples?" (Maine Secretary of State, 2012b, p. 3). According to *The New York Times* this vote represented the "only state where supporters of same-sex marriage put such an initiative on the ballot. Whenever the matter has gone to voters before, including here in 2009, it has been driven by opponents" (Seelye, 2012, para. 4). The outcome of this vote was intended to advise Maine's legislature to either legalize marriage equality or keep marriage in Maine restricted only to heterosexuals. The initiative was supported by the voters of Maine (with 51.5% approving, 46.2% not approving, and 2.3% of the ballots left blank on this question) (Maine Secretary of State, 2012a).

With Question 1's passage "same-sex couples in Maine [were] able to obtain marriage licenses by Jan. 5 [2013] and get married the same day" (Harrison, 2012, para 1). The two major campaigns working for and against this measure in the "Pine Tree" state were Mainers United for Marriage and Protect Marriage Maine. Mainers United for Marriage supported marriage equality, whereas Protect Marriage Maine was the organization working to defeat Question 1. As in each of the other three states with marriage equality ballot initiatives, NOM was the largest contributor to Protect Marriage Maine and Schubert was its campaign manager (Eckholm, 2012). Mainers United for Marriage was aided by the Human Rights Campaign, Gay & Lesbian Advocates & Defenders (GLAD), The Lesbian Super PAC (LPAC), and Equality Maine (Cover, 2012).

In each of these four states, the campaigns battling for and against marriage equality featured well-funded political advertising efforts. Such persuasive communication serves as the cornerstone of most any electoral endeavor, with candidates and political campaigns—including ballot initiatives—devoting considerable campaign resources to crafting and delivering messages designed to shape what voters think of candidates, or campaign issues, and appeals that seek to motivate supporters to take action in favor of a desired candidate or to support a particular issue. The ad messages sponsored by organizations in support of and against marriage equality represent important political messages worthy of analysis as this campaign discourse signifies a battle for interpretative dominance that contests the very definition of marriage in our society and offers competing interpretative frames that attempt to shape citizens' understanding of marriage equality. The following analysis explores these significant messages and particularly the arguments contained in rival campaign television ads, seeking to better understand the interplay and clash of these competing rhetorics that define marriage and the consequences of granting marriage equality to all citizens.

(Re)Defining Marriage?

A dominant feature of the televised campaign ads for and against marriage equality in each state was an obvious contestation over the very definition of what constitutes a marriage. Many of the advertisements against same-sex marriage went so far as to incorporate scare tactics in an attempt to persuade voters that "redefining" marriage could lead to the downfall of our society. In each state, the message of the anti-gay-marriage campaigns was clear: only heterosexual marriage should be viewed as "traditional" marriage; the institution of marriage was "ordained by God" and should be reserved for only one man and one woman; and traditional marriage is our only social institution whose express design is to propagate procreation (thus the necessity for only man and woman). The procreation appeals were often framed as a way to "protect" or pass on to "the next generation" the traditional institution of marriage that if destroyed would lead to the destruction of the nuclear family and eventually all of society (e.g., Mnformarriage, 2012a; MmanoOn6, 2012; PreserveMarriageWashington, 2012a; ProtectMarriageMaine, 2012). Minnesota, the one state in 2012 whose vote sought to restrict marriage to heterosexual couples, included heavy God appeals in their definition of marriage. In short, as one ad concluded, "Marriage ... was made by God for the creation and care of the next generation" (Mnformarriage, 2012a). The ads against marriage equality often argued that although one has every right to love any person she or he may choose, no one has the right to redefine the God created and ordained institution of marriage (MmanoOn6, 2012; Mnformarriage, 2012b; ProtectMarriageMaine, 2012).

The anti-gay-marriage ads not only defined marriage as the exclusive province of one man and one woman, and implored voters to not tinker with traditional marriage, but interestingly these ads also often sought to combat charges of intolerance against same-sex couples by arguing these couples already enjoyed the same legal rights as married couples. The premise advanced with this message is that one could simultaneously be against redefining traditional marriage and vote to restrict marriage to heterosexuals while also still being supportive of same-sex couples (ProtectMarriageMaine, 2012; Mnformarriage, 2012d; PreserveMarriageWashington, 2012c). One advertisement in Minnesota went so far as to suggest that voters "can support gays and lesbians without changing marriage," but "marriage is still about having a mom and a dad" (Mnformarriage, 2012d). Another ad in Washington stated emphatically, "You can oppose same-sex marriage and not be anti-gay" (PreserveMarriageWashington, 2012a).

The campaign ads in favor of marriage equality, in contrast, eschewed definitions of marriage in terms of societal tradition or strictly religious views in favor of marriage as recognition of one's commitment to and love for another human being (e.g., MainersUnited, 2012d; MDers4MarriageEqual, 2012b; MN4allfamilies, 2012d; WAUnitedForMarriage, 2012b); as a constitutionally granted freedom for all citizens no matter who they might love (e.g., MainersUnited, 2012c; MN4allfamilies, 2012b; WAUnitedForMarriage, 2012f); and as a civil right that acknowledges the dignity and equality of all citizens (e.g., MainersUnited, 2012f; MDers4MarriageEqual, 2012a; MN4allfamilies, 2012c; WAUnitedForMarriage, 2012a). Much like the ads against marriage equality, ads in favor of same-sex marriage also addressed the question of "redefining" traditional marriage. In many instances, testimonials were given by those who had originally favored "traditional" marriage, but over time had come to accept expanding—not necessarily redefining—marriage to include all committed couples no matter their sexual orientation (e.g., MainersUnited, 2012a; MN4allfamilies, 2012a). For example, John from Richfield, Minnesota, an elderly and ostensibly heterosexual married man (with wedding ring clearly visible), shared his evolution in thinking about marriage:

> Used to be there wasn't even this discussion. Marriage was a man and a woman. But times change, and I've thought about it more. My marriage is the most important thing in my life. Who am I to deny that to anybody, gay or straight? (MN4allfamilies, 2012b)

Stacey Fitts, a middle-aged father from Pittsfield, Maine, shown with his wife and two sons, shared:

> I've always been a Republican. I voted against same-sex marriage in 2009, but I know some gay people, and I've talked with them, and with my family. Deciding who you marry is the most important decision you'll ever make. I don't believe that government should tell anybody who they can love or who they can marry. Voting yes protects religious freedom and it protects individual freedom. To me, that's what our country is all about. (MainersUnited, 2012c)

Finally, Jeanette and Paul Rediker from Fort Fairfield, Maine, appeared together in an ad and shared, "My husband and I have been married 32 years [husband interjects: '42'],'" and as Jeanette laughs her husband continues, "We weren't always so gay friendly. We didn't even grow up in an era where it was even discussed." Jeanette then recounts that after learning their daughter was a lesbian, "There was a lot of emotions. We went to see a priest, and I will never forget the answer he told me 'She is the same person that you loved yesterday'" (MainersUnited, 2012a).

Across all four states, the ad messages supporting marriage equality had at least three features in common, as exemplified by the ads just described. First, in almost all of the pro marriage equality ads, the speakers and those appearing in the ads were heterosexual married couples and their extended families, with parents and grandparents often expressing just how much they wished their gay and lesbian family members would be allowed the very same freedom to marry that they enjoyed. Second, as illustrated in the preceding examples, many of those appearing in these ads shared stories of how their thinking about same-sex marriage had evolved over time. Yet, this evolution of views regarding marriage equality was in no way a redefinition of marriage but rather an expansion by which the institution of marriage would be more inclusive of all citizens. Finally, interestingly enough, religious and faith appeals were perhaps just as frequent in the pro same-sex marriage ads as were the many appeals to God and religion found in those ads against marriage equality. Although some of the ads supporting marriage equality included more cursory references to religion, such as the previous ads that described parents receiving affirmation from a minister upon learning their daughter is a lesbian or references to religious freedom, other ads were more explicit in their use of religion to endorse same-sex marriage.

For example, Reverend Rich Lang from Washington state, married 29 years to wife Cathy and with two sons, described his journey in accepting same-sex marriage: "I struggled with the notion of same-sex marriage, and it was compassion that broke in. My shift came when I realized that at the very core of my Christianity is the compassion that God has shown towards me" (WAUnitedForMarriage, 2012c). Also in Washington State, a 30 second ad titled "Faith" featured no fewer than four reverends, a bishop, and a friar all proclaiming their support for same-sex marriage (WAUnitedForMarriage, 2012b). Appearances in these ads from members of the clergy certainly served to assure voters that supporting same-sex marriage would not infringe on religious freedoms—that no church or religious organization would be forced by law to perform any marriage ceremony that contradicted the doctrine or tenants of a given faith. And, the frequent incorporation of religious talk and religious appeals in the pro marriage equality ads served to counter the dominant religious appeals found in the anti-gay-marriage ads.

A final major theme in the ad messages supporting marriage equality, and one related to the struggle to define marriage, described civil unions and domestic partnerships as an inadequate response and not equal to legal marriage. For example, Catharine and Phil Curtis from Biddeford, Maine, "married for almost 52 years" with three daughters, the youngest of whom, Katie, is gay, explained why a civil union is not good enough for their daughter:

> People will ask "Why wouldn't a civil union be enough for her?" When we were young we never dreamed about having a civil union or signing a piece of paper. We wanted to be married … [we] want our Katie to have what we have. The joy and security of marriage. A civil union is no substitute for marriage. We know that in our hearts. (MainersUnited, 2012b)

Yet another ad featured four generations of the Gardner family from Machias, Maine, seated around the dinner table. This ad begins with the matriarch of the family sharing that her granddaughter is gay, and noting "I would in my lifetime really like to see [her] get married legally. We want for her what we have. A marriage, not a domestic partnership." Grandfather Gardner concludes, "What has been so good for Dorothy and I is too good not to share with the people that we love" (MainersUnited, 2012e). Finally, in one of the few television advertisements that actually features a same-sex couple, domestic partners Angie Buysse and Cynthia Per-Lee from Washington state explain why a domestic partnership falls short of the protections afforded by legal marriage. Buysse begins the story of "their worst nightmare" when she was hospitalized and experienced complications during surgery. Per-Lee continues, "The nurse refused to tell me what was happening and how serious things had gotten, just because we weren't married." Buysse then concludes, "Only marriage guarantees that all couples can be there for each other … when it really matters" (WAUnitedForMarriage, 2012e).

As described, a primary task in the battle for interpretative dominance on the question of same-sex marriage was defining just what constituted marriage. For the forces against granting marriage equality, marriage was defined as a sacred institution created by God to be preserved only for a man and a woman, a union designed largely for procreation and the propagation of the family. To "redefine" marriage would lead to the destruction of the nuclear family. For those arguing in favor of marriage equality, they sought not to redefine but rather to enlarge this vital social institution to include all citizens. In so doing, an expanded notion of marriage would fulfill our nation's foundational promise of equality for all and recognize the social worth and dignity of all couples. Proponents of marriage equality did not ignore those arguments framed in religious terms by the anti same-sex marriage forces. Rather, their messages of expanding marriage sought to assure voters that legal recognition of same-sex marriage would in no way infringe on any religion's particular beliefs or practices. Finally, it was argued that full-fledged and legal marriage was needed, not substitutions such as domestic partnerships or civil unions.

The Consequences of Marriage Equality

Beyond attempts to define the central concept of marriage, the 2012 ballot ads also sought to persuade voters of the consequences—both good and bad—should voters sanction same-sex marriage. First, those against marriage equality depicted a rather grim society in which personal freedoms and fortune were to be sacrificed and innocent children to be preyed upon if same-sex couples were allowed to marry. For example, a Minnesota for Marriage ad offered a litany of dire consequences already suffered by those in states where same-sex couples could marry:

> When same sex marriage has been imposed elsewhere, it has not been "live and let live." People who believe marriage is one man and one woman have faced consequences. Small businesses fined, individuals fired, charities closed down, churches sued, same-sex marriage taught to young children in elementary school and parents have no legal rights to be notified or to take their children out of class that day. (Mnformarriage, 2012c)

Personal testimonials were provided by a number of affected citizens, including Jim and Mary O'Reilly from Lyndonville, Vermont, proprietors of the Wildflower Inn who were featured in ads that appeared in both Washington and Maine. Jim O'Reilly claimed "a lesbian couple sued us for not supporting their gay wedding because of our Christian beliefs. We had to pay $30,000 and can no longer host any weddings at our inn" (PreserveMarriageWashington, 2012b). Also featured in ads that appeared in both Washington and Maine, Damian Goddard shared that he "was a national sportscaster in Canada," yet "when a sports agent spoke out in favor of traditional marriage I sent a personal tweet that I agreed with him. The next day I was fired! Don't let this happen in Maine" (Protectmarriagme, 2012).

Perhaps the most calamitous consequence in granting marriage equality, at least according to the anti same-sex marriage forces, was the effect that "re-defining" marriage would have on the education of our children. In several anti-gay-marriage ads, children were depicted as innocent victims of those who wished to impose a "radical agenda" on our most vulnerable. These messages were characterized by a sense of foreboding urgency, complete with ominous music and visual depictions of orderly schoolrooms and happy children who needed protection from the menacing forces of marriage equality. For example, Massachusetts parents David and Tonia Parker were featured in ads that appeared in all four states warning voters that what had happened to them in Massachusetts could happen to families in other states should marriage equality be adopted:

> If gay marriage happens here, schools could teach that boys can marry boys. After Massachusetts re-defined marriage, local schools taught it to children in 2nd grade—including the school our son attended. Courts ruled parents had no right to take their children out of class, or to even be informed when this instruction was going to take place. If R 74 is approved, same-sex marriage could be taught in local Washington schools, just as it was in Massachusetts. Don't make the same mistake and think that gay marriage won't affect you. Don't re-define marriage. Reject R 74! (PreserveMarriageWashington, 2012c)

Those supporting marriage equality spoke of a society that would be more free and more equal should same-sex marriage be sanctioned. In Minnesota, for example, where marriage equality proponents were attempting to prevent a constitutional amendment prohibiting same-sex marriage, the theme of constitutionally protected individual liberties and personal freedom, including the freedom to choose whom one could love and marry, was developed:

> Government isn't telling people who they can fall in love with. So, government should not be telling people who they can marry. We're supposed to be the home of the brave, land of the free … Our constitution is supposed to protect our freedom, not take it away. (MN4allfamilies, 2012d)

Yet another ad from Minnesota suggested those against marriage equality were downright un-American in attempting to limit citizens' freedoms. This ad, featuring John Kriesel, a Republican member of the Minnesota House of Representatives and an Iraq war veteran, links patriotism and service to one's country with the freedom to choose whom one can marry. Rep. Kriesel first recounted, "I joined the military because I loved this country and I went to Iraq. I was in an incident and I nearly died. I remember lying there looking down and seeing my legs mangled. I thought about my family." Kriesel then went on to tell about a fallen comrade:

> Corporal Andrew Wilfahrt … he gave his life in Afghanistan protecting our freedoms. He was gay. I cannot look at this picture and say, "Corporal you were good enough to fight for your country and give your life, but you were not good enough to marry the person you love." (MN4allfamilies, 2012e)

Although opponents spoke of a world in which children needed protection from the forces of same-sex marriage, those supporting marriage equality argued that caring for and protecting those they loved, including their children, meant allowing individuals the freedom to choose whom they could marry. These messages featured families with gay and lesbian sons and daughters and also families that included same-sex parents and their children. For example, same-sex couple Rachel and Sandy Smith-Mosel from Federal Way, Washington, appeared in an ad shown with their three young children, with Rachel sharing, "I learned the importance of marriage from my mom and dad. It's not about politics; it's about family. It's about how we treat one another. Marriage matters to all our families" (WAUnitedForMarriage, 2012d). Another mother, Lisa, from Apple Valley, Minnesota, spoke of equality for all her children, including her gay son:

> I am a teacher, and a mother, and a wife. I have four sons in their twenties. My youngest son is gay. I don't see why one of my four sons should be treated differently. Marriage helps us to be the people that God means us to be. God says love your neighbor as yourself. Jason was made by God to be who he is. (MN4allfamilies, 2012c)

The consequences of allowing same-sex marriage were presented in starkly different terms by those supporting and opposing marriage equality. First, those against marriage for all spoke of a dystopian society with menacing forces threatening the destruction of the family unit, attempting to indoctrinate innocent children, and usurping citizens' freedoms of association and expression. Those supporting marriage equality, on the other hand, spoke of a world in which our nation's guiding principles of freedom and equality would actually be advanced through the realization of same-sex marriage, and with this change a society that grants all families and children equal dignity and respect.

Conclusion

Two competing visions of marriage were presented to citizens in four states in the 2012 November elections, asking voters to grant or deny marriage equality for same-sex couples. The forces opposing same-sex marriage argued that "re-defining" traditional marriage, an institution ordained by God, would destroy the nuclear family and society. Those arguing in favor of marriage equality based their appeals in freedom and equality; yet, not to be outdone by the voices favoring "traditional" marriage, the marriage equality appeals also included a heavy dose of "do unto others" dignity for "all God's children." In overall tone, these competing messages were characterized largely as appeals of negativity and pessimism (the ads against same-sex marriage) versus a message of hope for a more inclusive and loving future for all (the ads in favor of marriage equality). With the votes in all four states cast in favor of same-sex marriage, it appears—at least in the fall of 2012—that the arguments in support of marriage equality reigned supreme in the battle of interpretative dominance. Certainly, many factors play an important role in the outcome of elections and we feel a particularly important factor is voters' assessments of the arguments offered by candidates and issue campaigns. The doom and gloom appeals and arguments that our nuclear family, our children and our society stand in peril if man and man, woman and woman are granted legal marriage were perhaps viewed as overblown if not downright mean-spirited and did not hold sway in 2012. As we noted earlier in this chapter, the public acceptance of arguments against granting marriage equality were largely validated at the polls for more than a decade; it now appears that voters are less accepting of these appeals and now perhaps more likely to adopt the more inclusive vision of society articulated by those in favor of marriage equality.

Although we may well one day point to 2012 as the turning point in our national struggle regarding marriage equality, this social battle is far from over. Still, a majority of U.S. states have laws or constitutional amendments prohibiting same-sex marriage. Recent U.S. Supreme Court decisions, however, have bolstered the forces in favor of marriage equality. Just months after the string of ballot successes in 2012, the high court in *United States v. Windsor* (Lee, 2013) found the federal DOMA law unconstitutional; and, therefore, same-sex couples legally married in states granting such recognition are now regarded as legally married couples for purposes of federal recognition. At the same time, the U.S. Supreme Court also ruled in *Hollingsworth v. Perry* (Lee, 2013) that it would not overturn a California court's decision to invalidate Prop 8, the California ballot initiative approved by voters in 2008 limiting marriage in that state to heterosexual couples. Even with these two major decisions, the overturning of DOMA at the federal level and the overturning of Prop 8 in California, the U.S. Supreme Court did not use either of these two questions, as some had wished, to decree that same-sex marriage should be the law of the land throughout the United States. Rather, in making these decisions the U.S. Supreme Court reaffirmed the states' authority "to write their own laws defining marriage" (Erb, 2013, para. 4).

Thus, without a federal law or court ruling that all states must recognize a legal same-sex marriage performed in another state, or a ruling that the U.S. Constitution affords the right of marriage to all, our national debate regarding marriage equality will likely continue on a state-by-state basis. As one of the more contentious social issues our nation has now grappled with for more than a decade, this question has divided our electorate along so many of our predictable political fault lines, splitting Democrats and Republicans, conservatives and liberals, red states and blue states, even younger and older voters, as well as our most frequent and less frequent church attenders. If, however, we see a continued building of public acceptance and approval of granting legal and equal marriage to all couples—with now more than half of all voters indicating such opinion—and if we continue to see even more states follow the lead set by Minnesota, Washington state, Maryland and Maine in 2012, perhaps the deep divisions that have characterized this struggle will diminish.

References

Bowler, S., & Donovan, T. (2000). *Demanding choices: Opinion, voting, and direct democracy.* Ann Arbor, MI: The University of Michigan Press.

Calmes, J., & Baker, P. (2012, May 9). Obama says same-sex marriage should be legal. *The New York Times.* Retrieved from http://www.nytimes.com/2012/05/10/us/politics/obama-says-same-sex-marriage-should-be-legal.html

Cover, S. (2012, October 28). Same-sex marriage foes raise close to $950K in final weeks. *Morning Sentinel.* Retrieved from http://www.onlinesentinel.com/news/same-sex-marriage-foes-raise-close-to-_950k-in-final-weeks_2012-10-27.html

Eckholm, E. (2012, October 9). One man guides the fight against gay marriage. *The New York Times.* Retrieved from http://www.nytimes.com/2012/10/10/us/politics/frank-schubert-mastermind-in-the-fight-against-gay-marriage.html?_r=1&pagewanted=all

Equality Maryland. (2012). Marriage. Retrieved from http://www.equalitymaryland.org/issues/marriage

Erb, K. P. (2013, June 26). Supreme Court rules DOMA unconstitutional (and it was a tax case!). *Forbes.* Retrieved from http://www.forbes.com/sites/kellyphillipserb/2013/06/26/supreme-court-rules-doma-unconstitutional-and-it-was-a-tax-case/

Harrison, J. (2012, November 7). Same-sex couples could get marriage licenses by Jan. 5. *Bangor Daily News.* Retrieved from http://bangordailynews.com/2012/11/07/politics/elections/maines-question-1-approval-seen-as-national-tipping-point-for-same-sex-marriage/

Helgeson, B. (2012, September 26). Minnesota poll: Marriage vote splits state in two. *Star Tribune*. Retrieved from http://www.startribune.com/politics/statelocal/170192596.html?page=all&prepage=1&c=y#continue

Human Rights Campaign. (2012) Breaking news: Maryland voters approve marriage equality. *HRC*. Retrieved from http://www.hrc.org/states/maryland/

La Corte, R. (2012, February 13). Washington gay marriage bill signed into law by Governor Chris Gregoire. *The Huffington Post*. Retrieved from http://www.huffingtonpost.com/2012/02/13/washington-gay-marriage-signed-chris-gregoire_n_1273887.html

Lavers, M. K. (2012, November 5). State marriage campaigns make final election push. *The Washington Blade*. Retrieved from http://www.washingtonblade.com/2012/11/05/state-marriage-campaigns-make-final-election-push/

Leaderman, D. (2012, April 27). Same-sex marriage could rake in millions in Maryland, analysts say: Gay wedding revenue has been a boon to other states. *Gazette.net*. Retrieved from http://www.gazette.net/article/20120427/NEWS/704279651/1029/same-sex-marriage-could-rake-in-millions-in-maryland-analysts-say&template=gazette

Lee, R. (2013). DOMA and Prop 8: SCOTUS favors states' rights over federal rights. *PolicyMic*. Retrieved from http://www.policymic.com/articles/51345/doma-and-prop-8-scotus-favors-states-rights-over-federal-rights

Library of Congress. (1995–1996a). Bill summary & status 104th Congress (1995–1996) H.R. 3396 Major Congressional Actions. *United States Government Printing Office*. Retrieved http://thomas.loc.gov/cgi-bin/bdquery/z?d104:HR03396:@@@R

Library of Congress. (1995–1996b). Bill text 104th Congress (1995–1996) H.R. 3396 ENR. *Congressional Record Library of Congress*. Retrieved from http://thomas.loc.gov/cgi-bin/query/z?c104:h.r.3396.enr:

Library of Congress. (1996, September 10). Congressional Record—Senate (104th Congress): Defense of Marriage Act. *United States Government Printing Office*. p. S10100-S10125. Retrieved from http://thomas.loc.gov/cgi-bin/query/D?r104:19:./temp/~r104hvKlva::

MainersUnited. (2012a, October 3). *Yes on 1: Mainers United for Marriage—Jeanette & Paul Rediker*. [Video file]. Retrieved from http://www.youtube.com/watch?feature=player_embedded&v=rzGLqWjuu18

MainersUnited. (2012b, October 9). *Yes on 1: Mainers United for Marriage—Cathy & Phil Curtis*. [Video file]. Retrieved from http://www.youtube.com/watch?feature=player_embedded&v=TL48VDCsG-4

MainersUnited. (2012c, October 9). *Yes on 1: Mainers United for Marriage—Stacey Fitts*. [Video file]. Retrieved from http://www.youtube.com/watch?feature=player_embedded&v=LV8RogOJWDQ

MainersUnited. (2012d, October 19). *Yes on 1: Mainers United for Marriage—Pat & Dan Lawson of Monroe*. [Video file] Retrieved from https://www.youtube.com/watch?v=FdUCLgjxanQ

MainersUnited. (2012e, October 25). *Yes on 1: Mainers United for Marriage—the Gardner family*. [Video file]. Retrieved from https://www.youtube.com/watch?v=2dTdP-XLZzk

MainersUnited. (2012f, November 2). *Yes on 1: Mainers United for Marriage—Will & Arlene Brewster*. [Video file]. Retrieved from https://www.youtube.com/watch?v=rizfhtN6UVc

Maine Secretary of State. (2012a). *Tabulations for elections held in 2012: General election, November 6, 2012*. Retrieved from http://www.maine.gov/sos/cec/elec/prior12-13.htm#nov

Maine Secretary of State. (2012b). *Maine citizen's guide to the referendum election: Tuesday, November 6, 2012*. Retrieved from http://www.maine.gov/sos/cec/elec/2012/CITIZENS%20GUIDE.pdf

Maryland State Board of Elections. (2012, November 28). *Official 2012 presidential general election results for all state questions*. Retrieved from http://elections.state.md.us/elections/2012/results/general/gen_qresults_2012_4_00_t1.html

MDers4MarriageEqual. (2012a, October 9). *It's about fairness: Rev. Delman Coats for question 6.* [Video file]. Retrieved from http://www.youtube.com/watch?v=HjbuwRqpvck

MDers4MarriageEqual. (2012b, October 29). *Thinking through question 6.* [Video file]. Retrieved from http://www.youtube.com/watch?v=2VU99lghKDk

Merin, Y. (2002). *Equality for same-sex couples: The legal recognition of gay partnerships in Europe and the United States.* Chicago, IL: The University of Chicago Press.

Minnesota Secretary of State. (2012, November 9). *Results for constitutional amendments.* Retrieved from http://minnesotaelectionresults.sos.stte.mn.us/Results/AmendmentResultsStatewide/1

MMaNoOn6. (2012, October 7). *Marriage is more.* [Video file]. Retrieved from http://www.youtube.com/watch?v=FzNLuiLvTdM&feature=youtu.be

MN4allfamilies. (2012a, September 18). *Vote no TV ad #1: Kim & John.* [Video file]. Retrieved from http://www.youtube.com/watch?v=HYR_E-fYfRo

MN4allfamilies. (2012b, September 20). *Vote no TV ad #2: Pretty simple.* [Video file]. Retrieved from http://www.youtube.com/watch?v=8fIMeIrwPQ8

MN4allfamilies. (2012c, October 8). *Love your neighbor as yourself.* [Video file]. Retrieved from http://www.youtube.com/watch?v=oB6yhMn7YS4

MN4allfamilies. (2012d, October 11). *Vote no TV ad #3: Land of the free.* [Video file]. Retrieved from http://www.youtube.com/watch?v=_Gz7SvEJnhU

MN4allfamilies. (2012e, October 26). *Vote no TV ad #5: Freedom.* [Video file]. Retrieved from http://www.youtube.com/watch?v=aepSlHv3R_U

Mnformarriage. (2012a, October 1). *First Minnesota for Marriage TV ad: Good for marriage.* [Video File]. Retrieved from http://www.youtube.com/watch?feature=player_embedded&v=5z3QkveDGNk

Mnformarriage. (2012b, October 1). *First Minnesota for Marriage TV ad: Threat to marriage.* [Video file]. Retrieved from http://www.youtube.com/watch?feature=player_embedded&v=41KcIgoP4xQ

Mnformarriage. (2012c, October 18). *3rd TV ad: "Not live & let live": 30 TV.* [Video file]. Retrieved from http://www.youtube.com/watch?v=YqO9_I2akOQ&feature=plcp

Mnformarriage. (2012d, November 2). *Minnesota for Marriage releases 6th TV ad: We are all voting yes.* [Video file]. Retrieved from http://www.youtube.com/watch?v=Mi_ZHpGKI2Q

Newport, F. (2011, May 20). For first time, majority of Americans favor legal gay marriage: Republicans and older Americans remain opposed. *Gallup.* Retrieved from http://www.gallup.com/poll/147662/First-Time-Majority-Americans-Favor-Legal-Gay-Marriage.aspx

Newport, F. (2012, May 10). Half of Americans support legal gay marriage. *Gallup.* Retrieved from http://www.gallup.com/poll/154529/Half-Americans-Support-Legal-Gay-Marriage.aspx

Pew Research Center for the People & the Press. (2012, April 25). *More support for gun rights, gay marriage than in 2008, 2004. Retrieved from* http://www.people-press.org/files/legacy-pdf/4-25-12%20Social%20Issues.pdf

PreserveMarriageWashington. (2012a, October 11). *TV ad: Not about equality.* [Video file]. Retrieved from http://www.youtube.com/watch?feature=player_embedded&v=NRP6d0jOOBw

PreserveMarriageWashington. (2012b, October 23). *Reject Referendum 74 TV ad: Examples of consequences. Don't redefine marriage.* [Video file]. Retrieved from http://www.youtube.com/watch?v=iqcbDVDTTx0

PreserveMarriageWashington. (2012c, October 29). *Reject Referendum 74 TV ad: Schools could teach.* [Video file]. Retrieved from http://www.youtube.com/watch?v=-yWmSwLk9MA

ProtectMarriageMaine. (2012, October 6). *MME10512H MarriageServesMaine 1280x720.* [Video file]. Retrieved from http://www.youtube.com/watch?feature=player_embedded&v=VCW-cMx142Y

Protectmarriagme. (2012, October 19). *I was fired HD 15 MME101812H 640x360.* [Video file]. Retrieved from https://www.youtube.com/watch?v=rd_vn41m2gg

Public Religion Research Institute. (2012, May 9). Research note: Evolution of American opinion on same-sex marriage. *March PRRI/RNS Religion News Survey: Public Religion Research Institute.* Retrieved from http://publicreligion.org/research/2012/05/research-note-evolution-of-american-opinion-on-same-sex-marriage/

Rafter, D. (2012, November 7). It's official: Marriage victory in Washington. [Web log post]. Retrieved from http://www.hrc.org/blog/entry/its-official-marriage-victory-in-washington-state/

Rogers, J. (2010). The Defense of Marriage Act (DOMA) and California's struggle with same-sex marriage. *Regent University Law Review, 23*(1), 99.

Rogers, W. S. (2010). The constitutionality of the Defense of Marriage Act and state bans on same-sex marriage: Why they won't survive. *Howard Law Journal, 54*(1), 125.

Seelye, K. Q. (2012, June 25). Gay marriage again on ballot in Maine. *The New York Times.* Retrieved from http://www.nytimes.com/2012/06/25/us/politics/second-time-around-hope-for-gay-marriage-in-maine.html

Shannon, B. (2012, March 13). Update 3: Judge frees gay marriage referendum for signatures. *The Olympian.* Retrieved from http://www.theolympian.com/2012/03/13/2028285/judge-frees-r-74-for-signature.html

State of Hawaii. (1995, December 8). *Report of the Commission on Sexual Orientation and the Law.* Retrieved from http://hawaii.gov/lrb/rpts95/sol/pref.html http://hawaii.gov/lrb/rpts95/sol/soldoc.html

Stevens, B. (2002, April 23). *DOMA and its implications* (Unpublished honors thesis). Hamline University, Legal Studies Department, St. Paul, MN.

Wagner, J. (2012, October 24). "Deserving of death" scripture comment downplayed by Md. anti-gay marriage leader. *The Washington Post.* Retrieved from http://www.washingtonpost.com/local/md-politics/deserving-of-death-scripture-comment-downplayed-by-md-anti-gay-marriage-leader/2012/10/24/9e7dd696-1e1a-11e2-9cd5-b55c38388962_story.html

Washington Secretary of State. (2012a). *State of Washington voters' pamphlet: November 6, 2012 general election*. Retrieved from https://wei.sos.wa.gov/agency/osos/en/press_and_research/PreviousElections/2012/General-Election/Pages/Online-Voters-Guide.aspx

Washington Secretary of State. (2012b, November 27). Referendum measure No. 74 concerns marriage for same-sex couples. *November 06, 2012, general election results*. Retrieved from http://vote.wa.gov/results/20121106/Referendum-Measure-No-74-Concerns-marriage-for-same-sex-couples.html

WAUnitedForMarriage. (2012a, September 12). *Boehler*. [Video file]. Retrieved from https://www.youtube.com/watch?v=KcHeBWQJAXI

WAUnitedForMarriage. (2012b, October 1). *Faith*. [Video file]. Retrieved from http://www.youtube.com/watch?v=vWyi11noULM&feature=BFa&list=ULvWyi11noULM

WAUnitedForMarriage. (2012c, October 1). *Lang*. [Video file]. Retrieved from http://www.youtube.com/watch?v=omsr4AHtk9g&feature=channel&list=UL

WAUnitedForMarriage. (2012d, October 19). *Smith-Mosel*. [Video file]. Retrieved from https://www.youtube.com/watch?v=HRNb4o8zzQQ

WAUnitedForMarriage. (2012e, October 22). *Angie*. [Video file]. Retrieved from https://www.youtube.com/watch?v=SDwphILTP8g

WAUnitedForMarriage. (2012f, November 1). *Bandwagon*. [Video file]. Retrieved from https://www.youtube.com/watch?v=6b92JG2Mmjc

Note

1. Nevada had two votes (in 2000 and 2002) with the second vote completing the process to amend their state's constitution to restrict marriage to heterosexuals. California passed both a state statute in 2000 and then a constitutional amendment in 2008 limiting marriage to heterosexuals. Finally, Arizona first rejected a constitutional amendment in 2006 that sought to limit marriage to heterosexuals and would also have taken away domestic partnership rights, yet just two years later in 2008 the voters of Arizona approved a constitutional amendment solely limiting marriage to heterosexuals.

CHAPTER ELEVEN

Articulating Interests and Advocating Issues

An Analysis of Congresswomen's Political Speech after the 2012 Election

DIANNE G. BYSTROM AND VALERIE M. HENNINGS

Women voters, issues, and candidates garnered much attention in the 2012 election. Presidential candidates targeted appeals to women voters, with President Barack Obama's campaign charging that the Republicans were waging a "war on women" with their attacks on Planned Parenthood and mandatory insurance coverage of contraceptives, and former Governor Mitt Romney arguing that Obama, and not the Republican Party, had done the most damage to women by failing to turn around the economy quickly enough.

In addition to the presidential candidates, the media paid significant attention to "women's issues," including reproductive choice and pay equity, in the 2012 election (Ness, 2012). Public opinion polls showed that female and male voters cared about different issues. For example, an October 2012 survey of voters in 12 key swing states found that 39% of women respondents ranked abortion as their top issue whereas men chose jobs (38%) and the economy (37%) (Dugan, 2012). On Election Day, women were 10 percentage points more likely than men to vote for Obama (Center for American Women and Politics, 2012).

Women candidates also made their mark in the 2012 election. A record 184 women ran in the general election for seats in the U.S. Congress with a record 88 women winning their races. A record 101 women—20 in the Senate and 81 in the House, including three delegates representing a U.S. territory or Washington, D.C.—served in the 113th Congress in 2013.

This chapter examines the advocacy of women's interests and issues after the 2012 election through an analysis of the floor speeches of the 101 women serving in the U.S. Congress in 2013. We begin with a review of previous research on the speeches of women legislators, followed by our research questions, method, and results. We conclude with a discussion of the implications of our study as well as directions for future research.

Women's Political Speech in Legislative Bodies

Studies of women in state legislatures and the U.S. Congress often begin with the premise that their representation makes a difference in their policy interests and advocacy for women's issues and underrepresented constituencies, such as children and families. To examine whether or not female legislators make a difference, studies have looked at their legislative priorities (Reingold, 2000; Thomas, 1994); bill sponsorship (Bratton & Haynie, 1999; Thomas, 1994); voting patterns (Barnello, 1999; Clark, 1998; Dodson, 1998; Dolan, 1997; Frederick, 2013; Norton, 1999; Reingold, 2000; Swers, 1998, 2002; Thomas, 1989, 1994); and floor speeches (Osborn & Mendez, 2010; Pearson & Dancey, 2011a, 2011b; Shogan, 2002; Walsh, 2002).

Previous analyses of women's floor speeches delivered in the U.S. House of Representatives and U.S. Senate have documented differences in the rhetoric of female and male members in the constituencies they mention, personal experiences they share, and issues they discuss. For example, in her study of the floor debate of five major bills before the 104th Congress in 1995, Katherine Cramer Walsh (2002) found that women—more often than men—in the U.S. House mentioned the effect of legislation on "marginalized" constituencies, such as children and mothers; represented a broader array of constituencies; and included their personal experiences as women. Even when Democratic and Republican women took opposing stances on legislation, such as in the debate over "partial birth" abortion, they referred to their experiences as mothers to underscore their credibility and emphasize the sincerity of their views.

Similarly, a study of the floor speeches of Democratic and Republican women in the 105th Congress in 1997 (Shogan, 2002) found that women in the House of Representatives often discussed policies in terms of their effects on mothers and daughters. And, although female Republicans invoked women at the same frequency as Democratic women, the specific issues emphasized differed by political party. Republican women discussed how tax, business, and pension laws affected working women and Democratic women emphasized funding for welfare.

Several recent studies have analyzed the issues emphasized by female and male members of the U.S. Congress in their speeches. For example, in their content analysis of the floor speeches of women and men serving in the U.S. Senate in 1999 to 2000 (the 106th Congress), Tracy Osborn and Jeannette Morehouse Mendez (2010) found that females represented women's interests by speaking more frequently than men about such policy concerns as women's health and family issues. However, female and male senators devoted similar percentages of their speeches to talking about other issues traditionally related to women's roles, such as education and health care in general; specific women's policy issues, such as abortion; and issues not related to women's traditional roles, such as budget and monetary policy, agriculture, and the environment. They also found that women devoted a larger percentage of their total speeches to defense and foreign policy, contrary to stereotypes about women's policy interests.

Kathryn Pearson and Logan Dancey have examined the floor speeches of members of the U.S. House of Representatives by gender and partisanship. Although their analysis of more than 10,000 floor speeches from the 103rd and 109th Congresses did not systematically analyze speech content, they found that congresswomen of both political parties were more likely than congressmen to speak on a variety of issues, including stem cell research, family leave, abortion, and banning assault weapons but also on free trade and defense (Pearson & Dancey, 2011a).

In their analysis of more than 30,000 speeches delivered in the U.S. House from 1993 to 2008, Pearson and Dancey (2011b) found that female representatives from both political parties were significantly more likely than their male counterparts to mention women in their discussion of policies ranging from women's health to Afghanistan. They noted the importance of understanding the interactive effect of gender and partisanship on women's representation in an era marked by significant increases in the number of congresswomen and partisan polarization.

Our study of women's political speech at the beginning of the 113th Congress builds upon and expands previous research. First, we expand the scope of previous research by examining floor speeches by women in both the U.S. House of Representatives and U.S. Senate so that we can test for any differences in female political rhetoric between the two legislative bodies. Similar to previous research (Pearson & Dancey, 2011a, 2011b; Shogan, 2002), we are interested in comparing the floor speeches of Democratic and Republican women at a time when the overall representation of women reached record proportions in the U.S. Congress while partisan rhetoric overall continued.

Specifically, we are interested in examining the issues emphasized by Democratic and Republican women in the U.S. Congress; the constituencies they mention; and the ways in which they frame their rhetoric, including the use of personal experiences, personal tone, and addressing the audience as peers. Our frames for women's political rhetoric are based on Karlyn Kohrs Campbell's (1989) construct of "feminine style," which has been applied to analyses of the speeches of female (Dow & Tonn, 1993; Mayhead & Marshall, 2005) and female and male (Blankenship & Robson, 1995) political leaders; and speakers at national political party presidential nominating conventions (DeRosa & Bystrom, 1999). These studies have concluded that male and, especially, female politicians utilize a feminine rhetorical style in their political discourse.

Finally, like Osborn and Mendez (2010) and Pearson and Dancey (2011b), we are interested in whether or not years of service in the U.S. Congress affects the issues emphasized, constituencies mentioned, or frames used in the speeches of female members.

The time period after the 2012 election offers a unique opportunity to study the political rhetoric of Democratic and Republican women in the U.S. Congress. First, as previously noted, the months leading up to the November 6, 2012, general election featured appeals to women voters by both presidential campaigns, media attention on women's issues, and public opinion polls indicating that female and male voters were interested in different policy areas. Plus, record numbers of women were elected to serve in the 113th Congress. Following the 2012 election, female members of the House and, especially, the Senate were praised by the media (Lawrence, 2013; Roberts, 2013) for their collaborative efforts while the public's confidence in Congress as an institution dropped to an historic low of 10% in June 2013 (Mendes & Wilke, 2013).

Based on recent research on the political rhetoric of women in Congress, we seek to answer the following research questions:

RQ1: Are there differences in the issues emphasized, constituencies mentioned, or rhetorical frames used in the floor speeches of Democratic women as compared to Republican women in Congress?

RQ2: Are there differences in the issues emphasized, constituencies mentioned, or rhetorical frames used in the floor speeches of women serving in the U.S. House as compared to women serving in the U.S. Senate?

RQ3: Are there differences in the issues emphasized, constituencies mentioned, or rhetorical frames used in the floor speeches of women with more years of service as compared to women with fewer years of service in Congress?[1]

Method

To address these research questions, we conducted a content analysis of floor speeches by the 101 women—20 U.S. Senators, 78 U.S. Representatives, and

3 House delegates—serving in the 113th Congress in 2013 (Center for American Women and Politics, 2013).[2] We included speeches given on the floor of each chamber during the first six months of the session from January 3, 2013, through June 28, 2013, as printed in the Congressional Record. We utilized the THOMAS website by the Library of Congress to retrieve the transcripts used in our analysis.[3] Ultimately, we collected 1,097 speeches delivered by the women serving in the 113th Congress in 2013: 786 of these speeches were delivered on the floor of the U.S. House and 311 were presented in the U.S. Senate.

From this universe, we selected a random stratified sample of 546 speeches. This sampling approach included 341 House speeches and 205 Senate speeches and proportionately accounted for differences in the number of floor speeches delivered by each woman serving in Congress in 2013. The sample size meets a 95% confidence level and 4% margin of error.

To code the content of these speeches, we conducted a computer-assisted analysis. Computer-assisted content analysis affords a number of advantages. When compared to human coding, computer-assisted procedures allow researchers to efficiently analyze a large amount of data in a reliable, replicable manner, particularly when the coding unit is a word or phrase, as employed in the coding scheme described below (see Neuendorf, 2011; and Riffe, Lacy, & Fico, 2005 for additional discussion of the advantages and disadvantages of computer-assisted content analysis). We used Yoshikoder—which is open-source software that provides word frequencies, creates concordances for examining the usage of text in-context, and allows users to create custom dictionaries (Lowe, 2006)—for our analysis.

As a part of our coding scheme, we first constructed a dictionary of terms in the areas of interest—female issues, male issues, marginalized constituencies, other constituencies, and elements of feminine style. To ensure that the terms included in our dictionary were accurately measuring the underlying concept, we manually coded a randomly selected 10% subset (55 speeches) of our sample of speeches. This validity check confirmed the final dictionary used in our study correctly associated with the relevant concepts between 90% and 100% of the time.

Terms were selected and categorized based on previous research in the fields of communication and political science. We found some variety in the research as to how female vs. male issues (also known as feminine vs. masculine or women's vs. men's issues) were coded. We based our categorization of female and male issues primarily on the work of Kim Fridkin Kahn (Kahn, 1996; Fridkin, Carle, & Woodall, 2012). We also considered what issues were important to voters in the 2012 election, based on public opinion polls (Saad, 2012), as well as surveys indicating who was better—female or male political leaders—at handling a range of policy issues (Taylor, Morin, Cohn, Clark, & Wang, 2008).

Thus, we classified abortion, birth control, civil rights, contraception, child care, discrimination, domestic violence, education, the environment, equal rights, gay rights, gun control, health care, human rights, Medicare, pay equity, pollution, poverty, prescription drugs, racism, schools, social security, war on women, welfare, and women's rights as female issues. We categorized agriculture, Afghanistan, budget, crime, death penalty, debt, deficit, defense, economy, energy, gas prices, guns, hunting, farms, foreign affairs, immigration, Iran, Iraq, jobs, military, national security, North Korea, nuclear weapons, oil, safety, security, taxes, terrorism, trade, unemployment, and war as male issues.

Our categorization of constituencies as marginalized is based on research by Walsh (2002) on women's floor speeches in the U.S. House of Representatives. Thus, the terms children, disaster victims, families, handicapped, homeless, gays, immigrants, lesbians, mothers, poor people, rape victims, sick people, students, victims of domestic violence, and welfare recipients were coded as marginalized. We also coded for other constituencies based on appeals to key voting groups in the 2012 election as well as other phrases frequently used by political candidates that year. Thus, we coded African Americans, the American people, Christians, Latinos, men, the middle class, religious, and women as references to other constituencies.

Finally, we coded for five of the six elements of feminine style based on Campbell's research (1989) of women's rhetorical styles and strategies. Feminine style is characterized by an inductive structure; personal tone; addressing the audience as peers; use of personal experiences, anecdotes, and other examples; identifying with the experiences of others; and inviting audience participation. Thus, we coded for use of the terms I, we, and change to capture the women's use of personal tone, addressing the audience as peers, and inviting audience participation. Through concordance analysis, we also examined whether the women mentioned their personal experiences or identified with the experiences of others in their floor speeches.

Results

We began our analysis of congresswomen's floor speeches by examining word frequencies. Our sample of 546 speeches included 466,415 words, thus averaging about 855 words per speech. Comparing Democrats and Republicans, the average speech length was 859 words and 838 words, respectively. Between chambers, a clear difference was detected—the Senate average, 1,322 words per speech, was more than double the length of House speeches, which averaged 573 words.

Speeches by women who have served more years in Congress tended to be longer than those by women who have served less time—1,085 words on average as compared to 596 words. The shortest speech included in our sample was from the House; it included 115 words. However, brevity was just as likely in the Senate, where the shortest speech was 143 words. The longest speech included in our study was delivered on the floor of the Senate and had 7,005 words. The second longest speech had 6,797 words and was given in the House.

Overall, our sample of speeches used 16,374 different types of words. Among the 500 most common, which included those that appeared between 113 times across our sample (the word "protection") to 25,508 times ("the"), 29 of our 82 dictionary terms were found (see Table 1). The dictionary terms "we" and "I"—which indicate use of a feminine rhetorical style—appeared in women's floor speeches 6,910 times and 6,121 times, respectively. They were the most common of all of the items in our dictionary and ranked 9th and 10th overall among the most frequently used words in our sample of speeches (see Table 1).

Interestingly, terms identified as male issues comprised about half of the dictionary items, 15 out of the 29, ranked among the 500 most common words. The most frequently mentioned female issue was "school/s." "Women" was the most referenced item in the other key constituencies category, and "family/families" appeared the most often among the terms coded for marginalized constituencies.

From these word frequencies, we begin to see how women in the 113th Congress in 2013 articulated and advocated for various interests and issues through their floor speeches. Among the issues raised in floor speeches, male issues spanning topics such as the budget, security, immigration, and war were used more often than those we categorized as female issues. Congresswomen discussed marginalized constituencies including families, children, and students more frequently than other key constituencies. We also found indicators of a feminine style in the rhetorical frames present in women's political speeches.

Table 1. Top Dictionary Terms Used in Congresswomen's Floor Speeches by Frequency and Category

Term	Frequency	Category
We	6,910	Feminine Style
I	6,121	Feminine Style
Women	944	Other Constituencies
Budget	884	Male Issues
Tax*	841	Male Issues
Family*	821	Marginalized Constituencies
Child*	773	Marginalized Constituencies
Job*	663	Male Issues
Security	410	Male Issues

Term	Frequency	Category
Economy	408	Male Issues
Student*	373	Marginalized Constituencies
School*	353	Female Issues
Change	328	Feminine Style
Farm*	299	Male Issues
Energy	284	Male Issues
Military	277	Male Issues
Education	277	Female Issues
Deficit	222	Male Issues
Defense	209	Male Issues
Debt	196	Male Issues
Gun*	187	Male Issues
Safety	183	Male Issues
Immigration	163	Male Issues
Mom*	160	Marginalized Constituencies
Men	156	Other Constituencies
Medicare	152	Female Issues
Immigrant	149	Marginalized Constituencies
Mother*	125	Marginalized Constituencies
War	121	Male Issues

Note. Words marked with an asterisk (*) indicate terms that were coded using a wildcard search so as to include singular and plural versions of the word.

To better understand the content of congresswomen's floor speeches—and account for possible differences in the issues, constituencies, and frames used in their political discourse—we compared speeches given by women who differ in terms of partisanship, chamber, and length of service. Table 2 presents the results of this comparative analysis. We used two forms of information to illustrate these findings. First, we reported risk ratios, which reflected the relative probability of seeing each category of dictionary terms—female issues, male issues, marginalized constituencies, other constituencies, and feminine style—in the speeches of different groups of congresswomen. This measure was based on a ratio calculated from proportions—the number of words coded for each category divided by the total number of words—which accounts for differences in the length of speeches being compared.[4]

For example, to detect any differences in mentions of female issues between Democratic and Republican congresswomen, we divided the proportion of words in

Table 2. Differences in Issues, Constituencies, and Frames in Congresswomen's Floor Speeches

Category	Democrats or Republicans		House or Senate		More years or Fewer years	
N	418	128	341	205	288	258
Female Issues	**Democrats** % Change: 18.79 Risk Ratio: 1.19 [1.03, 1.37]*		**House** % Change: 56.32 Risk Ratio: 1.56 [1.39, 1.75]*		**Fewer years** % Change: -35.93 Risk Ratio: .74 [.65, .83]*	
Male Issues	**Republicans** % Change: -7.07 Risk Ratio: .93 [.88, .99]*		**Not Significantly Different** % Change: .39 Risk Ratio: 1.00 [.95, 1.10]		**Fewer years** % Change: -26.53 Risk Ratio: .79 [.75, .83]*	
Marginalized Constituencies	**Democrats** % Change: 23.12 Risk Ratio: 1.23 [1.11, 1.36]*		**House** % Change: 93.89 Risk Ratio: 1.94 [1.79, 2.10]*		**Fewer years** % Change: -109.05 Risk Ratio: .48 [.44, .52]*	
Other Constituencies	**Democrats** % Change: 175.66 Risk Ratio: 2.75 [2.27, 3.35]*		**House** % Change: 83.28 Risk Ratio: 1.83 [1.63, 2.10]*		**Fewer years** % Change: -38.72 Risk Ratio:.72 [.64, .81]*	
Feminine Style	**Democrats** % Change: 24.75 Risk Ratio: 1.25 [1.20, 1.30]*		**Senate** % Change: -32.41 Risk Ratio: .76 [.73, .78]*		**More years** % Change: 22.73 Risk Ratio: 1.23 [1.18, 1.27]*	

Note. Each cell identifies which groups of congresswomen—according to party, chamber, and length of service—were more likely to emphasize different issues and constituencies in their floor speeches and employ a feminine style. Percent change, risk ratio estimates, and 95% confidence intervals are also reported for each comparison.

*p < .05.

Democratic floor speeches that were coded as female issues by the same proportion of female issues mentions in Republican floor speeches; this produced a risk ratio of 1.19 (see Table 2). Ratios that were greater than 1 simply mean that the proportion from the first group of speeches listed in each set of comparisons—Democrats, women serving in the House, and those with more years of service (see Table 2)—is greater than the second group. The further away from 1 this ratio is, the greater the difference between the two groups compared. We also report a 95% confidence interval for each risk ratio.[5] If that interval does not include 1, the difference between the two groups—in this example, between Democrats and Republicans—is statistically significant (Lowe, 2006). Ultimately, we can then interpret this result as saying that Democratic congresswomen emphasized female issues in their floor speeches more often than Republican congresswomen and that this difference in emphasis is statistically significant.

Second, in Table 2 we report percent change. This allows us to consider how much of a difference is detected between the groups compared. Positive percent change, in those cases where a statistically significant ratio is detected, shows a greater likelihood of that category of content appearing in the speeches of the first group (Democrats, House members, and women serving more years) from each set of comparisons. Returning to the example discussed above, we see that the percent change in mentions of female issues between Democratic and Republican congresswomen is about 19% (see Table 2). Thus, speeches given by Democratic women were 19% more likely than those by Republican women to include mentions of female issues.

In response to our first research question, our overall comparison of speeches given by Democratic and Republican congresswomen revealed that Democrats were more likely to emphasize female issues whereas Republicans were more likely to emphasize male issues. These differences are statistically significant. When discussing female issues, the top three terms used by Democrats were "school/s" (28% of all female issues mentions), "education" (26% of female issues mentions), and "Medicare" (13% of female issues mentions). The following excerpt illustrates how the key term "school" from our dictionary was used in the context of a June 20, 2013, speech by Rep. Tammy Duckworth (D-IL), objecting to $20.5 billion in cuts to the Supplemental Nutrition Assistance Program:

> This is a very personal issue for me. I was one of those children. After my father lost his job for several years when I was a teenager, food stamps, school breakfast, and school lunch were the only things that saved me. They were there for me so I could worry about school instead of my empty stomach. They nourished me so I could develop the skills to serve my country for the next 20 years—all of the way here to Congress. (Duckworth, 2013, para. 2)

Speeches by Republican congresswomen were 7% more likely to mention male issues than those delivered by Democratic congresswomen. Republican congresswomen used the following items from our dictionary the most in their mentions of male issues: "tax/es" (25% of male issues mentions), "energy" (12% of male issues mentions), and "job/s" (9% of male issues mentions). The following excerpt from an April 11, 2013, speech by Sen. Deb Fischer (R-NE) on the president's proposed budget illustrates how taxes were discussed in the floor speeches of Republican congresswomen:

> I am disappointed that this budget amounts to more taxes, more spending, and more debt. The president's budget calls for $1.1 trillion more in taxes, on top of the $660 billion in tax hikes the president already demanded and won as part of the fiscal cliff deal enacted at the beginning of the year, before I arrived in Washington. That is a grand total of $1.8 trillion in tax hikes—before we add in another trillion dollar tax from "Obamacare." Yet, despite all of this new so-called "revenue," the president's budget would never balance. No amount of taxes will ever begin to address our nation's $17 trillion debt. (Fischer, 2013, para. 1)

Democratic congresswomen were significantly more likely to mention marginalized constituencies in their floor speeches as compared to Republican congresswomen—these mentions were 23% more likely in the floor speeches of the former than in the latter (see Table 2). Democrats most frequently mentioned marginalized constituencies by using such terms as "family/families" (33% of marginalized constituencies mentions), "child/ren" (33% of marginalized constituencies mentions), and "mom/s" (11% of marginalized constituencies mentions). The following excerpt from a February 5, 2013, speech by Rep. Janice Hahn (D-CA), on the female topic of gun control, demonstrates how marginalized constituencies were referenced in floor speeches:

> Now is the time to pass legislation that is necessary to protect our children and our families from these repeated patterns of senseless gun violence. Our children should not have to live in fear while learning their ABCs or college algebra or innocently waiting at a bus stop after school or seeing a movie. I believe America is ready to take common sense steps to keep our families and our communities safe. (Hahn, 2013, para. 2)

Democratic congresswomen also mentioned other key constituencies a great deal more that Republican congresswomen. References to other constituencies were 175%, or 1.75 times, more likely in the floor speeches by Democrats than by Republicans. Democrats mentioned key terms like "women" (83% of other constituencies mentions) and "men" (13% of other constituencies mentions) the most.

Democratic congresswomen were also more likely to use a feminine style in the rhetorical framing of their floor speeches. "We" was used more frequently than "I" (53% of instances of feminine style as compared to 45%). They also referred to their own personal experiences—as demonstrated in the excerpt quoted above from the June 20, 2013, speech by Rep. Tammy Duckworth (D-IL)—and/or identified with the experiences of others.

In response to our second research question, comparisons between women serving in the House and those serving in the Senate revealed that members of the House mentioned female issues at a significantly higher rate than those in the Senate. In fact, mentions of female issues were 56% more likely in House floor speeches than in Senate floor speeches. House members mentioned the following female issues terms from our dictionary most frequently: "education" (24% of female issues mentions), "school/s" (24% of female issues mentions), and "Medicare" (15% of female issues mentions). "Abortion" was the fourth most common female issues term raised in women's House floor speeches (12% of mentions). The following excerpt from a March 20, 2013, speech by Rep. Lynn Jenkins (R-KS) illustrates the discussion of Medicare as related to the federal budget, children, and families:

> Today, we are stealing from the next generation—our kids and our grandkids. We are making false promises that Medicare and Social Security benefits will be there to take care of folks when we know that Medicare is bankrupt in 8 to 12 years. It's time for Congress to do something to help Americans and their families. (Jenkins, 2013, para. 2)

Unlike mentions of female issues, we did not detect a significant difference between chambers in the attention male issues received. This should not be interpreted as evidence that male issues were not discussed by women in the House and Senate, but only that the proportions of words coded as male issues mentions were not significantly different between the two chambers' speeches. In fact, the proportion of words coded as male issues in the House speeches was 24% higher than the proportion of words coded as female issues; in the Senate, the proportion of male issues was 15% higher than female issues.

Women in the House also mentioned various constituencies, marginalized and otherwise, more often in their floor speeches than women in the Senate. These differences were statistically significant with the House emphasizing marginalized groups 94% more often and other constituencies 83% more often than the upper chamber. When discussing marginalized constituencies, women in the House mentioned "child/ren" (33% of marginalized constituencies mentions), "family/families" (30% of marginalized constituencies mentions), and "student/s" (19% of marginalized constituencies mentions) the most. "Women" and "men" were the most common terms from our dictionary coded as other key constituencies (84%

and 13% of other constituencies mentioned, respectively). In a May 20, 2013, speech, Rep. Joyce Beatty (D-OH) spoke on behalf of students:

> We must advance legislation that includes student loan reform in a way that provides realistic opportunities for our students to secure good jobs and pay off their student loans without falling into financial crisis. I will continue to advocate for better ways to lessen the financial burden of higher education for all students in this country. Our nation's students and families deserve an affordable education. (Beatty, 2013, para. 8)

Although women in the House tended to mention female issues and marginalized and other constituencies more often in their floor speeches than women in the Senate, we found the opposite to be true when it comes to employing a feminine style in the rhetorical frames used. Terms such as "we," "I," and "change" were 32% more likely to be used by women in the Senate than those serving in the House—this difference was statistically significant (see Table 2). In a February 28, 2013, speech in support of the Violence against Women Reauthorization Act, Sen. Lisa Murkowski (R-AK) demonstrated the use of a feminine rhetorical style with a personal tone, addressing the audiences as peers, and identifying with the experiences of others:

> I am pleased to stand with so many colleagues not only here on the Senate side but over in the House to recognize an accomplishment—an accomplishment of the Congress. I think it is important to recognize that in these times that are so contentious, where a lot of messages go back and forth but at the end of the day we haven't governed, we haven't done what we had hoped legislatively, we haven't really helped people, today we can be proud that we have worked to help people, particularly women … This ought not to be a Republican issue or a Democratic issue. It ought not be a woman's issue. It is an issue that should bother all of us when we cannot stand together and help those who have been victims of domestic violence. If we can't do that as a minimum, we really aren't doing our job, we really aren't doing service to people. (Murkowski, 2013, para. 1)

In response to our third research question, we examined differences between women who have been in Congress longer than the average number of years served by women in their chamber and those who have been in Congress for a shorter amount of time. Across all five content analysis categories, we detected significant differences between these two groups in the issues, constituencies, and frames emphasized (see Table 2).

Women who have served the average number of years or less for women in their chamber discussed female issues 36% more often than those who have served longer. As seen in our previous comparisons, the top terms used in these mentions of female issues were "education" (31% of female issues mentions), "school/s" (27% of female issues mentions), and "Medicare" (14% of female issues mentions). Women who have served fewer years also were more likely to emphasize male issues—27% more often—than women who have been in Congress longer. In coding for these mentions, we found that the male issues terms most frequently discussed were in relation to economic issues, including "tax/es" (22% of male issues mentions), "job/s" (11% of male issues mentions), and "budget" (10% of male issues mentions).

Women who have served fewer years also were more likely to talk about different constituencies in their floor speeches as compared to women who have spent more time in Congress. Women serving fewer years talked about marginalized groups a great deal more than their senior counterparts. More precisely, we found that the speeches by women serving less time referenced marginalized constituencies 109% more often than those by women serving more years. The terms most frequently used from this dictionary category were "family/families" (33% of marginalized constituencies mentions), "child/ren" (25% of marginalized constituencies mentions), and "student/s" (19% of marginalized constituencies mentions). In discussing other constituencies, women serving fewer years in Congress talked about "women" (82% of other constituencies mentions) and "men" (13% of other constituencies mentions) the most.

In an April 9, 2013, speech, Rep. Ann McLane Kuster (D-NH)—who was first elected to Congress in 2012—spoke on behalf of women and families on topics ranging from such female issues as education, health care, and retirement to the male issue of the economy:

> Women in my state of New Hampshire who work full time earn over $12,000 less every year than men. That wage gap has real consequences. Smaller paychecks make it harder for families to purchase health care, to send their kids to college, and to save for retirement. That doesn't just hurt women; it hurts our entire community and our economy. (Kuster, 2013, para. 2)

Feminine style was the only category where women with more years of service outpaced those serving fewer years in Congress; they employed this frame 23% more often than their junior colleagues. Women with more years of service used "we" most often (82% of feminine style mentions). In a February 13, 2013, speech against across-the-board-budget cuts, Sen. Susan Collins (R-ME)—who was first elected to Congress in 1996—used a feminine rhetorical style including a personal tone, addressing her colleagues as peers, and identifying with the experiences of others:

> If we are going to allow these mindless, indiscriminate cuts to go into effect, why are we here? We might as well have computers or robots making decisions for us. Our job

is to do the hard, painful work of setting priorities and making decisions. That is why I am so frustrated by the approach we appear to be on the verge of taking. While the Department of Defense would take a disproportionate impact from sequestration … there are other important programs that would be affected as well. The superintendents groups have met with me and talked about what it would mean for schoolchildren in Maine if … all of a sudden they get a reduction in Title I money that goes to low-income schools, to special education grants, to other important programs such as Head Start, and the TRIO Program, which helps low-income and first-generation students attend and excel in college. (Collins, 2013, para. 4)

In summary, our analysis of the content of floor speeches of women serving in the beginning six months of the 113th Congress in 2013 revealed that (1) Democrats were more likely than Republicans to emphasize female issues, mention both marginalized and other constituencies; and employ a feminine style; (2) Republicans were more likely than Democrats to emphasize male issues; (3) members of the House were more likely than those in the Senate to discuss female issues and mention marginalized and other constituencies; (4) women in the Senate were more likely than women in the House to employ a feminine style; (5) women with fewer years of service were more likely than women with more years to emphasize female and male issues and represent marginalized and other constituencies; and (6) women with more years of service were more likely than women with fewer years to employ a feminine style. Next, we discuss the implications of our findings, particularly for the direction of future research.

Conclusion

The purpose of our study was to examine the advocacy of women's interests and issues after the 2012 election through an analysis of the floor speeches of the 101 women serving in the 113th U.S. Congress in 2013. Would the attention on women voters and issues in the 2012 campaign and the record number of females serving in the U.S. Congress carry over into their speeches in 2013?

First, in examining the word frequencies of the key terms identified for our study, we note that male issues were raised more often than female issues in the speeches by the women serving in the 113th Congress. Of the top 18 issues mentioned, 15 were male issues—including the top five issues of budget, taxes, jobs, security, and the economy—and three were the female issues of schools, education, and Medicare. Although our analysis revealed that congresswomen spoke about a variety of issues—including abortion, agriculture, climate change, disaster relief, education, guns, health care, immigration, Iran, Medicare, pay equity, sexual assault in the military, student loans, veterans, violence against women, and voting rights—much of the debate in the early months of the 113th Congress focused on the budget sequestration (automatic spending cuts to federal programs). Thus, the impending "fiscal cliff" facing Congress in the opening months of 2013 may have led women to focus more on male, versus female, issues.

Still, when discussing issues—female or male—congresswomen were likely to mention "women" as well as such marginalized constituencies as families, children, students, mothers, and immigrants. Taken into consideration with the findings of previous research (Shogan, 2002; Walsh, 2002), this implies that women in Congress actively represent those who may not typically have a voice in governance. Also in keeping with previous research (Blankenship & Robson, 1995), congresswomen consistently employed feminine style as a rhetorical frame in advocating for issues and interests. Thus, although congresswomen's issues and interests may vary over time, they seem likely to continue to frame their arguments with such elements of feminine style as personal tone, addressing the audience as peers, and referring to their own experiences as well as the experiences of others.

Our comparative analysis based on political party, chamber of Congress, and length of service revealed interesting findings. As may be expected, Democratic women were more likely to emphasize female issues, marginalized constituencies, and other constituencies whereas Republicans were more likely to mention male issues. This underscores the importance of considering partisanship alongside gender in analyzing the issues advocated by female members of Congress, as suggested by previous research (Pearson & Dancey, 2011b).

Female Democrats also were more likely than female Republicans to use feminine style, perhaps indicating that women's experiences within their parties are different. As Denise Baer (2011) has argued, parties are differently gendered. So, perhaps a feminine rhetorical style is more acceptable for Democrats than for Republicans.

Women in the U.S. House of Representatives were more likely than women in the U.S. Senate to emphasize female issues and mention both marginalized and other constituencies. As women in both chambers were dominated by Democrats—77% of the women in the House and 80% of the women in the Senate—at the time of our study, we assume that this difference was not related to partisanship of individual members, per se. However, it could be related to which political party controlled each chamber. Democratic women in the U.S. House—which was controlled by the Republican Party in 2013—may have felt more compelled to represent their own gendered interests. Democratic women in the U.S. Senate—which was controlled by the Democratic Party in 2013—may have needed to pay more attention to balancing gender and partisanship interests in their floor speeches.

However, women in the U.S. Senate did employ a feminine style more often than those in the U.S. House. Perhaps this difference in rhetorical style results from members of the House representing—and speaking on behalf of—smaller constituencies back home whereas U.S. senators must frame their speeches to appeal to statewide constituencies. Thus, it is important for women senators to frame their rhetoric to appeal to "everyone." Again, this finding underscores the importance of considering the differences in governance culture and constraints across chambers as well as how best to appeal to their constituencies. Also, the speeches of women in the U.S. Senate tended to be longer on average than those delivered by women in the U.S. House. So, women senators had more time to incorporate personal experiences, anecdotes, and examples into their speeches.

Finally, women with fewer years of service were more likely to mention female and male issues and marginalized and other constituencies compared to women with more years of service in Congress. Perhaps women with less experience are motivated to represent agendas and constituencies more closely associated with their campaigns whereas women with more experience are more likely to recognize the congressional culture and constraints in which they must operate. However, women with more years of service were more likely to use feminine style, indicating that they feel more comfortable and confident governing as women over time through their use of a feminine rhetorical style. This finding also underscores the importance of including length of service in analyses of women (and men) serving in the U.S. Congress.

Our study also points to directions for future research. Although we focused on the political rhetoric of women serving in the 113th U.S. Congress, it is important to continue to compare the speeches of both female and male members. More research is needed on comparing the issues advocated by female and male members of Congress not only by gender, but also according to their political party, the chamber in which they serve, and their length of service. Through such analyses, we may better understand how Congress operates in representing our interests.

References

Baer, D. L. (2011). The gendered partisan divide and representation of women and women's organizations. In L. D. Whitaker (Ed.), *Women in politics: Outsiders or insiders?* (5th ed., pp. 89–112). Upper Saddle River, NJ: Pearson.

Barnello, M. (1999). Gender and roll call voting in the New York state assembly. *Women and Politics, 20,* 77–94.

Beatty, J. (2013, May 20). Remarks on the floor of the U.S. House at the U.S. Capitol in Washington, DC. Retrieved from http://www.gpo.gov/fdsys/pkg/CREC-2013-05-20/pdf/CREC-2013-05-20-pt1-PgH2795.pdf#page=1

Blankenship, J., & Robson, D. (1995). A "feminine" style in women's political discourse: An exploratory essay. *Communication Quarterly, 43*, 353–366.

Bratton, K., & Haynie, K. (1999). Agenda setting and legislative success in state legislatures: The effects of gender and race. *Journal of Politics, 61*(3), 658–679.

Campbell, K. K. (1989). *Man cannot speak for her: A critical study of early feminist rhetoric* (Vol. 1). New York, NY: Greenwood.

Center for American Women and Politics. (2012). *The gender gap: Voting choices in presidential elections.* Retrieved from http://www.cawp.rutgers.edu/fast_facts/voters/documents/GG-PresVote.pdf

Center for American Women and Politics. (2013). *Women serving in the 113th Congress.* Retrieved from http://www.cawp.rutgers.edu/fast_facts/levels_of_office/Congress-Current.php

Clark, J. (1998). Women at the national level: An update on roll call behavior. In S. Thomas & C. Wilcox (Eds.), *Women and elective office: Past, present and future* (pp. 118–129). New York, NY: Oxford University Press.

Collins, S. (2013, February 13). Remarks on the floor of the U.S. Senate at the U.S. Capitol in Washington, DC. Retrieved from http://www.gpo.gov/fdsys/pkg/CREC-2013-02-13/pdf/CREC-2013-02-13-pt1-PgS680.pdf#page=1

DeRosa, K. L., & Bystrom, D. (1999). The voice of and for women in the 1996 presidential campaign: Style and substance of convention speeches. In L. L. Kaid & D. G. Bystrom (Eds.), *The electronic election: Perspectives on the 1996 campaign communication* (pp. 97–111). Mahwah, NJ: Lawrence Erlbaum Associates Inc.

Dodson, D. (1998). Representing women's interests in the U.S. House of Representatives. In S. Thomas & C. Wilcox (Eds.), *Women and elective office: Past, present and future* (pp. 130–149). New York, NY: Oxford University Press.

Dolan, J. (1997). Support for women's interests in the 103rd Congress: The distinct impact of congressional women. *Women and Politics, 18*, 81–94.

Dow, B. J., & Tonn, M. B. (1993). "Feminine style" and political judgment in the rhetoric of Ann Richards. *Quarterly Journal of Speech, 79*, 286–302.

Duckworth, T. (2013, June 20). No child in America should go to school hungry. Retrieved from http://www.gpo.gov/fdsys/pkg/CREC-2013-06-20/pdf/CREC-2013-06-20-pt1-PgH3932-6.pdf#page=1.

Dugan, A. (2012, October 17). Women in swing states have gender-specific priorities. *Gallup.* Retrieved from http://www.gallup.com/poll/158069/women-swing-states-gender-specific-priorities.aspx.

Fischer, D. (2013, April 11). Remarks on the floor of the U.S. Senate at the U.S. Capitol in Washington, DC. Retrieved from http://www.gpo.gov/fdsys/pkg/CREC-2013-04-11/pdf/CREC-2013-04-11-pt1-PgS2581-2.pdf#page=1

Frederick, B. (2013). Gender and roll call voting behavior in Congress: A cross-chamber analysis. *The American Review of Politics, 34*, 1–20.

Fridkin, K., Carle, J., & Woodall, G. S. (2012). The vice presidency as the new glass ceiling: Media coverage of Sarah Palin. In M. Rose (Ed.), *Women and executive office: Pathways and performance* (pp. 33–52). Boulder, CO: Lynne Rienner Publishers.

Hahn, J. (2013, February 5). Gun violence. Retrieved from http://www.gpo.gov/fdsys/pkg/CREC-2013-02-05/pdf/CREC-2013-02-05-pt1-PgH353-7.pdf#page=1

Jenkins, L. (2013, March 20). Remarks on the floor of the U.S. House at the U.S. Capitol in Washington, DC. Retrieved from http://www.gpo.gov/fdsys/pkg/CREC-2013-03-20/pdf/CREC-2013-03-20-pt1-PgH1645-3.pdf#page=1

Kahn, K. F. (1996). *The political consequences of being a woman: How stereotypes influence the conduct and consequences of political campaigns.* New York, NY: Columbia University Press.

Kuster, A. M. (2013, April 9.) Equal pay day. Retrieved from http://www.gpo.gov/fdsys/pkg/CREC-2013-04-09/pdf/CREC-2013-04-09-pt1-PgH1848-6.pdf#page=1

Lawrence, J. (2013, July 12). Do women make better senators than men? *National Journal.* Retrieved from http://www.nationaljournal.com/women-of-washington/do-women-make-better-senators-than-men-20130711

Library of Congress. (2013). About the Congressional Record. *THOMAS.* Retrieved from http://thomas.loc.gov/home/cr_help.htm

Lowe, W. (2006, September). *Yoshikoder: An open source multilingual content analysis tool for social scientists.* Paper presented at the annual meeting of the American Political Science Association, Philadelphia, PA.

Mayhead, M. A., & Marshall, B. D. (2005). *Women's political discourse: A 21st century perspective.* Lanham, MD: Rowman & Littlefield Publishers Inc.

Mendes, E., & Wilke, J. (2013, June 13). American's confidence in Congress falls to lowest on record. *Gallup Politics.* Retrieved from http://www.gallup.com/poll/163052/americans-confidence-congress-falls-lowest-record.aspx.

Murkowski, L. (2013, February 28). Violence against women reauthorization act. Retrieved from http://www.gpo.gov/fdsys/pkg/CREC-2013-02-28/pdf/CREC-2013-02-28-pt1-PgS996.pdf#page=1

Ness, D. L. (2012, November 8). A good day for women, a good day for the country. *The Huffington Post.* Retrieved from http://www.huffingtonpost.com/debra-l-ness/women-voters-election-results_b_2092559.html

Neuendorf, K. A. (2011). Content analysis: A methodological primer for gender research. *Sex Roles, 64,* 276-289.

Norton, N. (1999). Uncovering the dimensionality of gender voting in Congress. *Legislative Studies Quarterly, 24,* 65–86.

Osborn, T., & Mendez, J. M. (2010). Speaking as women: Women and the use of floor speeches in Congress. *Journal of Women, Politics and Policy, 31*(1), 1–21.

Pearson, K., & Dancey, L. (2011a). Elevating women's voices in Congress: Speech participation in the House of Representatives. *Political Research Quarterly, 64*(4), 910–923.

Pearson, K., & Dancey, L. (2011b). Speaking for the underrepresented in the House of Representatives: Voicing women's interests in a partisan era. *Politics & Gender, 7*(4), 493–519.

Reingold, B. (2000). *Representing women: Sex, gender and legislative behavior in Arizona and California*. Chapel Hill, NC: University of North Carolina Press.

Riffe, D., Lacy, S., & Fico, F. G. (2005). *Analyzing media messages: Using quantitative content analysis in research* (2nd ed.). Mahwah, NJ: Lawrence Erlbaum Associates Inc.

Roberts, C. (2013, January 3). Hope abounds that record number of women in Congress will ease bipartisanship and action. *New York Daily News*. Retrieved from http://www.nydailynews.com/news/politics/record-female-congressional-presence-deemed-path-action-article-1.1232702

Saad, L. (2012, October 22). Economy is dominant issue for Americans as election nears. *Gallup Politics*. Retrieved from http://www.gallup.com/poll/158267/economy-dominant-issue-americans-election-nears.aspx

Shogan, C. J. (2002). Speaking out: An analysis of Democratic and Republican woman-invoked rhetoric of the 105th Congress. *Women and Politics, 23*(1/2), 129–146.

Swers, M. (1998). Are women more likely to vote for women's issue bills than their male colleagues? *Legislative Studies Quarterly, 23*(3), 435–448.

Swers, M. (2002). *The difference women make: The policy impact of women in Congress*. Chicago, IL: University of Chicago Press.

Taylor, P., Morin, R., Cohn, D., Clark, A., & Wang, W. (2008). *Men or women: Who's the better leader?* Retrieved from Pew Research Social and Demographic Trends: http://www.pewsocialtrends.org/2008/08/25/men-or-women-whos-the-better-leader/

Thomas, S. (1989). Voting patterns in the California assembly: The role of gender. *Women and Politics, 9*, 43–53.

Thomas, S. (1994). *How women legislate*. New York, NYJ: Oxford University Press.

Walsh, K. C. (2002). Enlarging representation: Women bringing marginalized perspectives to floor debate in the House of Representatives. In C. S. Rosenthal (Ed.), *Women Transforming Congress* (pp. 370–396). Norman, OK: University of Oklahoma Press.

Notes

1. Length of service is based on the average number of years women in the 113th Congress have served in each chamber as of January through June 2013. In the House, this average was nine years. In the Senate, the average length of service was 10 years. In our comparative analysis, we categorized congresswomen into one of two groups: those serving "more years" and "fewer years." Women who have served the average number of years for their chamber or less were classified in the "fewer years" group.

2. We thank Sue Cloud and Morgan Todd of the Carrie Chapman Catt Center for Women and Politics at Iowa State University for their assistance in collecting the samples of speeches for this study.

3. THOMAS can be found at http://thomas.loc.gov/home/thomas.php. The Congressional Record includes the verbatim account of floor proceedings of both chambers of Congress

as well as summaries of congressional activity (known as the "Daily Digest") and additional remarks and materials that members of Congress may insert into the public record at a later time (known as "Extensions of Remarks" for the House and "Additional Statements" for the Senate) (Library of Congress, 2013). When searching the Congressional Record, we included only transcripts of speeches as delivered on the floor in our data collection and analysis.

4. Stated as a formula, the risk ratio (RR) is:

$$RR = p_1 / p_2 \qquad \text{where}$$

p_1 = number of category terms in first sample/number of total words in first sample and

p_2 = number of category terms in second sample/number of total words in second sample

5. To generate a 95% confidence interval, we first calculate

$$\text{Ln(RR)} \pm 1.96 \sqrt{\frac{(n_1 - x_1)/x_1}{n_1} + \frac{(n_2 - x_2)/x_2}{n_2}}$$

and then take the antilog (exp) of the lower and upper limits. When the 95% confidence interval does not include the null value (RR = 1), the result is statistically significant.

Electorate

CHAPTER TWELVE

The Gender Gap in Presidential Vote Preference

KATE KENSKI

Although many predictors of vote preference are seemingly independent from campaign communication, elections are won by swaying voter margins through targeted messages to specific groups, or audiences, so that individuals in those groups will to go to the polls and cast their ballots a particular way. People possess different social identities, some more salient to the individuals than others. News media and candidate discourse can prime those identities influencing voting decisions. News outlets devote notable proportions of their campaign coverage trying to reveal candidate strategies and offer armchair speculation as to whether or not the strategies will in fact work on specific groups. Women are often one such group about whom the media offer their projections, some of which are based on evidence whereas others are based on gender stereotypes. Ultimately, by treating women as the malleable group and failing to acknowledge how other demographics interact with sex when it comes to vote decisions, the media cultivate gender stereotypes and overlook subpopulations that do not conform to media's gender predictions.

The purpose of this chapter is to explain the role that gender played in the 2012 presidential election and to provide a portrait of how gender was associated with the presidential vote. First, I will discuss why gender is believed to matter in political campaigns and what gender gaps exist. Second, the dominant gender frames put forth by the presidential campaigns and their parties will be described.

Early in 2012, a frame was offered for understanding the impacts that the Republican Party and its candidates had on public policy affecting women. The theme offered was the GOP's so-called "war on women." President Barack Obama and the Democrats won that framing battle, which hindered former Massachusetts Gov. Mitt Romney's ability to attract women, specifically undecided women. Third, the results of the 2012 Republican primaries and general election will be presented based on the exit poll data available. The data show that gender was associated with the outcome of the primaries and general election. Nevertheless, the data also show that certain demographic subgroups of women supported the Republican candidate over the presidential incumbent.

Why Gender Matters

Scholarly attention has been paid to gender and politics, not only because of the role that gender has played in voting outcomes, but also because women have not achieved political equality in both obvious and subtle ways. Although women currently vote in higher proportions than do men, they lag behind them in other forms of political participation (Burns, Schlozman, & Verba, 2001; Poole & Zeigler, 1985), expression of political interest (Bennett, 1986; Kenski, 2001), political knowledge (Delli Carpini & Keeter, 1996, 2000; Kenski, 2000; Kenski & Jamieson, 2001), expression of political opinion (Neuman, 1986), and elective representation (Center for American Women and Politics, 2013). The numerous inequalities that persist today call into question the image of American society as progressive.

Kathleen Hall Jamieson has observed that women face many Catch-22s or double binds. One such bind is the womb/brain bind, which pits female physiology against intellect. This bind perpetuates the notion of a duality between mind and body and assumes that women can either use their wombs for the purpose of creation or they can use their intellect, but not both. The womb/brain bind is based on the belief that a woman's natural role is determined by her body. "Although the womb/brain bind has been consigned to the history books, the assumption that women are driven by biology and are biologically defective persists in subtle ways," Jamieson has noted (1995, p. 133).

Entrenched societal beliefs about a woman's natural role are reflected in candidate campaign coverage and how media frame women candidates. When women run for political office, media coverage tends to treat female candidates differently from male ones. Although several studies have shown that male and female candidates receive the same amount of coverage (Bystrom, Robertson, & Banwart, 2001;

Devitt, 1999), gender stereotypes persist as women candidates are "described significantly more often than men in terms of their sex, marital status, and children" (Bystrom et al., 2001, p. 2009). James Devitt's study of gubernatorial candidates in 1998 revealed that issues were discussed more often in reference to male candidates than female ones, while "[n]ewspaper readers were more likely to read about a female candidate's personal life, appearance, or personality than that of a male candidate" (1999, p. 5).

When it comes to the presidency, no woman has ever been elected or secured a major party nomination. Only two women have made it onto major party tickets as vice presidential running mates: Democrat Geraldine Ferraro in 1984 and Republican Sarah Palin in 2008. Political communication scholars Erika Falk and Jamieson have argued that, "… the most significant barrier to a successful candidacy of a woman is the fact that so few occupy the positions that tend to be entryways to the White House" (2003, p. 45). Before we see women occupying as many positions at the federal level as men, gains must be made in local, state, and other federal offices. This means overcoming tough obstacles. "In communicating with both the media and voters, women candidates must overcome stereotypes about their viability and leadership skills," according to Dianne Bystrom, director of the Carrie Chapman Catt Center for Women and Politics (2003, p. 95). These stereotypes not only affect women candidates, but they shape women as citizen participants in the political process. Without women being empowered as citizens, it is unlikely that many women would want to take their involvement a step higher by running for office as candidates.

Media coverage of citizens has done little to dispel the belief that women are driven primarily by something other than rational thought or substantive issue concerns, which may contribute to biases—most of which may be subconscious—that prevent women from achieving equal voice and representation in government. A gender gap in political attitudes emerged in the 1980s. According to Kathleen A. Frankovic, a political scientist and former director of surveys for CBS News, little evidence from the 1940s to the 1970s suggests that gender played "a role in determining issue positions, candidate evaluations, or candidate preference" (1982, p. 439). This changed, however, during the 1980 presidential election between Jimmy Carter and Ronald Reagan. "Men favored Ronald Reagan by a large margin; women did not," Frankovic noted. "On election day, all major voter polls reported a 20-point margin in favor of Ronald Reagan among men, and an even division between Reagan and Jimmy Carter among women" (p. 440). After that election, media and scholarly attention to the relationship between gender and political attitudes increased. As Henry C. Kenski has noted, "The 1982 congressional election included extensive coverage of the contrasting voting patterns of men and women, while the 1984 election year was underscored by weekly commentary and analysis of the gender gap" (1988, p. 38). The gender gap has been a topic of public commentary and scholarly research since that time.

The media coverage of the gender gap in vote choice often has focused on women as a highly persuadable group. In 1996, the media speculated about how so-called soccer moms would influence the election (Carroll, 1999). In 2004, attention was paid to so-called security moms, although they did not seem to cohere as a group at the polls (Foster, 2010) despite the media proclaiming their existence. The "coveted female swing voter of 2012" was the waitress moms, according to *New York Times* correspondent Katharine Q. Seelye. "She has slipped a rung or two down the economic ladder from the soccer moms of the more prosperous 1990s, as indicated by her new nickname—waitress mom," she wrote. "Rather than ferrying children around the suburbs in minivans, she is spinning in the hamster wheel of a tight economy and not getting ahead" (2012, p. A1). The media storytelling has emphasized these subgroups as though they represent the whole.

Two problems emerge from the catchy narrative journalistic hooks that focus on one demographic as a lens for understanding the women's vote. First, the subgroup of focus is used to symbolize the larger whole, even when the subgroup's political behavior and needs may be quite different from other groups. As Carroll (1999) has noted, "Instead of empowering feminist and other women's organizations, the soccer mom news frame actually led to the disempowerment of most women through its narrow portrayal of women voters and their interests" (p. 11).

Second, although many stories discuss the women's vote, few journalists have framed the gender gap in terms of how men have behaved politically. The omission is serious given that history suggests that men have changed their political attitudes over time more so than have women. "American women have been the central feature of the gender gap story for the past twenty years, while men have most often been treated as the constant baseline against which the changing politics of women could be examined," political scientists Karen M. Kaufmann and John R. Petrocik have observed (2003, p. 865). Yet, this gender gap is mainly the outcome of the changing political preferences of men, not women. "Men have become increasingly Republican in their party identification and voting behavior since the mid-sixties while the partisanship and voting behavior of women has remained essentially constant" (2003, p. 865). Looking at percentages of the vote by gender over the last 60 years, men have been more likely than women, for example, to support third party candidates (Kenski & Kenski, 2013). Although women are more likely to say that they "don't know" for whom they plan to vote when asked, they are no less likely than men to express firm certainty for their decisions, once a substantive vote intention has been declared (Kenski, 2007). In other words, there is some evidence to suggest that men may be as persuadable as women.

Ultimately, gender mattered in 2012 because men and women have exhibited different vote preferences and because the media reported that the Republicans were struggling with the women's vote. Obama obtained a higher percentage of support from females who broke for the president at 55% than Romney obtained from males who broke for the Republican at 52% ("Exit Poll," 2012). Women made up a greater percentage of the voting electorate than did men, at 53% female compared to 47% male.

Gender Themes in the 2012 Election

The dominant gender frame of the 2012 campaign season was the so-called Republican war on women. An attempt to counter the frame with an alternative, Obama's "war on religion," was asserted in campaign communication, such as a television spot by the Romney campaign (Seligman, 2012), but the frame did not receive much media attention. Moreover, the war on women claim was put forth early in the campaign season and then seemingly supported by politically insensitive comments about rape made by two Republican politicians on separate occasions during the general election. Although the comments were denounced by prominent members of the Republican Party, they seemed to support the notion of a Republican war on women theme (see also Hennings & Bystrom, chapter 8, this volume for a discussion on the war on women as rhetorical strategy).

The war on women metaphor was used by Democrats to depict anti-abortion and anti-equal-pay legislation (Weigel, 2012). The phrase was created by a man in response to H.R. 3 (112th Congress): No Taxpayer Funding for Abortion Act, which was passed in the House but not in the Senate. On February 9, 2011, Democrat Rep. Jerry Nadler of New York claimed that the legislation "represents an entirely new front in the war on women and families" (Weigel, 2012). The phrase was then adopted by Democrat Rep. Debbie Wasserman Schultz of Florida in March 2011 and picked up by media. "For every Republican outrage, there was a three-word talking point in pocket, ready to drive the GOP up the wall. Between January 1 and April 12, *The New York Times* published 24 references to the 'war on women' and *The Washington Post* published 26 such references," noted *Slate* writer David Weigel (2012).

In February 2012, the House Oversight and Government Reform Committee had hearings on the requirements of insurance plans to cover contraception when the use of birth control violated the religious beliefs of entities, such as hospitals, that are affiliated with religious groups but are not the groups themselves. The Republican-controlled committee held hearings, but failed to include any testimony from women. The omission of women from testimony allowed for reinterpretation of the issues at stake. What had previously been considered a liability for Obama—an issue pegged on religious freedom (i.e., allowing religious organizations to not provide health insurance plans offering contraception)—became a Republican war on women. A picture of men offering testimony was diffused through social media with questions overlaid asking what was missing from the picture: women. When the committee's chairman, Republican Rep. Darrell Issa of California, was asked to include a female witness, the chairman said no, maintaining that the topic was one that centered on religious freedom, not reproductive rights. "The only question left: Is Darrell Issa a mole that's secretly working for the Democrats?" asked *Slate*'s Amanda Marcotte (2012). "If you wanted to send the message that Republicans have a serious problem with female sexuality and independence and are willing to move heaven and earth to take away the rights of ordinary women, you couldn't have concocted a better illustration than today's hearings."

The House Democrats held a hearing of their own as a response. A thirty-year-old Georgetown University law student named Sandra Fluke testified before the group. She argued that Georgetown's female population suffered undue financial hardships from the university's decision to provide health care that did not cover contraceptive drugs. She also noted that one of her friends had polycystic ovary syndrome that required contraceptive drugs to treat the disease. Owing to the treatment being contraception, the insurance company did not cover the needed medication. Conservative political talk radio personality Rush Limbaugh attacked Fluke on his show, calling her a "slut" and "prostitute." "[Fluke] essentially says that she must be paid to have sex—what does that make her? It makes her a slut, right? It makes her a prostitute," said Limbaugh. "She wants to be paid to have sex. She's having so much sex she can't afford the contraception. She wants you and me and the taxpayers to pay her to have sex" ("Year in review: Sandra Fluke's unexpected political stardom," 2012). The conservative icon lost advertisers over his comments. He later apologized to Fluke for having made them. Although many Republicans opposed the comments made by Limbaugh, the damage was done. His initial reaction was consistent with the Democrats' war on women claim.

Just as the war on women theme seemed to be dying down, two comments from Republican politicians brought the issue back to the fore. Missouri Republican senatorial candidate Todd Akin contended that women who were victims of "legitimate rape" rarely became pregnant. "People always want to make it into one of those things—well, how do you slice this particularly tough ethical question,"

Akin said in an interview in which he was trying to defend his position on abortion. "First of all, from what I understand from doctors, [pregnancy from rape] is really rare. If it's a legitimate rape, the female body has ways to try to shut that whole thing down" (Carroll, 2012). Doctors and rape experts, however, did not support such claims (Carroll, 2012). Akin later apologized and claimed that his remarks were cut short and taken out of context. He was defeated handily by Democratic incumbent Sen. Claire McCaskill in the November election. Although Romney had told the *National Review* that Akin's remarks on rape were "insulting, inexcusable, and, frankly, wrong" (Weiner, 2012), the entire Republican brand was harmed by them.

The second major Republican gaffe occurred during a senatorial debate in Indiana when the Republican candidate, Richard Mourdock, said that "even when life begins in that horrible situation of rape, that it is something that God intended to happen" (Weisman, 2012). The Mourdock campaign had released a television advertisement in which Romney was on camera endorsing him a couple days before the public relations blunder occurred. Romney disagreed with Mourdock on the rape position (Camia, 2012), but his campaign did not ask Mourdock to remove the endorsement ad. The Obama campaign used the comments to press "a message that the Republican Party is out of step with female voters" (Weisman, 2012). The instances were problematic for the Romney campaign, which had been trying to reach out to women voters.

Less controversial but treated as emblematic of the Republican's treatment of women occurred in the second presidential debate on October 16, 2012. Moderator Candy Crowley of CNN asked Romney about his position on pay equity for women. Romney responded:

> [W]e took a concerted effort to go out and find women who had backgrounds that could be qualified to become members of our cabinet. I went to a number of women's groups and said, "Can you help us find folks?" And they brought us whole binders full of women. (Commission on Presidential Debates, 2012)

Romney reported that he hired many women to join his cabinet. Social media lit up after he uttered the phrase "binders full of women." In addition to the reference being utilized in tweets, a Twitter account called Romney's Binder (@Romneys_Binder) acquired 12,300 followers and a Facebook page called Binders Full of Women had received 32,000 likes by the end of the October 16 debate (Johnson, 2012). User-generated pictures were uploaded to a Tumblr blog, Binders Full of Women, that made fun of the phrase. Photographs included a picture of actor Ryan Gosling with an open shirt that contained the words "HEY GIRL I WON'T PUT YOU IN A BINDER" and one of Patrick Swayze from his movie *Dirty Dancing* with the words "NO ONE PUTS BABY IN A BINDER." Another photo uploaded was a picture of Hillary Clinton texting on her phone with the overlaid words "Romney still uses binders? LOL."

It is hard to say why exactly "binders full of women" became such a popular meme acknowledging the awkwardness of the phrase. The social media environment was ready for pouncing on such moments of ineloquence. Romney's position was not helped by the fact that he ultimately did not answer Crowley's debate question about pay inequality, with or without binders. In his rebuttal, Obama stated, "I just want to point out that when Governor Romney's campaign was asked about the Lilly Ledbetter bill, whether he supported it? He said, 'I'll get back to you.' And that's not the kind of advocacy that women need in any economy" (Commission on Presidential Debates, 2012). He then used his rebuttal time as an opportunity to remind voters about their differences on the issue of contraception and Romney's proposal to eliminate funding for Planned Parenthood. "[T]here are millions of women all across the country who rely on Planned Parenthood for, not just contraceptive care, they rely on it for mammograms, for cervical cancer screenings. That's a pocketbook issue for women and families …," the president said.

The Democrats controlled the framing of how the campaign issues impacted women. Romney attempted to make arguments about the economy and health care in relation to women and families. He argued that Obama's policies had harmed the economy, which therefore had harmed women and their families. The Romney campaign released an ad called "Dear Daughter," in which a fictional mother tells her baby girl:

> Dear daughter. Welcome to America. Your share of Obama's debt is over $50,000. And it grows every day. Obama's policies are making it harder on women. The poverty rate for women—the highest in 17 years. More women are unemployed under President Obama. More than 5.5 million women can't find work. That's what Obama's policies have done for women.

The Washington Post gave the ad a two Pinocchio rating, as Hicks (2012) noted that the rates of poverty were on the rise before Obama took office and that the rate had increased faster during the previous George W. Bush administration.

Political consultant Peter Hart conducted focus groups during the 2012 election. On September 17, 2012, he had a discussion with undecided voters in Fairfax, Virginia. He found that the "undecided" voters in his group were not actually undecided. He also found "the degree to which Obama's attacks on Romney over abortion, contraception, and family planning had reached the targeted audience of women voters and threatened Romney's hopes of narrowing the gender gap" (Balz, 2013, p. 297). It is important to note that Obama's attacks on Romney were made early. The foundation was laid during the Republican nomination phase. Moreover, Romney's appeal to women was based on the argument that if the economy improved, everyone would benefit. In that sense, although he made that appeal to women, the appeal was not specific to women as a group. He tried to make his case through campaign surrogates, such as his wife Ann. By contrast, the Democrats had arguments that were specifically tailored to women and that a Romney presidency would harm their interests.

Gender and the Vote

Based on data from exit polls taken during the Republican primaries and general election, men and women expressed different preferences for the candidates.

The Republican Nomination

Exit polls were conducted in 15 states: Alabama, Arizona, Florida, Georgia, Illinois, Iowa, Massachusetts, Michigan, Mississippi, New Hampshire, Nevada, Ohio, South Carolina, Tennessee, and Wisconsin ("State-by-State Primary-Results," 2012). The data revealed that there was no state in which women outnumbered men in the Republican primaries or caucuses. The Republican voter composition varied from state to state. The gender gap in composition ranged from 0% to 14%. In Arizona, Alabama, and Mississippi, there was gender parity in turnout. In Iowa, however, 57% of caucus participants were male and 43% were female.

As shown in Table 1, in 10 of the 15 exit polls, women as a group supported the winning Republican with a wider margin than men did. The exceptions were in Arizona, Georgia, Illinois, South Carolina, and Tennessee. In Arizona, Romney had received a plurality from both men and women, but men supported him a bit more than did women (49% to 46%). In Georgia, Newt Gingrich was the favored candidate by both sexes, but men supported him more (50% to 45%). In Illinois, Romney acquired 48% of the vote from males and 46% from females. Gingrich captured South Carolina with 42% support from men and 38% support from women. In Tennessee, both men (38%) and women (37%) favored Rick Santorum. In all five states, even though men supported the winning candidate more so than did women, the candidate who won was the favored candidate among both sexes.

Table 1. Exit Poll Preferences from the Republican Primaries and Caucuses by Gender and State (%)

State		Bachmann	Gingrich	Huntsman	Paul	Perry	Romney	Santorum
IA	Male (57%)	4	14	1	24	10	23	23
	Female (43%)	5	12	0	19	10	25	27
NH	Male (54%)	0	10	17	25	0	39	8
	Female (47%)	0	9	17	20	1	40	11
SC	Male (51%)		42		14	1	26	14
	Female (49%)		38		12	0	29	20
FL	Male (51%)		36		9		41	13
	Female (49%)		28		5		45	14
NV	Male (53%)		20		23		48	9
	Female (47%)		22		14		52	12
AZ	Male (50%)		18		10		49	23
	Female (50%)		16		7		46	29
MI	Male (52%)		7		14		39	38
	Female (48%)		6		9		43	38
GA	Male (51%)		50		7		25	18
	Female (49%)		45		6		26	22
MA	Male (52%)		5		12		69	11
	Female (48%)		4		6		75	12
OH	Male (53%)		14		12		36	37
	Female (47%)		15		7		40	37
TN	Male (52%)		23		11		27	38
	Female (48%)		25		7		29	37
AL	Male (50%)		34		5		28	31
	Female (50%)		25		5		30	38
MS	Male (50%)		34		6		28	31
	Female (50%)		29		3		32	35
IL	Male (52%)		9		10		48	33
	Female (48%)		8		9		46	37
WI	Male (53%)		6		12		43	37
	Female (47%)		6		10		45	37

Note. Exit poll data from *The New York Times*. States are listed in the order of the date their caucus or primary was held in 2012.

In 11 of the 15 states, men were more likely to support Gingrich than were women (Nevada, Ohio, and Tennessee were the exceptions; parity in support was seen in Wisconsin). With the exception of Alabama, where there was gender parity in support, there were no states in which women offered more support than did men to Ron Paul. In 13 of 15 states, women supported Romney at higher rates than did men (Arizona and Illinois were the exceptions). In only one state (Tennessee) did men give greater support to Santorum than did women (with gender parity in Michigan, Ohio, and Wisconsin). When candidate support was averaged across the 15 states (with the state being the unit of analysis), the results showed that there was a 2.4% male preference for Gingrich, a 3.7% male preference for Paul, a 2.3% female preference for Romney, and a 2.8% female preference for Santorum.

In two states, Iowa and Ohio, men and women preferred different candidates when their pluralities were examined. In both cases, the women's vote decided the outcome. In Iowa, Santorum received the most votes. Men—who made up 53% of caucus participants—were equally split between Romney and Santorum at 23% each. Women, however, supported Santorum (27%) more than they supported Romney (23%), which gave Santorum the edge. In Ohio, where men made up a greater percentage of voters at 53%, women again gave the winning candidate Romney the edge. Ohio men supported Santorum (37%) slightly more so than they did Romney (36%). Ohio women, however, supported Romney (40%) more than they supported Santorum (37%).

In sum, the gender composition of the state presidential primary elections varied between gender parity and a gender gap of 14%, with males making up a greater proportion of voters. Support for the candidates by gender varied from state to state. Although the media often portray females as moderate voters, it is interesting to note that women supported Santorum, a socially conservative candidate, more so than did men. Romney and Gingrich were arguably the most moderate of the lot. Women gave the nod to Romney more so than did men. Men supported Gingrich more so than did women. Overall, female Republicans tended to support the winning candidates in the GOP primaries slightly more than male Republicans did. In Iowa and Ohio, it was the female vote that gave the winning candidates the edge.

The General Election

The gender gap, or the difference in how men and women vote for a candidate, exists and emerges during presidential general elections. Beginning in 1980, gender differences seemed more apparent on party identification, presidential job approval, issues, and candidate choice. Men tend to lean Republican whereas women lean toward Democrats. On issues, women are less inclined than men to favor the use of force in foreign policy and to express more support for domestic issues like education, health care, the environment, and financial support for the poor. Overall, men have been more supportive of Republican presidential candidates than have been women (Kenski & Kenski, 2009). Demographic shifts in turnout and candidate support occurred across the 2008 and 2012 general elections. Although Romney lost the election, he did slightly better overall than Republican presidential candidate John McCain had in 2008. In 2008, McCain captured 46% of the vote; in 2012, Romney received 48% of the vote (Kenski & Kenski, 2013).

Women increased their composition of the voting electorate in 2012 to 55% from 53% in 2008, as shown in Table 2. This was consequential for Obama. In terms of percentage of support from women, Obama actually did not do as well with women as a group in 2012 with 53% supporting him as he had done in 2008 with 56% supporting him. Nevertheless, more women overall supported Obama over the Republican candidate, and with the increase in women participating in the 2012 election, that net support helped contribute to his victory.

Table 2. Comparison of Gender Categories in Exit Polls, 2008 and 2012

Category	2008 (%)			2012 (%)		
	% of 2008 Total Vote	Obama	McCain	% of 2012 Total Vote	Obama	Romney
Total vote	100	53	46	100	51	48
Men	47	49	48	45	45	52
Women	53	56	43	55	53	44
White men	36	41	57	34	35	62
White women	39	46	53	38	42	56
Latino men	4	64	33	5	65	33
Latino women	5	68	30	6	76	23
Black men	5	95	5	5	87	11
Black women	7	96	3	8	96	3
Men with children	19	48	50	16	45	53
Women with children	21	57	41	20	56	43
Men without children	28	51	48	30	47	50
Women without children	32	56	43	34	54	45

Note. 2008 exit poll data from *CNN.com* and 2012 exit poll data from *NBC News.*

In 2008, males narrowly preferred Obama to McCain (49% to 48%), but Obama had made major inroads with women with a 56% to 43% advantage. Romney was successful in getting males to support his candidacy (52% to 45%). His success with male voters helped narrow Obama's victory. Nevertheless, there was a 2% drop in male composition of the electorate in 2012.

Focusing on the broad variable of gender, however, misses out on the nuances and diversity present in the electorate. Disaggregating the data by gender, race, and ethnicity shows a unique set of preferences between the subgroups. Table 2 presents data that disaggregates the vote by white men, white women, Latino men, Latino women, black men, and black women. Both white men and white women preferred the Republican presidential candidates over Obama in 2008 and 2012. In 2012, Romney increased support of white men and white women over what McCain had earned in 2008. Among white men, Republican candidate support increased from 57% in 2008 to 62% in 2012. Among white women, Republican candidate support increased from 53% in 2008 to 56%. It is important to note, however, that white men and white women dropped their percentage in composition of the electorate between the two elections by 2% for white men and by 1% for white women.

Obama's support among minority groups was high in both elections. He also managed to increase his already high levels of support among Latino men and women. Latino women were slightly more supportive than Latino males of Obama in 2008 (68% compared to 64%) and decisively more supportive in 2012 (76% versus 65%). Both Latino women and Latino men increased their presence in the voting electorate by 1% each, as shown in Table 2. In both 2008 and 2012, Obama was preferred by black women with 96% support over the Republican candidates 3% of support. Black women made up 7% of the voting electorate in 2008 and 8% in 2012. Among black men, Obama's support dropped from 95% in 2008 to 87% in 2012. Nevertheless, 87% support was still an impressive acquisition. Black male composition of the electorate did not change between the elections; in both elections, they made up 5% of the voting electorate.

Married men and women preferred Romney over Obama. Married men, who made up 29% of the voting electorate, supported Romney at 60% over Obama at 38%. Married females were not quite as enthusiastic about the Republican, but preferred him over the president by 53% to 46%. Married females composed 31% of the voting electorate. Unmarried men (18% of the voting electorate) and unmarried women (23% of the voting electorate) preferred the president over Romney. Among unmarried men, Obama received 56% of the vote to Romney's 40%. More than two-thirds (67%) of unmarried women preferred Obama to Romney (31%).

When having children is examined, the results show that men with and without children preferred Romney over Obama. Women with and without children preferred Obama over Romney.

The disaggregated results show that gender is affected by other group identities. Although women overall supported Obama, white women specifically preferred Romney. That said, white women did not show up at the polls as much as they did in 2008, suggesting lack of enthusiasm. Marital status also shapes our interpretation of gender's impact on the election. Married women preferred the Republican over the president in 2012. Although men overall preferred Romney, unmarried men preferred Obama.

Conclusion

There is no question that gender is associated with presidential vote preferences and matters to the outcome of elections. Differences in presidential preference emerged in 1980 and have continued ever since. However, there is more nuance to the voting patterns than what the media convey when they talk about "the women's vote" or when they focus on a subgroup of women (e.g., soccer moms). Although he lost the election, Romney increased his vote margin over what McCain had obtained in 2008 among some groups. For example, males overall had slightly preferred Obama to McCain in 2008, but they supported Romney in 2012. Romney also improved his support over 2008 support for McCain among women overall, white males, white females, and black males as well as both genders with and without children. Those increases in performance over McCain in 2008 were not enough, however, to lead him to victory. Although Romney did a better job than his Republican predecessor in many ways, some of the groups with whom he was preferred outright over Obama made up smaller proportions of the electorate in 2012. This was true of both white males and white females.

Given the state of the economy, it begs the question: Why were voters not enthusiastic about Romney to get to the polls? One speculation when it comes to gender is that the Obama campaign did a masterful job framing gender concerns as a Republican war on women. Romney's positions did little counter the questions that the Democrats had raised early in the Republican primary season. Gaffes by Republican congressional candidates about rape did not help the situation. Consequently, although people had misgivings about the president's first-term performance when it came to the economy, Obama had framed Romney as a risky alternative on a host of issues of relevance to women.

References

Balz, D. (2013). *Collision 2012: Obama vs. Romney and the future of elections in America.* New York, NY: Viking.

Bennett, S. E. (1986). *Apathy in America, 1960–1984: Causes and consequences of citizen political indifference.* Dobbs Ferry, NY: Transnational Publishers.

Burns, N., Schlozman, K. L., & Verba, S. (2001). *The private roots of public action: Gender, equality, and political participation.* Cambridge, MA: Harvard University Press.

Bystrom, D. (2003). On the way to the White House: Communication strategies for women candidates. In R. P. Watson & A. Gordon (Eds.), *Anticipating madam president* (pp. 95–105). Boulder, CO: Lynne Rienner Publishers.

Bystrom, D. G., Robertson, T. A., & Banwart, M. C. (2001). Framing the fight: An analysis of media coverage of female and male candidates in primary races for governor and U.S. senate in 2000. *American Behavioral Scientist, 44*(12), 1999–2013.

Camia, C. (2012, October 24). GOP's Mourdock says rape, abortion comments "twisted." *USA Today.* Retrieved from http://www.usatoday.com/story/news/politics/2012/10/24/mourdock-rape-god-intended-indiana-senate/1653745/

Carroll, L. (2012, August 20). Doctors appalled over Rep. Akin's comments that "legitimate rape" prevents pregnancy. *NBC News.* Retrieved from http://www.nbcnews.com/health/doctors-appalled-over-rep-akins-comments-legitimate-rape-prevents-pregnancy-954572?franchiseSlug=healthmain.

Carroll, S. J. (1999). The disempowerment of the gender gap: Soccer moms and the 1996 elections. *PS: Political Science & Politics, 32,* 7–11.

Center for American Women and Politics. (2013). *Women in elective office 2013.* Retrieved from http://www.cawp.rutgers.edu/fast_facts/levels_of_office/documents/elective.pdf

Commission on Presidential Debates. (2012, October 16). Debate Transcript. Retrieved from http://www.debates.org/index.php?page=october-1-2012-the-second-obama-romney-presidential-debate

Delli Carpini, M. X., & Keeter, S. (1996). *What Americans know about politics and why it matters.* New Haven, CT: Yale University Press.

Delli Carpini, M. X., & Keeter, S. (2000). Gender and political knowledge. In S. Tolleson-Rinehart & J. J. Josephson (Eds.), *Gender and American politics: Women, men, and the political process* (pp. 21–52). Armonk, NY: M.E. Sharpe.

Devitt, J. (1999). *Framing gender on the campaign trail: Women's executive leadership and the press.* New York, NY: Women's Leadership Fund.

Exit polls. (2012). *NBC News.* Retrieved from http://elections.nbcnews.com/ns/politics/2012/all/president/#exitPoll

Exit polls. (2008). *CNN.com.* Retrieved from http://www.cnn.com/ELECTION/2008/results/polls/#USP00p1

Falk, E., & Jamieson, K. H. (2003). Changing the climate of expectations. In R. P. Watson & A. Gordon (Eds.), *Anticipating madam president* (pp. 43–51). Boulder, CO: Lynne Rienner.

Foster, M. C. (2010). Security mom. In A. O'Reilly (Ed.), *Encyclopedia of Motherhood* (Vol. 1, p. 1104). Thousand Oaks, CA: SAGE Publications.

Frankovic, K. A. (1982). Sex and politics—new alignments, old issues. *PS: Political Science and Politics, 15*(3), 439–448.

Hicks, J. (2012, September 21). Fact checking a Romney appeal toward women. *The Washington Post.* Retrieved from http://www.washingtonpost.com/blogs/fact-checker/post/fact-checking-a-romney-appeal-toward-women/2012/09/21/314936c6-03e7-11e2-91e7-2962c74e7738_blog.html

Jamieson, K. H. (1995). *Beyond the double bind: Women and leadership.* New York, NY: Oxford University Press.

Johnson, M. W. (2012, October 16, updated October 17). Romney "binders full of women" debate remark inspires Tumblr, Facebook page and Twitter account. *Huffington Post.* Retrieved from http://www.huffingtonpost.com/2012/10/16/binders-full-of-women-tumblr-romney-debate_n_1972345.html

Kenski, H. C. (1988). The gender factor in a changing electorate. In C. M. Mueller (Ed.), *The politics of the gender gap: The social construction of political influence* (pp. 38–60). Newbury Park, CA: SAGE Publications.

Kenski, H., & Kenski, K. M. (2009). Explaining the vote in 2008. In R. E. Denton, Jr., (Ed.), *The 2008 presidential campaign: A communication perspective* (pp. 244–290). Lanham, MD: Rowman & Littlefield Publishers, Inc.

Kenski, H. C., & Kenski, K. M. (2013). Explaining the vote in the election of 2012: Obama's re-election. In R. E. Denton, Jr. (Ed.), *The 2012 presidential campaign: A communication perspective* (pp. 157–192). Lanham, MD: Rowman & Littlefield Publishers, Inc.

Kenski, K. (2000). Women and political knowledge during the 2000 primaries. *Annals of the American Academy of Political and Social Science, 572,* 26–28.

Kenski, K. (2001, November). *Explaining the gender gap in political knowledge: Tests of eighteen hypotheses.* Paper presented at the annual meeting of the National Communication Association in Atlanta, GA.

Kenski. K. (2007). Gender and time of voting decision: Decision certainty during the 2000 presidential election. *Journal of Political Marketing, 6,* 1–22.

Kenski, K., & Jamieson, K. H. (2000). The gender gap in political knowledge: Are women less knowledgeable than men about politics? In K. H. Jamieson (Ed.), *Everything you think you know about politics … and why you're wrong* (pp. 83–89, 238–241). New York, NY: Basic Books.

Kaufmann, K. M., & Petrocik, J. R. (2003). The changing politics of American men: Understanding the sources of the gender gap. *American Journal of Political Science, 43*(3), 864–887.

Marcotte, A. (2012, February 16). Darrell Issa's first panel on contraception coverage had zero female witnesses. *Slate.* Retrieved from http://www.slate.com/blogs/xx_factor/2012/02/16/issa_s_first_panel_of_witnesses_on_contraception_hearings_included_no_women_.html

Neuman, W. R. (1986). *The paradox of mass politics: Knowledge and opinion in the American electorate.* Cambridge, MA: Harvard University Press.

Poole, K. T., & Zeigler, L. H. (1985). *Women, public opinion, and politics: The changing political attitudes of American women.* New York, NY: Longman.

Seelye, K. Q. (2012, October 25). Crucial subset: Female voters still deciding. *The New York Times*, p. A1. Retrieved from http://www.nytimes.com/2012/10/25/us/politics/female-swing-voters-a-coveted-demographic.html?pagewanted=all&_r=0

Seligman, L. (2012, August 9). New Romney ad accuses Obama of "war on religion." *National Journal*. Retrieved from http://www.nationaljournal.com/2012-presidential-campaign/new-romney-ad-accuses-obama-of-war-on-religion--20120809

State-by-state primary results. (2012). *The New York Times*. Retrieved from http://elections.nytimes.com/2012/primaries/calendar

Weigel, D. (2012, April 12). The "war on women" is over. The life cycle of a political talking point, from birth to adolescence to death. Hilary Rosen just killed the Democrats' "war on women" talking point. *Slate*. Retrieved from http://www.slate.com/articles/news_and_politics/politics/2012/04/hilary_rosen_ann_romney_the_birth_adolescence_and_death_of_the_democrats_war_on_women_talking_point_.html

Weiner, R. (2012, August 20). "Insulting, inexcusable, and, frankly, wrong." *The Washington Post*. Retrieved from http://www.washingtonpost.com/blogs/post-politics/wp/2012/08/20/insulting-inexcusable-and-frankly-wrong/

Weisman, J. (2012, October 25). Rape remark jolts a senate race, and the presidential one, too. *The New York Times*. Retrieved from http://www.nytimes.com/2012/10/25/us/politics/using-mourdocks-rape-comment-against-romney.html

Year in review: Sandra Fluke's unexpected political stardom. (2012, December 31). *The Take Away with John Hockenberry*. Retrieved from http://www.thetakeaway.org/story/258714-year-review-sandra-flukes-unexpected-political-stardom/

CHAPTER THIRTEEN

Black, White, and Latino

Message Strategies for a Divided Electorate

CHARLTON MCILWAIN AND STEPHEN MAYNARD CALIENDO

President Barack Obama's 2008 election was historic because of its unique result: the election of the first African-American as president of the United States. His 2012 re-election was historic because it nullified that very same uniqueness. Many hailed 2008 as a turning point in America's racial history, the pinnacle achievement for a nation struggling to show that racial prejudice and discrimination were a thing of the past. Had the president lost his re-election bid in 2012, that achievement, no doubt, would have been deemed anomalous—a national error, a collective exercise of bad judgment, an American mistake. Thus, 2012 was in many ways more important than 2008 in that it provided a confirmatory stamp of approval on America's new image, an image of supreme leadership cloaked in historically tainted blackness.

Largely missing from the 2008 post-election storylines, however, was an electoral split that not only set the stage for Obama's first administration, but contributed greatly to the circumstances and candidates that emerged in 2012 to challenge his presidency. Beneath the dominant storyline of Obama's historic racial achievement and America's racial progress lay a significant fissure signaling a divided America. The bedrock evidence for what would become a narrative of racial division lies amidst the same data that confirmed Obama's 2008 election: that simple, final vote count in which Obama defeated U.S. Sen. John McCain by a handy seven-point popular vote margin.

While most newspaper headlines conflated Obama's historic election win with an equally historic victory for America's racial progress, news outlets could have easily justified a different headline, one that read something like this: "White America Chooses McCain, Non-White Voters Elect Obama." By a greater margin than that by which Obama edged out McCain, a majority of whites voting in 2008 cast their ballots for the white guy ("President: National Election Poll," 2008). In 2012, although Obama won the popular vote by about half of his margin four years earlier, the 12% racial gap became a 20% racial gap, as former Gov. Mitt Romney attracted 59% of the white vote ("President: Full Results," 2012).

The purpose of this chapter is to describe and provide reasonable explanations for how race factored into the 2012 presidential election—the candidates chosen to run, the messages they employed, the audiences they targeted, and the means by which they did so. The foundation for our description and explanations lies with a narrative of racial division whose kernel, as it were, is installed in those racially divided voting results from 2008. Continuing with the computing metaphor, this kernel of racial division serves as a primary mediating factor for interpreting the national mood of the electorate and modulated the strategic actions the Republican challengers made in 2012 in their quest to unseat President Obama.

To put it a different way, we argue that this notion and narrative of racial division was the primary animating message and mobilization strategy the Republican Party and its eventual standard bearer, Romney, relied on to mount their challenge. This strategy was premised on racial division. Specifically, we argue that the GOP set in motion a dual strategy to alienate and marginalize black and Latino voters as a way to captivate and capitalize on conservative white voters' own growing sense of alienation in a society where whites' numerical majority is declining. We seek to lay out an account of how and why the narrative of racial division took root in the empirical results of the 2008 election and ultimately pervaded the electoral climate and GOP vote strategy in 2012.

Specifying the Concepts: A Note About Our Approach

Political commentators and pundits rarely skip an opportunity to speculate on actors' racial intentions or to attribute a label such as "racist" to individuals or groups. It is seductive to try to "catch" a politician or celebrity saying something that reveals their hidden racism. Academics rarely take such an approach. For example, it is less important for social scientists interested in racialized campaign communication to discover if someone is secretly "a racist" than to understand the way that race-based communication can have an effect on candidate evaluation and, ultimately, vote choice. Accordingly, we center our analysis on the potential effects of race-based messages with particular attention to the contexts in which the messages are communicated and experienced.

To argue that the exploitation of racial divisions was a central component to the Republicans' 2012 presidential election strategy is not a direct claim that we can "know their hearts," to paraphrase former President George W. Bush; the conclusion reasonably follows from our analysis based on two interrelated strands of evidence: (1) the unique electoral context (i.e., challenging the re-election of the nation's first president of color) and structure of the Electoral College rendered such an approach the most plausible for the Republicans and (2) evidence from both the content of communication and the exit poll results of voting behavior in the election supports our contention.

It is also important to understand that we employ terms more precisely than the way they are used in colloquial settings. For instance, we differentiate between "racist" messages and "racial" messages. The former are messages that invoke race and gain persuasive advantage because of the history of white supremacy in the United States. The latter are messages that invoke race but do so in ways that do not gain advantage because of America's racist past. For example, a black candidate who argues that she "works hard" and "gained success the right way" is a reference to the racist stereotype that African-Americans are lazy and cheat to get ahead. Such a message is racial, but rather than benefitting from structural and attitudinal racism, it works to counteract it or inoculate the candidate from such accusations—direct, implied, or merely assumed. A vast and growing literature in cognitive psychology, social psychology, and social neuroscience has demonstrated that individuals socialized in a racist culture absorb racist messages that continue to reside—often latently—in their subconscious (Amodio, Devine, & Harmon-Jones, 2008; Amodio & Devine, 2006; Richeson & Trawalter, 2008).

As a result, invocation of both racist and racial messages is often not conscious. This reality renders the messages even more effective because they operate outside of conscious-level filters related to norms of racial equality. In other words, when whites in particular recognize that race is being used as a rhetorical lever—often called "playing the race card"—they are resistant to the messages. When race-based messages escape the filters, they have a greater potential for effect.

Related to this is the differentiation we borrow from other scholars that race-based messages can be either explicit or implicit. Implicit appeals often use images or code words to carry a racist or racial message. Implicit racist messages, in particular, have been found to be more effective with white audiences than explicit racist messages and they have the additional benefit of affording plausible deniability to their source (Mendelberg, 2001).

These distinctions are central to our argument here, as we do not attribute conscious racial animosity to Romney or Republican leadership. The race-based messages in 2012 are predictably implicit and, therefore, can always be denied. Absent a death-bed confession—such as that issued by Lee Atwater in 1991 (Associated Press, 1991)—there will never be evidence to support direct, conscious intentionality.[1] Rather, we offer support for our argument that a strategy rooted in racial divisions was central to the efforts to defeat President Obama in 2012. As will become clear, this strategy was not unique to 2012, but the election of Obama in 2008 and the Republican narrative that was structured around his first term created a new dynamic for race-based appeals.

We Never Were Postracial: The 2008 Election

Political scientists and other close observers of U.S. politics were more surprised than anyone when it was clear that Obama was to be elected president in 2008. Although most Americans appreciate the historical achievement, there is a structural element that adds significant additional weight to this accomplishment. Because U.S. presidents are chosen based on the Electoral College model, there are essentially 51 separate presidential elections—one in each state and in the District of Columbia. Forty-nine of those entities use a "winner-take-all" system, which means that a candidate must win the plurality of the popular vote in the state to be awarded the state's electoral votes. Since Reconstruction, only five African-Americans had been elected to high-profile statewide office (i.e., U.S. Senator or governor), so it seemed very unlikely that an African-American candidate could win enough states to be elected. As a result, although most Americans—even many whites who supported McCain—felt a sense of pride on Election Day night in 2008, those who attend to the nuances of U.S. political history were even more amazed at what had taken place.

However, a kind of divided consciousness gripped the United States that night. On the one side, as noted above, there was certainly a sense of national overcoming. As we wrote about extensively in our book, *Race Appeal* (2011), and was detailed in other ways in McIlwain's (2012) article on the president's successful narrative, Obama capitalized on a message of racial progress. His campaign established and cultivated this narrative and the news media largely latched on to it in their reporting (McIlwain, 2012). In short, this narrative situated Obama's candidacy within a historical trajectory of race struggle and, thus, presented his election as a crowning achievement of a social movement to square national principles of racial equality with concrete and meaningful practice. This narrative— primarily because it was first established with Obama's 2004 Democratic National Convention speech in Boston—largely overshadowed the more immediate racial opposition he faced throughout 2012.

But this was the other side of the story in 2008. White, racist opposition was present, even as it was, in most instances, supplanted by this more enduring narrative of racial progress. Appeals to Obama's otherness—as black, as un-American, as Muslim, as terrorist sympathizer, socialist, communist, dangerous radical, and the like—circulated *ad nauseum* throughout the right-wing rumor mill, conservative blogosphere, and social networks where racist ridicule based on a wide array of black stereotypes also ran rampant (Joseph, 2011; Piston, 2009). The July 21, 2008, *New Yorker* magazine cover featuring the Obamas' infamous "terrorist fist bump" was indicative of how more mainstream media outlets and elite voices viewed this kind of explicitly racist opposition. Although some viewed the cover as trading on multiple appeals to the Obamas' otherness, one could also clearly see the way in which the cover ridiculed the kind of twisted and warped racial thinking that could turn the Obamas into such caricatures in the first place. "This is what Barack and Michelle Obama look like to the racist lunatic fringe" is how many read the cover—a nod to the fact that such sentiment was out there, but a repudiation of it as so far afield of mainstream American values that it could only be seen as a caricature.

Beyond this, almost every expression of implicit or explicit racial appeals made by candidates and/or their supporters was met with media criticism, if not outright rebuke. This was the case for Democratic remarks during the primaries—i.e., Vice President Joe Biden's reference to Obama as "clean" and, thus, a "storybook" (Thai & Barrett, 2007); Bill Clinton's marginalizing Obama's South Carolina primary win (Callebs, 2008); Hillary Clinton's claim that she was better suited because she could win white voters (Kiely & Lawrence, 2008); and former Democratic vice presidential nominee Geraldine Ferraro's adamant claim that Obama's success in the primaries was because of, rather than in spite of, his race (Seelye & Bosman, 2008)—as well as remarks from Republicans during the general election campaign.

The point of recalling all of this history is to draw attention to the fact that two racial currents pervaded the voting population during and up through the 2008 election. Understanding the way race played out in 2012 is contingent on recognizing the important fact that currents of white optimism ran parallel to white racial anxieties and fears that fueled the overall opposition of whites to Obama's candidacy. Counter to the popular postracial narrative, election night evidence—in the form of exit polls—demonstrated a nation at least as embroiled in racial matters as had been overcome. This set of racial contradictions is exemplified in the opening statement reporting on the election results by *The New York Times*:

> Even during the darkest hours of his presidential campaign, Senator Barack Obama of Illinois held on to his improbable, unshakable conviction that America was ready to step across the color line. Millions of voters—white and black, Hispanic and Asian, biracial and multiracial—put their faith and the future of their country into the hands of a 47-year-old black man who made history both because of his race and in spite of it. (Swarns, 2008, para. 1–3)

Despite the clear recognition of 2008's racial underbelly, the "in spite of" aspect of the election contest remains sublimated beneath Obama's victory. But that "in spite of" was nevertheless present through election year sentiments and in the voting patterns of whites. Thus, the first step to understanding race in the 2012 presidential campaign is to reframe 2008 from a display of racial unity to one of acute division along W.E.B. Dubois's "color line," separating whites from the "darker peoples of the earth," who, by their majorities, voted against and for Obama, respectively.

Before we detail the messages that Romney and the GOP deployed throughout the 2012 election, we first briefly consider demographic data about the national electorate that may have provided empirical support for the campaign choices made by Romney and the wider Republican establishment. We look to this data to point out the potential it had to support a particular course of action and to later describe how it ran counter to many of the message choices actually made by the Romney and the GOP team.

The Racial Divide in Presidential Approval

Our central aim is to explain the message strategy and demographic targets characterizing the opposition that the GOP and its presidential standard bearer Romney imagined in 2012. More importantly, we aim to describe how race, specifically racially divisive themes, factored into the messages they targeted to different swaths of American voters. To do so, we begin with data that could have provided a road map for the campaign—data that may have influenced decisions about what messages to deploy and to whom in order to strategically garner the necessary votes to unseat President Obama. Specifically, we examine a core set of data measuring American citizens' approval or disapproval with the way President Obama governed the country in this first term.

In many ways, elections involving incumbents can be reduced to a single basic question: Does the incumbent's performance in office warrant the status quo—reelection—or change? For guidance on this question, we consulted Gallup's weekly presidential job approval ratings, which span 198 weeks from January 19, 2009, (one day prior to Inauguration Day) to November 5, 2012, (Election Day). These data—particularly the breakdown by demographic characteristics—provide a reasonable basis for explaining the similarly racial (meaning that race was taken into account) though different message strategies the GOP aimed at black and Latino voters in 2012.

First, there is a clear racial disparity between whites, blacks, and Latinos with respect to average ratings over the entire period. Blacks gave Obama the highest ratings, averaging 88%, while whites ranked him the lowest, at 41%. Rankings by

Latinos fell in between these two extremes at 61%, placing them well above the 50% mark, but closer to the ratings of whites than blacks. The three groups also differed significantly with respect to the range of ratings they gave the president over this period. Latinos showed the highest rate of variability, ranging 41 points from a low of 44% to a high of 85%; followed by whites, 32 points, 41% to 63%; and finally blacks, 17 points, 79% to 96%.

When it comes to potential for electoral persuasion and mobilization, these data alone suggested that whites provided the most favorable targets. The bulk of white support existed for a short time at the beginning of the president's tenure—the so-called "honeymoon period"—quickly waned, and remained consistently low despite changes in presidential actions that took place during the period under examination (see Figure 1). As such, whites' rating trajectory was one of pre-job, tacit approval that gave way to a general pattern of steady and sustained dissatisfaction with the president. Blacks, on the other hand, demonstrated stalwart support for the president, apparently despite any particular actions taken by him over the course of his first term. As such, they provided little potential for movement toward a challenger seeking to erode the president's 2008 coalition.

Although there are moments when approval declined, the ratings never fell below a point that cast any suspicion on blacks' overwhelming support. And, although Hispanics highly approved of Obama's performance overall, the level of variability suggests that their approval may be more closely contingent on factors related to specific actions taken—or not taken—by the president. Thus, from the differential ratings by racial groups alone, it would seem that Romney and the Republicans had a clear opening to target whites in general and a somewhat slimmer potential to persuade at least some measurable part of the Hispanic citizenry toward voting against the president in 2012.

Despite the clear racial disparity in presidential approval ratings, however, we know that race alone is not enough information to rely on for precise demographic targeting. Race, combined with other characteristics, helps further narrow the focus. When we look at the ratings gap between the highest and lowest scores across multiple variables, we get a better picture of what constituencies might respond more favorably to the GOP message. Figure 2 shows the percentage gap between the lowest and highest favorable ratings for each demographic group available to identify the range of variability in ratings within each segment. We find a familiar cluster of variables that, in this case, signify the largest disparities in presidential approval: party identification, ideology, and race. Specifically, conservative whites who identify with the Republican Party express the least approval with Obama's presidential performance—significantly more than even moderate/independent-leaning members of the Republican Party.

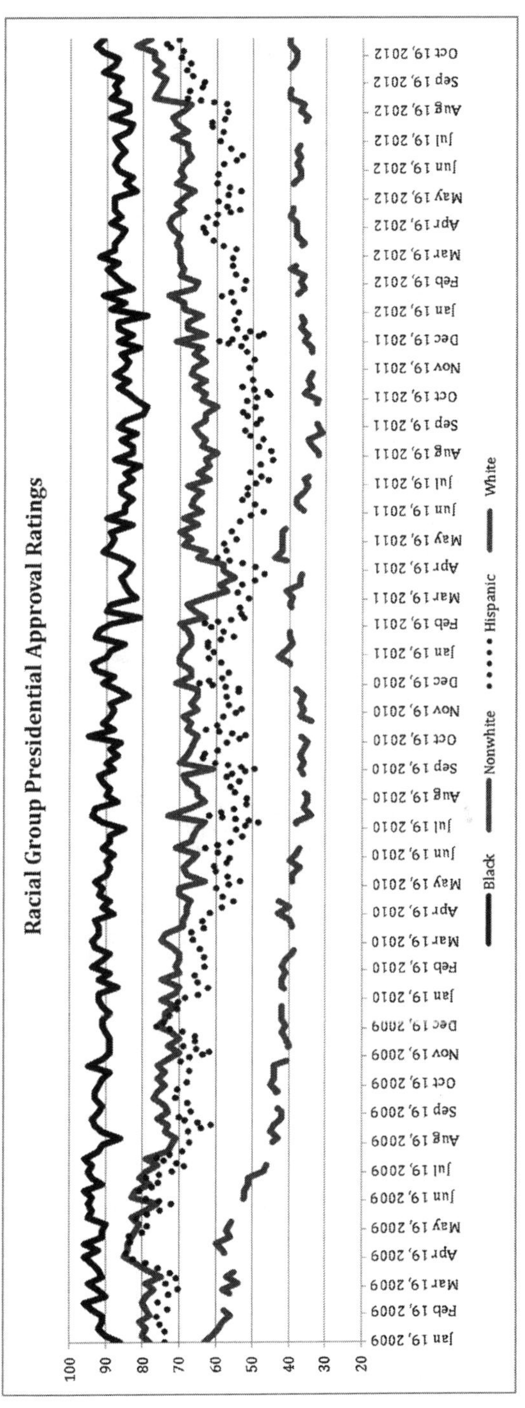

Figure 1. Racial Group Presidential Approval Ratings Over Time
Note. Figure includes Gallup presidential approval ratings data from 2009 through 2012 retrieved from Gallup.com.

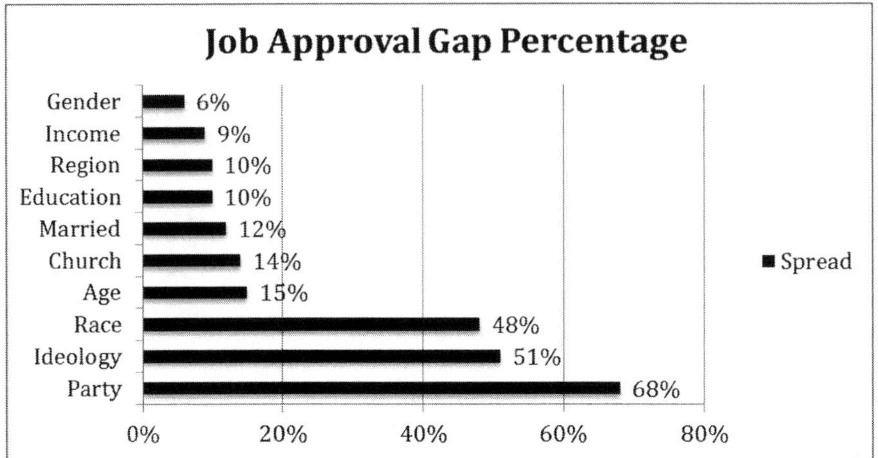

Figure 2. Difference Between Lowest and Highest Approval Percent for Specified Variables
Note. Figure includes Gallup presidential approval ratings data from 2009 through 2012 retrieved from Gallup.com. From bottom to top, the lowest ratings given by the demographic group in each category are: Republican, conservative, white, 65+, church-going, married, no higher education, South, $70K+ annual income, and male.

Although these three variables are tied to the largest gaps in presidential performance ratings, ideology and party identification are not essential for this analysis. The U.S. electoral system is structured in a way that promotes a two-party system, and ideology is closely related to party identification for most Americans within that context. In other words, because the "game" in the general election is Republicans versus Democrats, and that distinction is closely tied to conservatives versus progressives/liberals, the most interesting of the three most notable variables revealed in Figure 2 is race.

To summarize, what we find in these data is a well-established pattern of racial, ideological, party, and class division that set in early during Obama's first presidential term. As many have noted (most significantly, Kinder & Winter, 2001), it is difficult given the political history of the United States to disentangle race and ideology—and in more contemporary contexts, political party. In fact, the strong relationship these factors have with each other is what frequently provides cover for explicit racial appeals masked in implicit language and imagery (McIlwain & Caliendo, 2011; Mendelberg, 2001). Frequent assertions that Republicans attacked Obama because of his race were (and are) met with an equally frequent refrain in response: "We don't object to Obama's race, but his policies."

Although race figures into the presidential approval ratings as an intersection with ideology, party, and class, the racial dimensions—particularly Obama's blackness—become a salient, not sublimated, element of that juncture. For instance, given the high volatility of President George W. Bush's second term—with respect to both political circumstances that emerged and Bush's responses to them—one might expect the same level of division in approval ratings if party and ideology were the most significant factors driving the ratings. However, when we compare ratings from Obama's first term and Bush's second, the black-white difference in approval is significantly less—by half (24%)—during Bush's tenure than it is for Obama's.

Cashing in on Old Stereotypes: The 2012 Election

Unlike in 2008, there was no primary contest for Obama in 2012, so attacks came steadily throughout the nomination season from all of the candidates vying for the Republican nomination. By the time the general election was in full swing and as Election Day 2012 approached, a media narrative of racial polarization widely framed the presidential contest. Racial divisions in presidential approval undergird a message strategy based on differentiation. However, that racial polarization was exacerbated by a Republican Party/Romney strategy that seemed to run counter to the data at hand. That is, the data presented here suggests that a fruitful course of action might have involved targeting conservative, Republican, and wealthy whites; disregarding (that is, ignoring) blacks; and targeting at least a segment of the Latino population.

However, what took place over the course of the GOP primary and general election was not consistent with this approach. The Romney campaign appeared to, indeed, target the white, conservative, Republicans that comprise the Republican base, but it also invoked an economic message that was targeted toward the wealthy—an approach that had the potential to proactively alienate and marginalize many black and Latino voters. More precisely, Romney's message—embodied both in his advertising and high-profile rhetoric—deployed the welfare issue for blacks and immigration for Latinos as vehicles to utilize an economic message that galvanized the most conservative white, working class, and wealthy citizens while alienating blacks and Latinos. In addition, this approach ran the risk of offending socially moderate whites if Obama supporters' or media critics' claims of "racism" were to gain hold.

Although hindsight is always 20/20, Romney's approach was inconsistent with a potentially winning electoral strategy. That is, Romney seemed to reason that in order to garner and mobilize the "white vote," he had to alienate a group (blacks) that he had no chance of winning and to act with hostility toward a group (Latinos) whom, data suggested, he may have a chance of winning over in margins necessary to make him more competitive.

Campaigning for the "White Vote"

Our assessment of Romney's strategy is based largely on his speeches and paid political advertisements, though it is increasingly important to consider that advocacy for Romney and attacks against President Obama were also made by surrogates, such as national and local political parties, PACs, 527 groups, and super PACs. The concept of plausible deniability can be extended even further when one considers the illegality of a campaign coordinating with third-party entities, so we focus our discussion here specifically on campaign communication from the Romney campaign and the Republican Party.

The approach that we find to be counter-intuitive has two distinct prongs: a focus on welfare and a focus on deportation as a centerpiece to immigration reform. Both of these elements ran the risk of alienating segments of the population that either were firmly in the Obama camp to begin with—and, therefore, not available to Romney, i.e., most African-Americans and some Latinos—or potential Romney voters who might be offended by the policy proposals, i.e., socially moderate whites and some Latinos.

The welfare narrative did not begin in the general election. Republican presidential hopeful and former Speaker of the U.S. House of Representatives Newt Gingrich famously remarked that Obama was the "food stamp president" (Elliott, 2012), referring to the increase in the number of individuals who were enrolled in the Supplemental Nutrition Assistance Program since Obama was inaugurated. Many commentators and fact checkers rushed to discredit the largely inaccurate claims (Jackson, 2012), and others pointed out that there was a racial undercurrent to the charge (Mosely, 2012).

For his part, Romney continued to attempt to leverage the increased poverty rates—which resulted from the Great Recession and cannot be attributable to Obama since it began in the summer of 2008—and concomitant jump in rates of federal assistance programs to the president. For a period of time, the Romney website featured an image of a winding line of people queuing up before a sign that read "unemployment office" with the caption "Obama Isn't Working" (McNally, 2012)—a phrase that served as a double entendre to invoke a surface message that the president's programs have contributed to (or at least not abated) poverty as well as playing on stereotypes of lazy African-Americans who choose public assistance over hard work.

The most notable example of Romney invoking the "lazy black" stereotype, however, was his persistent claim over a number of weeks leading up to the Republican National Convention that Obama secretly removed the work requirement for welfare recipients. There were two related ads on this message. In one, former President Clinton signs the Personal Responsibility and Work Opportunity Act of 1996 while a narrator notes that "[s]ince 1996, welfare recipients were required to work." The image of Clinton fades to a quote noting that the requirement was successful, while the narrator adds that the reform was bipartisan and resulted in reduced welfare rolls. The next image shown in this ad is a smiling President Obama—with an on-screen text that reads "President Obama Ended Work Requirements for Welfare"—while the narrator notes that "[o]n July 12, President Obama quietly ended the work requirement, gutting welfare reform." The narrator then reads a quote from what he calls "one of the most respected newspapers in America" (the *Richmond* [VA] *Times-Dispatch*), which claimed that the move was "nuts" because removing incentives to work would not reduce unemployment. The narrator then notes that "Mitt Romney's plan for a stronger middle class will put work back in welfare." This statement is supported by an onscreen image of a smiling Romney at a rally with the text "Put Work Back in Welfare" on the screen.

A second ad used some of the same language and format, but added multiple video images of whites working factory jobs as well as voiceover narration that claimed, "Under Obama's plan, you wouldn't have to work and wouldn't have to train for a job. They just send you your welfare check," as the on-screen text reads "They just send you your welfare check." The narrator continues, "And welfare to work goes back to being plain old welfare." The video footage of white workers transitions to two brief scenes of footage of Romney talking to white workers in factory settings while the narrator notes that "Mitt Romney will restore the work requirement, because it works."

According to several fact checking organizations, the claims in these ads were false. FactCheck.org ("Does Obama's Plan," 2012) and CNN (Foreman & Marrapodi, 2012) pointed out the inaccuracy of the claim. PolitiFact rated it "pants on fire" ("Mitt Romney Says," 2012). Glenn Kessler, *The Washington Post's* "The Fact Checker," issued its harshest rating of four Pinocchios (Kessler, 2012), and PolitiFact further noted that it was one of the top six "biggest falsehoods of the presidential campaign" of the 800 facts that they checked in 2012 (Adair, 2012). The new policy, which was a response to state officials who asked for more flexibility in the work requirement, allows states to request a waiver from federal rules that require individuals enrolled in the Temporary Assistance to Needy Families program to engage in specific activities. PolitiFact noted that the new policy was designed to work with states to strengthen the work requirement, not weaken it ("Mitt Romney Says," 2012). Romney and his surrogates ("Rick Santorum Repeats," 2012) continued to make the claim for more than a month (Delaney, 2012) and never admitted that the ads were misleading (at best).

It is important to consider why a campaign would make such a clearly false claim and then defend it in the face of overwhelming evidence that it was untrue. If the assertion was not consistent with long-standing, deeply rooted stereotypes, it would likely not have been made at all. As it stands, however, it was easy for

Americans to believe—at least initially—that a black man would: (1) look to take care of his own, (2) be interested in making it easy for African-Americans to be paid (from hard-working white taxpayers' money) without working, and (3) acted in secret to push the policy through. Three persistent negative stereotypes about African-Americans are packed tightly into this claim, which made it easy to sell.

The ease with which this racialized message was sold, seemingly without regard to its inaccuracy, also had much to do with the increasingly sophisticated ability to directly target individuals in the digital era. On the one hand, this increasing phenomenon that Gronbeck and Wiese (2005) refer to as "repersonalization," allows presidential candidates to use digitally derived data about the electorate to target voters most likely to respond to their message. More important, however, may be the related aspect of segmentation—partitioning off parts of the electorate (African-Americans, Latinos, etc.) that could be strategically disregarded. In this sense, Romney may have seen his implicitly racist message as no risk at all, inasmuch as it was communicated often directly to voters, delivered in ads airing only in specific areas, or delivered online where it was directly accessed by voters most likely to receive Romney's message.

On the other hand, the increasing ability to micro-target the electorate because of new technologies also allows for what Bennett and Manheim (2006) refer to as a move to a one-step flow of influence. That is, the ability to directly communicate with individual members of the electorate largely bypasses the influence that the media and other opinion elites have in framing presidential candidates' messages. Indeed, one of the reasons the Romney campaign could stridently defend their racialized message strategy was not only because it could be targeted to a segmented audience. Its direct communication to that audience almost ensured that individuals would accept it and take it at face value prior to, and in spite of, any third-party or elite framing that might take place. Simply put, by specifically targeting an audience already known to be maximally receptive to the message, the Romney campaign minimized the influence that opinion leaders—especially critical ones—might have.

Similarly, Romney's policy on immigration reform traded in on stereotypes of Latino criminality—a stereotype that is so powerful that it has become embodied in the very notion of Latinos themselves as "illegal," irrespective of their individual immigration or citizenship status. During the nomination season, Romney accused some of his Republican challengers of being soft on immigration. He espoused a policy of "self-deportation," which meant that he would enact a set of laws that would make day-to-day life so difficult for undocumented workers that they would choose to leave on their own. After Romney secured the nomination, he softened his rhetoric significantly, arguing that he would simply give undocumented immigrants "the choice to leave if they wished" (Foley, 2012).

Romney continued to pledge to complete a high-tech fence along the border with Mexico, force employers to be diligent in checking legal status before hiring by way of a new national database, and expand the temporary worker program for seasonal farm labor (Lauter, 2012). He continued to firmly oppose any amnesty program as well as most of the DREAM Act, which would legalize the status of undocumented individuals who were brought to the United States when they were children and who are pursuing higher education or military service ("A Start on the Dream," 2012). However, he began to air a series of Spanish-language campaign advertisements in the summer of 2012 touting his bipartisan work on the issue as governor of Massachusetts and pledging to do the same as president (Madison, 2012). Some immigration advocacy groups called foul on Romney's claim of his past efforts (Foley, 2012), but it was clear that he sensed an opportunity when the president's numbers with Latinos showed signs of wavering (Cillizza, 2011; Rojas, 2012; Shahid, 2012). Those small dips—from 72% to 67% in early October (Rojas, 2012)—were anomalous, however; Obama carried the Latino vote by a margin of 71% to 27% in 2012 ("President: Full Results," 2012), which represents an 8% increase over his 2008 margin ("President: National Exit Poll," 2008). In post-election analysis, Romney claimed that Obama won the election by giving "gifts" to blacks and Latinos throughout his first term ("Mitt Romney Says Obama Won," 2012).

Conclusion

We do not have access to the minds of Romney, the Republican Party, or the GOP primary candidates. Nor do we know the motives and decisions of their strategists. Judging from the content of the campaign messages and the state of the electorate, however, our explanation for the role that race played in the 2012 presidential election is as follows. First, according to presidential job performance data, Romney had the potential to easily garner support from the Republican base—white, ideologically conservative Republicans. He had little chance of persuading even a marginal percentage of African-Americans. However, he had some potential to persuade a marginal number of Hispanic voters, which—in an ideal circumstance—may have given him enough voters to win, or at least lose by a lower margin.

Second, we argue that Romney lost by the margin he did because his message targeted to these diverse swaths of the electorate ran counter to Obama's presidential approval data. Given the inconsistency between the data and the Romney message, we naturally ask the question, "why?" Why did Romney engage African-American citizens at all? He may have reasoned that to ignore them might turn into a backlash. But one can hardly speak of a potential backlash when more than 90% of a voting bloc is already poised to vote against you. Why did Romney choose to engage forthrightly and with such harsh rhetoric about deportations, knowing the importance of the immigration issue to Hispanics? Why did he not craft a more nuanced response that may have still garnered an acceptable number of Hispanic votes?

Our answer is that Romney found himself in a catch-22 of sorts. Given the racial polarization in the electorate and his overwhelming support singularly from white conservatives, Romney was faced with the challenge of how to mobilize as much of that support as possible—perhaps enough from that constituency that he might cobble together a win with them and a slim number of other voters. We contend that faced with a decision about how to best mobilize white conservatives—especially those of the Tea Party variety who gained power and influence during Obama's first term—Romney retreated to what history had demonstrated worked.

Again, we are not saying that Romney and the Republicans deliberately mobilized race as an explicit and deliberate strategy, but their message had that effect. They chose to target blacks as the subject of their economic message—the message that said the economy will grow if we don't vote for the guy whose policies favor freeloaders. They did not have to do so. They chose to double down on the rhetoric of deportation and Hispanic criminality rather than rejecting it and developing a specific, moderate immigration policy. Why risk alienating one minority constituency when you don't have to do so? Why risk alienating another minority group when a simple policy and rhetoric adjustment might secure some votes?

Irrespective of intent, we believe it was apparent to Romney and the GOP that these alienating messages targeted to and centered around blacks and Hispanics were ignited, energized, and promised to mobilize that core base of support that Romney knew he must have if he was to have any shot at winning the presidency. Romney campaigned for the white vote; he had to deliver a message that would thus mobilize that vote. We should note that this observation is not ours alone. For example, before the 2012 GOP convention, Republican U.S. Sen. Lindsay Graham said, "The demographics race we're losing badly … we're not generating enough angry white guys to stay in business for the long term" (Helderman & Cohen, 2012). And, Ron Brownstein of the conservative publication the *National Journal* wrote—after breaking down the racial demographics underlying each presidential candidate's voter strategy—that "a GOP coalition that relies almost entirely on whites could squeeze out one more narrow victory in November. But if Republicans can't find more effective ways to bridge the priorities of their conservative core and the diversifying Next America, that weight will grow more daunting every year (2012, para. 12).

Romney hoped his coalition of mostly whites would squeeze out one more narrow victory, and his message demonstrated that if that was to happen, he needed to mobilize enough angry white guys and others. His communications also made it clear that alienating blacks and Hispanics might do the trick.

References

A start on the dream. (2012, June 3). *The New York Times*. Retrieved from http://www.nytimes.com/2012/06/04/opinion/a-start-on-the-dream-act.html

Adair, B. (2012, November 1). Biggest falsehoods of the presidential campaign. *PolitiFact.com*. Retrieved from http://www.politifact.com/truth-o-meter/article/2012/nov/01/biggest-falsehoods-presidential-campaign/

Amodio, D. M., & Devine, P. G. (2006). Stereotyping and evaluation in implicit race bias: Evidence for independent constructs and unique effects on behavior. *Journal of Personality and Social Psychology, 91*(4), 652–661.

Amodio, D. M., Devine, P. G., & Harmon-Jones, E. (2008). Differences in the regulation of intergroup bias: The role of conflict monitoring and neural signals for control. *Journal of Personality and Social Psychology, 94*(1), 60–74.

Associated Press. (1991, January 13). Gravely ill, Atwater offers apology. *The New York Times*. Retrieved from http://www.nytimes.com/1991/01/13/us/gravely-ill-atwater-offers-apology.html

Bennett, W. L., & Manheim, J. B. (2006). The one-step flow of communication. *The Annals of the American Academy of Political and Social Science, 608*(1), 213–232.

Brownstein, R. (2012, August 24). Obama needs 80% of minority vote to win 2012 presidential election. *National Journal*. Retrieved from http://www.nationaljournal.com/thenextamerica/politics/obama-needs-80-of-minority-vote-to-win-2012-presidential-election-20120824

Callebs, S. (2008, March 17). Bill Clinton: What happened in South Carolina a "myth." *CNN-Politics.com*. Retrieved from http://www.cnn.com/2008/POLITICS/03/17/clinton.bill/

Cillizza, C. (2011, September 18). With Hispanic support for Obama waning, could Latino vote be up for grabs in 2012? *The Washington Post*. Retrieved from http://articles.washingtonpost.com/2011-09-18/politics/35273316_1_hispanic-unemployment-rate-hispanic-voters-latino-decisions

Delaney, A. (2012, August 22). Romney defends bogus welfare ads, dismissing fact-checkers. *The Huffington Post*. Retrieved from http://www.huffingtonpost.com/2012/08/22/romney-obama-welfare-ads_n_1823462.html

Does Obama's plan "gut welfare reform." (2012, August 9). *FactCheck.org*. Retrieved from http://www.factcheck.org/2012/08/does-obamas-plan-gut-welfare-reform/

Elliott, D. (2012, January 17). "Food stamp president": Race code, or just politics? *National Public Radio*. Retrieved from http://www.npr.org/2012/01/17/145312069/newts-food-stamp-president-racial-or-just-politics

Foley, E. (2012, October 18). Immigrant groups call for Romney to take down ad. *The Huffington Post*. Retrieved from http://www.huffingtonpost.com/2012/10/18/immigration-romney-television-ad_n_1981091.html

Foreman, T., & Marrapodi, E. (2012, August 30). Fact check: Romney's welfare claims wrong. *CNN.com*. Retrieved from http://www.cnn.com/2012/08/23/politics/fact-check-welfare

Gronbeck, B. E., & Wiese, D. R. (2005). The repersonalization of presidential campaigning in 2004. *American Behavioral Scientist, 49*(4), 520–534.

Helderman, R. S., & Cohen, J. (2012, August 29). As Republican convention emphasizes diversity, racial incidents intrude. *The Washington Post*. Retrieved from http://articles. washingtonpost.com/2012-08-29/politics/35490241_1_latino-voters-convention-stage-party-with-black-people

Jackson, B. (2012, February 6). Fact check: Gingrich's faulty food stamp claim. *USA Today*. Retrieved from http://usatoday30.usatoday.com/news/politics/story/2012-01-18/fact-check-gingrich-obama-food-stamps/52645882/1

Joseph, R. L. (2011). Imagining Obama: Reading overtly and inferentially racist images of our 44th president. *Communication Studies, 62*(4), 389–405.

Kessler, G. (2012, August 8). Spin and counterspin in the welfare debate. *The Washington Post*. Retrieved from http://www.washingtonpost.com/blogs/fact-checker/post/spin-and-counterspin-in-the-welfare-debate/2012/08/07/61bf03b6-e0e3-11e1-8fc5-a7dcf1fc161d_blog.html#pagebreak

Kiely, K., & Lawrence, J. (2008, August 5). Clinton makes case for wide appeal. *USA Today*. Retrieved from http://usatoday30.usatoday.com/news/politics/election2008/2008-05-07-clintoninterview_N.htm

Kinder, D. R., & Winter, N. (2001). Exploring the racial divide: Blacks, whites, and opinion on national policy. *American Journal of Political Science, 45*, 439–453.

Lauter, D. (2012, October 17). Latinos may hold sway over immigration reform. *The Chicago Tribune*. Retrieved from http://articles.chicagotribune.com/2012-10-17/site/ct-nw-issues-day3-immigration-20121017_1_immigration-reform-deportations-latino-voters

Madison, L. (2012, July 18). With eye on Latino vote, Romney ad talks immigration. *CBSNews. com*. Retrieved from http://www.cbsnews.com/8301-503544_162-57474878-503544/with-eye-on-latino-vote-romney-ad-talks-immigration/

McIlwain, C. D. (2012). From deracialization to racial distinction: Interpreting Obama's successful racial narrative. *Social Semiotics, 23*(1), 119–145. doi: 10.1080/10350330.2012.707039

McIlwain, C. D. (2011). Racialized media coverage of minority candidates in the 2008 Democratic presidential primary. *American Behavioral Scientist, 55*(4), 371–389.

McIlwain, C. D., & Caliendo, S. M. (2011). *Race appeal: How candidates invoke race in U.S. political campaigns*. Philadelphia, PA: Temple University Press.

McNally, M. (2012, April 20). Hey Tommy Christopher, you can thank Maggie Thatcher for Romney's "Obama isn't working" slogan. *PJ Tattler*. Retrieved from http://pjmedia. com/tatler/2012/04/20/hey-tommy-christopher-you-can-thank-maggie-thatcher-for-romneys-obama-isnt-working-slogan/

Mendelberg, T. (2001). *The race card: Campaign strategy, implicit messages, and the norm of equality*. Princeton, NJ: Princeton University Press.

Mitt Romney says Barack Obama's plan for welfare reform: "They just send you your welfare check." (2012, August 6). *PolitiFact.com*. Retrieved from http://www.politifact.com/truth-o-meter/statements/2012/aug/07/mitt-romney/mitt-romney-says-barack-obamas-plan-abandons-tenet/

Mitt Romney says Obama won by giving "gifts" to Latino voters. (2012, November 15). *Fox News Latino*. Retrieved from http://latino.foxnews.com/latino/politics/2012/11/15/mitt-romney-says-obama-won-by-giving-gifts-to-immigrant-voters/

Mosely, W. (2012, January 26). "Food stamp president": Gingrich's poetry of hate. *CNN.com*. Retrieved from http://www.cnn.com/2012/01/26/opinion/mosley-gingrich-food-stamp-president

Piston, S. (2010). How explicit racial prejudice hurt Obama in the 2008 election. *Political Behavior, 32*(4), 431–451.

President: Full results. (2012). Retrieved from http://www.cnn.com/election/2012/results/race/president

President: National exit poll. (2008). Retrieved from http://www.cnn.com/ELECTION/2008/results/polls/#val=USP00p1

Richeson, J. A., & Trawalter, S. (2008). The threat of appearing prejudiced and race-based attentional biases. *Psychological Science, 19*(2), 98–102.

Rick Santorum repeats Romney claim that Obama is ending work requirement in welfare. (2012, August 28). *PolitiFact.com*. Retrieved from http://www.politifact.com/truth-o-meter/statements/2012/aug/28/rick-santorum/Santorum-Romney-claim-Obama-ending-welfare-work/

Rojas, N. (2012, October 15). Presidential election polls 2012: Obama sees drop in Latino support, Romney continues to lag behind. *Latinos Post*. Retrieved from http://www.latinos-post.com/articles/5487/20121015/presidential-election-polls-2012-obama-sees-drop.htm

Seelye, K. Q., & Bosman, J. (2008, March 12). Ferraro's Obama remarks become talk of campaign. *The New York Times*. Retrieved from http://www.nytimes.com/2008/03/12/us/politics/12campaign.html

Shahid, A. (2012, January 26). Hispanic voters' support for Obama drops as GOPers Romney and Gingrich spar over immigration in Florida. *New York Daily News*. Retrieved from http://www.nydailynews.com/news/politics/hispanic-voters-support-obama-drops-gopers-romney-gingich-spar-immigration-florida-article-1.1012326

Swarns, R. L. (2008, November 5). Vaulting the racial divide, Obama persuaded Americans to follow. *The New York Times*. Retrieved from http://www.nytimes.com/2008/11/05/us/politics/05race.html

Thai X., & Barrett, T. (2007, February 9). Biden's description of Obama draws scrutiny. *CNNPolitics.com*. Retrieved from http://www.cnn.com/2007/POLITICS/01/31/biden.obama/index.html

Note

1. Atwater suggested, however, that although his attacks on Democratic presidential candidate Michael Dukakis in 1988 were improper and cruel, they were not racist. His apology noted that the attacks made him "sound racist, which I am not." Atwater, like most Americans, was conflating subconscious racism with conscious, explicitly racist intentions. We argue that whether he is personally "racist" or not is beside the point; the invocation of Willie Horton was, indeed, racist, because it gained persuasive advantage from powerful and persistent stereotypes of black criminality and sexual aggression toward white women. That is, the message can be racist without some objective validation of the source of the message having racist attitudes or intentions.

CHAPTER FOURTEEN

Defying Expectations

Young Citizens' Political Attitudes and Participation in the 2012 Election

LESLIE A. RILL AND MITCHELL S. MCKINNEY

A prediction heard frequently before the 2012 presidential election was that young citizens who had supported Barack Obama in large numbers in 2008 were some-how now "disillusioned" with the political process and would "not turn out to carry Obama to victory again" (Frosch & Peyron, 2012, para. 1). Just days before the November 2012 election, the Institute of Politics at Harvard University reported in its "Survey of Young Americans' Attitudes Toward Politics" a number of indicators that foretold the almost certain decline in young citizens' electoral participation (McKenna, 2012). Specifically, the Harvard study pointed to a 16% decrease in youth voter registration from 2008 and a substantial decrease in young citizens reporting they were "definitely voting" (at 48% in 2012 down from 66% in 2008). Yet, despite widespread predictions to the contrary, young voters (18 to 29 year olds) delivered a relatively strong performance on Election Day and one that some have argued was decisive in the re-election of President Obama.

Although, overall, the youth vote did decline slightly from 2008 (with 45% turnout, down 6% from their 51% participation in 2008) and Obama's support from young voters also declined just slightly in 2012 (as he netted 60% of the 18-to-29-year-old vote in 2012 compared to his 66% in 2008), voting among all ages in 2012 actually declined with 62% of all eligible voters participating in the November election (down from 64% in 2008) (The Youth Vote, 2013). Yet, and perhaps more important than overall turnout, the electoral participation of young voters held steady where it counted most—in key battleground states. In fact, in the few toss-up states that proved crucial to Obama's re-election, youth turnout was at 50%, almost matching the overall 51% turnout that young voters produced in 2008. Also, in 2012, young citizens' 50% turnout in battleground states was significantly higher than their voting cohort's 43% turnout in non-battlegrounds (The Youth Vote, 2013).

Analysis by Peter Levine, director for the Center for Information and Research on Civic Learning and Engagement (CIRCLE), showed that Obama's relatively close re-election victory might well be attributed to his success with young voters: "The edge young voters gave to Mr. Obama proved decisive in several states. According to CIRCLE analysis, in the battleground states of Florida, Ohio, Pennsylvania, and Virginia, if young people had not voted, or if only half of them had supported the president in those states, Mr. Romney would have won the election" (Lipka, 2012, para. 17).

Thus, the presumed disillusioned young citizen of 2012 actually proved to be a pivotal and committed voter, especially for President Obama. In fact, for more than a decade now, young citizens have recorded a noticeable and impressive turnaround in their electoral participation—at least in presidential elections. Yet, to what factor or factors might we attribute young voters' improved electoral performance? Certainly, there are many considerations that influence voter mobilization; and although a single study is unable to encompass the myriad of influences affecting voter participation, the analysis presented here examines key attitudes of democratic engagement that have been found to predict voting behavior. Drawn from a national longitudinal study of young citizens' political attitudes, we explore the influence of political cynicism and political information efficacy on young citizens' candidate choice and decision to participate in the electoral process. First, before positing our research questions regarding young voters' political cynicism and information efficacy, we provide a brief historical overview of young citizens' participation in presidential elections. Finally, in our discussion of this study's results, we point to the important role of campaign communication targeted specifically to young citizens in achieving a more engaged youth electorate.

Young Citizens' Electoral Engagement

In tracing the voting behaviors of young citizens, we find that they traditionally have been the least represented at the ballot box. Until most recently, only about one-third of 18 to 29 year olds regularly voted in presidential elections, compared to approximately two-thirds of those 30 years and older (Levine & Lopez, 2002).

The fact that older citizens vote in larger numbers than young voters, by itself, is not a new phenomenon nor is it necessarily surprising. This has always been the case, largely because of the less settled and still developing (economically, educationally, politically, socially, etc.) nature of younger citizens. Still, if we view voting in national elections as a gauge of young citizens' involvement in political and civic matters, recent improvement in young voters' electoral performance provides some reason to believe that our youngest citizens are now more politically engaged than before.

When the voting age was lowered (from 21 years of age) to include 18 year olds in 1972, young voters achieved their "high-water mark" of electoral participation at 55.4%. For the next 20 years, the participation of young citizens in presidential elections charted a steady decline. Then, in 1992, driven largely by young citizens turning out in greater numbers to vote for Bill Clinton, youth voting increased to 52%, which still stands as youth voters' second highest rate of participation since 1972. This achievement, however, was short lived as 18 to 29 year olds followed their 1992 increased participation by recording their lowest level of voter turnout in 1996 at 34%, once again returning young citizens to their more traditional one-third rate of participation in presidential balloting (Levine & Lopez, 2002).

Great alarm was sounded by scholars, pundits, and political campaign practitioners following the 1996 presidential election regarding young citizens' disengagement in political and civic affairs (see, for example, Kaid, McKinney, & Tedesco, 2000; McKinney & Banwart, 2005; McKinney, Kaid, & Bystrom, 2005). Curtis Gans (2005, p. 79), director of the Committee for the Study of the American Electorate, lamented the "decline of American civic participation" and described the "apparent dangers for our democratic system" caused by an intergenerational pattern of civic disengagement in which nonvoting young citizens were now growing into disengaged older citizens. In short, Gans' assessment of voting data in presidential elections since the 1960s found that the ranks of our more active senior voters representing the so-called "greatest generation" were not being replenished with replacement voters who had taken up their civic responsibility during their formative years as young citizens.

Beginning with the 2000 presidential election, however, young voters have produced a noticeable and sustained improvement in their electoral performance. Still, each of the past four national elections have been accompanied by the rather pessimistic predictions regarding young citizens with which this chapter began, suggesting any electoral gains made by young voters would be short lived. Our contention, however, which we develop more fully later in this chapter, is that the increased youth mobilization may well be in response to campaign messages targeted specifically to young citizens using the language, modes, and channels of communication most common to these voters. Indeed, the past decade of successive presidential elections marked by young citizens' improved electoral participation has substantially narrowed the voter participation gap between younger and older voters. In 2000, voter turnout for 18 to 29 year olds increased from 34% in 1996 to 40%, compared to 65% for citizens 30 years and older (a 25% gap); in 2004, younger citizens' rate of voting increased again to 49%, compared to older voters at 68% (a 19% gap); in 2008, younger voters recorded a 51% rate of participation, compared to older voters' 67% participation (a gap of 16%); and, finally, although the overall turnout between younger and older voters in 2012 was 45% to 66% (a 21% gap), again—in the all-important battleground states—the participation gap held steady at only 17.5% (The Youth Vote, 2013).

Exploring Young Citizens' Attitudes of Political Engagement

As we seek to better understand what might produce a voting—and nonvoting— young citizen, our analysis explores key attitudes of democratic engagement that limited research suggests may in fact predict voting behavior. Our exploration of young citizens' attitudes of political engagement supports Michael Pfau's (2003) admonishment, to which we enthusiastically respond, that political communication scholars must attempt to untangle the complex domain of political attitudes and processes of persuasion that may lead to greater engagement in political and electoral affairs; and, as Pfau concluded, "There are no other more important effects that scholars could document" (p. 32). Our analysis in the current study focuses on two such important normative democratic attitudes, political information efficacy and political cynicism.

Perhaps the cornerstone of a participatory democracy is the informed voter. Although several scholars have focused their attention on the cognitive dimensions of political knowledge, chiefly the acquisition and processing of requisite political facts and information (e.g., Delli Carpini & Keeter, 1996; Popkin, 1991), another important element of political knowledge is the attitudinal dimension of knowledge attainment—specifically, how confident one is in what they know about politics. Here, Kaid, McKinney, and Tedesco (2007) first developed the concept of Political Information Efficacy (PIE), an attitudinal construct with important theoretical links between general political efficacy and one's feelings of confidence in the political knowledge they possess. Although traditional political efficacy has been defined as an individual's feeling that he or she has the ability to influence the political process (Campbell, Gurin, & Miller, 1954), the concept of political information efficacy is defined as the level of confidence one has in their political knowledge and that one possesses sufficient knowledge to engage the political process through such behaviors as voting and persuading others how to vote (Kaid et al., 2007).

A number of studies have analyzed how PIE works in the context of an ongoing presidential campaign and how particular forms of campaign communication affect this important political attitude. For example, McKinney and Warner (2013) report that citizens' PIE grows stronger over the course of a long campaign, with PIE at its lowest levels during the early stages of a presidential primary, increasing substantially by the conclusion of the primary campaign, and continuing to strengthen even more throughout the fall presidential campaign. Also, studies have consistently found that exposure to a televised campaign debate strengthens citizens' PIE (e.g., McKinney & Chattopadhyay, 2007; McKinney & Rill, 2009; McKinney, Rill, & Gully, 2011; McKinney & Warner, 2013); and at least one study (Kaid, Postelnicu, Landreville, Yun, & LeGrange, 2007) found that presidential debates are more helpful than political ads in strengthening young voters' PIE. Finally, in their initial testing of PIE, Kaid et al. (2007) utilized both National Election Studies survey data and a pilot experimental investigation that showed younger voters reported significantly less confidence in their political knowledge than older voters; also, confidence in one's political knowledge was significantly related to voting. Specifically, those with less PIE were significantly less likely to vote.

In the present study, we are particularly interested in pursuing the relationship between PIE in younger citizens who are voters and those who chose not to participate in the electoral process. With limited research on this point, we thus posit the following question:

> RQ 1: Is there a difference between the Political Information Efficacy (PIE) of young citizens who vote and those who do not vote?

Among the broad range of political attitudes and values, Delli Carpini (2004, p. 398) has identified political cynicism as a principal attitude affecting citizens' democratic engagement. As with PIE, a number of studies have examined how particular forms of campaign communication affect political cynicism. Several studies have found, for example, that exposure to a televised campaign debate significantly decreases viewers' political cynicism (Kaid et al., 2000; McKinney & Banwart, 2005; McKinney & Chattopadhyay, 2007; McKinney & Rill, 2009; McKinney & Warner, 2013). Additional research (e.g., Kaid et al., 2000) has found that political advertising intensifies one's political cynicism. Finally, at least one study of young citizens' political cynicism (Kaid et al., 2000) identified a link between political cynicism and voting—specifically, the political cynicism of nonvoters was significantly higher than that of voters. Again, with limited research on this point, we ask the following question:

> RQ 2: Is there a difference between the political cynicism of young citizens who vote and those who do not vote?

Finally, as we attempt to more fully illuminate young citizens' democratic engagement attitudes of PIE and political cynicism, our analysis also explores the relative influence of additional factors that may relate to both PIE and cynicism. Here, we explore the influence of such factors as one's campaign interest and attention, political ideology, and candidate vote choice. We ask:

> RQ 3: Does campaign interest, campaign attention, political ideology, or vote choice predict young citizens' level of political information efficacy (PIE)?

> RQ 4: Does campaign interest, campaign attention, political ideology, or vote choice predict young citizens' level of political cynicism?

Method

The current research was conducted as part of a larger national election study that examined young citizens' political attitudes and behaviors throughout the 2012 presidential campaign. The overall analysis employed a three-wave panel design, with Time 1 as participants' responses before viewing a presidential or vice presidential debate in early to mid-October, Time 2 as post-debate responses, and Time 3 as post-election responses collected during a one-week period following the election (November 7–14, 2012). The analysis reported in the current study explores participants' post-election (Time 3) responses.

Sample

A total of 277 participants, undergraduate students from 11 universities across the nation, completed the post-election survey.[1] Of these, 199 (74%) were female and 69 (26%) were male (with nine participants not reporting their gender). Participants ranged in age from 18 to 60 years old with a mean age of 20.67 (SD = 4.62). Although the sample was primarily composed of Caucasian respondents (71%), also represented in the study were Hispanic or Latino (8%), African-American (7%), Asian or Pacific Islanders (6%), and multiracial or mixed-raced (4%) participants, with four percent not reporting their racial/ethnic identity. The majority of our participants (74%) reported voting in the 2012 presidential election. Political affiliation among the respondents was distributed as follows: 40% Republican, 37% Democrat, and 23% independent.

Procedures

During the second wave of data collection (post-debate viewing), participants were asked to provide their email address if they were willing to allow researchers to contact them during later phases of the campaign season. Following Election Day, participants indicating a willingness to be contacted again received an email with a link to an online survey that contained a series of items designed to measure their political cynicism, political information efficacy, campaign interest and attention as well as vote behavior, candidate choice, and demographic information. Subjects received a $10 Amazon gift card in exchange for participation in the post-election survey.

Measures

Political cynicism. Young citizens' political cynicism was assessed using a political cynicism scale (Rill & Cardiel, in press) that was adapted from the National Election Studies (Rosenstone, Kinder, & Miller, 1997) and with an earlier version of the current scale also used in previous election studies (Ansolabehere & Iyengar, 1995; Kaid et al., 2000; McKinney et al., 2011; Pinkleton, Um, & Austin, 2002; Sweester & Kaid, 2008). For the present study, political cynicism was assessed using a series of eight 5-point Likert scales anchored at 1 = strongly disagree and 5 = strongly agree. The mean score of the eight items was used to determine the level of trust or confidence that individuals had in politicians, with higher scores indicating a greater level of political cynicism. Example items included, "politicians are corrupt," "politicians are dishonest," and "politicians are more interested in power than in what the people think." The scale demonstrated good reliability at the post-election measurement (Cronbach's α = .91).

Political information efficacy. Respondents' political information efficacy (PIE) was measured by indicating the level of agreement (using a five-point scale from 1 = strongly disagree to 5 = strongly agree) on four statements reflecting their level of confidence in their political knowledge. Items included: "I consider myself well-qualified to participate in politics," "I think that I am better informed about politics and government than most people," "I feel that I have a pretty good understanding of the important political issues facing our country," and "If a friend asked me about the presidential election, I feel I would have enough information to help my friend figure out who to vote for." As in past research, the four-item measure of PIE demonstrated good reliability (Cronbach's α = .92).

Campaign interest. A single item measure was used to assess young citizens' interest in the ongoing 2012 campaign. Participants were asked to indicate how interested they were in the presidential campaign using a five-point Likert scale, with answers ranging from 1 = very uninterested to 5 = very interested, (M = 4.30, SD = .86).

Campaign attention. The degree to which individuals perceived themselves as following the 2012 presidential campaign was measured by asking participants to rate how informed they thought they were about the campaign on a five-point Likert scale, with 1 = very uninformed and 5 = very well informed, (M = 3.89, SD = .89).

Political ideology. To measure political ideology, participants were asked to place themselves on a scale from 1 (extremely liberal) to 10 (extremely conservative).

Vote choice. Vote choice was determined by first asking participants if they had voted in the 2012 presidential election. Again, 74% indicated they voted whereas 26% of our sample reported they did not vote. If participants indicated that they voted in the 2012 election, they were then instructed to specify for whom they voted. Interestingly, our sample of young citizens' vote choice mirrored almost exactly the national presidential vote, with 51% of our participants indicating they voted for Obama and 47% reported voting for Mitt Romney. The remaining 2% chose "other."

Analysis

For research questions one and two, independent samples t-tests were computed for PIE and cynicism of voters and nonvoters. Regression analysis was used to answer research questions three and four. The alpha level was set at .05 *a priori*.

Results

In answering our first research question, whether or not a difference exists between the Political Information Efficacy (PIE) of young citizens who voted and those who did not vote, independent samples t-test indicated that the PIE of voters (M = 3.77, SD = .88) was significantly higher than for nonvoters (M = 3.09, SD = 1.01), t(277) = 5.43, p < .01. For research question two, whether or not a difference exists between the cynicism of young citizens who voted and those who did not vote, although voters' cynicism (M = 3.03, SD = .77) was lower than nonvoters (M = 3.15, SD = .65), this difference was not found to be statistically significant, t(277) = -1.21, p = .23.

Our third research question asked if campaign interest, campaign attention, political ideology, or vote choice predicted young citizens' level of Political Information Efficacy (PIE). Before determining which if any of these factors predicted PIE, a correlation analysis was conducted. The results revealed that there was no significant relationship between political ideology and PIE, $r(268) = -.04, p = .57$. However, PIE did have significant positive relationships with campaign attention, $r(274) = .69, p < .001$, and campaign interest, $r(273) = .51, p < .001$. Thus, to determine the predictors of PIE, a regression model was created using campaign attention, campaign interest, and vote choice while controlling for sex, race, and political ideology. The results indicated that campaign attention and interest positively predicted political information efficacy among young citizens (see Table 1). For campaign attention, as individuals felt more informed about the presidential campaign, their confidence in their political knowledge increased. Similar results were present for campaign interest. As young citizens' interest in the presidential campaign increased, so did their level of confidence in their political knowledge.

Table 1. Regression Analysis for Variables Predicting Political Information Efficacy

Variable	B	SE B	B	t	p
Sex	.02	.11	.01	.23	.82
Race	.18	.11	.09	1.64	.10
Vote Choice	.13	.15	.08	.89	.38
Ideology	.01	.03	.02	.20	.85
Attention	.65	.06	.63	10.64	.00
Interest	.17	.07	.13	2.22	.03

Note. $R^2 = .48$ ($N = 193, p < .001$) male = 0, female = 1; vote choice Obama = 1, vote choice all others = 0

Finally, our fourth research question asked if campaign interest, campaign attention, political ideology, or vote choice predicted young citizens' level of political cynicism. Preliminary analysis revealed that political cynicism is negatively correlated with one's degree of interest in the presidential campaign, $r(273) = -.15, p = .01$. In other words, as political cynicism increased, young citizens' interest in the presidential campaign decreased. However, political cynicism was not related to campaign attention, $r(274) = -.39, p = .52$. Further, correlation results indicated a positive correlation between political cynicism and political ideology, $r(268) = .15, p = .01$. Here, results showed that the more cynical young voters reported being, the more conservative their political views.

To further explore the predictors of political cynicism, regression analysis was employed using the variables with which political cynicism was significantly correlated as well as individual vote choice. As Table 2 indicates, while holding sex and race constant, the results revealed that campaign interest is a predictor of political cynicism. Specifically, the less interested one is in the presidential campaign, the more cynical they are of politicians. Although political ideology did not hold its significance in the regression model, an interesting finding did surface: respondents' vote choice was a predictor of their level of political cynicism. Specifically, young citizens who reported voting for Obama were significantly less cynical of politicians.

Table 2. Regression Analysis for Variables Predicting Political Cynicism

Variable	B	SE B	B	t	p
Sex	-.07	.12	-.04	-.56	.57
Race	.14	.13	.08	1.07	.29
Vote Choice	-.55	.17	-.36	-3.18	.00
Ideology	-.04	.03	-.12	-1.11	.27
Interest	-.15	.08	-.14	-1.94	.05

Note. R^2 = .12 (N = 194, p < .001) male = 0, female =1; vote choice Obama = 1, vote choice all others = 0

Discussion

Our findings provide an interesting picture of the political motivations and attitudes of young citizens, with results both confirming extant research and also suggesting that young voters may think and behave differently than older voters. First, our analysis reveals that younger citizens who vote have greater PIE—they feel more confident in the political knowledge they possess—than nonvoting young citizens. This finding, we believe, both validates this important political engagement construct and also is encouraging from a normative perspective. It seems rather intuitive that if people are more confident in their political knowledge they may, therefore, be more likely to act on this knowledge.

Conversely, those citizens with less knowledge, at least those who believe they know less, may not represent the most informed or enlightened voter. Although we may desire that all citizens exercise their right and obligation to participate in the electoral process, we are particularly pleased to see that among our sample of younger citizens those who believe they know more are more likely to vote. Our findings also revealed that younger citizens who vote are less cynical about politics and politicians than nonvoting young citizens, and it is quite likely that our much smaller sample of nonvoters (26% of our study's 277 participants) prevented this difference from reaching a level of statistical significance. Still, future research should continue to explore the impact of political cynicism on voting behavior, particularly among younger voters.

In examining the specific factors that influence young citizens' PIE and cynicism, this study uncovered several noteworthy relationships that allow us to better understand young citizens' political behavior and also point to potentially fruitful areas for future research. First, regression analysis revealed that as one's campaign interest and attention increases, so too does one's confidence in the political knowledge one possesses, leading to greater participation through voting and persuading others how they should vote. Thus, taken together, our findings provide tentative support for the formulation of a model of young citizens' electoral engagement by which campaign interest and attention leads to greater PIE, and those young citizens with greater PIE are more likely to be among the ranks of voters.

Yet, our analysis also reveals that political cynicism diminishes campaign interest—as young citizens' cynicism increased, their interest in the campaign decreased—and, at least tentatively, among our sample of young citizens, we found that those with greater political cynicism were more likely to be among the group of nonvoters. On this point, much more analysis is needed to help us better understand the role of political cynicism and its effect on young citizens' voting behavior. Interestingly, and somewhat counter to the present results, past research has shown that political cynicism is not necessarily deleterious to political engagement. Cappella and Jamieson's (1997) *Spiral of Cynicism* actually found that those with greater political cynicism were among the heaviest viewers of political and public affairs news, and these individuals were also among the most likely to vote. Yet, it may well be that political cynicism has different effects on younger voters that may in fact discourage their electoral participation. Again, more research is needed on this front.

Finally, our results also point to a relationship between ideology and cynicism—those who reported being more conservative were more cynical—and we also found that young citizens who reported voting for Obama were significantly less cynical. It is possible that these results speak to a potential cynicism effect following the outcome of the 2012 election. Those who are more conservative, and more likely Romney supporters, registered greater cynicism following the election, whereas Obama supporters who were obviously pleased with the election's outcome reported significantly less cynicism.

Returning to our suggested model of young citizen electoral engagement proffered above, if we begin the process of engagement with interest and attention—which leads to greater PIE and less cynicism, both key engagement attitudes related to voting and nonvoting—a crucial antecedent in this dynamic of political engagement is the question of just what might induce greater campaign interest and attention among young citizens? It is here that we insert the key role of campaign communication, and particularly appeals targeted specifically to younger citizens. When considering the history of young citizens' electoral participation recounted earlier in this chapter, we might view from a macro perspective the empirical evidence of young voters' turnout in presidential elections throughout the past several decades and note especially those few instances in which their participation increased.

Since 1972 and the "high watermark" of youth voting, the second highest moment of youth electoral participation came in 1992 when Clinton's campaign specifically targeted young citizens, a voting segment that most all presidential campaigns found unworthy of expending candidate attention or campaign resources. Yet, from his saxophone and shades on late night TV to his MTV appearance with college students—where he responded "usually briefs" to the burning question from a young female voter "Is it boxers or briefs?"—candidate Clinton appealed directly to young citizens using their language and dominant media. Next, beginning with the 2000 presidential election and much in response to young citizens' historic low voter participation in 1996, it seemed that a national movement was afoot to get young citizens involved in the political process. From MTV's "Rock the Vote" and "Choose or Lose" to P. Diddy and Lil' Kim's "Vote or Die" advertising blitzes, voting was marketed to young citizens as the "hip" thing to do (McKinney & Banwart, 2005). Since 2000, as noted previously, we've now witnessed increased and sustained electoral participation of young citizens in successive presidential elections, helping to narrow the once sizeable gap between more older vs. fewer younger citizens voting.

Certainly, our case studies of targeted campaign appeals generating greater numbers of young voters would be incomplete without documenting Obama's "digital revolution" in campaign communication. Much has been written about team Obama's ability to identify with, organize, and turn out a generation of "digital natives"—citizens for whom digital technologies have been an integral part of their entire lives—by developing campaign messages and appeals that use the very communicative practices and language of these young citizens (e.g., McKinney & Banwart, 2011; Palfrey & Gasser, 2008). Describing Obama's 2008 quest for the presidency, *The New York Times* went so far as to label his loyal following of youth voters "Generation O." Indeed, Obama developed a seemingly personal relationship with his following of young supporters, forged by a steady stream of digital communication perhaps best typified in the exchange that took place just seconds after the national news networks called the history-making 2008 election for America's first African-American president. Before addressing the nation and world in an otherwise "old school" televised victory address, the president-elect first sent his throng of digital followers a text signed simply "Barack" that informed his online supporters, "I'm about to head to Grant Park to talk to everyone, but I wanted to write to you first. All of this happened because of you. We just made history" (Cave, 2008, para. 4).

In 2012, team Obama continued to build and refine its impressive digital campaign operation of 2008, with particular efforts to maintain his connection with and support among young citizens. In terms of winning the social media race alone, it was no contest. Just as Romney secured the Republican presidential nomination, the digital media and technology magazine *Mashable* posed the question "Who's winning the Twitter and Facebook 2012 presidential election?" reporting that "President Barack Obama's Facebook and Twitter following leaves the Republican presidential candidate in the dust ... Obama still is the social-media-savvy candidate who reaches out to voters on the online platforms where they communicate" (Skelton, 2012, para. 3). "Votes" for the two candidates via social media tallied to well over 25 million people who "liked" Obama on Facebook compared to Romney's Facebook following of 1.5 million people. Also, Obama had nearly 13 million Twitter followers in 2012, with the president personally tweeting an average of four times each day throughout the campaign (Skelton, 2012).

Following his re-election, the magnitude of team Obama's digital dominance became even more clear with reports of how the campaign's technology "nerds" developed sophisticated algorithms that sifted through massive amounts of voter, online, and social media data resulting in strategically targeted messages to likely and desired voters, including large numbers of young citizens. Eschewing mass appeals through televised advertising and other traditional means of campaign communication, Obama's frequent campaign appeals were instead targeted at the individual voter with personalized messages and delivered via digital and social media. Such campaign messaging allowed Obama to connect more efficiently with likely voters all the way down to the neighborhood, voter precinct, and county level in the handful of battleground states that would decide the 2012 contest (Madrigal, 2012).

As noted earlier in this chapter, Obama's voting models and corresponding communication strategies accurately predicted that his campaign messaging would allow him to maintain his level of youth vote in areas where these voters were needed—as well as maintain or enhance other needed voting blocs—thus ensuring his re-election. Much to the astonishment of Republican strategist Karl Rove on election night as the returns came in (Blake, 2012) and also Mitt and Ann Romney who were reportedly "shell-shocked" when the networks called the election for Obama (Crawford, 2012), the Obama voting models—and messaging machine—produced victory. In the end, as *The Atlantic's* Alexis Madrigal (2012, para. 1) concluded, it was "a dream team of engineers from Facebook, Twitter and Google who built the software that drove Barack Obama's re-election."

Obama's success in attracting young voters through his use of digital technologies and social media in both his initial and re-election efforts serves as illustration to support our central argument regarding young voters' political and electoral engagement. The "macro" evidence is rather compelling. When candidates strategically target and craft appeals designed particularly for young citizens, such activity captures the attention and interest of these citizens who respond through greater electoral engagement. As previously noted, the election cycles in which young voters came near matching their cohort's record high rate of participation in 1972—Clinton's campaign of 1992 and Obama's 2008 and 2012 efforts—happen to be elections in which the candidates, both regarded as "new" or younger generation, devoted considerable time and campaign resources to communicating with young citizens; and these campaigns communicated by adopting the language and channels used most by young citizens. In these instances, young voters responded in record numbers.

Without doubt, we must be cautious in making claims and connections between candidates' campaign messaging activity and its likely effects on voter behavior, particularly when analyzing aggregate or macro-level data. Still, we are aware of at least one micro-level study of specific campaign communication that supports our contention that when candidates craft appeals targeted directly to young citizens, they respond with increased attention and interest in the campaign and also achieve heightened political efficacy and decreased cynicism, attitudes that the current study relate to one's likelihood of voting. McKinney and Banwart (2005) examined college students' reactions to a presidential primary debate designed expressly for young voters—MTV's "Rock the Vote" debate, which took place in fall 2003 and featured the Democratic presidential primary candidates. In this comparative study, young citizens also were exposed to a "traditional" primary debate not targeted explicitly to youth voters. McKinney and Banwart found that the youth-targeted debate, significantly more so than a "traditional" candidate debate, encouraged greater campaign interest and identification between young citizens and the candidates. Also, viewers of the "Rock the Vote" debate expressed greater political efficacy, heightened political trust, and decreased political cynicism.

Conclusion

Much more research is needed that examines the role and performance of young citizens in the electoral process, and specifically work that allows us to better understand how campaign communication affects both attitudes of democratic engagement and behaviors such as voting. Although the present study has uncovered a number of important findings and suggests several fruitful endeavors for additional research in this area, our study—as with all research endeavors—has its limitations. First, our panel data collected throughout the fall 2012 campaign captured a much smaller number of nonvoters than we would have liked to more fully compare with those young citizens who reported voting. Also, we realize that although our convenience sample of college students may represent the age cohort of young citizens that were of interest to our analysis, our sample is not particularly representative of all young citizens and especially those citizens who are not college educated. Finally, future research should avoid single-item measurements for such constructs as campaign interest and attention as was utilized in the present study.

The foundation of a vibrant democracy requires the participation and representation of all segments of society. Although our youngest citizens have traditionally been viewed, and often treated by candidates, as an inconsequential segment of the electorate, the voices—and votes—of young citizens represent a vital element of our democratic process. The evidence presented in this chapter suggests that when political candidates acknowledge and incorporate the concerns of young citizens as an important part of their campaign message and communicate with these citizens using the language and modes of communication most readily adopted by young voters, these good citizens respond with enthusiasm.

References

Ansolabehere, S., & Iyengar, S. (1995). *Going negative: How political advertisements shrink and polarize the electorate.* New York, NY: The Free Press.

Blake, M. (2012, December 5). Fox news reportedly benches Karl Rove after election meltdown. *Los Angeles Times.* Retrieved from http://articles.latimes.com/2012/dec/05/entertainment/la-et-st-fox-news-benches-karl-rove-dick-morris-20121205

Campbell, A., Gurin, G., & Miller, W. E. (1954). *The voter decides.* Evanston, IL: Row Peterson & Co.

Cappella, J. N., & Jamieson, K. H. (1997). *Spiral of cynicism: The press and the public good.* New York, NY: Oxford University Press.

Cave, D. (2008, November 9). Generation O gets its hopes up. *The New York Times*, p. ST1. Retrieved from http://www.nytimes.com/2008/11/09/fashion/09boomers.html

Crawford, J. (2012, November 8). Adviser: Romney "shell-shocked" by loss. *CBSNews.com*. Retrieved from http://www.cbsnews.com/8301-250_162-57547239/

Delli Carpini, M. X. (2004). Mediating democratic engagement: The impact of communications on citizens' involvement in political and civic life. In L. L. Kaid (Ed.), *Handbook of political communication research* (pp. 395–434). Mahwah, NJ: Lawrence Erlbaum.

Delli Carpini, M. X., & Keeter, S. (1996). *What Americans know about politics and why it matters*. New Haven, CT: Yale University Press.

Frosch, J., & Peyron, J. (2012, June 11). Can the "youth vote" carry Obama to victory again? *France24 International News*. Retrieved from http://www.cbsnews.com/8301-250_162-57547239/

Gans, C. (2005). Low voter turnout and the decline of American civic participation. In M. S. McKinney, L. L. Kaid, D. G. Bystrom, & D. B. Carlin (Eds.), *Communicating politics: Engaging the public in democratic life* (pp. 79–85). New York, NY: Peter Lang.

Kaid, L. L., McKinney, M. S., & Tedesco, J. C. (2000). *Civic dialogue in the 1996 presidential campaign: Candidate, media, and public voices*. Cresskill, NJ: Hampton Press.

Kaid, L. L., McKinney, M. S., & Tedesco, J. C. (2007). Political information efficacy and young voters. *American Behavioral Scientist, 50*, 1093-1111. doi:1177/0002764207300040

Kaid, L. L., Postelnicu, M., Landreville, K., Yun, H. J., & LeGrange, A. G. (2007). The effects of political advertising on young voters. *American Behavioral Scientist, 50*, 1137-1151. doi:10.1177/0002764207300039

Levine, P., & Lopez, M. H. (2002). *Youth voter turnout has declined, by any measure*. Retrieved from www.civicyouth.org/research/areas/pol_partic.htm

Lipka, S. (2012, November 7). Defying expectations, half of young voters cast ballots, 60% for Obama. *The Chronicle of Higher Education*. Retrieved from http://chronicle.com/article/Defying-Expectations-Half-of/135620/

Madrigal, A. C. (2012, November 16). When the nerds go marching in. *The Atlantic*. Retrieved from http://www.theatlantic.com/technology/archive/2012/11/when-the-nerds-go-marching-in/265325/

McKenna, I. (2012, November 5). Lower youth turnout expected for election day 2012. *The Observer*. Retrieved from http://www.fordhamobserver.com/lower-youth-turnout-expected-for-election-day-2012/

McKinney, M. S., & Banwart, M. C. (2005). Rocking the youth vote through debate: Examining the effects of a citizen versus journalist controlled debate on civic engagement. *Journalism Studies, 6*, 153–163. doi:10.1080/14616700500057171

McKinney, M. S., & Banwart, M. C. (2011). The election of a lifetime. In M. S. McKinney & M. C. Banwart (Eds.), *Communication in the 2008 election: Digital natives elect a president* (pp. 1–9). New York, NY: Peter Lang.

McKinney, M. S., & Chattopadhyay, S. (2007). Political engagement through debates: Young citizens' reactions to the 2004 presidential debates. *American Behavioral Scientist, 50*, 1169–1182. doi:10.1177/0002764207300050

McKinney, M. S., Kaid, L. L., & Bystrom, D. G. (2005). The role of communication in civic engagement. In M. S. McKinney, L. L. Kaid, D. G. Bystrom, & D. B. Carlin (Eds.), *Communicating politics: Engaging the public in democratic life* (pp. 3–26). New York, NY: Peter Lang.

McKinney, M. S., & Rill, L. A. (2009). Not your parents' presidential debates: Examining the effects of the CNN/YouTube debates on young citizens' civic engagement. *Communication Studies, 60*, 392–406. doi:10.1080/10510970903110001

McKinney, M. S., Rill, L. A., & Gully, D. (2011). Civic engagement through presidential debates: Young citizens' attitudes of political engagement throughout the 2008 election. In M. S. McKinney & M. C. Banwart (Eds.), *Communication in the 2008 U.S. election: Digital natives elect a president* (pp. 121–141). New York, NY: Peter Lang.

McKinney, M. S., & Warner, B. R. (2013). Do presidential debates matter? Examining a decade of campaign debate effects. *Argumentation and Advocacy, 49*, 238–258.

Palfrey, J., & Gasser, U. (2008). *Born digital: Understanding the first generation of digital natives.* New York, NY: Basic Books.

Pfau, M. (2003, March). *The changing nature of presidential debate influence in the new age of mass media communication.* Paper presented at the 9th annual Conference on Presidential Rhetoric, Texas A&M University, College Station, Texas.

Pinkleton, B. E., Um, N., & Austin, E. W. (2002). An exploration of the effects of negative political advertising on political decision making. *Journal of Advertising, 31*, 13–25.

Popkin, S. L. (1991). *The reasoning voter: Communication and persuasion in presidential campaigns.* Chicago, IL: University of Chicago Press.

Rill, L. A., & Cardiel, C. (in press). Funny, ha ha: The impact of user generated political satire on political attitudes. *American Behavioral Scientist.*

Rosenstone, S. J., Kinder, D. R., Miller, W. E., & the National Election Studies. (1997). *American National Election Study 1996: Pre- and post-election survey* [Computer file]. Ann Arbor, MI: University of Michigan, Center for Political Studies (Producer) and Inter-University Consortium for Political and Social Research (Distributor).

Skelton, A. (2012, February 18). Who's winning the Twitter and Facebook presidential election? *Mashable.com*, p. 9. Retrieved from http://mashable.com/2012/02/18/presidential-election-infographic/

Sweetser, K. D., & Kaid, L. L. (2008). Stealth soapboxes: Political information efficacy, cynicism and uses of celebrity weblogs among readers. *New Media & Society, 10*, 67–91. doi:10.1177/1461444807085322

The Youth Vote in 2012. (2013, May 10). *CIRCLE Fact Sheet.* The Center for Information & Research on Civic Learning & Engagement. Retrieved at www.civicyouth.org.

Note

1. Campuses participating in this study included: Auburn University, Emerson College, Georgia College and State University, Marquette University, Ohio University, Portland State University, Radford University, Rhodes College, Texas State University-San Marcos, University of Georgia, and University of Missouri.

CHAPTER FIFTEEN

Altar Calls

Religious Segmentation in Campaign Appeals

BRIAN T. KAYLOR

Civil rights leader Martin Luther King, Jr., a Baptist minister, popularized a critique of U.S. churches for enacting segregation. Speaking at the National Cathedral in Washington, D.C., just days before his assassination, King proclaimed, "We must face the sad fact that at eleven o'clock on Sunday morning when we stand to sing 'In Christ There is no East or West,' we stand in the most segregated hour of America" (King, 1968, para. 16). Fifty years later, his words likely still ring true. Yet, since that time, houses of worship across the land have shifted to create another form of segmentation. When King preached, Americans mostly divided by denominational lines when they entered the ballot boxes. Those attending Catholic and evangelical Protestant churches generally punched their ballots for the Democratic candidates, while those occupying pews in mainline Protestant churches typically favored the Republicans.

Within a few years of King's death, these denominational voting trends started dissipating with voting trends more likely to be seen on matters of church attendance or other religious behaviors (Putnam & Campbell, 2010). Within many denominations and religious traditions, conservative and liberal congregations emerged with parishioners more likely to change their church and religion than change their politics (Putnam & Campbell, 2010). Segregated by race, income, culture, geography, and even—if not especially—politics, houses of worship mirror—and perhaps magnify—the nation's polarized and divided electorate.

In recent decades, many politicians hit the campaign trail to preach about God while some religious leaders played the role of political pundits on cable news programs and attempted to transform their followers into grassroots political movements. Scholars increasingly join political strategists and religious leaders in giving attention to the intersections of religion and politics. Often these scholarly analyses examine how presidential candidates invoke the divine on the campaign trail. Among those especially receiving scholarly attention: John Kennedy, the first Catholic to occupy the Oval Office; Jimmy Carter, a born-again Sunday school teacher who often injected his faith into his speeches; ministers Jesse Jackson, Pat Robertson, and Mike Huckabee as they sought to move from the pulpit to 1600 Pennsylvania Avenue; Ronald Reagan and George W. Bush, two heroes for conservative Christians; and Bill Clinton and Barack Obama, two crusaders for liberal religious causes.[1] Other politicians receiving scholarly scrutiny for religious-political appeals have included Ted Kennedy and Mario Cuomo, two liberal Catholics who articulated their policy disagreements with the conservative Catholic positions; Joe Lieberman, the first Jewish vice presidential nominee for a major political party; and Mitt Romney, the first Mormon nominee for president by a major political party.[2]

In each of the nine presidential elections from 1976 through 2008, the most religiously outspoken general election candidate prevailed (Kaylor, 2011b). Winning candidates (and many of the contenders) used a form of "confessional politics" with religious rhetoric that is testimonial, partisan, sectarian, and liturgical in form (Kaylor, 2011b). Heading into 2012, both parties seemed to understand the electoral need to find God on the campaign trail.

As Democrats and Republicans increase the sophistication of their campaign outreach and mobilization efforts, political currents within religion have not gone unnoticed. With the path to the White House often appearing to run through religious congregations, both Republicans and Democrats utilize faith-based appeals in hopes of finding political salvation in the ballot box. Although each of the two major political parties mined for votes in religious communities during the 2012 campaign, few churches and faith leaders found themselves targeted from both directions. The 2012 campaign brought a shift from recent elections when Democrat Obama sought to win over Republican-leaning evangelical Protestants in 2008 and Republican Bush hoped to pry away Democratic-leaning black Protestants in 2000 and 2004.

During the 2012 campaign, the religious-political rhetoric came not as broad-based or unifying arguments, but instead as carefully micro-targeted messages. Obama and the Democratic National Committee focused on fewer religious groups than in 2008 as they narrowed their appeals to get out the vote among key populations. Similarly, Romney and the Republican National Committee centered their religious appeals on exciting their base constituents. With these targeted religious-political messages, the parties focused less on winning over new converts and more on sparking revivalistic energy to mobilize their followers. This chapter will explore the religious rhetoric offered by the presidential campaigns and the parties based on both rhetorical analysis of public arguments and ethnographic insights from attendance at Republican and Democratic religious-political events during the campaign. This chapter will explore a critical area of political campaigning that often goes unnoticed and will demonstrate how even churches, synagogues, and mosques are divided into red and blue camps.

Red Church

Waking up on the morning of Wednesday, November 3, 2010, many Republicans could scarcely hold their glee. The U.S. House of Representatives turned red in one of the most historic landslide elections, and the U.S. Senate edged rightward. Attention quickly turned to the next mission: defeating President Obama in 2012. With the energy of the "Tea Party" thought by many to be the key, Republican presidential hopefuls elbowed each other as they framed themselves as the most anti-Obama candidate and as the resurrection of President Reagan. As the candidates crisscrossed between Iowa, New Hampshire, and South Carolina during much of 2011, evangelical Christian churches and gatherings became key stops. On any given Sunday, a candidate could be found in one of those states sitting in a church pew and being referenced by a preacher or even standing behind the pulpit to testify.

U.S. Rep. Michele Bachmann often spoke in churches, as did former U.S. Senator Rick Santorum and Texas Gov. Rick Perry (including in an Iowa church the Sunday before Christmas while his holiday ad blanketed the state calling himself a Christian and attacking "Obama's war on religion"). U.S. Rep. Ron Paul picked up religious-political adviser Doug Wead (who helped both George H. W. Bush and George W. Bush on religious outreach), launched "Evangelicals for Ron Paul," and increased the use of biblical references in speeches when compared to 2008. Bachmann, Perry, and former pizza mogul Herman Cain each spoke about being "called" by God to run for president, and Newt Gingrich took to the campaign trail to confess his past moral failings and preach about finding forgiveness from God. Meanwhile, former Massachusetts Gov. Romney dropped fliers in South Carolina stressing his "faith" (although without mentioning Mormonism). Especially when courting voters in Iowa and South Carolina, it seemed each campaign playbook featured the old Christian hymn "Victory in Jesus."

One exemplary moment that demonstrates the evangelical focus of the race came in June 2011 as most Republican presidential hopefuls found themselves standing before about 1,000 conservative Christian activists at the Renaissance Hotel in Washington, D.C., for the conference hosted by the Faith & Freedom Coalition (FFC). FFC's founder, Ralph Reed, previously led the Christian Coalition before entering Republican politics as a candidate. However, after the Jack Abramoff lobbying scandal dashed Reed's personal electoral rise, he returned to religious-political activism by creating the FFC in 2009 in large part to mobilize Christians against Obama. At Reed's invitation, Republican presidential hopefuls left the early primary states and headed to the heart of the city they preached against in their stump speeches.

Former Minnesota Gov. Tim Pawlenty, former Ambassador to China Jon Huntsman, Romney, Bachmann, Santorum, Paul, Cain, Gingrich, and even will-he-won't-he-run businessman Donald Trump all spoke and peppered their remarks with evidence of their Christian credentials. Even Huntsman, a Mormon candidate who on other occasions referred to himself as "spiritual" instead of "religious," worked in references to "Jesus," "religion," "soul," and "values" (Kaylor, 2011c, para. 7–12). Pawlenty started his speech by quoting the Bible, Paul worked scriptural quotations into his libertarian message, and Bachmann led the group in a long prayer asking God to fix the nation. Trump took the faith-based pandering even further as he held up a picture of his Presbyterian confirmation class as a child—which also appeared on the large video screens—to prove he had, in fact, gone through confirmation. As the crowd applauded his confirmation photo, a beaming Trump even confessed this political ploy: "Good, right? That doesn't always play, but in this crowd it plays" (Kaylor, 2011d, para. 11). For the Republican presidential hopefuls, the crowd to play for was the group gathered in that room: conservative evangelicals.

Two months later, the candidates descended on Iowa State University's campus in Ames for the Iowa Straw Poll. As the kickoff event for modern Republican presidential contests came to life on the morning of Saturday, August 13, 2011, a man wearing a National Rifle Association T-shirt and driving a golf cart for Bachmann's campaign plowed into a group of people. Before day's end, Bachmann's campaign similarly rode to victory—in large part because of her religious outreach. Although everyone hit by the golf cart—including myself (attending with a press pass)—was okay, Pawlenty's campaign did not survive the day as the once-favored Iowa candidate fell to a distant third behind the near-tie showings of Bachmann and Paul.

Part political rally, part state fair, and part music festival, the 2011 Iowa Straw Poll attracted 17,000 Iowans to cast their nonbinding preference ballot.

To understand Bachmann's victory in the event that tests the organizational strength of campaigns, one must look to church pulpits and pews. On the Sunday before the straw poll, Bachmann attended the nondenominational Point of Grace Church in Waukee, a suburb of Des Moines. During the service, Bachmann read from Philippians 4, after which the congregation cheered. Jeff Mullen, the church's pastor, then joined Bachmann at the pulpit, declaring as he held up Bachmann's Bible: "There are some candidates who start running, and have this come-to-Jesus moment. … What I love about this Bible … is how well it's used" (Novogrod, 2011, para. 5).

A few days before the church service, Bachmann's campaign released a list of more than 100 Iowa pastors and church leaders who endorsed her candidacy (Ball, 2011). The list of pastors unknown to national observers—such as Mullen, the pastor who would praise Bachmann from the pulpit just a couple of days later—demonstrated her campaign's focus on mobilizing the evangelical Christian community in mostly under-the-radar ways. Similarly, Bachmann's campaign worked to mobilize the home school movement to turn out for her at the straw poll. This mostly behind-the-scenes effort mirrored a key component of former Arkansas Gov. Huckabee's surprise second-place finish in the 2007 Iowa Straw Poll that launched him from also-ran status to contender.

As attendees at the 2011 straw poll arrived at Bachmann's air-conditioned tent, they could pick up information about the candidate and fill up on free hot dogs, corn dogs, ice cream, cinnamon rolls, and "beef sundaes" (beef topped with mashed potatoes and gravy with a plum tomato on top). As the campaign sought to energize her supporters, attendees could also enjoy a full schedule of speakers and performers, including country music star Randy Travis and the worship leader for Thomas Road Baptist Church (started by the late Jerry Falwell). Indicative of Bachmann's electoral focus, one of the main speakers in her tent was Rick Green of WallBuilders, a conservative evangelical Christian group that argues the United States was created by its founders to be an explicitly Christian nation and that writes Christian "history" books for Christian private school and homeschoolers.

Bachmann also joined the "Values Bus," a political outreach effort by FRC Action (the political action committee of the Family Research Council), the National Organization for Marriage, and the Susan B. Anthony List to make social issues a top priority among straw poll voters. Other candidates who joined the "Values Bus" for various Iowa stops were Pawlenty, Santorum, Cain, and quixotic candidate U.S. Rep. Thaddeus McCotter of Michigan. After crisscrossing the state to rally evangelical voters, the "Values Bus" parked itself at the straw poll along with numerous other religious and political groups handing out fliers and trinkets.

As with other candidates, Pawlenty particularly sought to beat Bachmann by appealing to conservative evangelicals. In addition to serving free barbecue and Dairy Queen Blizzards, Pawlenty's tent featured the Christian band Sonicflood singing worship songs to God as Pawlenty staffers handed out campaign paraphernalia. Huckabee, still a star among conservative evangelicals even though he was not running for president, briefly joined Sonicflood at Pawlenty's tent to play the bass guitar. Huckabee also briefly joined musicians at the straw poll tents of Santorum and Cain, both of whom featured much smaller setups with simpler food indicative of their small campaign budgets. While Cain wooed voters with Godfather's pizza and Coke (and a bounce house and corn hole for children), Santorum's campaign flipped burgers in a parking lot. Meanwhile, Paul's large tent included many libertarian-themed children's games (like the inflatable "Sliding Dollar" slide and the "Dump Ben Bernanke" dunk tank) and a full-course outdoor summer feast with hot dogs, barbecue, potato salad, grilled corn-on-the-cob, and baked beans. With God, food, and music, the Republican presidential candidates battled each other in the hot August sun. As Pawlenty packed his bags and Bachmann beamed, another candidate looked to enter the race with a prayer.

Although multiple 2012 Republican presidential candidates mentioned praying as part of their exploratory process, Texas Gov. Perry out-prayed them all with a massive prayer rally at the Reliant Stadium, home of the Houston Texans professional football team. More than 30,000 people gathered for the August 6, 2011, event, which was dubbed "The Response: A Call to Prayer for a Nation in Crisis." Perry, who once worked as a door-to-door Bible salesman, wove several Bible verses and prayer into his 13-minute speech as he spoke about his personal beliefs on sin and salvation. He highlighted Joel 2:12–17, a passage he had used to promote the event. During his presentation, Perry prayed:

> Father, our heart breaks for America. We see discord at home. We see fear in the marketplace. We see anger in the halls of government and, as a nation, we have forgotten who made us, who protects us, who blesses us, and for that, we cry out for your forgiveness. (Fernandez, 2011, para. 2)

Perry's remarks drew strong applause from the crowd, as did the remarks of other speakers, which included Republican Kansas Gov. Sam Brownback, Republican Florida Gov. Rick Scott (via pre-recorded video), David Barton of Wallbuilders, Focus on the Family founder James and Shirley Dobson, controversial pastor John Hagee, the FRC's Tony Perkins, and evangelist James Robison. The crowd often applauded during prayers, such as when Vonette Bright, widow of Campus Crusade for Christ founder Bill Bright, prayed for the Ten Commandments and prayer to be allowed in public schools.

Barton, Dobson, Hagee, Perkins, Robison, and the late Bright have all previously campaigned for Republican presidential candidates. In between prayers and short speeches from leaders of Perry's rally, the crowd joined music leaders in singing numerous hymns and praise music. The event also included times when those in the stadium broke into small groups to pray about specific topics. Although the day was billed as one for prayer and fasting, concession stands at the stadium were open and attracting lines of hungry participants.

Despite organizers insisting the prayer rally remained unconnected to a potential Perry run—which he did not officially announce until just over a week later—Perry had said before the rally that he felt called by God to run. Additionally, Perry credited two individuals for inspiring him to host the prayer rally: conservative religious-political organizer David Lane and evangelist and conservative political cheerleader James Robison. In June 2011, Perry secretly met with a group of nearly 80 conservative evangelical Christians leaders in Texas, including Robison (who organized the meeting); Lane; Vonette Bright; Richard Land, the Southern Baptist Convention's top politico; Ruth Graham, daughter of the famed evangelist Billy Graham; former Republican U.S. Rep. Bob McEwen, who often focuses on mobilizing conservative Christian leaders; controversial evangelist Rod Parsley, who endorsed John McCain in 2008 (before McCain rejected his endorsement and that of Hagee, who spoke at "The Response"); Jerry Boykin, a former Pentagon official rebuked for speaking in churches in uniform and who media reports connected to the Abu Ghraib prison abuses; Jim Garlow, a pastor who ran a religious-political organization started by Gingrich; and Don Wildmon of the politically-active American Family Association.

Several of those at the June 2011 meeting spoke at "The Response" in August 2011 or served in leadership roles for its planning. Perry's presence at the behind-closed-door meeting, the timing of which matches when Perry later said he decided to run for president, initially escaped public reporting (Kaylor, 2011e). Robison led a similar effort of secret religious-political strategy meetings prior to the 1980 presidential election as he sought to defeat then-President Carter. That effort culminated in an August 1980 rally in Dallas, Texas, with then-Republican presidential nominee Reagan as the key speaker. Perry and Robison speaking at a religious rally in Texas to assist a presidential campaign clearly echoed that earlier Reagan-Robison effort that served as a key milestone in the creation of the so-called "religious right."

Although Perry's campaign ultimately fell apart due to his devastating "oops" debate performance, his prayer rally launched him to the front of the pack as soon as he officially entered the presidential race, thus wiping out Bachmann's post-Iowa boost. Perry's collapse would give rise to later evangelical surges for Cain, Gingrich, and Santorum, with the latter two splitting the evangelical vote as Romney slowly snatched up delegates. Although Romney did not reach out to conservative evangelicals during the primary as strongly as he did with his "Faith in America" speech four years earlier, he did not need to with the evangelical base badly splintered after Perry's self-destruction. Four years earlier, Romney faced a more united evangelical front behind former Southern Baptist pastor Huckabee and struggled with moderate Republican voters thanks to McCain. Yet despite evangelical opposition to Romney during the primaries, he quickly gained their support once he wrapped up the nomination. For instance, Southern Baptist pastor Robert Jeffries, who attended the June 2011 meeting with Perry and attacked Romney as a cult member during a campaign event on Perry's behalf, endorsed Romney against President Obama. Romney also worked to ease evangelical concerns about him as their standard-bearer, such as by giving a faith-filled speech in May 2012 at Liberty University (founded by the late "Moral Majority" founder Jerry Falwell), talking with prominent evangelical leaders in phone calls and private meetings, and making a pilgrimage to the North Carolina mountains to meet with Billy and Franklin Graham. At Liberty, Romney made several references to "Christ," spoke of the importance of "trusting in God," and gave "thanks to the grace of God" (Romney, 2012b, para. 25, 27). He testified:

> Christianity is not the faith of the complacent, the comfortable or of the timid. It demands and creates heroic souls like Wesley, Wilberforce, Bonhoeffer, John Paul the Second, and Billy Graham. Each showed, in their own way, the relentless and powerful influence of the message of Jesus Christ. May that be your guide. (Romney, 2012b, para. 15)

The alliance uniting Romney and conservative evangelicals might have been an awkward, arranged marriage, but he seemed determined to at least say the vows to their liking.

In addition to reaching out to evangelicals, Romney's campaign sought to win over conservative and moderate white Catholics. The "swingingest" of religious groups, Catholics backed the popular vote winner in each election since 1972. Romney's selection of Paul Ryan as his running mate highlighted this effort as Ryan became only the second Catholic on a national Republican ticket (the other being Barry Goldwater's running mate, William Miller, in 1964). As Romney proclaimed during his announcement that Ryan would join the ticket:

> Paul is in public life for all the right reasons—not to advance his personal ambitions but to advance the ideals of freedom and justice; and to increase opportunity and prosperity to people of every class and faith, every age and ethnic background. A faithful Catholic, Paul believes in the worth and dignity of every human life. (Romney, 2012c, para. 9)

The argument Romney used to introduce Ryan's Catholicism represented the key religious argument Romney used as he sought conservative Catholic and evangelical voters: religious liberty. In particular, Romney claimed that Obama—and especially "Obamacare"—represented a threat to the religious liberty rights of conservative Christians. Romney and Ryan peppered their speeches with this argument, which both Catholic bishops and evangelical preachers advanced. For instance, Romney declared (and repeated in other speeches): "President Obama orders religious organizations to violate their conscience. I will defend religious liberty and overturn any regulation that tramples on our first freedom, our right to worship as we choose" (Romney, 2012a, para. 33). Yet, Romney's argument clearly focused on conservative Christians—as opposed to other interpretations of religious liberty—since he redefined the concept to mean that Christians receive preferential treatment from the government. As he declared during a speech to a gathering of conservative Christian activists:

> Our heritage of religious faith and tolerance has importantly shaped who we have become as a people. We must continue to welcome faith into the public square and allow it to flourish. Our government should respect religious values, not silence them. We will always pledge our allegiance to a nation under God. (Romney, 2011, para. 41)

A nation of religious tolerance as long as God is given allegiance was just the rhetoric conservative Catholics and evangelical leaders wanted to hear. So Romney kept tooting that horn and ignored references to his Mormon faith, other than allowing Mormons to talk about his church work during the final night of the Republican National Convention. Romney instead put his electoral prayers in mobilizing conservative Catholics and evangelicals.

Blue Church

As other chapters in this book detail, President Obama's victory in 2012 came from a strategic ground game that sliced and diced the electorate as they identified and mobilized voters. Religion proved no different as the Obama campaign targeted key religious groups, ignoring many of those sought by the Romney campaign as well as the Obama campaign in 2008. During his first presidential campaign, Obama cast a wide net as he reached out to various religious groups, including conservative evangelicals. After Obama's acceptance address at the 2008 Democratic convention, conservative evangelical mega church pastor Joel Hunter offered the benediction. Hunter, who previously had been chosen to lead Pat Robertson's Christian Coalition (although he parted with the group before it officially started), also spoke on a "Faith Caucus" panel during the convention. Other evangelical leaders who prayed or spoke at the Democratic convention events included author Don Miller, professor David Gushee, and author Jim Wallis as well as John Dilulio (who led George W. Bush's White House Office of Faith-Based and Community Initiatives).

Obama also targeted evangelicals with faith-based messages and campaign brochures in key swing states. Although Obama's share of the white evangelical vote in 2008 only barely improved on John Kerry's showing in 2004, he saw larger gains among evangelicals in key swing states like Indiana where the campaign focused its evangelical outreach. By 2012, however, the Obama campaign appeared to accept conventional wisdom that white evangelicals would be the least likely religious group to vote for him (or any other Democratic candidate). The only white Protestant clergy member—evangelical or mainline—to speak at faith events at the 2012 Democratic National Convention was Welton Gaddy (who also spoke at the 2008 convention). Gaddy, however, did not appear merely because he is a Baptist minister but also because he leads the Interfaith Alliance (a cause not shared by conservative evangelicals). Although Hunter continued to offer pastoral guidance to Obama, he disconnected from political participation following Obama's public support for same-sex marriage. Obama's campaign seemed content to leave white evangelicals for Romney.

Although the Democrats went from early 2009 until late 2011 without someone leading faith issues, they started the process of gearing up for the 2012 election in October of 2011. The Democratic National Committee (DNC) hired Reverend Derrick Harkins, an African American Baptist pastor in Washington, D.C., to lead its religious outreach. Harkins, a board member for the moderate-conservative National Association of Evangelicals and the progressive Faith in Public Life, is well connected within Christian circles. Harkins led the DNC's faith outreach along with an assistant. Joshua DuBois, who led Obama's religious outreach during the 2008 campaign, had in 2009 become head of the White House Office of Faith-Based and Neighborhood Partnerships. In May 2012, the Obama campaign filled the role DuBois had played by hiring 24-year-old Michael Wear to serve as the campaign's faith vote director. Wear had previously interned on religious outreach during Obama's 2008 campaign and worked for DuBois in the White House. After the election, DuBois and Wear both left their Obama jobs to start their own religious-political organization, Values Partnerships.

As Democrats gathered in Charlotte, N.C., to push for the re-election of President Obama, two images of the party's position on religion emerged: one in the media and one on the ground. Although numerous religion reporters flocked to Tampa the week before for the Republican National Convention, most packed their bags and headed home without offering similar treatment for the Democratic

National Convention. As I attended the Democratic convention faith events with a press pass, I noted how few reporters attended and how the most covered faith story was initially written by a reporter not even in Charlotte. Early during the convention, Democratic leaders found themselves criticized for removing the word "God" from the party platform. The attacks—and the disorganized response—undermined the faith outreach of the DNC, but primarily played into an evangelical reading of the document. Harkins, the DNC's faith outreach director, pushed back against news reports that Democrats removed the sole reference to God in the platform. Noting that the removed reference to "God" came in an economic statement and not a faith section, he defended the platform as sufficiently religious without the reference to God:

> The word "faith" is used, I believe, 11 times, the word "religion" is used nine times—you can tell I've been talking with our communications department—the word "clergy" is used once. The word "God" was mentioned 30 times last night by various speakers up on the podium. ... Faith is an integral part of the Democratic Party." (Kaylor, 2012a, para. 5–7)

Illustrating the difference between the focus of evangelicals on publicly talking about faith and the focus of other religious traditions on deeds, Harkins added:

> I had someone a long time ago say to me, "It's not what you write down, it's how you live it out." And the temerity of individuals to cast aspersions on the value of faith because of a shift in a paragraph that wasn't even speaking about faith ... [and] that somehow means that God is excised from our work and from who we see ourselves as part of the American story is just unconscionable. ... How dare anybody say that faith is not an integral part of who we are as a party! (Kaylor, 2012a, para. 8)

As Harkins worked to defend the Democratic Party's platform, he also struggled to make the convention seem faith-filled, even though many of the faith events came together at the last moment and featured hand-made signs instead of the professionally-printed ones that other events at the convention received.

Even as Harkins defended the Democratic platform as religious enough without the "God" clause, DNC leaders relented to the media criticism. Platform Committee Chairman Ted Strickland, a former Ohio governor noted for his faith outreach during his 2006 campaign (Spiker, 2008), brought the floor amendment to reinstate the "God" clause. However, the vote, which also included reinserting a different clause referring to Jerusalem as the capital of Israel, did not go according to script. As Los Angeles Mayor Antonio Villaraigosa presided over the voice vote that appeared to be fairly evenly split, he paused and seemed confused instead of reading the teleprompter text declaring two-thirds had voted in the affirmative. Like a biblical story, he asked for the vote three times before finally reading the script that contradicted the sound. What had been designed to create religious cover for the Democrat Party instead ended with boos filling the air, more media criticism, and perhaps an apt metaphor for the Democrats faith outreach efforts.

Although Democratic leaders fought to seem as the party for the faithful—as well as those of no faith—they also narrowed their focus from four years earlier. The 2012 Democratic convention faith events included fewer white Protestant clergy than 2008. Most panelists were African-American Christians, with a mix of other Christian, Mormon, Jewish, Muslim, and Hindu figures. Overall, there were more Jewish rabbis and more Mormon leaders than white Protestant clergy or Hispanic leaders. The group that received courting from both Democrats and Republicans—white Catholics—was particularly notable as Democrats booked Cardinal Timothy Dolan to pray at their convention after Republicans pegged him to pray at theirs. As Harkins entered the room to a faith event, he visited with his clergy friends. Even during the mostly empty morning prayer gatherings, Harkins did not work his way around to meet the few delegates and guests present as he delayed the start—each morning—in hopes of more people coming. However, Harkins did rally his fellow African-American clergy to attend and pledge to use church connections to mobilize for the campaign.

Throughout the faith events at the Democratic convention, the rhetoric focused on Obama as a divinely chosen leader, and numerous speakers attacked Republicans for being inauthentic or too narrow on faith matters. At times the rhetoric seemed a mirror image of the Republican religious-political claims that often spark media controversy. For instance, Michael Blake, deputy director for Operation Vote and a lay African Methodist Episcopal minister, argued at a convention Faith Council meeting that Obama was divinely chosen to lead the nation. Recounting a biblical story from Judges 4, Blake argued:

> [Deborah] looked out and needed a new leader, she needed a new commander, the word says. Now the new commander could've had any name that could've been out there, but surprisingly and appropriately his name was Barak. Barak was the commander that Deborah called out and said "I need you to help lead this army" and the people were glad. And there were many thousands that were against them but they were not afraid about the tens of thousands against them because they had an assignment. … I'm just hoping, Democrats, that we will say that we are the ones who will accept our assignment and stand in Barack's army. (Kaylor, 2012b, para. 6–7)

Other speakers during the convention's various faith events praised Obama's policies as an embodiment of their religious beliefs and attacked Republicans for embodying poor values (especially in terms of being religiously narrow with little diversity). Rabbi Fred Guttman, who fired up the crowd with proclamations as to why Jewish beliefs aligned more closely with voting for Obama than Romney, even showed off his "Rabbis for Obama" button and his "Obama Yarmulke" (or as he called his sacred symbol stamped with a political logo, "Obamulke"). U.S. Rep. Emanuel Cleaver, an African-American congressman from Missouri who is also a United Methodist minister, compared those who questioned the faith of Democrats to the biblical Pharisees. Far from what the media buzz suggested based on the missing "God" clause in the platform, the Democrats filled their political philosophy and strategizing with faith-based rhetoric. And the targeted faith communities at the Democratic convention faith events often filled the air with applause, cheers, and shouts of "amen!"

Obama toned down his religious references in 2012 compared to his 2008 speeches. This may have come because Obama did not reach out as much to white evangelicals, did not have a religious controversy like in 2008 when his pastor Jeremiah Wright stole the headlines, and because he was not working to convince people he was not a secret Muslim (although the percentage of people holding that belief did not dissipate, Obama may have realized those individuals were among the least likely to vote for him). However, Obama still wore his faith on his sleeves at times, showing an ability to discuss key theological concepts in a way that Romney, as a Mormon, shied away from doing. For instance, at an Easter prayer breakfast in April 2012, Obama reflected on the occasion:

> It's an opportunity for us to reflect on the triumph of the resurrection, and to give thanks for the all-important gift of grace. And for me, and I'm sure for some of you, it's also a chance to remember the tremendous sacrifice that led up to that day, and all that Christ endured—not just as a son of God, but as a human being. (Obama, 2012a, para. 7)

Obama also quoted from scriptural passages and talked about his own faith—a level of testifying that Romney never publicly reached. In a video speech to the Q Conference (a Christian gathering) just as Romney became the presumptive nominee, Obama again talked about his personal faith in Christ and then connected his religious principles to public policies like feeding children, budget priorities, and international assistance. But he also praised the Christian leaders at the event for "the values you bring to the public square" and for working to improve society since "we also know that government isn't the only answer" (Obama, 2012b, para. 9–10). Like other recent presidents, Obama's bully pulpit often borrowed language from church pulpits.

Conclusion

This analysis of religious targeting during the 2012 presidential campaign reveals important implications. Both parties—and the nominees of both parties—clearly continued to engage in deliberate religious outreach with explicit religious (mostly Christian) rhetoric. Although this follows other recent campaigns as the more rhetorically religious candidate in the general election won (Kaylor, 2011b), this observation still runs counter to a common media narrative that blames the Republicans and "religious right" for bringing religion into politics. Yet, Obama proved more comfortable preaching about Christ than Romney. Perhaps some of the problem comes because white evangelicals often dominate the national religious-political discussion. Even factors used to show the so-called "God gap" in voting (which paints Republicans as the church party and Democrats as the more godless party) are based on factors that favor an evangelical view of spiritual faithfulness. Thus, some scholars question the pervasiveness of the so-called "God gap" (Roof, 2011). Additionally, other scholars argue that the factors usually used in such analyses are biased toward behaviors that evangelical Christians prioritize (e.g., frequent church attendance, daily prayer, and Bible reading), while tradition-adjusted scales—those which test each individual's religiosity according to what their religious tradition places more value upon—produce only modest differences (Mockabee, Monson, & Grant, 2001).

Another key finding in this chapter concerns how the parties divided up religious traditions: Republicans getting white Protestants (evangelical and mainline) and Mormons; Democrats getting minority Christians (Protestant and Catholic), those of other religions, and those of no religion; and the two parties fighting over Catholics. Although white Catholics joined white Protestants in supporting Romney, all other faith groups backed Obama (including Catholics overall). The political targeting of voters based on religious affiliation speaks loudly about the political importance of faith—and the politicization of faith—in contemporary presidential politics. These demographics, however, should concern Republicans as white Protestants and white Catholics will not create a solid electoral base as whites continue to make up a smaller percentage of the U.S. population. Additionally, younger Americans are more likely to call themselves "nones" (meaning they do not identity with a religious faith but also do not call themselves atheists) and these younger "nones" are more progressive (Putnam & Campbell, 2010). These demographic shifts in racial and religious terms suggest that the Republican Party will not find political salvation with the same evangelical focus that helped usher George W. Bush and Ronald Reagan into the White House. Perhaps 2016 will bring new religious-political strategies, especially for Republicans. If so, white evangelical leaders may find it more difficult to demand the attention of candidates as African-American and Hispanic preachers find politicians of both parties knocking on their church doors. The evangelical era of U.S. politics that started in the late 1970s might not last through another decade.

References

Abelman, R. (1990). News on the "700 Club" after Pat Robertson's political fall. *Journalism Quarterly, 67,* 157–152.

Bailey, D. C. (2008). Enacting transformation: George W. Bush and the Pauline conversion narrative in "A Charge to Keep." *Rhetoric & Public Affairs, 11,* 215–241.

Ball, M. (2011, August 5). Michele Bachmann releases faith endorsement list in Iowa. *Politico.* Retrieved from http://www.politico.com/news/stories/0811/60764.html

Barrett, H. (1964). John F. Kennedy before the Greater Houston Ministerial Association. *Central States Speech Journal, 15,* 259–266.

Berggren, D. J. (2005). "I had a different way of governing": The living faith of President Carter. *Journal of Church and State, 47,* 43–61.

Boase, P. H. (1989). Moving the mercy seat into the White House: An exegesis of the Carter/Reagan religious rhetoric. *Journal of Communication and Religion, 12*(2), 1–9.

Boller, Jr., P. F. (1979). Religion and the U.S. presidency. *Journal of Church and State, 21,* 5–21.

Branham, R. J., & Pearce, W. B. (1987). A contract for civility: Edward Kennedy's Lynchburg address. *Quarterly Journal of Speech, 73,* 424–443.

Cohen, D. B., & Wells, J. W. (2007). In the eye of the storm: Bill Clinton, the culture war, and the politics of religion. *Journal of Religion & Society, 9.* Retrieved from http://moses.creighton.edu/jrs/2007/2007-28.pdf

Crick, N. (2012). Barack Obama and the rhetoric of religious experience. *Journal of Communication and Religion, 35,* 35–49.

Crosby, R. B. (2013). Mitt Romney's paralipsis: (Un)veiling Jesus in "Faith in America." *Rhetoric Review, 32,* 119–136.

Detwiler, T. (1988). Viewing Robertson's rhetoric in an Augustinian mirror. *Journal of Communication and Religion, 11*(1), 22–31.

Domke, D., & Coe, K. (2008). *The god strategy: How religion became a political weapon in America.* New York, NY: Oxford University Press.

Erickson, K. V. (1980). Jimmy Carter: The rhetoric of private and civic piety. *Western Journal of Speech Communication, 44,* 221–235.

Farrell, T. B. (1978). Political conventions as legitimation ritual. *Communication Monographs, 45,* 293–305

Fernandez, M. (2011, August 6). Perry leads prayer rally for "nation in crisis." *The New York Times.* Retrieved from http://www.nytimes.com/2011/08/07/us/politics/07prayer.html

Flint, A. R., & Porter, J. (2005). Jimmy Carter: The re-emergence of faith-based politics and the abortion rights issue. *Presidential Studies Quarterly, 35,* 28–51.

Flowers, R. B. (1983). President Jimmy Carter, evangelicalism, church-state relations, and civil religion. *Journal of Church and State, 25*, 113–132.

Frank, D. A. (2011). Obama's rhetorical signature: Cosmopolitan civil religion in the presidential inaugural address, January 20, 2009. *Rhetoric & Public Affairs, 14*, 605–630.

Friedenberg, R. V. (2002). Rhetoric, religion and government at the turn of the 21st century. *Journal of Communication and Religion, 25*, 34–48.

Glenn, G. D. (1988). Rhetoric and religion in the 1984 campaign. *Political Communication & Persuasion, 5*, 1–13.

Goldzwig, S. R. (2002). Official and unofficial civil religious discourse. *Journal of Communication and Religion, 25*, 102–114.

Granberg, D. (1985). An anomaly in political perception. *Public Opinion Quarterly, 49*, 504–516.

Hahn, D. F. (1980). One's reborn every minute: Carter's religious appeal in 1976. *Communication Quarterly, 28*, 56–62.

Hart, R. P. (1977). *The political pulpit.* West Lafayette, IN: Purdue University Press.

Hart, R. P., & Childers, J. P. (2005). The evolution of candidate Bush: A rhetorical analysis. *American Behavioral Scientist, 49*, 180–197.

Hattery, J. W. (1967). The presidential election campaigns of 1928 and 1960: A comparison of "The Christian Century" and "America." *Journal of Church and State, 9*, 36–50.

Hostetler, M. J. (1998). Gov. Al Smith confronts the Catholic question: The rhetorical legacy of the 1928 campaign. *Communication Quarterly, 46*, 12–24.

Hostetler, M. J. (2002). Joe Lieberman at Fellowship Chapel: Civil religion meets self-disclosure. *Journal of Communication and Religion, 25*, 148–165.

Johnson, A. E. (2012). Avoiding phony religiosity: The rhetorical theology of Obama's 2012 National Prayer Breakfast Address. *Journal of Contemporary Rhetoric, 2*, 44–53.

Kaylor, B. T. (2011a). No Jack Kennedy: Mitt Romney's "Faith in America" speech and the changing religious-political environment. *Communication Studies, 62*, 491–507.

Kaylor, B. T. (2011b). *Presidential campaign rhetoric in an age of confessional politics.* Lanham, MD: Lexington Books.

Kaylor, B. (2011c, June 6). Religious conservatives cheer Trump at conference. *Ethics Daily.* Retrieved from http://ethicsdaily.com/religious-conservatives-cheer-trump-at-conference-cms-18007

Kaylor, B. (2011d, June 7). Huntsman avoids "faith" questions at evangelical event. *Ethics Daily.* Retrieved from http://ethicsdaily.com/huntsman-avoids-faith-questions-at-evangelical-event-cms-18011

Kaylor, B. (2011e, July 5). Conservative Christian group met with Rick Perry. *Ethics Daily.* Retrieved from http://ethicsdaily.com/conservative-christian-group-met-with-rick-perry-cms-18156

Kaylor, B. (2012a, September 10). Democrats struggle with faith outreach. *Ethics Daily.* Retrieved from http://ethicsdaily.com/democrats-struggle-with-faith-outreach-cms-19979

Kaylor, B. (2012b, September 11). Democratic Party's religious rhetoric deifies Obama, demonizes GOP. *Ethics Daily.* Retrieved from http://ethicsdaily.com/democratic-partys-religious-rhetoric-deifies-obama-demonizes-gop-cms-19984

Kengor, P. (2004). *God and George W. Bush: A spiritual life.* New York, NY: ReganBooks.

King, Jr., M. L. (1968, March 31). *Remaining awake through a great revolution.* Retrieved from http://mlk-kpp01.stanford.edu/index.php/encyclopedia/documentsentry/doc_remaining_awake_through_a_great_revolution

Lee, R. (2002). The force of religion in the public square. *Journal of Communication and Religion, 25,* 6–20.

Linder, R. D. (1996). Universal pastor: President Bill Clinton's civil religion. *Journal of Church and State, 38,* 733–749.

Medhurst, M. J. (2002). Forging a civil-religious construct for the 21st century: Should Hart's "contract" be renewed? *Journal of Communication and Religion, 25,* 86–101.

Medhurst, M. J. (2009a). Evangelical Christian faith and political action: Mike Huckabee and the 2008 Republican presidential nomination. *Journal of Communication and Religion, 32,* 199–239.

Medhurst, M. J. (2009b). Mitt Romney, "Faith in America," and the dance of religion and politics in American culture. *Rhetoric & Public Affairs, 12,* 195–221.

Mockabee, S. T., Monson, J. Q., & Grant, J. T. (2001). Measuring religious commitment among Catholics and Protestants: A new approach. *Journal for the Scientific Study of Religion, 40,* 675–690.

Muir, Jr., W. K. (1992). *The bully pulpit: The presidential leadership of Ronald Reagan.* San Francisco, CA: Institute for Contemporary Studies Press.

Murphy, J. M. (2011). Barack Obama, the Exodus tradition, and the Joshua generation. *Quarterly Journal of Speech, 97,* 387–410.

Novogrod, J. (2011, August 8). Bachmann attends church service denouncing homosexuality. *NBC.* Retrieved from http://firstread.nbcnews.com/_news/2011/08/08/7304701-bachmann-attends-church-service-denouncing-homosexuality

Obama, B. (2012a, April 4). Remarks at Easter prayer breakfast. Retrieved from http://www.whitehouse.gov/the-press-office/2012/04/04/remarks-president-easter-prayer-breakfast.

Obama, B. (2012b, April 10). Message to the Q Conference. Retrieved from http://sojo.net/blogs/2012/04/10/president-obama-young-evangelicals-god%E2%80%99s-hand-moving-through-his-people

Ofulue, N. I. (2002). President Clinton and the White House prayer breakfast. *Journal of Communication and Religion, 25,* 49–63.

O'Leary, S., & McFarland, M. (1989). The political use of mythic discourse: Prophetic interpretation in Pat Robertson's presidential campaign. *Quarterly Journal of Speech, 75,* 433–452.

Patton, J. H. (1977). A government as good as its people: Jimmy Carter and the restoration of transcendence to politics. *Quarterly Journal of Speech, 63,* 249–257.

Porter, L. W. (1990). Religion and politics: Protestant beliefs in the presidential campaign of 1980. *Journal of Communication and Religion, 13*(2), 24–39.

Putnam, R. D., & Campbell, D. E. (2010). *American grace: How religion divides and unites us.* New York, NY: Simon & Shuster.

Romney, M. (2011). Remarks at the Values Voter Summit in Washington, D.C. Retrieved from http://www.presidency.ucsb.edu/ws/index.php?pid=97898

Romney, M. (2012a, February 4). Remarks in Las Vegas following the Nevada caucuses. Retrieved from http://www.presidency.ucsb.edu/ws/index.php?pid=99395

Romney, M. (2012b, May 12). Commencement address at Liberty University in Lynchburg, Virginia. Retrieved from http://www.presidency.ucsb.edu/ws/index.php?pid=101158

Romney, M. (2012c, August 11). Remarks introducing Representative Paul Ryan as the 2012 Republican vice presidential nominee in Norfolk, Virginia. Retrieved from http://www.presidency.ucsb.edu/ws/index.php?pid=101715

Roof, W. C. (2011). Obama and the polls: The contrarian weekly + religious attenders. *Review of Religious Research, 52,* 323–333.

Smith, C. R. (2011). Compromising the Manichaean style: A case study of the 2006 State of the Union address. *American Communication Journal, 13,* 23–43.

Solomon, M. (1978). Jimmy Carter and *Playboy*: A sociolinguistic perspective on style. *Quarterly Journal of Speech, 64,* 173–182.

Spielvogel, C. (2005). "You know where I stand": Moral framing of the war on terrorism and the Iraq war in the 2004 presidential campaign. *Rhetoric & Public Affairs, 8,* 549–570.

Spiker, J. A. (2008). Ohio's rhetorical "road to renewal": Governor Ted Strickland's 2007 inaugural address. *Ohio Communication Journal, 46,* 131–144.

Toulouse, M. G. (1989). Pat Robertson: Apocalyptic theology and American foreign policy. *Journal of Church and State, 31,* 73–99.

Troup, C. L. (1995). Cuomo at Notre Dame: Rhetoric without religion. *Communication Quarterly, 43,* 167–181.

Van Der Slik, J. R., & Schwark, S. J. (1998). Clinton and the New Covenant: Theology shaping a new politics or old politics in religious garb? *Journal of Church and State, 40,* 873–890.

Willhite, K. (1989). "God and country" in Ronald Reagan's address to the National Religious Broadcasters: A "faith" that backslides or perseveres? *Journal of Communication and Religion, 12,* 38–42.

Wilson, P. (1996). The rhythm of rhetoric: Jesse Jackson at the 1988 Democratic National Convention. *Southern Communication Journal, 61,* 253–264.

Wolfe, J. S. (1980). Exclusion, fusion, or dialogue: How should religion and politics relate? *Journal of Church and State, 22,* 89–106.

Wood, Jr., J. E. (1984). Religion and politics–1984. *Journal of Church and State, 26,* 401–411.

Notes

1. Key studies on these presidential candidates are: Kennedy (Barrett, 1964; Boller, 1979; Hart, 1977; Hattery, 1967; Hostetler, 1998; Wolfe, 1980); Carter (Berggren, 2005; Boase, 1989; Erickson, 1980; Farrell, 1978; Flint & Porter, 2005; Flowers, 1983; Hahn, 1980; Patton, 1977; Porter, 1990; Solomon, 1978; Wolfe, 1980); Jackson (Wilson, 1996; Wood, 1984), Robertson (Abelman, 1990; Detwiler, 1988; O'Leary & McFarland, 1989; Toulouse, 1989); Huckabee (Medhurst, 2009a); Reagan (Boase, 1989; Domke & Coe, 2008; Muir, 1992; Willhite, 1989; Porter, 1990; Wood, 1984); Bush (Bailey, 2008; Domke &

Coe, 2008; Friedenberg, 2002; Goldzwig, 2002; Hart & Childers, 2005; Kengor, 2004; Lee, 2002; Medhurst, 2002; Smith, 2011; Spielvogel, 2005); Clinton (Cohen & Wells, 2007; Kengor, 2004; Lee, 2002; Linder, 1996; Ofulue, 2002; Van Der Silk & Schwark, 1998), and Obama (Crick, 2012; Frank, 2011; Johnson, 2012; Murphy, 2011).

2. Key studies on these politicians are: Kennedy (Branham & Pearce, 1987; Glenn, 1988; Granberg, 1985); Cuomo (Glenn, 1988; Troup, 1995); Lieberman (Hostetler, 2002); and Romney (Crosby, 2013; Kaylor, 2011a; Medhurst, 2009b).

CHAPTER SIXTEEN

Working Together at Arm's Length

Bipartisan Rhetoric in the 2012 Presidential Campaign

MIKE MILFORD

Voters have become increasingly frustrated with the apparent inability of Democrats and Republicans to work together. Since the 2008 election voters have blamed this lack of cooperation for a perceived stagnation in legislative and executive action. The Pew Center's 2012 American Values Survey ("Partisan Polarization," 2012) found an 18-percentage point difference between Democrat and Republican perceptions of major issues that contributed to a lack of cooperation between the parties. As Jensen, Kaplan, Naidu, and Wilse-Samson (2012) demonstrated, this divergence played out rhetorically as bipartisan agreements in presidential and congressional speech became increasingly rare (p. 42). Legislation slowly ground to a halt as each party blamed the other for stoppages.

Eventually voters grew weary of the blame game and turned their ire on Congress as a whole. Some polls registered as high as 89% of voters voicing an intense distrust and disapproval of the Senate and House (Carpathios, 2012, para. 1). As the 2012 presidential election neared, voters became pessimistic that their concerns would be overwhelmed by partisan obstructionism (McNeil, 2012, para. 4). Morris (2012) summed up voter frustration succinctly: "voters just want the war to end and the parties to come to an agreement" (para. 2). This made bipartisanship the "key national goal of American voters" and a crucial deciding factor for much-sought-after undecided and independent voters (Morris, 2012, para. 3).

Sensing voters' dissatisfaction with the dissonance between the parties, both candidates in the 2012 election worked to incorporate bipartisan terminology into their campaign rhetoric. In high profile events both candidates professed an "eagerness to work across party lines and end gridlock in Washington" (Espo & Pace, 2012, para. 2). For instance, Republican presidential nominee Mitt Romney pledged a "spirit of cooperation," the same he showed as governor of Massachusetts, should he win the office (Peoples & Hunt, 2012, para. 1; Wines, 2012, para. 3). Incumbent President Barack Obama followed suit, promising to work across the aisle with Congress if he was re-elected (MacQuarrie, 2012, para. 6).

From a rhetorical standpoint, this bipartisan exigence put the Romney and Obama campaigns in an awkward position. The introduction of "bipartisan" into the campaign lexicon added to the complexity of an already intricate rhetorical situation. The campaign is typically a time to delineate the parties and their candidates from one another as much as possible while still appealing to the center. The bifurcated nature of the campaign suggests that rhetoric which leaned on bipartisanship too strongly might damage its relationship with the much-needed partisan base. But, because bipartisanship was a primary concern for voters, the candidates were compelled to incorporate the terminology into campaign messages.

In this chapter, Kenneth Burke's concept of identification is used to elucidate how the Romney and Obama campaigns rhetorically framed bipartisanship to dramatize the perceived political gridlock. In response to voters' frustrations about gridlock, the Romney and Obama campaigns deployed "bipartisan" as a dramatic agon. According Burke (1973), an agon occurs when rhetors subdivide "competing principles" into "protagonist and antagonist" that are "strongly identified with one another" (p. 76). The rhetors set these terms against one another in order to establish a symbolic conflict. In the 2012 campaign, each party established such a conflict by dramatizing "bipartisan" in order to cast its opponent as the antagonist to blame as well as cast its candidate as the protagonist with the cure. This demonstrates Burke's assertion that rhetors will often define in-groups through the use of negative rhetorical space: the in-group is the "not" of the out-group.

In a broad sense, campaigns are about creating identification with potential voters. However, one can also create identification not through terms that produce unity, as in being for a common term, but also through terms that are against a common term, the rhetorical equivalent of making friends from an enemy's enemies. In Engels's (2009) terms, the use of bipartisan rhetoric in the 2012 election highlighted the murky border between identification and division. He writes, "the relationship between identification and division is unclear" to the point that "the lines between the two blur completely and identification can become the means to division and vice versa" (p. 38). Campaigners for both parties internalized this principle as they worked to frame the opposing party as the one unwilling to make the necessary steps toward bipartisanship, and thus the cause of the ever-infamous gridlock, in an effort to create sympathy for their own candidates.

Bipartisan, Identification, and Division

Bipartisanship is typically framed as a good thing in political discourse. It is used to signify those instances where politicians from both parties set aside their political agendas in allegiance to higher values. It is represented by terminology that celebrates "widespread two-party support" and "country above party" (Patterson, 1970, p. 284). In a Burkean sense, "bipartisan" has traditionally been a term of transcendence that provides "symbolic bridging and merging" through an appeal to an elevated value (Burke, 1984, pp. 92, 179-180). Terms of transcendence are particularly useful to political rhetors, allowing them to "overcome symbolically perceived negative manifestations" (Goldzwig, 2003, p. 41). For instance, Patterson (1970) demonstrates how Sen. Arthur Vandenberg was able to overcome party conflicts after World War II by appealing to values such as patriotism and security in order to find consensus on important legislation (p. 288). Carcasson (2006) similarly examined how President Bill Clinton used "bipartisan values of work, responsibility, family, and opportunity" to transcend competing concepts of welfare (p. 672). Rowland (2011) also explored how President Obama sought out "bipartisan legislation" in his efforts to pass the Affordable Care Act (p. 695).

However, in the 2012 campaign, both Obama and Romney used "bipartisan" as a dramatic rather than a transcendent term in order to create identification with voters. First, both candidates sought to frame themselves as "bipartisan" by aligning their values with those of their audience, which represents a classic application of Burke's theory of identification. Burke (1969) argues that persuasion stems from identification: "You persuade a man only insofar as you can talk his language by speech, gesture, tonality, order, image, attitude, idea, identifying your ways with his" (p. 55). The symbols are chosen to be a "manifestation of those common properties" that establish a "common interest, value, or form" with voters (Gaines, 1979, p. 200; Sanbonmatsu, 1971, p. 36). Through the "selected use of symbols" that contain "implicit, and sometimes explicit, appeals to others" candidates invite voters to "join with or oppose the identities which are proffered" (Gusfield, 1989, p. 59).

Second, and more importantly, both candidates used bipartisan terminology to dramatically frame the opposing party as partisan and directed the audience to blame the opposing party for the current political gridlock. In this case, identification did not develop from the commonalities the candidates shared with the audience but through their collective frustration with other partisan politicians. Burke (1973) writes that terms such as "bipartisan" may be "analytically subdivided into competing principles" allowing rhetors to frame the "protagonist and antagonist" and polarize the audience (p. 76). Through a "dramatic realignment" of the terms, rhetors are able to cast the opposition as antithetical to the audience's values (Rueckert, 1982, p. 86). This allows rhetors to cast a wider "we" against the backdrop of a more unlikeable "they" (Engels, 2009, p. 43). The analysis, then, becomes not an examination of "what goes with what," but rather "what does against what" (Berthold, 1976, p. 304).

In a political sense, this principle undergirds much of a candidate's rhetoric. Smith (2010) has asserted that a campaign is "less a search for common ground than it is a search for the phrases that divide the country into a majority supporting one candidate and a minority who do not" (p. 245). As such, political rhetors illustrate this idea by arguing that a vote for me is more importantly a vote against them. In the 2012 election this meant that each candidate was able to establish a bipartisan image while also casting blame on the opposition.

In the following analysis, I demonstrate how both candidates used bipartisan terminology in their campaign speeches to create identification in two distinct ways. First, both candidates emphasized examples that illustrated their ability to act in a bipartisan manner, establishing an image of a "bipartisan candidate." Second, both candidates also framed their opponents as incapable of bipartisan action, as the genesis of the gridlock voters so vehemently despised. Finally, I examine the implications of the dramatic dénouement each candidate offered in alleviating partisan tensions.

I focused on the candidates' campaign speeches, analyzing each speech for instances of bipartisan language, such as references to the opposing candidate or party and phrases such as "working together," or "working with the other party" or "across the aisle" in an effort to flesh out how each candidate approached this pivotal issue. My texts were drawn from The American Presidency Project sponsored by the University of California at Santa Barbara. The American Presidency Project is an impressive collection of presidential election and governing documents gathered by John Woolley and Gerhard Peters. They have collated major inaugural and State of the Union addresses, news conferences, party platforms, editorial endorsements, and campaign documents, including stump speeches. I examined 105 of Obama's campaign speeches and 54 excerpts and speeches from Romney. Though the sample sizes were uneven, they were comparable in content because many of Obama's speeches were nearly identical speeches delivered to a range of audiences with only slight modifications.

Competing Campaign Agons: Collaborative Courage versus The Heroic Stand

Both Obama and Romney worked to portray a bipartisan image but did so by dramatizing the term, identifying a protagonist and an antagonist in order to position their policies in a positive light, and perhaps more importantly, vilify their opponent. First, each candidate began by referencing a bipartisan past, thus removing himself from blame for Washington's current political climate, in an effort to appeal to an audience exasperated by political division.

Obama's Collaborative Courage

Obama made a concerted effort to remind the audience of his bipartisan past throughout each phase of the campaign. His speeches, though separated over months of campaigning and delivered to dozens of audiences in both supportive and battleground states, showed a remarkable consistency of message. First, Obama dramatized his bipartisan past by framing it as an answer to the recent economic crisis. He began by setting a scene of economic devastation. He spoke repeatedly of facing the "worst economic crisis of our lifetimes" (Obama, 2012d, para. 32–33). He also highlighted the challenges voters faced when "millions of people lost their jobs or lost their homes or lost their savings" (Obama, 2012f, para. 18).

In answer to this crisis, Obama offered the "basic bargain," his reframing of the American Dream, as a transcendent value that allowed him to overcome partisan conflicts. It was this "basic bargain" that made "America the greatest nation on Earth," "an economic superpower," and "the most prosperous economy that the world has ever known" (Obama, 2012g, para. 28; Obama, 2012j, para. 21). It was centered on the belief that "if you put in enough effort, if you act responsibly, then you should be able to find a job that pays the bills" (Obama, 2012h, para. 13). Occasionally, in educational settings such as campaign rallies at universities or schools, he would add a component about "education and opportunity" that would allow children to "dream even bigger and do even better than we did," but overwhelmingly he was consistent in his portrayal of the "basic bargain" as the hub of the American middle class wheel (Obama, 2012n, para. 38). Through an allegiance to the "basic bargain," Obama (2012b) was able to garner the support of "Democrats, but also independents and, yes, some Republicans" to solve this crisis (para. 20–21).

In supporting his "basic bargain," politicians working with Obama (2012e) were able to demonstrate that they weren't "Democrats or Republicans first" but "Americans first" (para. 26). Thus, by uniting the parties in bipartisan harmony, Obama (2012d) was able to overcome the "worst economic crisis in our lifetimes" and other economic challenges that threatened the "basic bargain" essential to the American dream (para. 32–33).

As Election Day inched closer, Obama bolstered his bipartisan drama by including other instances where he secured bipartisan support. He still retained the specter of the economic crisis, but, in response to some of Romney's criticisms, he reshaped his bipartisan image as a cost-cutter as well as an economic-stimulator. Keeping the overarching theme of middle class economics, Obama (2012o) consistently referenced the "$1 trillion in spending" he cut to balance the federal budget (para. 57). This remarkable feat was only accomplished because he was able to work "with Republicans and Democrats" (Obama, 2012p, para. 48). Other times he referenced success with social issues, such as the repeal of "Don't Ask, Don't Tell," which required the cooperation of "brave Republicans" (Obama, 2012s, para. 65). Each of these instances was provided as proof that Obama's (2012v) principles were not "partisan." Instead, these examples offered evidence that Obama advanced "the cause of middle class and working class families," which is the essence of the "basic bargain" (para. 64–66).

Obama pitted the partisan forces, which were solely interested in selfishly maintaining the status quo that generated the crisis, against the heroic politicians that joined him in answering the economic crisis. Obama (2012b) made consistent references throughout the campaign trail to what he called the "stalemate in Washington" (para. 32). The stalemate stemmed from a tension between those who would "move forward" and the opposition who had been "on our ankles and pulling us back" (Obama, 2012c, para. 31; Obama, 2012a, para. 30). It was a stalemate not because of a "lack of technical solutions," but one born of "politics in Washington" (Obama, 2012i, para. 22–24).

Obama centered the blame for the stalemate on his opponents who were unwilling to make the necessary compromises needed for bipartisan progress. Obama (2012l) asserted that it was the "folks who think compromise is a dirty word," a phrase Obama used with remarkable consistency, who were preventing economic recovery (para. 22). It was they who were responsible for the "gridlock and stalemates and dysfunction" (Obama, 2012k, para. 18). He warned that, given the chance, his opponents would go back "to the same top-down economics that got us into this mess in the first place" (Obama, 2012m, para. 19). In light of the dire economic scene, Obama created this antagonistic portrayal of Republicans that was certainly polarizing.

In Obama's drama, the antagonists were motivated not only by an allegiance to the "basic bargain" of the American Dream and middle class economic success but also by adherence to a status quo that all but gutted that dream, privileging the few at the expense of the many. Obama (2012h) spoke of his opponents' "uncompromising view" that the best solutions were the "same, tired solutions that got us into this mess in the first place" (para. 27). He contended that they had "fought…every step of the way" to prevent reforms that restored the "basic bargain" (Obama, 2012u, para. 47–52). He argued, "That's not bipartisanship. That's not change. That's just surrendering to the same status quo that's hurt middle class families for way too long" (Obama, 2012t, para. 51).

Obama asserted that the gridlock was a deliberate construction on the part of these antagonists. Obama (2012r) vilified his opponents by insisting, "Their strategy from the start was to engineer pure gridlock, refusing to compromise on ideas that both Democrats and Republicans had supported in the past" (para. 63). He reasoned that their obstructionism was designed to foster apathy in voters, which would allow them to maintain their positions and "advocate the very same policies that got us into this mess" (Obama, 2012s, para. 62). Obama (2012v) specifically mentioned the Affordable Care Act's similarity to Romney's health care plan as governor in Massachusetts as an example of this obstructionism. He argued that the health care similarities exemplified a policy that "worked fine when a Republican was sponsoring it" but was "terrible when a Democrat put it forward" (para. 60). Obama's rhetoric carefully constructed antagonists who were to blame for the ills of the community (i.e., the economic crisis and political gridlock) and who used their position for selfish gain.

In the final dénouement of Obama's drama, he invited the audience to join him and break partisan gridlock with their votes. Obama (2012q) explained that if the audience wanted relief from "the gridlock in Congress" they should vote for those who followed his example of bipartisanship (para. 45). Obama (2012s) positioned himself as the prime bipartisan and advocated for those who imitated his "willingness to work with anybody of any party to move this country forward" (para. 67). He magnanimously admitted that these leaders may be "Democrats, Republicans, or independents" but they would have the same consistent thread he embodied: they were "people who are willing to put people first instead of putting elections first" (Obama, 2012t, para. 49–50). Thus, Obama's drama culminated in a call for audiences who share his interests in breaking the gridlock in Washington to join him. At the same time, his dramatization of the term "bipartisan" inhibited the audience's ability to identify with his opposition: they are the genesis of the stagnation in legislation.

Romney's Heroic Stand

Romney flipped the script on Obama in a similar fashion by framing Obama as the truly partisan politician in Washington. Much like Obama, Romney worked to demonstrate his bipartisan roots. Like Obama, Romney (2012j) believed that through "extraordinary unity…we were able to overcome challenges that many thought would be impossible" (para. 7–8). The most significant difference in the two dramas was causal: where Obama blamed purposeful partisan gridlock, Romney blamed weak, ineffectual leadership. As a result, their solutions to the current crises were very different: where Obama championed a collaborative "we" laden style of bipartisanship, Romney advocated a "firm hand" approach that was necessitated by crisis situations.

Romney couched his bipartisan pedigree in a story of strong leadership overcoming partisan problems. For instance, Romney (2011) frequently mentioned the fact that as governor of Massachusetts his legislature was "over 85% Democrat," yet he was able to pass significant legislation (para. 13). Through strong leadership, he was able to eradicate a "$3 billion budget shortfall and left office with a $2 billion rainy day fund" (Romney, 2012c, para. 20–21). Romney (2012d) asserted that he was strong enough to make the tough choice: when faced with "a program, an agency, or a department that needed cutting, we cut it," regardless of its popularity (para. 48). Because of his more authoritarian approach to government, Romney was able to withstand challenges such as union dissention about educational reforms in his state (Romney, 2012e, para. 66). As a result, his brand of bipartisanship was more about earning opposition support for his causes than collaborating with opponents to find new solutions (Romney, 2012h, para. 3–4). If elected president, Romney promised to continue in this vein and vowed to "work with Republicans and Democrats" to generate support for his plans (Romney, 2012g, para. 31). He pledged to lead "both parties" full of "men and women of integrity, decency, and humility" to new heights (Romney, 2012h, para. 48).

Similar to Obama, Romney emphasized the transcendent nature of "bipartisanship" by highlighting the greater values needed to transcend the partisan divide. He called on legislators to "rise above politics" to "win this fight for America's future" (Romney, 2011, para. 11). He pledged to "work with Republicans and Democrats" in Congress, to "find those good men and women on both sides of the aisle who care more about the country than about the politics," echoing Obama's appeal to be Americans first (Romney, 2012l, para. 36). Interestingly, he frequently used Seal Team Six's elimination of Osama bin Laden as an example of bipartisan unity. Often, he commented that when the team went after bin Laden they did so "not as Republicans or Democrats or independents, they did so as Americans" (Romney, 2011, para. 11). He carried the analogy further, commenting that "the final image that Osama bin Laden took with him straight to hell was not a party symbol—not a Republican elephant or a Democrat donkey—but an American flag" (Romney, 2011, para. 19). A strange analogy on the surface, but perhaps an apt one for the military-friendly conservative audiences he often addressed.

However, in the midst of his bipartisan pledges, Romney maintained his vision of a strong, central leadership, asserting that he had the necessary answers for the country's current crises. Romney (2012b) declared that his first act as president would be to "tell the American people how it is and tell Congress what we really need to do" (para. 38). He made multiple comments about instructing Congress on proper legislative action, including sending them legislation and "several fundamental reforms" that they would be expected to adopt (Romney, 2012l, para. 27–28). One of the more overt claims to central leadership was his comment that he would use the State of the Union address to "lay out an agenda that will get our … fiscal house in order" (Romney, 2012b, para. 38). He stated that he would not waste time "blaming others for how we got in this mess" but would instead "explain how we're going to get out of it" (Romney, 2012b, para. 38).

Like Obama, Romney also dramatized "bipartisan" in order to vilify his opposition. However, while Obama targeted the Republican Party, Romney targeted Obama. Romney put the blame for the bipartisan gridlock squarely on Obama's shoulders by pointing out that Obama had "promised to bring people together" but instead created more partisan problems (Romney, 2012a, para. 5). But, where Obama framed his opposition as being purposefully partisan for selfish gain, Romney blamed the gridlock in Washington on Obama's weak leadership. In Romney's (2012i) drama, Obama was guilty of "playing politics" instead of stepping up and fixing problems (para. 42). In Romney's terms it was Obama who "divided us with the bitter politics of envy" (Romney, 2012a, para. 21). He also blamed Obama's administration for "pitting one side against another," which resulted in "failure and mediocrity" and made the "federal establishment … hostile [and] remote" (Romney, 2012e, para. 7; Romney, 2012f, para. 11).

Romney reasoned that Obama's interest in political games, coupled with weak leadership, fostered an environment of political inactivity. Romney (2012i) pointed out that despite the fact that Obama had "majorities in both houses of Congress … the president never even offered up a bill" (para. 43). Romney (2012k) characterized Obama's decisions as contradictory and ineffectual, citing instances where Obama "promised to cut the deficit in half, but … doubled it," as well as Obama's budget that "failed to win a single vote, Republican or Democrat" (para. 9). In Romney's (2012l) eyes, Obama had "promised to be the first 'post-partisan president' but he became the most partisan" because he was not able to lead the country with the firm hand necessary to lead (para. 8).

Romney's "bipartisan" drama played out in a much different fashion than Obama's. Obama vilified conservatives for putting a selfish agenda ahead of the "basic bargain" of the American Dream and called on voters to seek out those candidates who were willing to work together. Conversely, Romney vilified Obama for failing to have a strong enough hand to direct the country out of partisanship and called on voters to look to his record of determined leadership as evidence of his appropriateness for the position. In both cases, "bipartisan" maintained its status as a transcendent term as each candidate defined it as the ability to find a common value elevated above political conflicts. However, in order to create a sense of identification with voters, each candidate dramatized "bipartisan" with a different agon, one a sense of collaboration and the other strong leadership.

Conclusion

In sum, campaign speeches by Obama and Romney illustrate the potency of a dramatized term. This chapter is concerned with the ways political rhetors seek to create identification by dramatizing an event in order to orient the audience to see the event in bifurcated terms. The analysis here highlights the extent to which political rhetors make use of "division" as a means to foster "identification." Identification, as one of Burke's (1969) core components of persuasion, is "compensatory with division" (p. 22). He writes that rhetoric "considers the ways in which individuals are at odds with one another, or become identified with groups more or less at odds with one another" (p. 22). As Wolin (2001) notes, "whenever we say we identify with an idea, a principle, a philosophy, a person, or a group, we are necessarily saying that we are divided from something else" (p. 178). In Engels' (2009) terms, "the relationship between identification and division is unclear," to the point that "the lines between the two blur completely and identification can become the means to division and vice versa" (p. 38).

In the 2012 campaign, the principles of identification and division played out in the competing dramas around the term "bipartisan." The partisan gridlock that irritated voters became the scene in which the candidates staged their drama, carefully casting protagonists and antagonists in such a way as to engender ideological sympathy for the former and animosity for the latter. In doing so, each candidate exhibited, through the reflexive nature of their own terministic screens, glimpses into their concept of the term (Burke, 1966, p. 45). Obama exhibited a collaborative approach to bipartisanship that focused on collective action. Romney proffered a leadership approach to bipartisanship centered on strong authority designed to withstand crises.

Interestingly, despite its obvious political utility in governing, one must question the role "bipartisan" rhetoric has in a campaign. One of the foremost goals of presidential campaigns is to delineate one candidate's party from the other, a mission seemingly antithetical to bipartisan terminology. Its utility in governance has been proven, particularly in the face of external threats (Patterson, 1970, p. 286). For instance, Goodwin's (2005) thorough examination of President Lincoln's "team of rivals" demonstrates how a president can use an external threat to create a strong sense of unity that transcends party lines. However one could also argue that too strong an emphasis on partisan delineation could have ramifications for a newly elected president. For instance, Ornstein (2001) points out that President George W. Bush's divisive rhetoric in the 2000 campaign limited his "opportunity for bipartisan cooperation and action" (p. 100).

In hindsight, this principle could partially explain Obama's struggles with Republicans during his second term. Where Romney focused on Obama the candidate as his enemy, Obama zeroed in on the Republican Party. Thus, when he took office, the foe that he had created was still before him. For instance, the short-lived government shutdown in October 2013 was spurred on by a virulent strain of GOP partisanship, spearheaded by Tea Party legislators such as U.S. Sen. Ted Cruz (R-TX), who spoke openly about blocking any of Obama's actions (Reid, 2013).

From the perspective of this research, their overt obstructionism could be attributed to a backlash against Obama's party-centered attacks during the 2012 election. In choosing to dramatize Republicans as his antagonist instead of Romney, Obama may have painted himself into a corner. The trick seems to be finding that nice middle ground where parties and candidates can create a singular identity unique from their opposition, but one that allows for collaboration once the campaign is over. Like so much rhetorical practice, politicians would be wise to heed Aristotle's (2007) advice and adhere to Chilon's maxim: "Nothing too much" (p. 150).

References

Aristotle. (2007). *On rhetoric: A theory of civic discourse* (2nd ed.). (G. A. Kennedy, Trans.). Oxford, NY: Oxford University Press.

Berthold, C. A. (1976). Kenneth Burke's cluster-agon method: Its development and an application. *Central States Speech Journal, 27,* 302–309.

Burke, K. (1966). *Language as symbolic action.* Berkeley, CA: University of California Press.

Burke, K. (1969). *A rhetoric of motives.* Berkeley, CA: University of California Press.

Burke, K. (1973). *The philosophy of literary form* (3rd ed.). Berkeley, CA: University of California Press.

Burke, K. (1984). *Attitudes toward history* (3rd ed.). Berkeley, CA: University of California Press.

Carcasson, M. (2006). Ending welfare as we know it: President Clinton and the rhetorical transformation of the anti-welfare culture. *Rhetoric & Public Affairs, 9,* 655–692.

Carpathios, C. (2012, March 10). Independent voters urge reforms to limit partisan political power. *Cleveland Plain Dealer*. Retrieved from http://www.cleveland.com/opinion/index.ssf/2012/03/independent_voters_urge_reform.html

Engels, J. (2009). Friend or foe?: Naming the enemy. *Rhetoric & Public Affairs, 12*, 37–64.

Espo, D., & Pace, J. (2012, November 5). Rivals stress differences and bipartisanship hopes. *Associated Press*. Retrieved from http://bigstory.ap.org/article/obama-focuses-turnout-romney-pennsylvania

Gaines, R. N. (1979). Identification and redemption in Lysias' *Against Eratosthenes*. *Central States Speech Journal, 30*, 199–210.

Goldzwig, S. R. (2003). LBJ, the rhetoric of transcendence, and the Civil Rights Act of 1968. *Rhetoric & Public Affairs, 6*, 25–53.

Goodwin, D. K. (2005). *Team of rivals*. New York, NY: Simon & Schuster.

Gusfield, J. R. (1989). Scientism and dramatism: Some quasi-mathematical motifs in the work of Kenneth Burke. In H. W. Simons & T. Melia (Eds.), *The legacy of Kenneth Burke* (pp. 55–73). Madison, WI: University of Wisconsin Press.

Jensen, J., Kaplan, E., Naidu, S., & Wilse-Samson, L. (2012). Political polarization and the dynamics of political language: Evidence from 130 years of partisan speech. *Brookings Papers on Economic Activity*, 1–81.

MacQuarrie, B. (2012, November 4). President Obama pledges principled, bipartisan push in New Hampshire rally. *Boston.com*. Retrieved from http://www.boston.com/politicalintelligence/2012/11/04/president-obama-pledges-principled-bipartisan-push-new-hampshire-rally/yEh7riCvbTAiWQ4kagjOQO/story.html

McNeil, T. (2012, August 10). AARP poll: Older voters bemoan partisan gridlock in Washington. *WAMU*. Retrieved from http://wamu.org/news/morning_edition/12/08/10/older_voters_bemoan_partisan_gridlock_in_washington_in_aarp_poll

Morris, D. (2012, October 6). Bipartisanship: A new winning issue. *Real Clear Politics*. Retrieved from http://www.realclearpolitics.com/articles/2012/10/06/bipartisanship_a_new_winning_issue_115695.html

Obama, B. H. (2012a, July 5). Remarks at a campaign rally in Parma, Ohio. Retrieved from http://www.presidency.ucsb.edu/ws/?pid=101322

Obama, B. H. (2012b, July 5). Remarks at a campaign rally in Maumee, Ohio. Retrieved from http://www.presidency.ucsb.edu/ws/?pid=101324

Obama, B. H. (2012c, July 6). Remarks at a campaign rally in Pittsburgh, Pennsylvania. Retrieved from http://www.presidency.ucsb.edu/ws/?pid=101330

Obama, B. H. (2012d, July 13). Remarks at a campaign rally in Hampton, Virginia. Retrieved from http://www.presidency.ucsb.edu/ws/?pid=1013493. 3

Obama, B. H. (2012e, July 13). Remarks at a campaign rally in Roanoke, Virginia. Retrieved from http://www.presidency.ucsb.edu/ws/?pid=101347

Obama, B. H. (2012f, July 14). Remarks at a campaign rally in Glen Allen, Virginia. Retrieved from http://www.presidency.ucsb.edu/ws/?pid=101348

Obama, B. H. (2012g, July 16). Remarks at a campaign rally and question-and-answer session in Cincinnati, Ohio. Retrieved from http://www.presidency.ucsb.edu/ws/?pid=101380

Obama, B. H. (2012h, August 1). Remarks at a campaign rally in Akron, Ohio. Retrieved from http://www.presidency.ucsb.edu/ws/?pid=101677

Obama, B. H. (2012i, August 2). Remarks at a campaign rally in Leesburg, Virginia. Retrieved from http://www.presidency.ucsb.edu/ws/?pid=101675

Obama, B. H. (2012j, August 2). Remarks at a campaign rally in Winter Park, Florida. Retrieved from http://www.presidency.ucsb.edu/ws/?pid=101676

Obama, B. H. (2012k, August 12). Remarks at a campaign rally in Chicago, Illinois. Retrieved from http://www.presidency.ucsb.edu/ws/?pid=101721

Obama, B. H. (2012l, August 13). Remarks at a campaign rally in Council Bluffs, Iowa. Retrieved from http://www.presidency.ucsb.edu/ws/?pid=101723

Obama, B. H. (2012m, August 14). Remarks at a campaign rally in Oskaloosa, Iowa. Retrieved from http://www.presidency.ucsb.edu/ws/?pid=101729

Obama, B. H. (2012n, August 15). Remarks at a campaign rally in Davenport, Iowa. Retrieved from http://www.presidency.ucsb.edu/ws/?pid=101731

Obama, B. H. (2012o, September 26). Remarks at a campaign rally in Kent, Ohio. Retrieved from http://www.presidency.ucsb.edu/ws/?pid=102301

Obama, B. H. (2012p, October 17). Remarks at a campaign rally in Mount Vernon, Iowa. Retrieved from http://www.presidency.ucsb.edu/ws/?pid=102386

Obama, B. H. (2012q, October 25). Remarks at a campaign rally in Green Bay, Wisconsin. Retrieved from http://www.presidency.ucsb.edu/ws/?pid=102560

Obama, B. H. (2012r, November 1). Remarks at a campaign rally in North Las Vegas, Nevada. Retrieved from http://www.presidency.ucsb.edu/ws/?pid=102579

Obama, B. H. (2012s, November 1). Remarks at a campaign rally in Boulder, Colorado. Retrieved from http://www.presidency.ucsb.edu/ws/?pid=102595

Obama, B. H. (2012t, November 2). Remarks at a campaign rally in Lima, Ohio. Retrieved from http://www.presidency.ucsb.edu/ws/?pid=102593

Obama, B. H. (2012u, November 3). Remarks at a campaign rally in Mentor, Ohio. Retrieved from http://www.presidency.ucsb.edu/ws/?pid=102619

Obama, B. H. (2012v, November 4). Remarks at a campaign rally in Cincinnati, Ohio. Retrieved from http://www.presidency.ucsb.edu/ws/?pid=102616

Ornstein, N. J. (2001). The legacy of Campaign 2000. *Washington Quarterly, 24*, 99–105.

Partisan polarization surges in Bush, Obama years: Trend in American values: 1987–2012. (2012) Pew Research Center. *2012 American values survey* [Data file]. Retrieved from http://www.people-press.org/values/

Patterson, J. W. (1970). Arthur Vandenberg's rhetorical strategy in advancing bipartisan foreign policy. *Quarterly Journal of Speech, 56*, 284–295.

Peoples, S., & Hunt, K. (2012, November 4). Presidential candidate Mitt Romney pledges bipartisanship in final push. *News Net 5*. Retrieved from http://www.newsnet5.com/dpp/news/political/presidential-candidate-mitt-romney-pledges-bipartisanship-in-final-push

Reid, T. (2013, October 11). Tea Party calls Ted Cruz a hero; some others see disaster. *Reuters*. Retrieved from http://www.reuters.com/article/2013/10/11/us-usa-fiscal-cruz-idUSBRE99A0LW20131011

Romney, W. M. (2011, September 2). Remarks to the Republican National Hispanic Assembly in Tampa, Florida. Retrieved from http://www.presidency.ucsb.edu/ws/?pid=97896

Romney, W. M. (2012a, January 10). Remarks in Manchester following the New Hampshire primary. Retrieved from http://www.presidency.ucsb.edu/ws/?pid=98865

Romney, W. M. (2012b, January 24). Remarks in Tampa, Florida on President Obama's State of the Union. Retrieved from http://www.presidency.ucsb.edu/ws/?pid=99284

Romney, W. M. (2012c, February 4). Remarks to the Conservative Political Action Conference. Retrieved from http://www.presidency.ucsb.edu/ws/?pid=99343

Romney, W. M. (2012d, April 4). Remarks to the Newspaper Association of America in Washington, D.C. Retrieved from http://www.presidency.ucsb.edu/ws/?pid=100576

Romney, W. M. (2012e, May 23). Remarks on education at the Latino Coalition's annual economic summit in Washington, D.C.: A chance for every child. Retrieved from http://www.presidency.ucsb.edu/ws/?pid=101160

Romney, W. M. (2012f, June 15). Remarks in Stratham, New Hampshire. Retrieved from http://www.presidency.ucsb.edu/ws/?pid=101164

Romney, W. M. (2012g, June 21). Remarks in Stratham, New Hampshire. Retrieved from http://www.presidency.ucsb.edu/ws/?pid=101164

Romney, W. M. (2012h, July 11). Remarks at the NAACP convention in Houston, Texas. Retrieved from http://www.presidency.ucsb.edu/ws/?pid=101443

Romney, W. M. (2012i, September 17). Remarks to the U.S. Hispanic Chamber of Commerce 33rd annual convention in Los Angeles, California. Retrieved from http://www.presidency.ucsb.edu/ws/?pid=102451

Romney, W. M. (2012j, September 25). Remarks to the Clinton Global Initiative in New York City. Retrieved from http://www.presidency.ucsb.edu/ws/?pid=102450

Romney, W. M. (2012k, October 26). Remarks on the economy in Ames, Iowa. Retrieved from http://www.presidency.ucsb.edu/ws/?pid=103076

Romney, W. M. (2012l, November 2). Remarks in West Allis, Wisconsin: Real change from day one. Retrieved from http://www.presidency.ucsb.edu/ws/?pid=103104

Rowland, R. C. (2011). Barack Obama and the revitalization of public reason. *Rhetoric & Public Affairs, 14*, 693–726.

Rueckert, W. H. (1982). *Kenneth Burke and the drama of human relations* (2nd ed.). Berkeley, CA: University of California Press.

Sanbonmatsu, A. (1971). Darrow and Rorke's use of Burkeian identification strategies in *New York v. Gitlow. Communication Monographs, 38*, 36–48.

Smith, C. A. (2010). *Presidential campaign communication*. Malden, MA: Polity Press.

Wines, M. (2012, October 5). Romney claims of bipartisanship as governor face challenge. *The New York Times*. Retrieved from http://www.nytimes.com/2012/10/06/us/politics/romney-claims-of-bipartisanship-as-governor-face-challenge.html?pagewanted=all&_r=0

Wolin, R. (2001). *The rhetorical imagination of Kenneth Burke*. Columbia, SC: University of South Carolina Press.

CHAPTER SEVENTEEN

Affective Polarization from Campaign Communication

Alienating Messages in the 2012 Presidential Election

BENJAMIN R. WARNER AND MOLLY GREENWOOD

The 2012 election was historic not only because the outcome would influence the future of the nation but also because of the potentially alienating "divide and conquer" strategies that are now so prevalent in modern political campaigns. With the campaigns of former Massachusetts Gov. Mitt Romney and President Barack Obama attempting to maximize the support and enthusiasm of their committed political base of support while also reaching out to increasingly fragmented and narrow segments of voters, it is worth asking whether the divisive communication of the 2012 election polarized the electorate and, if so, through what means?

Although a great deal of research has examined polarization as a political phenomenon (Abramowitz & Saunders, 2008; Fiorina, Abrams, & Pope, 2011; McCarty, Poole, & Rosenthal, 2006) and as a consequence of political communication (Binder, Dalrymple, Brossard, & Scheufele, 2009; Lin, 2009; Stroud, 2010; Warner, 2010), only recently have researchers begun to test the effects of campaign communication on political polarization (Cho & Ha, 2012; Iyengar, Sood, & Lelkes, 2012; Warner & McKinney, 2013). In this chapter we contribute to the emerging literature on the polarizing influence of political campaigns by testing whether exposure to the 2012 campaign increased polarization and exploring what role political communication played in the polarization process.

And, our findings suggest that 2012 was in fact a polarizing election. In other words, people who were more attentive to campaign communication and those who engaged in frequent communication about the campaign were more likely to be polarized. Furthermore, the polarizing effect of political campaigns may be self-reinforcing, as those who were more polarized were also less cynical and possessed more information efficacy. Finally, through this study we found evidence that, as the election progressed and people had more time to engage in election communication, they were likely to be more polarized. In what follows, existing research about political polarization is reviewed, a study of the polarizing effect of the 2012 election is presented, and the implications of our findings are discussed.

Polarization and Political Communication

Polarization, or the growing bi-modality of political alliances at the extremes of the ideological spectrum, is widely believed to be on the rise ("Partisan Polarization Surges," 2012). Although there is still debate about the extent of this polarization (see Abramowitz & Saunders, 2008; Fiorina et al., 2011), political communication researchers have established a number of features of the current political climate that affects polarization. From the evolving media landscape, to the policymakers who shape the legislative process, to diversity in discussion networks, a number of factors influence the level of political polarization in the United States. Granted, there is some academic controversy regarding the extent of political polarization. One school of thought claims that, whereas the elite (e.g., policymakers, media) are becoming more polarized (Fiorina et al., 2011; McCarty et al., 2006) the general public are not; there are not fewer moderates nor is there an increase in stronger partisans (Fiorina et al., 2011). However, elite polarization can lead to individual polarization. Individuals respond to increases in elite-level polarization not by changing their attitudes toward the parties, but rather by changing their issue attitudes to align with their political party (Layman & Carsey, 2002). Furthermore, even if fewer people describe themselves as moderate there is evidence of mounting polarization among the electorate. Although the congressional parties' respective electoral constituents are far apart, their primary electoral constituencies are even more so (Jacobson, 2012). There is also evidence that partisans are becoming more polarized—both in terms of intensity of attitude and ideological consistency (Abramowitz & Saunders, 2008; Iyengar et al., 2012)—and that moderates are increasingly opting out of the political conversation (Prior, 2007).

What factors shape polarization among such constituencies? Concerns about polarization have been the impetus of a number of studies about which communication and social phenomena are associated with increased polarization. Much research focuses on the digital media revolution, particularly online news media in part because digital media offer significant choices to consumers. This high-choice environment allows moderates to avoid political content (Prior, 2007) just as partisans are able to consume information that reinforces their predispositions (Sunstein, 2007). The tendency for partisans to select attitude-consistent information while avoiding attitude-dissonant information has therefore been central to polarization research (Iyengar & Hahn, 2009; Knobloch-Westerwick & Meng, 2011; Warner, 2010). Such selective exposure can result in a media echo chamber, which happens when we only encounter echoes of our own views (Sunstein, 2007). This trend is more pronounced among the highly partisan and operates from the premise that people prefer ideologically consistent information (Brannon, Tagler, & Eagly, 2007; Tewksbury, 2005) and partisans who select attitude-consistent information are more polarized than partisans who select more diverse media diets (Stroud, 2010).

Although partisans may prefer attitude-consistent information, this does not mean they avoid opinion challenges (Brundidge, 2010; Garrett, 2009; Gentzkow & Shapiro, 2011). Granted, exposure to opinion challenges may not be sufficient to curtail polarization, because partisans tend to rate attitudinally congruent information as more accurate and counter argue with counter-attitudinal messages (Taber & Lodge, 2006). This phenomenon is known as confirmation and disconfirmation bias, which can lead to attitude polarization (Taber & Lodge, 2006). In other words, when people encounter political information that challenges their predispositions, they use partisan processing to discount dissonant claims (Baum & Groeling, 2008; Coe et al., 2008; Taber & Lodge, 2006). This may help explain findings that ideological media use spurs polarization (Lin, 2009; Stroud, 2010; Warner, 2010).

This type of confirmation bias offers an interesting link with the principle of homophily (Yardi & Boyd, 2010)—which says that people associate with other groups of people who are like themselves—to reduce exposure to difference and minimize the influence of different perspectives when they are encountered. For instance, replies to comments on social network sites between like-minded individuals strengthen group identity, whereas such replies between different-minded individuals reinforce in-group and out-group affiliation (Yardi & Boyd, 2010). Furthermore, partisans tend to view agreeable content as less biased, more interesting, and more informative (Coe et al., 2008). As an additional accelerant to polarization among the most politically engaged, Dilliplane (2011) found that people who consume more ideological news become more involved in politics. The result is that the most politically active also tend to be the most polarized.

Group homogeneity is also thought to increase polarization, as like-minded individuals reinforce and strengthen one another's attitudes. So when people talk politics with like-minded groups, there is an increase in not only polarization but also an increase in extreme attitudes and affective polarization specifically (Binder et al., 2009; Sunstein, 2009).

Much communication research concerns ideologically fragmented media and homogeneous social networks, and some studies have identified personality characteristics as potential sources of polarization. For instance, traits such as "authoritarianism" and "dogmatism" have predicted greater polarization (Hetherington & Weiler, 2009), as have views on humanity—if people have high levels of trust in others they tend to be strong Democrats and if they have little trust in others they tend to be strong Republicans (Kaltenthaler & Miller, 2012). Extroversion, agreeableness, and openness have also predicted strength of partisan identification (Gerber, Huber, Doherty, & Dowling, 2011). More extroverted and agreeable people were more likely to be strong partisans, and more open people were less likely to be strong partisans (Gerber et al., 2011).

Whereas selective exposure and individual personality traits have been studied fairly extensively for contribution to polarization, political campaigns have received less attention. Iyengar and colleagues (2012) found that increased exposure to campaign communication was associated with more affective polarization—operationalized as a strong dislike (even hatred) for political opponents. People in battleground states were more polarized than similar voters in non-battleground states, and voters who were exposed to more negative advertisements were more polarized than those who were not (Iyengar et al., 2012). Exposure to presidential debates may also increase polarization (Cho & Ha, 2012; Warner & McKinney, 2013)—though most of the polarization is experienced by the least politically engaged (Warner & McKinney, 2013) and does not generate strong partisans in the sense discussed by most polarization literature (e.g., Fiorina et al., 2011; Iyengar et al., 2012).

Although these findings suggest that political campaigns likely increase polarization and that greater exposure to political communication can exacerbate this, there is little empirical work on the effects of campaign communication in general. This study seeks to advance current understanding of how political campaigns contribute to polarization by looking to the 2012 presidential election between President Barack Obama and former Massachusetts Gov. Mitt Romney. Based on Iyengar and colleagues' (2012) finding that greater exposure to campaign communication was associated with more affective polarization, we hypothesized that people would be more polarized later in the campaign, that people who were more attentive to the campaign would be more polarized, and that people who engaged in frequent campaign communication would be more polarized:

H1: People will become more polarized as the election progresses.

H2: People who pay close attention to the election will be more polarized.

H3: People who participate in more political communication will be more polarized.

In addition to these questions about the effects of campaign communication on polarization, we also sought to understand how polarization influenced communication about the campaign. Prior (2007) has argued that those who are politically moderate are more likely to opt out of the conversation, whereas Dilliplane (2011) found that, as people become more polarized, they are more likely to participate in politics. However, it is unclear what effect polarization has on the normative attitudes associated with increased participation. We therefore sought to determine the effect of polarization on political information efficacy and political cynicism, two normative attitudes associated with political engagement.

RQ1: Will people who are polarized have higher political information efficacy?

RQ2: Will people who are polarized be less cynical?

Finally, in addition to testing the linear relationship between time, attention, communication, and polarization, we also wished to explore more dynamic relationships. Indeed, as an election progresses (i.e., time passes) people have more opportunity to be attentive to the campaigns and to communicate about them. It is therefore possible that time has an indirect effect on polarization through attention and communication. Hence we propose our final research questions:

RQ3: Is there an indirect effect of time on polarization such that those who pay close attention to the election will be more polarized the later they complete the survey?

RQ4: Is there an indirect effect of time on polarization such that those who engage in more political communication will be more polarized the later they complete the survey?

Method

Participants and procedure

Data for this study was collected from five independent samples over the course of the 2012 presidential election campaign. The first four samples were taken from participants in university-sponsored debate-watch events prior to the live broadcast of each of the four general election debates (three presidential and one vice presidential). Participants completed a survey in person via an online survey link provided to them just prior to the debate viewing. The fifth sample was collected via an electronic survey emailed to participants in the final week prior to the election. Participants were recruited from 14 universities across the United States as part of a national election research project. States with participating universities included: Alabama, Georgia, Iowa, Kansas, Massachusetts, Missouri, Ohio, Oregon, Tennessee, Texas, Virginia, and Wisconsin. In some cases participants were offered course credit or extra credit though the specific recruitment strategies varied by university. In total, 2,092 people completed the survey. The sample ranged in age from 18 to 77 with a mean age of 22.55 (SD = 3.99). Of the participants, 754 (36%) were male and 1,328 (64%) were female with 700 (34%) identifying themselves as Democrats, 812 (39%) as Republicans, and 574 (27%) as affiliated with neither major party.

Measures

Polarization was calculated from "feeling thermometer" scales commonly used in the National Election Studies survey to measure candidate favorability (Rosenstone, Kinder, Miller, & the National Election Studies, 1997). Participants were asked to indicate their overall feelings toward both the Democratic and Republican presidential candidate before the debate and then again afterward. Participants were told that a score between 0 and 49 indicated an unfavorable feeling with 0 being the most unfavorable and 49 being only slightly unfavorable, that 50 indicated a neutral evaluation, and that a score between 51 and 100 demonstrated a favorable evaluation with 100 the most favorable and 51 only slightly favorable.

To compute polarization from the feeling thermometer scores Romney's evaluation was subtracted from Obama's evaluation and the absolute value was taken. In this way, 0 would represent no polarization at all (an equal evaluation of both candidates) and 100 would represent absolute polarization (where one candidate was evaluated as maximally unfavorable—a score of zero—and the other was evaluated as maximally favorable—a score of 100). This approach is similar to polarization measures used in past research (e.g., Skitka, Bauman, & Sargis, 2005; Stroud, 2010). Combining all samples, the overall mean polarization score for the pretest was 48.92 (SD = 31.16). The minimum observed score was 0 and the maximum was 100.

Time. To determine whether responses from later in the election were more polarized than early responses we created a variable that represented the day on which the survey was completed. Because the first set of responses were recorded immediately prior to the first presidential debate on October 3, 2012, the first of

October was selected as the zero-point for this measure. All participants in the first debate study were therefore assigned a time score of three; those in the vice presidential debate were assigned 11; those who completed the survey prior to the second presidential debated received a time score of 16; all who completed the survey prior to the third debate were assigned a score of 22; and those who completed the survey in the final week of the campaign were assigned a score ranging from 32–36 depending on the day that they completed the survey.

Attention. To determine how closely respondents followed the campaign we asked two questions: "How informed do you think you are about the presidential campaign?" (1 = very uninformed, 5 = very well informed) and "How interested would you say you are in the presidential campaign?" (1 = very uninterested; 5 = very interested). The items were sufficiently correlated to justify combining them into a single measure of campaign interest, Pearson's $r(2031) = .624, p < .001$.

Political communication. To determine the amount of political communication respondents engaged in they were asked two questions, one regarding their media exposure to election content and one regarding their interpersonal conversations about the election. The questions asked the respondents to indicate, on a 1 to 5 scale (1 = very rarely; 5 = very often): "How often have you been exposed to media coverage of the campaign in the past week?" and "How often have you talked with other people about the campaign in the past week?" The items were sufficiently correlated to justify combining them into a single measure of political communication, Pearson's $r(1520) = .646, p < .001$. The political communication items were only asked in the debate studies, thus the fifth study is excluded from analysis of H3 and RQ4.

Political Information Efficacy. A four-item scale was used to measure political information efficacy (PIE). Participants were asked to indicate their level of agreement (using a five-point scale from strongly agree to strongly disagree) on four statements reflecting one's level of confidence in their political knowledge. The items include: "I consider myself well qualified to participate in politics," "I think that I am better informed about politics and government than most people," "I feel that I have a pretty good understanding of the important political issues facing our country," and "If a friend asked me about the presidential election, I feel I would have enough information to help my friend figure out who to vote for". Consistent with several past studies in which this measure has been used (e.g., Kaid, McKinney, & Tedesco, 2007; McKinney & Chattopadhyay, 2007; McKinney & Rill, 2009; McKinney et al., 2011), the measure was reliable, $a = .901$.

Political cynicism. Political cynicism was measured with an eight-item scale used in previous campaign research (e.g., McKinney & Warner, 2013), with participants responding to a five-point scale ranging from 1 (strongly disagree) to 5 (strongly agree). The items include: "Politicians are more interested in power than what people think," "Politicians are corrupt," "Politicians make promises that are never kept," "Politicians cannot be trusted," "Politicians are too greedy," "Politicians always tell the public what they want to hear instead of what they actually plan to do," "Politicians are dishonest," and "Politicians are more concerned about power than advocating for citizens." The measure has demonstrated strong reliability in research utilizing this scale (McKinney & Warner, 2013; Warner, Turner McGowen, & Hawthorne, 2012) and achieved strong reliability, α = .886.

Results

On the basis of previous findings that campaign communication increases affective political polarization (Cho & Ha, 2012; Iyengar et al., 2012; Warner & McKinney, 2013), it was hypothesized that people who completed the survey later in the election cycle would be exposed to more polarizing messages from the campaign and would thus be more polarized. To test this hypothesis, a two-step multiple regression analysis was conducted with age, sex, ethnicity, and political party entered as covariates in the first block and time entered as the independent variable in the second block. As can be seen in Table 1, time was not a significant predictor of polarization. People who completed the survey later in the election were no more likely to be polarized. With the same rationale, the second hypothesis predicted that people who were highly attentive to the election would be more polarized. Following the same procedure, a multiple regression model indicated that attention to the campaign was a significant predictor of polarization. The full results are presented in Table 1. Attention to the election explained approximately 10 percent more of the variance in polarization above and beyond that which was accounted for by the covariates. People who followed the election more closely were subsequently more likely to express affective polarization.

Because political communication has previously been associated with greater polarization (Binder et al., 2009; Stroud, 2010), the final hypothesis predicted that people who participated in more political communication would be more polarized. Following the previous procedure a two-step multiple regression was conducted to test this hypothesis. As can be seen in Table 1, political communication positively predicted affective polarization above and beyond party identification, sex, race, and age. Political communication explained approximately seven percent more of the variance in polarization than the covariates alone. Those who engaged in more mediated and interpersonal communication about the election were significantly more likely to express affective polarization.

Table 1. Predictors of Political Polarization

	Covariate Model		Predictor Model		
	R^2	β	R^2	ΔR^2	β
Time					
Model	.132***		.132***		
Age		.008			.008
Democrat		.423***			.423***
Republican		.338***			.338***
Female		.019			.019
Race/Ethnicity		-.015			-.015
Time					.022
Attention					
Model	.131***		.228***	.097***	
Age		.005			-.034
Democrat		.421***			.365***
Republican		.338***			.295***
Female		.019			.064**
Race/Ethnicity		-.013			-.005
Attention					.321***
Political Communication					
Model	.131***		.197***	.065***	
Age		.019			-.024
Democrat		.427***			.399***
Republican		.34***			.328***
Female		.011			.045
Race/Ethnicity		-.04			-.031
Political Communication					.263***

Note. To allow uniform interpretation, regression weights are presented as standardized coefficients.

*$p < .05$, **$p < .01$, ***$p < .001$

Previous findings revealing that people who are more polarized tend to be more engaged in politics (Dilliplane, 2011) and that moderates are more likely to opt out (Prior, 2007) in turn suggest that there may be a relationship between polarization and other normative political attitudes associated with polarization. To explore this possibility, the first research question asked whether people with higher levels of polarization would also have more political information efficacy relative to less polarized individuals. To answer this question a two-step multiple regression analysis was conducted with age, sex, ethnicity, and political party entered as covariates in the first block and affective polarization entered as the independent variable in the second block. As can be seen in Table 2, affective polarization is a positive predictor of political information efficacy above and beyond political party, sex, age, and ethnicity. Polarization explained approximately seven percent more of the variance in political information efficacy. Those who were more polarized were more likely to have high amounts of information efficacy. The second research question asked if polarized respondents would be less cynical. To test this, a multiple regression analysis was conducted following the above procedure. Affective polarization significantly predicted political cynicism. The relationship was negative such that, as polarization increased, cynicism decreased. Polarization explained approximately one percent of the variance in cynicism above and beyond that which was explained by the covariates. Polarized respondents were slightly less likely to be cynical than those who were less polarized.

Table 2. Prediction of Cynicism and Information Efficacy from Polarization

	Covariate Model		Predictor Model		
	R^2	β	R^2	ΔR^2	β
Information Efficacy					
Model	.048***		.116***	.068***	
Age		.098***			.094***
Democrat		.083**			-.035
Republican		.074**			-.021
Female		-.171***			-.176***
Race/Ethnicity		-.045			-.041
Affective Polarization					.28***
Cynicism					
Model	.042***		.051***	.01***	
Age		.068**			.023**
Democrat		-.192***			-.148***
Republican		-.165***			-.129***
Female		-.105**			-.069**
Race/Ethnicity		-.047			-.047
Affective Polarization					-.105***

Note. To allow uniform interpretation, the regression weights are presented as standardized coefficients.

*p < .05, **p < .01, ***p < .001

The third and fourth research questions asked whether there was an indirect effect of time on polarization through either attention to the campaign or political communication. In other words, was the increased exposure to the campaign facilitated by the passage of time associated with more political polarization? To test the third research question, whether there was an indirect effect of time on polarization through attention, a simple mediation model was tested using the PROCESS macro for SPSS designed by Andrew Hayes (2013). In the model, age, sex, ethnicity, and political party were entered as covariates, time was specified as the independent variable, and attention to campaign was specified as the mediating variable. The bootstrapping procedure recommended by Preacher and Hayes (2004) was used to determine if there was a statistically significant indirect effect. As with the previous finding, there was no direct effect of time on polarization. The indirect effect of time on polarization through attention was also not statistically significant; the 95% bias-corrected bootstrap confidence interval was not above zero (-.0270 to .0544). Following the same procedure, a simple mediation model was tested to determine whether there was an indirect effect of time on polarization through campaign communication. Although there was no direct effect of time on polarization, the indirect effect of time on polarization through political communication (.2001) was statistically significant as the 95% bias-corrected bootstrap confidence interval was entirely above zero (.1368 to .2750). In other words, the passage of time was associated with more political communication and those who engaged in more political communication were more polarized the later in the election cycle they completed the survey.

Discussion

This results reported in this chapter confirm that campaign communication significantly influenced political polarization in the 2012 election. This finding contributes to a growing body of research about polarization as a political phenomenon (Abramowitz & Saunders, 2008; Fiorina et al., 2011; Jacobson, 2012; McCarty et al., 2006) and as a consequence of political communication (Binder et al., 2009; Lin, 2009; Stroud, 2010; Warner, 2010) as well as adds to the more recent scholarship examining effects of campaign communication on political polarization (Cho & Ha, 2012; Iyengar et al., 2012; Warner & McKinney, 2013). From this current study, we contribute three core findings to this ongoing research program. First, our findings suggest that people who are more attentive to campaign communication and people who more frequently engage in political communication about the campaign are likely to be more polarized. Second, the polarizing effect of political campaigns may be cyclical. In other words, those who are more polarized are not only less cynical but also possess more information efficacy—and are therefore more likely to participate in the political process than less polarized citizens. Finally, our findings provide preliminary evidence that polarization is a process which unfolds at pace with the election through political communication. Each of these findings will be discussed in the following section.

Because existing research suggests that campaign communication increases polarization (Cho & Ha, 2012; Iyengar et al., 2012), our first hypothesis predicted that, as time passed and the election progressed, people would become more polarized. However, time was not associated with greater polarization by itself. This may be due to the study design. First, the study was not longitudinal and we were therefore unable to compare within-subject changes in polarization as the election advanced. Instead, we were only able to compare between subject effects at different times in the election. Furthermore, the first four sets of data were reported on the evenings of a presidential debate. This may not have provided sufficient variability in time—a majority of respondents would have one of four scores—and the effect may have been masked.

Finally, no data was collected in the early stages of the campaign either in the period leading up to the party conventions or the period of time between the conventions and the first debate. As a result, the earliest polarization scores were collected after participants may have already been exposed to a great deal of campaign advertising and media coverage. It is possible that much of the hypothesized polarization occurred prior to the first debate and the absence of a significant finding was due to a ceiling effect. Future studies should incorporate a longitudinal design and collect data in the early phases of the campaign to determine if individual subjects become more polarized over the course of an election.

Our second hypothesis, which predicted that those who were more attentive to the campaign would be more polarized, was confirmed. This is consistent with previous findings that those who are exposed to more campaign information are more likely to be polarized (Iyengar et al., 2012) and suggests that elections are polarizing for those who follow them more closely. As with attention to the campaign, those who engaged in more frequent political communication were also more likely to express high levels of affective polarization. Respondents who reported frequent conversations about the election and high levels of attention to media about the campaign were more polarized. This is consistent with previous findings about non-campaign political communication (Binder et al., 2009; Stroud, 2010) and post-debate political communication (Cho & Ha, 2012). This study, therefore, reinforces the finding that political communication is polarizing and strengthens the emerging case that campaign communication is especially polarizing.

Because the responses were cross-sectional we cannot attribute causality to attention—it is entirely plausible that those who are more polarized are more likely to be highly attentive to the campaign because they have more at stake in the outcome. In fact, the best explanation is probably cyclical. If campaign exposure is polarizing and those who are most polarized already are more likely to have high exposure to campaign communication, the two processes may be mutually reinforcing. Nevertheless, partisanship was included as a covariate and should provide some control against the possible spurious or reverse causal associations between polarization and attention/communication. In other words, whereas partisans are more likely to engage in campaign communication and are also more likely to be polarized, those who engage in campaign communication are more polarized than committed partisans who do not. Future researchers should strengthen this finding by testing these relationships over the course of a campaign using a within-subjects design to better assess causality.

In addition to the first set of findings regarding attention and communication, we sought to determine whether polarization was associated with greater political information efficacy and less cynicism. Research shows that those who are less polarized are more likely to opt out of politics (Prior, 2007) and that when people become more polarized they are more likely to be actively engaged in politics (Dilliplane, 2011). We wanted to know if those who were more polarized were also likely to express more political information efficacy—were more confident that they possessed the requisite knowledge to participate in the political process—and whether they were less cynical and presumably less likely to opt out of the political process. Our results suggest that people who are more polarized do express more political information efficacy and less cynicism. Although the relationship between cynicism and polarization was considerably smaller than the others we observed, it helps explain why people who are more polarized are also more likely to be highly engaged in the political process.

The finding that people who are polarized are also less cynical suggests a possible connection with the phenomenon of political ambivalence. Recently researchers have indicated that political ambivalence is not necessarily the result of an inability to decide between the two major political parties. Rather, individuals may simultaneously hold positive and negative evaluations toward a given party or candidate (Sung-jin, 2010). Because ambivalence (strong conflicting feelings) is often at odds with polarization (a clear-minded and straightforward candidate preference), the fact that those who are less polarized are also more cynical may suggest that a general distrust of politicians causes people to be conflicted about both candidates. As a result, the findings in this study regarding cynicism and polarization suggest a possible connection between polarization and political ambivalence that provides an important direction in future analyses of campaign communication and its effects on normative political attitudes.

The third set of findings, resulting from our final two research questions, illustrates the important role of communication in the process of polarization. Whereas there was no direct effect of time on polarization, there was an indirect effect of time through political communication. As time passed and the election entered the later phases, frequent political communicators became more polarized. In other words, although we did not observe an overall change in polarization at different points in the election, the passage of time allowed the effect of political communication on polarization to manifest. Those who engaged in frequent political communication were more polarized the later in the election they were surveyed. This finding strengthens the case for a causal relationship between campaign communication and polarization, as there was no direct effect of the evolution of the campaign on polarization (via time) but only an indirect effect when respondents were engaged in frequent political communication during the time lag between respondents. Granted, this mediation process was not evident for attention to the campaign, yet the political communication questions were only asked in the debate studies so the discrepancy in the finding could be a result of a peculiarity in the data from the fifth survey. And, there may be an important distinction between passive engagement in a campaign (i.e., attention) and more active processing (i.e., communication) due to the potential that the difference is a function of the discrepancy in questionnaires between surveys one through four and survey five. Future research might explore the possibility of an active/passive distinction.

Conclusion

The findings presented in this chapter advance a growing body of research on the effects of political communication in general and campaign communication more specifically on political polarization in the American electorate. This study contributes valuable information to our understanding of how alienating messages functioned in the 2012 campaign, although there are limitations that merit discussion. First, the participants were recruited from a convenient sample of university students. Using this pool of subjects allowed for a national sample of people from many universities and permitted a larger and more dynamic survey than would be possible under other circumstances. Nevertheless, student samples always pose problems for generalizing results. Meta-analyses have found no significant differences in effect sizes between student and adult samples in studies of campaign advertisements (Lau, Sigelman, Heldman, & Babbit, 1999) and debates (Benoit, Hansen, & Verser, 2003), so there is reason to suspect that bias introduced by convenience sampling would not substantially alter the nature or direction of the results presented here. But, until similar research is done with a more generalizable sample, these findings should be treated as preliminary. The research is also limited by the cross-sectional design. Future studies should attempt to capture the dynamic relationships between polarization, engagement, and campaign communication with longitudinal research designs.

Finally, because the research was derived from a broader data-collection effort that sought to test numerous different campaign communication phenomena, some of measures variables here were not as dynamic as would be ideal. Specifically, political communication was only measured with two self-report items about talk and media, and these questions were not asked in the final survey. Future studies should develop more dynamic and comprehensive scales to measure political communication in a way that better captures the nuance and diversity of political communication.

The 2012 presidential election was both historic and divisive. Although this may be a unique feature of the emerging digital communication landscape, a function of the increasing divisiveness on Capitol Hill, or a feature of many previous elections that is only now receiving scholarly attention, our findings suggest that the 2012 campaign was in fact polarizing. The more closely people followed the contest between Obama and Romney, and the more frequently they discussed the campaign, the more polarized they became. Furthermore, as people became more polarized they expressed greater confidence in their ability to participate, increasing the likelihood that the polarized voices would be the most commonly heard in the public sphere.

References

Abramowitz, A. I., & Saunders, K. L. (2006). Exploring the bases of partisanship in the American electorate: Social identity vs. ideology. *Political Research Quarterly, 59*(2), 175–187.

Baum, M. A., & Groeling, T. (2008). New media and the polarization of American political discourse. *Political Communication, 25,* 345–365. doi: 10.1080/10584600802426965

Benoit, W. L., Hansen, G. J., & Verser, R. M. (2003). A meta-analysis of the effects of viewing U.S. presidential debates. *Communication Monographs, 70,* 335–350. doi: 10.1080/0363775032000179133

Binder, A. R., Dalrymple, K. E., Brossard, D., & Scheufele, D. A. (2009). The soul of a polarized democracy: Testing theoretical linkages between talk and attitude extremity during the 2004 presidential election. *Communication Research, 36,* 315–340. doi: 10.1177/0093650209333023

Brannon, L. A., Tagler, M. J., & Eagly, A. H. (2007). The moderating role of attitude strength in selective exposure to information. *Journal of Experimental Social Psychology, 43*, 611–617. doi:10.1016/j.jesp.2006.05.001

Brundidge, J. (2010). Encountering "difference" in the contemporary public sphere: The contribution of the Internet to the heterogeneity of political discussion networks. *Journal of Communication, 60*, 680–700. doi:10.1111/j.1460–2466.2010.01509.x

Cho, J., & Ha, Y. (2012). On the communicative underpinnings of campaign effects: Presidential debates, citizen communication, and polarization in evaluations of candidates. *Political Communication, 29*, 184–204. doi:10.1080/10584609.2012.671233

Coe, K., Tewksbury, D., Bond, B. J., Drogos, K. L., Porter, R. W., Yahn, A., & Zhang, Y. (2008). Hostile news: Partisan use and perceptions of cable news programing. *Journal of Communication, 58*, 201–219. doi:10.1111/j.1460–2466.2008.00381.x

Dilliplane, S. (2011). All the news you want to hear: The impact of partisan news exposure on political participation. *Public Opinion Quarterly, 75*, 287–316. doi: 10.1093/poq/nfr006

Fiorina, M. P., Abrams, S. A., & Pope, J. C. (2011). *Culture war?: The myth of a polarized America*. New York, NY: Pearson Longman.

Garrett, R. K. (2009). Politically motivated reinforcement seeking: Reframing the selective exposure debate. *Journal of Communication, 59*, 676–699. doi:10.1111/j.1460–2466.2009.01452.x

Gentzkow, M., & Shapiro, J. M. (2011). Ideological segregation online and offline. *The Quarterly Journal of Economics, 126*, 1799–1839. doi: 10.1093/qje/qjr044

Gerber, A. S., Huber, G. A., Doherty, D., & Dowling, C. M. (2011). Personality and the strength and direction of partisan identification. *Political Behavior, 34*, 653–688. doi: 10.1007/s11109-011-9178-5

Hayes, A. F. (2013). *Introduction to mediation, moderation, and conditional process analysis: A regression-based approach*. New York, NY: Guilford Press.

Hetherington, M. J., & Weiler, J. D. (2009). *Authoritarianism and polarization in American politics*. New York, NY: Cambridge University Press.

Iyengar, S., & Hahn, K. S. (2009). Red media, blue media: Evidence of ideological selectivity in media use. *Journal of Communication, 59*, 19–39. doi: 10.1111/j.1460–2466.2008.01402.x

Iyengar, S., Sood, G., & Lelkes, Y. (2012). Affect, not ideology: A social identity perspective on polarization. *Public Opinion Quarterly, 76*, 405–431. doi: 10.1093/poq/nfs038

Jacobson, G. C. (2012). The electoral origins of polarized politics: Evidence from the 2010 Cooperative Congressional Election Study. *American Behavioral Scientist, 56*, 1612–1630.

Kaid, L. L., McKinney, M. S., & Tedesco, J. C. (2007). Introduction: Political information efficacy and young voters. *American Behavioral Scientist, 50*(9), 1093–1111. doi: 10.1177/0002764207300040

Kaltenthaler, K., & Miller, W. J. (2012). The polarized American: Views on humanity and the sources of hyper-partisanship. *American Behavioral Scientist, 56*, 1718–1734. doi: 10.1177/0002764212463357

Knobloch-Westerwick, S., & Meng, J. (2011). Reinforcement of political self through selective exposure to political messages. *Journal of Communication, 61*, 394–368. doi: 10.1111/j.1460–2466.2011.01543.x

Layman, G. C., & Carsey, T. M. (2002). Party polarization and "conflict extension" in the American electorate. *American Journal of Political Science, 46*(4), 786. doi: 10.1017/S000305541000016X

Lin, C. A. (2009). Selective news exposure, personal values, and support for the Iraq war. *Communication Quarterly, 57*, 18–34. doi: 10.1080/01463370802662440

Lau, R. R., Sigelman, L., Heldman, C., & Babbitt, P. (1999). The effects of negative political advertisements: A meta-analytic assessment. *American Political Science Review, 93*, 851–875.

McCarty, N., Poole, K. T., & Rosenthal, H. (2006). *Polarized America: The dance of ideology and unequal riches.* Cambridge, MA: MIT Press.

McKinney, M. S., & Chattopadhyay, S. (2007). Political engagement through debates: Young citizens' reactions to the 2004 presidential debates. *American Behavioral Scientist, 50*(9), 1169–1182. doi: 10.1177/0002764207300050

McKinney, M., S., & Rill, L. (2009). Debating with YouTube: Examining the effects of a targeted debate message on the intended audience. *Conference Papers—International Communication Association*, 1–23.

McKinney, M. S., & Warner, B. R. (2013). Do presidential debates matter? Examining a decade of campaign debate effects. *Argumentation and Advocacy* (forthcoming).

"Partisan Polarization Surges in Bush, Obama Years" (2012, June 4). *Pew Research Center for the People and the Press.* Retrieved from http://www.people-press.org/2012/06/04/partisan-polarization-surges-in-bush-obama-years/

Preacher, K. J., & Hayes, A. F. (2004). SPSS and SAS procedures for estimating indirect effects in simple mediation models. *Behavior Research Methods, Instruments, and Computers, 36*, 717–731.

Prior, M. (2007). *Post-broadcast democracy: How media choice increases inequality in political involvement and polarizes elections.* New York, NY: Cambridge University Press.

Rosenstone, S. J., Kinder, D. R., Miller, W. E. (1997). *American National Election Studies.* Ann Arbor, MI: Center for Political Studies/Inter-university Consortium for Political and Social Research, University of Michigan.

Skitka, L. J., Bauman, C. W., & Sargis, E. G. (2005). Moral conviction: Another contributor to attitude strength or something more? *Journal of Personality and Social Psychology, 88*(6), 895–917. doi:10.1037/0022-3514.88.6.895

Stroud, N. J. (2010). Polarization and partisan selective exposure. *Journal of Communication, 60*, 556–576. doi: 10.1111/j.1460-2466.2010.01497.x

Sung-jin, Y. (2010). Two types of neutrality: Ambivalence versus indifference and political participation. *Journal of Politics, 72*(1), 163–177.

Sunstein, C. R. (2007). *Republic.com 2.0.* Princeton, NJ: Princeton University Press.

Sunstein, C. R. (2009). *Going to extremes: How like minds unite and divide.* New York, NY: Oxford University Press.

Taber, C. S., & Lodge, M. (2006). Motivated skepticism in the evaluation of political beliefs. *American Journal of Political Science, 50*, 755–769. doi: 10.1111/j.1540-5907.2006.00214.x

Tewksbury, D. (2005). The seeds of audience fragmentation: Specialization in the use of online news sites. *Journal of Broadcasting & Electronic Media, 43*, 322–348. doi: 10.1207/s15506878jobem4903_5

Warner, B. R. (2010). Segmenting the electorate: The effects of exposure to political extremism online. *Communication Studies, 64*, 430–444. doi: 10.1080/10510974.2010.497069

Warner, B. R., Turner McGowen, S., & Hawthorne, J. (2012). Limbaugh's social media nightmare: Facebook and Twitter as spaces for political action. *Journal of Radio & Audio Media, 19*(2), 257–275. doi: 10.1080/19376529.2012.722479

Yardi, S., & Boyd, D. (2010). Dynamic debates: An analysis of group polarization over time on Twitter. *Bulletin of Science, Technology & Society, 30*(5), 316–327.

Reflections on the 2012 Election

An Agenda Moving Forward

DIANNE G. BYSTROM AND MARY C. BANWART

As we reflect on the analyses of the 2012 presidential campaign presented in the preceding chapters—now more than a year after the election—we find ourselves as a nation still emerged in divisive and partisan political rhetoric. The effects of such partisan polarization is evidenced not only by the gridlock in Congress—which led to a 16-day government shutdown in October 2013—but also by public opinion polls showing American citizens largely fed up by the constant bickering, unwillingness to compromise, and lack of action by their political leaders.

For example, the public's approval of Congress dipped to an all-time low of 9% in November 2013 with the majority of respondents citing "party gridlock, bickering, and not compromising" for their disdain (Newport, 2013). President Barack Obama's approval ratings averaged in the mid-40s for most of 2013, with an all-time low of 37% in November 2013 (Dutton, De Pinto, Salvanto, & Backus, 2014). Political parties fared even worse, with only 34% of citizens approving of the performance of Democrats in Congress and an even fewer 25% approving of congressional Republicans in January 2014 (Langer, 2014).

Still, will the public's discontent about their political institutions, leaders, and representatives make a difference in the approaching 2014 midterm and 2016 general elections? Or, as Langer (2014, para. 2) suggests, can both political parties take solace in these "hold-your-nose" polling results because "however unloved, somebody's got to win"?

Although the partisan polarization and alienation gripping our nation may well continue into the 2014 midterm and 2016 general elections, we still hope that voters, the media, politicians, and researchers can learn from our analyses of the 2012 presidential campaign. Thus, we summarize our thoughts concerning the 2012 campaign communication as deduced from the preceding chapters, present our expectations for upcoming elections, and set an agenda for future research.

Consequences of Divisive Communication Strategies for Political Campaigns

As this book focuses on campaign communication and effects during the 2012 election, our concluding thoughts examine the consequences of media and candidate messages on voters as well as the representation of top issues and targeted appeals to a diversity of voters.

The Media, Their Messages, and Effects

First, it appears clear that the news media—both traditional and new—feeds the frenzy for division, competition, and polarization in their coverage of political campaigns. As Dimitrova finds in Chapter 1, the media once again relied on horse-race coverage in reporting the 2012 presidential election. Through media coverage that lacked thematic and issue framing as well as a substantive discussion of policy issues and emphasized conflict through a winner-versus-loser strategic game frame, viewers were exposed to a divisive style of discourse.

In other studies, scholars have suggested that one unintended consequence of the strategic game frame is the increased level of cynicism toward politicians and the political process in general. It is not likely that anytime soon the media will change its propensity for drama and hyper-emphasis on the competition implicit. However, these results remind us of the need for voters to be critical consumers of media messages, seeking out those sources that provide substantive issue discussion and contribute to a more informed—and, thus, empowered—polity.

As the media feeds divisiveness in their political campaign coverage, voters also are becoming increasingly partisan and polarized. As Hawthorne and McKinney found in Chapter 2, presidential debates—one of the primary forms of candidate communication with voters—can actually threaten some viewers' worldview and, thus, not only strengthen their political partisanship but also their polarization and, ultimately, their political aggression. Similarly, in Chapter 17, Warner and Greenwood found that increased engagement in campaign communication results in more political polarization. As both of these studies clearly demonstrate, the implications of political polarization and aggression demand continued study and analysis. When combined with a media that reinforces political divisions and competition, there remains an increasingly important need to explore whether these forms of polarization and aggression generate long-term effects similar to those identified in the short-term.

However, as some chapters demonstrate, political campaign communication can have positive effects on voters. For example, although Warner and Greenwood found evidence of increased polarization among voters from engagement in campaign communication, these voters also were less cynical, more politically efficacious, and more likely to participate in the political process. And, one way that young voters are more likely to participate in the political process is through digital media channels. As explained by Sweetser in Chapter 4, political participation has changed and, for young voters, has far more of a digital presence and set of activities than researchers have typically acknowledged.

Political communication channels—both traditional in the form of television advertisements and digital in the form of social media memes—also can affect voter evaluations of candidates, as several chapters show. Political campaign advertising on television—although routinely denounced by voters in public opinion surveys—remains an effective strategy for candidates in enhancing their favorability and perceptions of sincerity with voters, as demonstrated by the results presented by Winfrey, Banwart, and Warner in Chapter 3. Although exposure to social media messages in the form of memes had mixed effects on young voters, as shown by Jasperson in Chapter 5, they did lower the evaluations by Republicans of Mitt Romney's personal and professional attributes. Both of these chapters found that campaign messages targeted toward female voters had differing effects, with women reporting more favorable evaluations than men—especially toward President Obama.

Issue Framing and Effects

As several chapters demonstrate, the framing of issues in the 2012 election was critical—and effective—particularly on the concerns most important to voters. For example, as Childers and Stangler observed in Chapter 6, President Obama's rhetorical use of "synechdochic sound bites" to discuss the issue of the economy within the framework of fairness—and emphasize Romney's own words against him—may have proven uniquely powerful with voters. The authors also provide valuable insight as to why it remains critical for presidential contenders—and ultimately candidates in general—to present the issues in a way that connects with voters' identities of what they want their future to hold, in this case, their economic security.

Whereas both Obama and Romney discussed the economy within the rhetorical framework of fairness, they took different approaches when crafting their appeals about health care as demonstrated in Chapter 7 by Gordon, Robertson, and Sparks. Second to the economy among the top issue concerns among voters, health care was discussed by Romney within the frameworks of family, the economy, and religion and by Obama within the frameworks of egalitarianism. Advertisements by both campaigns were deeply negative, fueling confusion and uncertainty among voters about the content and nature of health care reforms that have persisted in the months following the 2012 election.

Although immigration did not emerge as a top concern discussed by the candidates or cited by a majority of voters in public opinion polls during the 2012 campaign, it has taken on more prominence in political discussions since the election as 1.4 million more Latinos voted in 2012 as compared to 2008 (Lopez & Gonzalez-Barrera, 2013) and primarily (71%) for President Obama. Thus, the analysis by Jarvis and De Castilla in Chapter 9 on how English and Spanish language newspapers framed Arizona's immigration legislation is important in understanding how the use of language can help define a demographic group's right to have a participatory role in the political process.

Similarly, the analysis by Cole and McKinney in Chapter 10 of the political debate over same-sex marriage referendums in four states contributes to our understanding of the effectiveness of competing rhetorical strategies in a time when 52% of citizens nationwide favor equal rights for such unions (Saad, 2013). The findings of this chapter further establish the important role of communication and voters' desire to connect with, emotionally, the issues being discussed. And, by finding a dominant theme of negativity and pessimism throughout the televised advertisements sponsored by opponents of same-sex marriage and a dominant theme of inclusivity and hope in televised advertisements sponsored by proponents, these results may indicate that voters do respond to appeals that are more united than divided.

Finally, with women once again comprising a key constituency during the 2012 campaign, two chapters explore the rhetorical styles and strategies used to frame these voters and their issues—both during and after the election. In Chapter 8, Hennings and Bystrom contribute to our understanding of how the term "war on women" was, and continues to be, used by traditional and social media—including those with neutral, liberal, and conservative ideologies—in ongoing debates that divide political parties and voters. And, in Chapter 11, Bystrom and Hennings offer insights into how women serving in the 113th Congress address various constituencies and advocate for "female" and "male" issues in their floor speeches. Taken together, these chapters illustrate how the media, political candidates, and elected officials use different strategies to frame women's issues and appeal to women voters.

Campaign Messages for a Divided Electorate

This volume also contributes to our understanding of how campaign messages can be crafted to appeal to an electorate separated into potential voting constituencies by gender, race and ethnicity, age, and religion and, in some cases, lead to further divisions. Taken together, Chapters 12 through 17 demonstrate that nuances exist within each demographic and successful campaigns—and their messages must take these subtle differences into account.

More specifically, in Chapter 12, Kenski provides a deeper dive into the demographic group of women through her analysis of the gender gap in the 2012 election. Confirming that the gender gap is far more nuanced than portrayed by the media, this chapter also demonstrates how political candidates can be successful—or not—in the way they tailor their appeals to women voters.

Gender, of course, was not the only way in which voters were divided—and to which campaign communication was targeted—in 2012. In Chapter 13, McIlwain and Caliendo offer an important examination of how race and ethnicity were discussed in the 2012 campaign as a "mobilization strategy." Specifically, they argue that the Republican Party, in an effort to unseat the nation's first African-American president, set in motion a dual strategy to alienate and marginalize black and Latino voters as a way to captivate and capitalize on conservative white voters' own growing sense of alienation in a society where their numerical majority is declining.

As the electorate also can be divided—and targeted by campaign messages—according to the age of voters, Rill and McKinney shed new light on the political participation of young citizens in Chapter 14. Not only are young voters significantly more likely to rate higher than young nonvoters on a variety of political socialization variables—such as interest, political information efficacy, and political knowledge—they also are less likely to be cynical about politics. Thus, this chapter provides important connections on how political campaigns can deliver a youth vote through targeted communication strategies employed in both traditional and digital media.

As religion continues to be an important consideration in today's presidential campaigns, Kaylor contributes to our understanding of faith-based appeals in Chapter 15. Although both presidential candidates targeted voters with faith-based messages in 2012, Kaylor shows the potential challenges faced by Republican candidates using religious appeals as members of nontraditional religious organizations and, especially, young voters with no religious identification tended to support Obama and Democratic candidates.

In addition to messages targeted to demographics based on gender, race and ethnicity, age, and religious affiliation, the 2012 campaign featured rhetorical strategies designed to appeal to voters fed up with partisanship. In Chapter 16, Milford shows how the rhetorical strategies of both candidates—and the dramas created—around the term "bipartisanship" ultimately resulted in developing more divisiveness and differentiation in the election. The effects of such "divide and conquer" campaign strategies are confirmed in Chapter 17, as Warner and Greenwood present strong evidence that people who are more attentive to and more frequently engaged in communication about the campaign are likely to be more polarized.

Yet, even with the growing polarization emerging from more exposure to campaign messages, Warner and Greenwood also report that as polarization increases so does confidence in one's ability to participate in the political process. Instead of collective caution around the idea of political polarization, are we being called to recognize a silver lining? Is a silver lining emerging that finds a more polarized electorate is actually less cynical, more efficacious, and more likely to participate in the political process? Ironically, isn't that an outcome for which we would hope in most elections? Certainly our field is ripe for continued study and analysis of such questions.

Based on our observations of campaign communication and effects during the 2012 election, we now turn to predictions for the 2014 midterm and 2016 general election campaigns as well as suggestions for future research.

Predictions for the 2014 and 2016 Elections

Ultimately, in a hyper-mediated campaign environment—with the media; candidates; and the variety of political actors, elites, and third-party supporters each representing the complexities of the voting public and all seeking attention and time—it is not likely we will enjoy or embrace a unifying communication dialogue any time in the near future. We see no indication that the media will embrace a campaign coverage framework that is focused more on the issues—and providing substantive information to voters—rather than on reporting political news as competing conflicts and strategic games between winners and losers. Television news has long been known to ascribe to the maxim that "what bleeds, leads," and we do not expect this to change in their coverage of upcoming elections.

However, we can be hopeful that the increasing number of sources now available to follow political campaigns will result in more fully informed, engaged, and knowledgeable voters. Today's voter can follow political campaigns on not only local, national network, and cable television news shows but also through other traditional mediums such as newspapers, news magazines, and radio stations;

emerging nontraditional digital sources such as Facebook, Twitter, and political blogs; and the candidate's own communication efforts through political ads, debates, websites, and social media. Voters, however, need to take the time to seek out the variety of information available through these sources to become more fully informed about the issues and candidates in any election.

Similarly, we do not predict that political candidates and campaigns will become more unifying—and less divisive—in their political communication efforts in the upcoming elections. Gerrymandered congressional districts that favor candidates for U.S. House races espousing the extremes of conservative and liberal viewpoints, divisions of power between Democrats and Republicans within executive and legislative bodies, and an electorate that remains almost evenly divided on such issues as health care reform, marriage equality, and reproductive rights for women will continue to produce rhetoric that is more divisive than unifying. And, the heightened micro-targeting by political candidates and campaigns around the factors that make U.S. citizens different—such as gender, race and ethnicity, age, religious affiliation, and economic status—will increase the likelihood of voting in "my interests" rather than "our interests" in upcoming elections.

Despite these somewhat pessimistic predictions, we do see some examples in the research presented in this volume that voters can—and do—respond to more positive and hopeful campaign messages on issues with which they identify on an emotional level. For example, the most effective campaign messages about the economy, health care, and marriage equality were framed in the values of fairness, egalitarianism, and inclusivity. Also, on a positive note—and contrary to the findings of most recent research—women's interest in the 2012 election was at a level similar to that of men. This suggests many of the gaps that have kept women from seeing themselves as active participants in the political arena—beyond the voting booth—may in fact be slowly narrowing. Finally, the most partisan and polarized of voters actually report also being less cynical, more informed, and more likely to participate in the political process.

Suggestions for Future Research

A number of promising avenues for future research on political campaign communication are proposed by the chapters included in this volume.

For example, many of our authors who explored the content of media and candidate messages recommend employing experimental and longitudinal designs to measure the effects of campaign communication on voters. What are the effects of the frames used by the media—both traditional and new—on consumers of their content?

Do the frames used by traditional media—such as television and newspapers—have different effects on citizens than those used by new media channels, such as Facebook and Twitter? In addition to measuring the effects of the content of campaign communication on voters, future studies could survey the purveyors of such information—journalists, candidates, and campaign managers—to learn more about their intentions when framing news stories and campaign messages.

Studies employing longitudinal panel research designs would be particularly useful in helping us understand the ebb and flow of the media's coverage of politics, candidate messaging, and the public's interest in key issues over the course of the campaign. For example—as several of the chapters analyzing messages, issues, and targeted constituencies demonstrate—appeals to female voters and the framing of "women's issues" ebbed and flowed through the 2012 campaign, flowing one way when the question was Obamacare's coverage of birth control and another way after Romney's "binders full of women" debate remark.

Also, the authors who explored the effects of various channels of political campaign communication suggest that more work needs to be done on messages targeted toward specific demographic groups, including women, young voters, and political independents. Which messages specifically targeted toward key voting constituencies work the best, when do they work, and through which channels do they work the best?

In addition, we suggest the collective findings in the volume reveal a need for an increase in the research that makes connections between campaign styles and governing styles. For example, do the rhetorical strategies used by candidates during a campaign to frame such issues as the economy, health care, and marriage equality as well as target appeals to women, racial and ethnic groups, young voters, and members of religious organizations differ from the styles they use when elected to office? Such analyses will help reveal how campaign and governing communication styles are different, or the same, and ultimately lead to a better understanding of how government and its political leaders operate as well as can be held accountable.

Finally, additional research is needed on relationships between the various channels of campaign communication and political polarization, political aggression, and alienation—the central themes of this volume. Future studies should attempt to capture the dynamic relationships between polarization, engagement, and campaign messages with longitudinal research designs that use comprehensive scales to better measure the nuance and diversity of political communication efforts leading up to elections.

As the research reported in this volume demonstrates, the 2012 election raised complex, dynamic, and intriguing questions for political communication researchers. And, the results reported herein not only underscore the need for further examination of how the media, candidates, and other political actors communicate with voters, but also on how voters communicate with one another and ultimately choose to participate in the political process. Undoubtedly the 2014 midterms and 2016 election cycles promise to unveil opportunities for further careful examination of many similar and still important questions and findings as we seek to determine whether we will remain an *alieNATION*. As political communication scholars research the ways in which all forms of political actors—and their campaign communication—highlight and reinforce differences, perhaps it is through the lens of our scholarship that we might also find the spaces in which we as a country can ultimately agree.

References

Dutton, S., De Pinto, J., Salvanto, A., & Backus, F. (2014, January 23). Poll: Americans split on Obama approval. *CBSnews.com*. Retrieved from http://www.cbsnews.com/news/poll-americans-split-on-obama-approval/

Langer, G. (2014, January 15). Dems, GOP in Congress: Unlucky in love. *ABCnews.com*. Retrieved from http://abcnews.go.com/blogs/politics/2014/01/dems-gop-in-congress-unlucky-in-love/

Lopez, M. H., & Gonzalez-Barrera, A. (2013, June 3). *Inside the Latino electorate*. Retrieved from the Pew Research Hispanic Trends Project website: http://www.pewhispanic.org/2013/06/03/inside-the-2012-latino-electorate/

Newport, F. (2013, November 12). Congressional approval sinks to record low. *Gallup.com*. Retrieved from http://www.gallup.com/poll/165809/congressional-approval-sinks-record-low.aspx

Saad, L. (2013, July 29). In U.S., 52% back law to legalize gay marriage in 50 states. *Gallup Politics*. Retrieved from http://www.gallup.com/poll/163730/back-law-legalize-gay-marriage-states.aspx

About the Contributors

Mary Christine Banwart (Ph.D., University of Oklahoma) is an associate professor of communication studies at the University of Kansas, where she also directs the university's interdisciplinary leadership studies minor. Her current research focuses on political campaign communication and the influence of gender, with specific attention on political advertising, campaign websites, and mixed-gender debates. She is the co-author of a book examining gender and politics, co-editor of a book on the 2008 election, and has published book chapters and journal articles on the strategic use of advertising in political campaigns, the gender gap, and news coverage of mixed-gender races.

Dianne Bystrom (Ph.D., University of Oklahoma) is the director of the Carrie Chapman Catt Center for Women and Politics at Iowa State University. Her research focuses on the styles and strategies used by female and male political candidates in their campaign communication as well as their news coverage by the media. A frequent commentator on political and women's issues for state, national, and international media, Bystrom is the co-author of a book on gender and candidate communication and co-editor of five books. She has contributed chapters to another 13 books and has published several journal articles, primarily on women and politics.

Stephen Maynard Caliendo (Ph.D., Purdue University) is a professor of political science at North Central College in Naperville, Ill. He studies political psychology and political communication to better understand the potential effects of racialized communication in the context of U.S. elections. He is the author of *Inequality in America: Race, Poverty, and Fulfilling Democracy's Promise* (2014) and the co-author of *Race Appeal: How Candidates Invoke Race in U.S. Political Campaigns* (2011).

Jay P. Childers (Ph.D., University of Texas) is an associate professor in the Department of Communication Studies at the University of Kansas. His research focuses on understanding the ways in which democratic politics and citizenship are articulated and practiced in the United States. In addition to many articles and book chapters, he is the author of *The Evolving Citizen: American Youth and the Changing Norms of Democratic Engagement* (2012) and co-author of *Political Tone: How Leaders Talk and Why* (2013).

Hayley J. Cole is a Ph.D. student in the Department of Communication at the University of Missouri. Her current research focuses on gender and sexuality issues and campaign rhetoric, including television advertising and web advertisements.

Daniela V. Dimitrova (Ph.D., University of Florida) is an associate professor and director of graduate education at the Greenlee School of Journalism and Communication at Iowa State University. Her research focuses on news media framing of political news and cross-cultural journalism studies. Dimitrova is a member of the Association for Education in Journalism and Mass Communication, the largest U.S. organization for journalism educators, and most recently served as head of its communication technology division.

Ann Gordon (Ph.D., University of Southern California) is associate dean and director of the Henley Social Science Research Laboratory at Chapman University in Orange, Calif. Her current research interests include methodology, women and politics, political communication, and public opinion. She is co-editor of *Anticipating Madam President* (2002), author of *Playing Politics: An Active Learning Approach to American National Government* (2004), co-author of *When Stereotypes Collide: Race, Gender, and Videostyle in Congressional Campaigns* (2005), and has published several journal articles.

Molly Greenwood is a Ph.D. student in political communication at the University of Missouri. Her research focuses on political polarization, political ambivalence, and social media. She is a contributor to two books and has published two journal articles.

Joshua Hawthorne is a Ph.D. student in political communication at the University of Missouri. His research focuses on the political use of social media and the effects of political rhetoric. Hawthorne's work has been published in several journal articles and edited book chapters.

Valerie M. Hennings (Ph.D., University of Wisconsin-Madison) is an assistant professor of political science at Morningside College in Sioux City, Iowa. Her current research examines candidate training programs and their influences on women's political ambition. In addition to publishing several studies focused on women, politics, and the media, she teaches courses on gender and leadership, gender and politics, political behavior, and state and local government.

Sharon E. Jarvis (Ph.D., University of Texas) is an associate professor in the departments of Communication Studies and Government and the associate director for research at the Annette Strauss Institute for Civic Life at the University of Texas. She teaches and conducts research on political communication, language use, and persuasion. She is the author of *The Talk of the Party: Political Labels, Symbolic Capital & American Life* and a co-author of *Political Keywords: Using Language that Uses Us*. Her work on Latino politics has appeared in the *Journal of Communication* and *Howard Journal of Communication* among other outlets.

Amy E. Jasperson (Ph.D, University of Minnesota) is the department chair and an associate professor of political science at Rhodes College in Memphis, Tenn. Her current research focuses on media framing and its resonance with citizens, communication during crises, campaign advertising strategies, and citizens' moment-to-moment responses to candidate campaign messages. She served as an American Political Science Association congressional fellow during the 109th Congress.

Brian T. Kaylor (Ph.D., University of Missouri) is an associate professor of communication studies at James Madison University in Harrisonburg, Va. His research focuses on religious and political rhetoric, particularly the intersection of the two. He is the author of several journal articles and two books on religion and politics, most recently *Presidential Campaign Rhetoric in an Age of Confessional Politics*.

Kate Kenski (Ph.D., University of Pennsylvania) is an associate professor of communication and government and public policy at the University of Arizona, where she teaches political communication, public opinion, and research methods. Her co-authored 2010 book, *The Obama Victory: How Media, Money, and Message*

Shaped the 2008 Election, won the 2011 International Communication Association's Outstanding Book Award and the 2012 National Communication Association's Diamond Anniversary Book Award. Her current research focuses on incivility in online forums and multimedia teaching strategies to mitigate cognitive biases.

Charlton McIlwain (Ph.D., University of Oklahoma) is an associate professor of media, culture, and communication at New York University. His research examines the role that race plays in electoral politics, social movements, and digital media. He is the co-author of *Race Appeal: How Candidates Invoke Race in U.S. Elections* (2011).

Mitchell S. McKinney (Ph.D., University of Kansas) is professor and chair of the Department of Communication at the University of Missouri, courtesy professor with the MU School of Journalism, and director of the university's Political Communication Institute. He is the co-author/co-editor of seven books and has written numerous articles appearing in major communication, journalism, and interdisciplinary journals. His research interests include presidential debates, political campaigns, civic engagement, media and politics, and presidential rhetoric.

Mike Milford (Ph.D., University of Kansas) is an assistant professor in the School of Communication and Journalism at Auburn University. His current research focuses on the ways politics and sports use metaphors and popular narratives to make ideological arguments in the public sphere. Milford's work has been published in numerous international, national, and regional journals.

Leslie A. Rill (Ph.D., University of Missouri) is an assistant professor in the Department of Communication Studies at the University of Nevada, Reno. Her current research focuses on the influence of interpersonal and media messages on democratic behaviors and attitudes.

Brett Robertson is a senior research fellow at Chapman University in Orange, Calif. His interests include political campaign communication, health-care reform rhetoric, and organizational communication technologies.

Clariza Ruiz De Castilla (Ph.D., University of Texas) is a speech professor at San Jacinto Community College in Pasadena, Texas. Her current research focuses on English and Spanish news media portrayals of immigrants and Latino populations in light of the Arizona Senate Bill 1070 (The Support Our Law Enforcement and

Safe Neighborhoods Act). She currently teaches courses on oral, interpersonal, and business communication.

Lisa Sparks (Ph.D., University of Oklahoma) is the Foster and Mary McGaw endowed professor in behavioral sciences at Chapman University in Orange, Calif., where she also directs the graduate program in health and strategic communication in the Department of Communication Studies. She is the author and editor of more than 10 books in the areas of communication, health, and aging with a focus on the intersections of provider-patient interaction and family decision-making as related to cancer communication science.

R. McKay Stangler (Ph.D., University of Kansas) is an assistant professor of mass media at Baker University in Baldwin City, Kan. His research focuses on discourse relating to economics, technology, and science.

Kaye D. Sweetser (Ph.D., University of Florida) is an associate professor of public relations at San Diego State University in the School of Journalism and Media Studies. Her research focuses on politics as public relations campaigns. The majority of her work examines digital political public relations and looks at the use of various social media and online tools in campaigns and their effects on the electorate.

Benjamin R. Warner (Ph.D., University of Kansas) is an assistant professor in the Department of Communication at the University of Missouri. His research focuses on political polarization, extremism, new media, and campaign communication effects. He has published a number of articles and book chapters about the effects of partisan media, presidential debates, and social media.

Kelly L. Winfrey (Ph.D., University of Kansas) is a lecturer at Iowa State University with the Carrie Chapman Catt Center for Women and Politics. Her research focuses on gender differences in campaign messaging. She has published several articles and book chapters examining the effect of campaign messaging on women's vote choice and political engagement.

General Editors
Bruce Gronbeck and Mitchell S. McKinney

At the heart of how citizens, governments, and the media interact is the communication process, a process that is undergoing tremendous changes as we embrace a new millennium. Never has there been a time when confronting the complexity of these evolving relationships been so important to the maintenance of civil society. This series seeks books that advance the understanding of this process from multiple perspectives and as it occurs in both institutionalized and non-institutionalized political settings. While works that provide new perspectives on traditional political communication questions are welcome, the series also encourages the submission of manuscripts that take an innovative approach to political communication, which seek to broaden the frontiers of study to incorporate critical and cultural dimensions of study as well as scientific and theoretical frontiers.

For more information or to submit material for consideration, contact:

> BRUCE GRONBECK
> Email: bruce-gronbeck@uiowa.edu
>
> OR
>
> MITCHELL S. MCKINNEY
> Department of Communication, University of Missouri
> Email: McKinneyM@missouri.edu

To order other books in this series, please contact our Customer Service Department:

> (800) 770-LANG (within the U.S.)
> (212) 647-7706 (outside the U.S.)
> (212) 647-7707 FAX

Or browse online by series:
> WWW.PETERLANG.COM